THE DEMOCRATIC CLASS STRUGGLE

W 5065557 4

THE DEMOCRATIC CLASS STRUGGLE

Walter Korpi

ROUTLEDGE & KEGAN PAUL
London, Boston, Melbourne and Henley

First published in 1983
by Routledge & Kegan Paul plc
39 Store Street, London WC1E 7DD,
9 Park Street, Boston, Mass. 02108, USA,
296 Beaconsfield Parade, Middle Park,
Melbourne, 3206, Australia, and
Broadway House, Newtown Road,
Henley-on-Thames, Oxon RG9 1EN
Printed in Great Britain by
Billing & Sons Ltd., Worcester

Library of Congress Cataloging in Publication Data

Korpi, Walter.
The democratic class struggle.
Bibliography: p.
Includes index.
1. Political participation - Sweden. 2. Trade-unions - Sweden - Political activity. 3. Strikes and lockouts. 4. Social conflict. 5. Welfare state. I. Title.
JN7945.K66 1983 324'.042'.09485 82-23183

ISBN 0-7100-9436-1

CONTENTS

PREFACE

This book combines a case study of class relations, politics and voting in Sweden with a comparative analysis of distributive conflicts and politics in eighteen OECD countries. Its underlying theoretical theme is the development of class relations in free-enterprise or capitalist democracies. The different chapters of the book are connected more by their relation to common theoretical issues than by a continuous narrative thread. In a few chapters I have drawn on previously published materials.

The comparative analysis of industrial conflict presented in Chapter 8 as well as the cross-national data introduced in Chapter 3 derive from a research project carried out in collaboration with Michael Shalev of the Hebrew University of Jerusalem. Our collaboration started during a contemporaneous sojourn on the shore of Lake Mendota in Wisconsin. I wish to thank Michael for intellectual stimulation, generous friendship and unspared energy.

Among my colleagues at the Swedish Institute for Social Research I want to give my special thanks to Christian Berggren, Ulla Carlstedt, Eva Carlsson, Robert Erikson, Anne-Maj Folmer-Hansen, Sven E. Olsson, Eleanor Rapier, Miljan Vuksanović and Eskil Wadensjö for advice and assistance. I have benefited from valuable comments on the manuscript made by Olof Frändén, Olof Petersson, Levi Svenningsson and Rune Åberg. My thanks are also due to Karin Busch, Sören Holmberg, Hans Nordlöf and Staffan Sollander for helpful assistance in the data analysis and to Diane Sainsbury for the translation into English as well as for perceptive comments.

The work with this book has been partly supported by research grants from the Swedish Delegation for Social Research and from the Bank of Sweden Tercentennial Foundation.

W.K.
Stockholm

1 INTRODUCTION: CLASS, POWER AND SOCIAL CHANGE

How important are class and power for conflict and change in Western societies? This question opens up a set of perennial issues in the social sciences. The economic crisis which in the early 1980s was holding the industrialized nations in its grip brought these issues to the fore for the social sciences as well as for politics.

The heritage from Marx points to the central role of class divisions in shaping political struggles and societal change. In the Marxian perspective, the conflicts of interest expressed in and mediated by the roles and rights of individuals and collectivities in the sphere of production are seen as an enduring base for social and political cleavages. These conflicts of interest introduce a structural instability into the organization of production and are, in the long run, expected to transmute the capitalist mode of production.

Departing from Weber's critique of Marx, during the postwar period many social scientists have seen class as gradually losing its importance as a basis for cleavages and as a driving force for change in modern societies. With the development of production technology the structure of the labour force changes, a process which is seen as transforming the once existing class society into a mass society. In the mass society a multitude of cross-cutting lines of cleavage gives politics a more amorphous structure, increasingly distant from the class base which it once may have had. Old cleavages such as religion, race and ethnicity are seen as overtaking the socio-economic ones as bases for conflict. New issues divorced from class propel themselves into the centre of the political struggles in post-industrial, post-materialist societies. The structural stability of a mode of production based on private enterprise is often seen as fortified by the evolution of the welfare state. If anything, the stability of welfare capitalism is threatened not from the left but from the right as a reaction against the political crippling of market mechanisms.

'From class to mass' thus summarizes the evolution of mainstream social science conceptualizations of the structural bases for cleavages in Western societies. The progress of the concept of power has, however, been more discordant. Hobbes once conceived of power as the present means to secure some future good. Although the term 'power' rarely appears in the writings of Marx, it is obvious that power in the Hobbesian sense plays a central role in his thought. In the view of Marx, the sphere of production is an institutionalization of unequal power. However, Marx introduces the seeds for structural change in his theoretical model by indicating that, through organizations for collective action, the powerless groups can gradually improve their power position and potentially overtake their superiors.

An optimistic view on the role of organizations for collective action in the mobilization of power is also found in pluralist thought. The pluralists, however, combine it with the assumption of a fragmentation of the bases of cleavages and thus of collective action in the mass society. This re-combination leads to the conclusion that the capitalist democracies provide their multifarious interest groups with relatively equal opportunities to mobilize power and to act as pressure groups, something which largely evaporates the need to transmute the capitalist mode of production.

In the 1970s the pluralist position came under vigorous attacks from scholars congregating around the concept of neo-corporatism. Many neo-corporatist writers argue for a pessimistic interpretation of the role of organizations for collective action such as unions in modifying the distribution of power in Western nations. Rather than being only or primarily vehicles for the advancement of the interests of the subordinated groups, these organizations are seen as gradually becoming perverted into instruments of social control on behalf of the dominant interests. Also, scholars leaning toward the Leninist interpretation of Marx have largely dismissed the possibility that, through their organizations for collective action, the wage-earners can significantly decrease their subordination in capitalist societies.

The purpose of this book is to discuss some of the theoretical issues central to the social science debate on class, power and political alignments in Western nations, and to bring together empirical evidence of relevance for illuminating the relative fruitfulness of alternative theoretical approaches to the understanding of politics and social change in the capitalist democracies. The book combines a partial comparative analysis of eighteen OECD countries with a case study of the development and future alternatives of one of these countries, Sweden. Both in the comparative analyses and in the case study, an attempt is made to incorporate the historical dimension. The analysis is focused on the potential for structural changes in the economic organization of production in Sweden.

SWEDEN IN A COMPARATIVE PERSPECTIVE

In many Western nations, the years since the late 1960s have been marked by drastic political and economic readjustments. Sweden, one of the most stable democracies in the world, experienced these changes rather abruptly in the latter half of the 1970s. After three Social Democratic electoral setbacks the bourgeois parties formed a government in the autumn of 1976 for the first time in forty-four years. Economic growth, to which the Swedes had become accustomed during the postwar period, gave way to industrial crisis and declining real wages. Issues related to nuclear energy and the environment appeared to open up a new cleavage in politics, divorced from the traditional left-right dimension. Women's demands for equality grew in intensity. Sweden's much acclaimed industrial peace was shattered by the largest industrial conflict in its history. The Social Democrats and the trade unions discussed proposals for wage-earners' funds which could challenge the cardinal principle of capitalism - the control of large shareholders over the major corporations. The bourgeois governments proposed cutbacks in ingrained social benefits. After the 1982 elections, however, a Social Democratic government was returned to power.

From a historical perspective, the 1970s stand out as a break with the past in Swedish politics. A reliable model for managing social conflicts then ceased to function. This model had emerged during the 1930s as a result of a 'historical compromise' between capital and labour, based on a relatively strong labour movement and the new but apparently stable Social Democratic hold over governmental power. The division of governmental and economic power between the most important collectivities of citizens formed the precondition for politics in Sweden during the next four decades. It generated a welfare capitalism which gave Sweden an element of uniqueness among the Western countries. The country also came to be viewed as the prototypical case of neo-corporatist interest politics. During the 1970s, however, it became clear that the basis of the model had crumbled and that its methods were no longer effective.

Since Sweden is the country in which a reformist socialist government has been strongest and has had a record tenure in government position, it is an important test case for the study of class relations and conflicts of interest in the advanced industrial nations. The dramatic changes in its political life during the 1970s suggest that Sweden may have come to a crossroad in its development. Do these problems and changes signal that the welfare state has developed beyond its proper limits and that Sweden will have to search its way back to the mainstream of the Western nations with a much larger dose of capitalism in its mixed economy? Or will the still strong labour movement be able to seek solutions to the crisis in ways which will move the country closer to an economic democracy, where all citizens can participate, on an equal basis, in the making of decisions concerning business and the economy which now are reserved for the select few? 'More capitalism' or 'economic democracy' are thus the signposts at the crossroads where the Swedes will have to make a choice during the 1980s.

This book attempts to analyse the development and future alternatives of Swedish politics from the perspective of historical and international comparisons. In the theoretical discussion we shall look at the writings of pluralist and neo-corporatist scholars from the point of view of an alternative approach, where class and the distribution of power resources play central roles. A historical analysis of the development of unions, left political parties and the distribution of power in the Western nations gives a context for the discussion of our test case, Sweden. The empirical analysis of Sweden is focused on the development of class relations, politics and voting behaviour. We return to a comparative analysis to examine the evolution of one of the classical expressions of class conflict in the Western nations - strikes and lockouts - and also to analyse the development of welfare states and inequality in the capitalist democracies. The question underlying these analyses concerns the direction of change in the possibilities for a labour movement to transmute a capitalist democracy into an economic democracy.

In this book the conflicts of interest manifested in the political arenas of Western nations are conceived of as a democratic class struggle. This concept addresses itself critically to different bodies of thought. It is thus directed against the pluralists in the mainstream of academic thought, who have tended to de-emphasize the significance of power and politics in societal change and the role of the class structure in generating conflicts of interest in modern Western societies. But to conceive of parliamentary politics as a democratic class struggle also goes against the Leninist interpretation of Marx, which emphasizes the importance of classes but holds that in the capitalist democracies class conflict does not significantly manifest itself in the contests for parliamentary power. The concept of democratic class struggle also implies criticism of neo-corporatist writers, who tend to view political competition for government power as overshadowed by new institutional structures created by the major interest groups outside the parliamentary setting. Finally, the concept also indicates that under certain conditions the democratic class struggle can focus on the class structure itself, i.e., on the question of the economic organization of production.

'Der Leitfaden' of my study is that, in order to understand the functioning and development of the Western nations, we have to focus on the distribution of power resources between the main classes within these societies. The book argues that in a capitalist democracy the probability of a development in the direction of economic democracy depends primarily on changes in the distribution of power resources between its major classes and collectivities. Since the 1930s the Swedish wage-earners have developed increasingly strong organizations. During the postwar period the level of unionization has grown to include practically all wage-earners, an internationally unique situation. By joining class-based organizations for collective action, the wage-earners in Sweden have greatly decreased their internal competition and have thereby reduced their disadvantage in power resources. Through this process they have undermined the foundation of the capitalist system of wage labour.

PLAN OF THE BOOK

In Chapter 2 we shall discuss critically two major approaches to the understanding of the development of the advanced industrial societies: on the one hand pluralist thought, based on 'the logic of industrialization', and on the other hand the various conceptions of neo-corporatism. An alternative approach based on class structure and the distribution of power resources between classes is outlined. Chapter 3 analyses the development of union movements and left parties in eighteen OECD countries and examines the development of class relations in Sweden.

In order to influence the political process, the citizens must participate in it. Against the background of international comparisons, Chapter 4 discusses how different groups of citizens in Sweden, since the introduction of universal suffrage, have become involved in the democratic class struggle through voting. Differences in other forms of political participation between various groups are also examined. Chapter 5 deals with the long-term factors determining voter preferences and loyalties. It also elucidates changes in the parties' support among different occupational groups and classes during the postwar period.

The electoral geography of Sweden is treated in Chapter 6 in view of the fact that the units of political decision-making are geographically demarcated. We trace the changes in the 'red' and the 'blue' Sweden since the 1920s, examine influences of the social environment on the socialist vote, and discuss the special case of voters in the metropolitan centres. The movement of voters between the parties and political blocs can be followed in election statistics and opinion polls. These data provide the basis for Chapter 7, which analyses the increasing volatility of the electorate. This chapter also takes up the question of whether the classic left-right dimension in Swedish politics is now complemented by a new dimension involving environmental issues and other types of 'new politics'. It includes an analysis of the referendum on nuclear power that was held in the spring of 1980.

Chapter 8 is comparative and takes up the clashes between labour and capital in the form of strikes and lockouts since the turn of the century in eighteen OECD countries. The dramatic decline in the level of industrial conflict in Sweden following the historical compromise in the 1930s is taken as an example of the role of politics in industrial strife. The central theme in this chapter is an analysis of the conditions under which the centre of gravity of distributive conflicts can be moved from the labour market into politics. Chapter 9 is also largely comparative, although in a more preliminary way. Here we broach the question of what importance the political composition of the executive can be expected to have for social policy and the development of the welfare state. We devise a set of concepts for analysing cross-national variations in welfare state development and examine empirical data illuminating the effects of politics on inequality in different countries.

In the final chapter, we attempt to tie together the threads from the preceding chapters. Against the background of the discussions, we here return to the central question of the book concerning the direction of change in the possibilities of the labour movement to remould the foundations of a capitalist society.

2 THE DEMOCRATIC CLASS STRUGGLE

How fruitful are the presently dominant social science theories on structure and change, power, conflict and politics in modern societies? In this chapter we shall discuss the basic ideas in two important streams of thought - the pluralist industrial model of society and neo-corporatism - both of which offer interpretations and explanations of the development of advanced industrial societies. An alternative approach, based on class and the distribution of power resources between collectivities and classes, will be outlined. Against the background of these theoretical approaches, we shall then discuss the role of interest organizations in the making of public policy and the relative importance of different bases for cleavages in the Western nations during the postwar period.

FROM PLURALISM TO CORPORATISM?

During the postwar period numerous contributions centring around the concepts of 'pluralist industrial society' and 'modernization' have dominated in attempts to explain the development of contemporary societies. This theoretical approach was developed largely as an alternative to the Marxian perspective, which was seen as negated by the actual course of development in Western societies. The body of thought on pluralist industrial society forms an imaginative and relatively coherent interpretation of the past, present and future of modern societies. In spite of vigorous criticisms, its basic premises continue to influence the mainstream of social science thought in the 1980s. The many scholars who have written within this tradition are not necessarily in agreement on all major issues.[1] Nevertheless, there is a sufficient common ground between them to invite an attempt to lay out the basic tenets of this body of thought into a 'synthetic' view.

A fundamental idea underlying the pluralist industrial model is that the unceasing development of industrial technology is the most important force of societal change. The Industrial Revolution crushed the old agrarian society and its institutions. Subsequently, industrial societies are assumed to develop according to an inherent logic of industrialization and along converging lines of movement.

According to this logic of industrialization, the ever-growing complexity of industrial technology generates an increasingly specialized and educated labour force and thereby dissolves the class structure of early industrial society. Increasing geographic and social mobility hastens this process. The basic division into two opposed classes, labour and capital, in early industrialism thus gives way to a pluralism of smaller, more narrowly based interest groups. The working class in particular becomes fragmented and gradually merges into the 'middle mass', which becomes the most significant category in the advanced industrial societies. In place of a few antagonistic classes, the advanced industrial society thus develops a multiplicity of cleavages and interest groups. Through multiple and overlapping associational memberships, criss-crossing lines of interest conflicts emerge.

Because of the dual impact of the deprivations suffered by large groups of the population and the breakdown of the old institutions of social integration and conflict regulation at the onset of industrialization, the magnitude and intensity of internal conflict are expected to peak in the early phase of the industrialization process. While conflicts of interest remain, with the erosion of the old class structure and the accompanying decline of congruent and cumulated cleavages, the manifestations of conflicts of interest are expected to become less serious. Increasing standards of living contribute to this decline. A crucial development, furthermore, is the gradual establishment of new institutions for conflict regulation in place of those torn down at the onset of industrialization.

The new institutional order includes two key elements: on the one hand, political democracy and universal suffrage, and on the other hand, the growth of trade unions and the institutionalization of collective bargaining. As universal suffrage gave everybody 'political citizenship', the establishment of collective bargaining is seen as giving workers 'industrial citizenship'. The granting of 'social citizenship' in the welfare state tends to be viewed as a more or less natural response to the requirements of industrial society.

In industrial society interests are assumed to be mediated by shifting combinations of spontaneously generated groups with multiple allegiances, which exert influence on the state in relation to issues of special interest to them. These pressure groups are assumed to have enough power to be able to veto decisions which go against their basic interests. The state is seen as neutral in relation to these different groups.

The pluralist industrial model thus projects the picture of a changing, yet structurally stable, society where there is no need for fundamental institutional changes. Ideologies are assumed to fade. A key assumption in this body of thought is that the institutional stability and sublimation of conflicts in the advanced industrial societies is not based on the domination of one or a few interest groups over others. A pluralist society is instead assumed to give all groups roughly equal opportunities to mobilize power. Differences in power resources between groups and collectivities therefore tend to be seen as unproblematic and as being of limited importance for the functioning of these societies.

The assumption of a rough balance of power is implicit, for instance, in the stress on the role of collective bargaining in extending 'industrial citizenship' to the workers, which tends to be equated with universal suffrage and political democracy. The countervailing sanctions available to workers under collective bargaining are assumed to equalize the power resources of labour and capital or, at least, to render the differences unproblematic to the integration of the working class into capitalist society.

Since the 1960s the pluralist interpretation of advanced industrial societies has been increasingly challenged by social scientists using the Marxian perspective in their analyses of contemporary Western societies. Many of the writers who have proclaimed themselves as 'Marxists' have however converged towards a Leninist interpretation of Marx. Crudely summarized, the main tenet of the Leninist interpretation is that under capitalism the state acts on behalf, if not at the behest, of the economically dominant class and its different fractions. Therefore, in capitalist societies the composition of parliaments and governments is of no major significance for the actions of the state. Parliamentary democracy tends to be seen, in Lenin's words, as 'the best possible shell' for capitalism.[2]

In terms of widespread scholarly acceptance, however, the most successful attack on the pluralist body of thought was launched in the 1970s by writers who used the concept of corporatism (with or without prefixes like 'societal', 'liberal' or 'neo') as a descriptive term and a catalyst for alternative views on the development of interest intermediation and policy formation in Western societies during the postwar period. The term 'corporatism' was found appetizing by writers coming from very different starting points and therefore came to span the spectrum of writers, from pluralists to Marxist-Leninists.[3] This led to a rather diversified interpretation of the concept. The term 'corporatism' has thus been used, inter alia, to refer to possible changes not only in modes of interest mediation (from pluralism to corporatism), but also in the mode of production (from capitalism to corporatism) and in the form of the state (from parliamentarism to corporatism). Some writers use the term to describe specific types of institutions for and modes of organizing conflictual interests, others to identify ways of making and implementing public policy. One writer notes that 'as the quantity of work on corporatism has expanded, it has been difficult to discern whether definitional convergence has really tended to outpace definitional refraction'.[4]

The common core in the corporalist writings, however, appears to be shared views on the modes in which conflicting interests are organized, represented and mediated in advanced industrial societies, views which clearly differ from those assumed by the pluralists. The differences concern partly institutional forms. Instead of being manifold, independent, competing and voluntary, the interest organizations are assumed to be few, closely related to the state, monopolistic and with compulsory memberships. Rather than being intermittent seekers of access and influence, the interest organizations are seen as having an intimate relationship to the state, including a continuing participation in policy-making and policy implementation. A crucial assumption in corporalist thought is that in public policy-making interest organizations do not only or even primarily represent the interests of their members. With the development of corporatism the processes of representation of member interests by the organizations are assumed to become more or less perverted. To a large extent the organizational leaderships are assumed, instead, to mediate state interests to their members, to exercise social control over their members on behalf of state interests, and to place the organizations in the service of their own interests.

During the postwar period the novel aspect of the relationships between the state and the interest groups was that, among the latter, organized labour appeared with increased strength. The focus of attention among corporatist writers has thus frequently been on the tripartite relations between the state and the organizations of labour and capital, especially in the areas of industrial relations and in economic and incomes policies.

In an article which seems to have been the spark that ignited a growth industry, Philippe C. Schmitter outlined two subtypes of corporatism.[5] One subtype is the traditional or 'state corporatism', historical examples of which existed during the 1930s in Italy, Germany and Portugal. During the postwar period the second subtype, 'societal corporatism', has developed gradually and to differing extents in the countries of Western Europe, where the once existing pluralism has decayed. This new system of interest mediation includes the following characteristics. Its constituent units, the organizations of interest, are functionally differentiated and have become limited in number. Each of them represents the interests of a specific section of the population, defined primarily in terms of economic function in the division of labour. Membership in these organizations is de facto compulsory.[6] The organizations do not compete with each other for members. Internally the organizations have generated a bureaucratic hierarchy which separates the organizational leadership from the members. The organizations have developed a mutual understanding with the state, which grants them recognition and representational monopoly in return for the observance of certain controls on their selection of leaders and in the articulation of their demands. With the development of societal corporatism, political parties fade into the background.

To explain the emergence of neo-corporatism, Schmitter argues that

> [the roots of] societal corporatism can be traced primarily to the imperative necessity for a stable, bourgeois-dominant regime, due to processes of concentration of ownership, competition between national economies, expansion of the role of

> public policy and rationalization of decision-making within the state to associate or incorporate subordinate classes and status groups more closely within the political process.[7]

Yet although the class structure and conflicting interests in capitalist society have played a key role in generating societal corporatism, Schmitter assumes that, once the institutions and systems of interest representation have developed, the participating organizations tend to acquire a relative independence from, and even disregard for, the interests of the individuals, sectors and classes that they supposedly represent. The leaderships of the organizations do not only or primarily 'represent' the interests of their members in decision-making at different levels of the state. The organizational leadership also assumes a very significant function of social control by 'mediating' interests, i.e., by transmitting, teaching and imposing state interests on their own members.[8] Once in operation, societal corporatism thus becomes a relatively stable and resilient means for the dominant groups in bourgeois society to maintain their dominance.

Although Schmitter explicitly wanted to challenge the pluralist interpretation, somewhat surprisingly he thus assumes the institutional arrangements of societal corporatism to create a stability in the capitalist democracies reminiscent of the stability generated by the institutions for conflict resolution in the pluralist industrial model. Nevertheless, in Schmitter's view the viability of neo-corporatist institutions is to some extent threatened, e.g., by the possible establishment of single-issue movements and by a declining economic performance which may undermine the weakly legitimated neo-corporatist institutions.[9]

In contrast to Schmitter, another leading writer on neo-corporatism, Leo Panitch, has argued that the neo-corporatist system of interest mediation is continuously destabilized by the marked imbalance in what the different parties get out of the corporatist arrangements. Panitch views neo-corporatism as 'a political structure within advanced capitalism which integrates organized socio-economic producer groups through a system of representation and cooperative mutual interaction at the leadership level and mobilization and control at the mass level'.[10] He locates the origins of corporatism in the need for the state to foster economic growth by facilitating capital accumulation. In the view of Panitch, corporatism thus becomes primarily state-induced collaboration, designed to contain the organized working class in the capitalist state. It involves organized labour in institutional representation and administration of state policy, which makes the functional interest groups of labour and capital interact at the level of the state. However, since the interests of labour are weakly represented through the neo-corporatist institutions, the imbalance in outcomes for the different classes generates contradiction which tends to undermine these institutions through outbursts of militancy from below.

Bob Jessop also views corporatism as relatively unstable.[11] He regards parliamentarism and corporatism as alternative state forms, with tripartism, involving cooperation between labour, capital and the state, as a contradictory hybrid of the two. Jessop assumes that corporatist tendencies develop as responses to political crisis within parliamentarism which restrict its ability to function on behalf of capital. Such crises can be generated, e.g., by splits among parties or between the parties and their supporters which make governments inefficient. They can also be generated by the substantial representation in the parliament of revolutionary parties or if the parties choose to use public spending to compete for voters rather than to ensure capital accumulation. In such situations corporatism can become a strategy to maintain bourgeois domination, since it can disorganize the forces of opposition and find an adequate social base in the working class.

Jessop assumes that social democracy plays a key role in the development of corporatism. Social democratic parties 'prevent or weaken the development of autonomous forms of working class mobilization that threaten to unify economic and political struggles against the rule of capital'.[12] Therefore, the importance of social democracy as a social base for capital accumulation has increased both in monopoly and in state monopoly capitalism. Jessop concludes that

> the dominant tendency in the modern state is towards a social democratic tripartism based on the articulation of corporatism and parliamentarism and unified through the location of a social democratic party at the apex of both the corporatist and the parliamentary system.[13]

While writers using the pluralist industrial model generally conceive of pluralism as an ideal for the development of their societies, the above summary of the views of leading corporatist writers indicates that the concept of neo-corporatism originated as a critical concept. It has thus been used to draw attention to developments in modern societies which, from pluralist, semi-syndicalist, neo-Marxist or neo-Leninist points of view, have appeared as negative aspects. However, the concept of neo-corporatism remains vague, something which probably has enhanced its use by scholars coming from very diverse starting points.[14]

Undoubtedly the writings on pluralist industrial society and on neo-corporatism contain many significant and relevant observations on the development of Western societies. Yet I think that their explanations of the development of capitalist democracies remain inadequate. In my judgment the most serious weaknesses in the pluralist industrial model derive from the assumptions that class divisions and inequalities in power no longer are significant in structuring the processes of change in these societies. The weakness of the Leninist perspective is its reverse assumption that the distribution of power resources under capitalism is given by the mode of production and is almost completely unequal. The Leninist interpretation of Marx is highly problematic. Marx was, in fact, clearly ambiguous on the role of political democracy as a means to restructure capitalist society. In one of his more optimistic moments he wrote: 'Universal Suffrage is the equivalent of political power for the working classes . . . where the proletariat forms the large majority of the population. . . . Its inevitable result . . . is the political supremacy of the working class.'[15]

In comparison with the pluralist industrial model, the neo-corporatist view offers a more fruitful and realistic interpretation of the development of capitalist democracies in some important respects. This is true above all with respect to its conceptualization of the forms in which organized interests participate in the formation of public policy. To the extent that neo-corporatist writers view class and power as relevant for the structure and functioning of politics and distributive processes in capitalist democracies, they move beyond the pluralist model. Yet in my view the neo-corporatist interpretations harbour serious difficulties, several of which stem from an inadequate conceptualization of the role of power in the emergence and functioning of what are called neo-corporatist institutions.

In retrospect, it would appear that, in conceptualizing state and societal corporatism as two subtypes of the same syndrome and as essentially functional equivalents in the service of the needs of the dominant groups in society, Schmitter closed many questions which should have been left open. One of these questions concerns the origins of the tripartite relations between the state and the organizations representing labour and capital. By assuming that neo-corporatist institutions serve to stabilize the position of the dominant groups in capitalist society, attention was diverted away from the possibility that these institutions are manifestations of serious conflicts of interest generated by significant changes in the distribution of power resources between classes and interest groups.

The neo-corporatist assumption that corporatist organizations largely have replaced political parties as important actors leads to an inadequate analysis of the role of the state in the tripartite relations. Many neo-corporatist writers tend to view state organs by and large as representing the interests of the economically dominant groups in the capitalist democracies. In my view a more fruitful hypothesis is that the actions of state representatives and the pattern of coalition formations in the tripartite bargaining between state, labour and capital can be significantly affected by changes in the strength of working-class-based organizations and by the nature and extent of left party control of the government. The neo-corporatist assumption of a near stability in the functioning of the institutions of interest intermediation accords the institutions of conflict regulation the same semi-independent role as does the pluralist industrial model. It prevents attention being paid to the ways in which the functioning of institutions is conditioned by the distribution of power resources in society.

Schmitter's assumption of a massive 'goal displacement' within the interest organizations, from representation of membership interest to the stabilization of the position of the organizational leadership and social control over the members, turns upside down the views on the role of interest organizations such as unions found in Marxian as well as in pluralist traditions. This assumption is difficult to reconcile with a model of individual members as rational actors. The view that organizations such as unions de facto have a compulsory membership, and are non-competitive as well as monopolistic, has tended to preclude attention to the sizeable variations found, e.g., in levels of unionization between different countries, variations which cannot be explained by measures which are compulsory in the common meaning of this word. Such assumptions have inhibited analyses of the conditions under which workers enter into collective action on a large scale, what organizational tendencies come to be seen by them as more promising than others and of the extent to which organizational leaders remain responsive to membership interests.

In my view many of the phenomena which pluralist, Leninist and neo-corporatist writers have identified can be dealt with more fruitfully through an analytical approach which takes class and the distribution of power resources in society as the point of departure. In contrast to the pluralist views, my guiding hypothesis is that in a capitalist society the working class is a subordinated class in relation to capital. However, in contrast to the Leninist interpretation of Marx, my hypothesis is that, through its political and union organizations, the working class can decrease its disadvantage in power resources in relation to capital. Therefore in the capitalist democracies the degree of disadvantage of the power resources of the wage-earners can vary significantly over time and as well as between countries. In this power resource perspective some parts of the neo-corporatist syndrome come to be seen as variables dependent on the power resource distribution, other aspects as indicators of the power resource distribution and still other parts as intervening variables.

POWER RESOURCES

The stability implied in the pluralist industrial model of society rests on the assumption that the distribution of power resources between various groups and collectivities in the capitalist democracies is potentially equal. Schmitter's assumption of relative stability of neo-corporatist arrangements appears to imply an unequal yet fairly stable distribution of power resources. The Leninist interpretation of Marx similarly implies an unequal but stable power distribution in the capitalist democracies. Such assumptions must be questioned. One way of elucidating the distribution of power is to analyse what instruments and resources of power different groups and collectivities in society have at their disposal in the interaction which takes place between them over long periods of time.[16]

What, then, are power resources? Power resources are characteristics which provide actors - individuals or collectivities - with the ability to punish or reward other actors. These resources can be described in terms of a variety of dimensions. Power resources can thus vary with regard to domain, which refers to the number of people who are receptive to the particular type of rewards and penalties. They can also differ in terms of scope - the various kinds of situations in which they can be used. A third important dimension is the degree of scarcity of a power resource of a particular type. Furthermore, power resources can vary in terms of centrality; i.e., they can be more or less essential to people in their daily lives. They also differ with regard to how easily they are convertible into other resources. The extent to which a power resource can be concentrated is a crucial dimension. Of relevance are also the costs involved in using a power resource and in its mobilization, i.e., in making it ready for use. Power resources can furthermore differ in the extent to which they can be used to initiate action or are limited to responses to actions by others.

It is important to realize that power resources need not be used or activated in order to have consequences for the actions of other people. An actor with the ability to reward or punish need thus not always do so to influence others.[17] Since every activation of power resources entails costs, it actually lies in the interests of power holders to increase efficiency in the deployment of power resources. This can be achieved through what we may call the investment of power resources. Thus, power resources can be invested through the creation of structures for decision-making and conflict regulation, whereby decisions can be made on a routine basis and in accordance with given principles.[18] Investments of power resources can be made in institutions for conflict resolution such as laws, ordinances and bureaucracies, in technologies, in community and national planning, and in the dissemination of ideologies.

Some types of power resources can be described as basic in the sense that they in themselves provide the capacity to reward or to punish other actors. Through processes of investment, from basic power resources actors can derive new types of power resources. These derived power resources, however, ultimately depend on the basic power resources for their effectiveness. The distinction between basic and derived power resources is not easy to make but appears fruitful. It indicates, for instance, that power resources such as ideologies can be seen as ultimately based on resources which provide the capability to apply positive or negative sanctions.

Let us now look briefly at the characteristics of some of the more important basic power resources in Western societies. Among resources familiar to students of power, means of violence have traditionally been considered important. In terms of the aforementioned dimensions, means of violence have a large domain, wide scope and high concentration potential, as well as a relatively high convertibility. Although the legitimate use of violence is typically reserved for the state, resources for violence are not scarce. Their essential drawback is the high costs associated with their use.

Two types of power resources are central and their dimensions important for the theoretical controversy between pluralists and Marxist social scientists. The first type of power resource consists of capital and control over the means of production. The second type is what economists often call 'human capital', i.e., labour power, education and occupational skills. The pluralist approach assumes that persons possessing control over capital and the means of production do not have appreciably greater power resources at their disposal than persons with only human capital. Yet in terms of the aforementioned dimensions, capital and control over the means of production are power resources which differ drastically from human capital, making parity between them extremely problematic.

As power resources, capital and the means of production have a large domain, wide scope and high concentration potential, as well as high scarcity and convertibility. The costs involved in mobilizing and using these resources are relatively low. Furthermore, control over the means of production has high centrality, since it affects people's livelihood. Capital is also typically used to initiate action.

When regarded as a power resource, human capital is characterized by serious limitations. Usually it has a fairly small domain and narrow scope. Since everybody has some of it, human capital is generally not a highly scarce resource. Where labour power is offered on the labour market, its value depends on demand from capital, and its ability to initiate action is limited. Human capital has low convertibility and a low concentration potential. In an era of mass education, formal training beyond a certain level can at times yield diminishing returns. To be effective, the human capital of various individuals and groups must therefore be coordinated on a broad basis. This requires investments in organizations for collective action and hence fairly large mobilization costs.

In the Western countries, most human capital is utilized in the labour market. Economists often discuss the labour market as one of supply and demand where commodities are bought and sold. But human labour power is a very special commodity, since it is inseparable from its owner. Thus it cannot be sold; that would be slave trade. Labour can be hired only for a certain time, and the buyer acquires the right to make use of the seller's labour capacity during hours of work. Once the employment contract has been concluded, the owner of human capital cannot shed it like an overcoat but must deliver his labour power at the workplace, and on the job must personally subordinate himself to the directives of management.[19] Thus the system of wage labour creates relationships of authority and subordination among people and the basis for a division into classes.

The possibility of increasing the effectiveness of the power resources of individuals through collective action provides a rational explanation for the origin of unions to promote the interests of wage-earners in disputes with employers. It also offers an explanation of why wage-earners organize themselves into political parties. As the growth of 'juristic persons' and corporate actors during the past centuries indicates, other actors also have organized for collective action to increase the efficiency of their power resources. Alongside capital and control over the means of production, organizations to co-ordinate wage-earners' actions - primarily trade unions and political parties - belong to the strategically important power resources in the capitalist democracies.

Are, then, either of these types of strategic power resources - on the one hand control over capital and the means of production, and on the other hand control over human capital co-ordinated through the organizations of wage-earners - dominant in the capitalist democracies? Let us look more closely at the clearest confrontation between them, viz., at the workplace. Control over the means of production forms the basis of management's right of command over labour. It is capital which hires labour, not labour which hires capital. The subordination of labour is, however, a matter of degree inasmuch as the prerogatives of the representatives of capital have been restricted by legislation and by collective bargaining, the effectiveness of which in turn is influenced by the market situation. The prerogatives of management still confirm that, in terms of power resources, the wage-earners in these societies are in a position of inferiority vis-à-vis capital. The maintenance of a system of authority and subordination based on control over the means of production is a major problem confronting the dominant groups in the capitalist democracies.

I agree with the pluralist view on power distribution in the capitalist democracies to the extent that in these societies power is probably more widely shared than in other contemporary societies with different political and economic systems. However, I object to the next and crucial step in pluralist thought: that the assumed equal opportunities to mobilize power has generated a distribution of power resources in these societies that is sufficiently equal to no longer warrant our attention. If we view the development of wage-earners' collective organizations as essential for the effectiveness with which their 'human capital' can be applied in the conflicts of interest with capital, it appears evident that the distribution of power resources in Western societies can vary considerably over time as well as between countries. Once we drop the assumptions of the distribution of power resources implicit in the pluralist, neo-corporatist and neo-Leninist models, a host of interesting questions concerning distributive processes, social consciousness and patterns of conflict, as well as institutional functioning and stability, come to the fore.

SOCIAL CHANGE

In Western societies variations in the difference in power resources between labour and business interests, along with their allied groups, can be expected to have a variety of consequences. This difference can influence:

(a) the distributive processes in the society;
(b) the social consciousness of the citizens;
(c) the level and patterns of conflicts in the society; and
(d) the shaping and functioning of social institutions.

The processes of distribution in society can be viewed as exchange relations where, for example, the right to control labour power is exchanged for wages. These exchanges, however, need be neither in accordance with principles of equity nor mutually balanced. Instead, we must assume that the distribution of power resources influences the outcomes of the exchange processes and consequently the degree of inequality in society. Stronger groups thus will often get the 'lion's share' of what is to be distributed. Power resources, which can be regarded as stocks of values, thus influence the flow of values between individuals and collectivities.

But the distribution of power resources is also critical for the social consciousness and levels of aspiration of citizens as well as for the way in which they define their interests. Perceptions of what is just, fair and reasonable vis-a-vis other groups of citizens are largely dependent upon the power relations between these groups. Weak groups often learn, or are taught to accept, circumstances which stronger groups would consider unjust. Strong actors also tend to develop more long-range definitions of their interests than weaker groups.

The distribution of power resources is of major importance for the levels and patterns of conflict in society. Even if a weak group feels that an exchange relationship is unjust, the group may have to accept the terms of exchange because it lacks better alternatives and opposition may lead to reprisals of various kinds. But when the power resources of actors increase, they can offer resistance in situations which they previously had to accept. They can also attempt to change conditions which they find unjust. The distribution of power resources and its changes thus influences the levels of conflicts in society. Since changes in the distribution of power resources also affect the alternatives for action open to the actors, they can be expected to influence the actors' strategies of conflict and thus the pattern of conflict between them.

From this perspective, changes in the distribution of power

resources between different collectivities or classes can thus be assumed to be of central importance for social change. Such changes will affect the levels of aspiration of the actors and their capacity to maintain or to change existing social structures. Social change can be expected to emerge from various types of bargaining, but will sometimes involve manifest conflicts. Since open conflicts are costly to all parties, it is in the interests of the actors to limit their length and frequency. Through settlements following bargaining and/or manifest conflicts, the terms of exchange between the parties are thus moulded.

Where parties are involved in long-term interactions, settlements between them generally tend to involve different types of compromises. Such compromises may lead to the creation of new social institutions or changes in the functioning of existing institutions. Social institutions and arrangements related, e.g., to processes of distribution and decision-making can thus be seen as outcomes of recurrent conflicts of interest, where the parties concerned have invested their power resources in order to secure favourable outcomes. Such institutions thus need not be viewed as neutral or objective arrangements for conflict resolution. Instead, the ways in which they were created and function reflect the distribution of power in society. When the distribution of power resources is altered, the form and functioning of such institutions and arrangements are also likely to change.

The distribution of power resources between the major collectivities or classes in society will thus shape people's actions in a variety of ways. These actions, in turn, will affect social structure as well as the distribution of power. A continuous interplay between human action and the structure of society arises. The approach outlined here comes close to the perspective of Marx, according to which structural change is the result of people, through co-operation or conflict, seeking solutions to what they define as important social problems. The definitions of social problems are, however, not objectively given but depend largely on the distribution of power resources in society. The alternative solutions considered and ultimately chosen are also affected by the power distribution.

In this perspective the state can be conceived of as a set of institutional structures which have emerged in the struggles between classes and interest groups in a society. The crucial aspect of this set of institutions is that they determine the ways in which decision-making on behalf of the whole society can legitimately be made and enforced. The state must not however, be seen as an actor in itself, or as a pure instrument to be used by whichever group that has it under its control. While the institutional structures and the state can be used to affect, e.g., distributive processes in the society, these structures also affect the way in which power resources can be mobilized and are, in turn, affected by the use of power resources.[20]

Conflicts of interest between different groups or collectivities continuously generate bargaining, manifest conflicts and settlements. At some points, however, the settlements are the outcomes of important changes in the distribution of power resources and are of such a nature that they significantly affect institutional arrangements and strategies of conflict for long periods of time. In connection with such settlements or 'historical compromises', the patterns and conceptions of 'normal politics' change.

In the capitalist countries, the acceptance of the wage-earners' right to organize in unions and parties and to participate in political decision-making via universal and equal suffrage are examples of such historical settlements. The winning of political democracy was the result of a decrease in the disadvantage of working-class power resources brought about through organization and often through alliances with middle-class groups. It limited the legitimate use of means of repression by the state and opened up legitimate avenues for the citizens to participate in the decision-making of state organs. In many Western countries, the historical settlements concerning political democracy came around World War I. These institutional changes significantly affected the patterns of interest conflicts in the years to come.

SOCIETAL BARGAINING

With the exception of setbacks in countries like Italy, Germany and Spain, during the interwar period the strength of the unions and working-class parties increased in the Western nations. In the period after World War II this trend has by and large continued. Through increasing levels of organization the wage-earners have considerably strengthened their bargaining position in the distributive conflicts in the capitalist democracies. This has affected strategies of conflict and patterns of institutional arrangements. It is my hypothesis that the tripartite 'neo-corporatist' institutional arrangements largely reflect the compromises and settlements generated by the decreasing differences in the distribution of power resources between wage-earners and representatives of capital and allied groups in these countries. The decreasing disadvantage in wage-earner power resources has generated institutional arrangements and practices in reaching settlements involving major interest groups, which we can describe as 'societal bargaining'.[21] The notion of bargaining implies that the outcome of the interaction cannot be predetermined.

The choice of the term 'societal bargaining' to describe arrangements and practices which others have termed 'corporatism' is made not only to avoid a word which many have found hard to swallow. In my view, societal bargaining of the tripartite type that was developed in some countries of Western Europe during the postwar period clearly differs from traditional corporatist arrangements. It is therefore misleading to regard the two as more or less functional equivalents in the way several writers on neo-corporatism have done.

Traditional state corporatism, e.g., in Italy, Germany and Spain, must be seen as a successful attack on the working class and its organizations in a situation where the power gap between classes was very large. State corporatism was used to widen that gap. The institutional arrangements of societal bargaining, however, have come about in situations where the disadvantage in power resources of the wage-earners is much smaller than where the traditional 'state corporatist' solutions have been practised. Societal bargaining involving the organizations of the wage-earners must, by and large, be seen as reflecting an increasingly strongly organized working class. Whether societal bargaining benefits the wage-earners or not is an empirical question, which cannot be settled through definitions. We must assume, instead, that its long-term as well as the short-term outcomes can vary and are dependent on the distribution of power resources between the parties. From the power resource perspective the institutional arrangements of societal bargaining (i.e., the 'neo-corporatist' institutions) appear as intervening variables between, on the one hand, the distribution of power resources in society and, on the other hand, the pattern and outcome of distributive conflicts.

The spread of societal bargaining in Western nations during the postwar period is the result of an important shift in the lines separating decision-making through markets and politics. Since the breakthrough of political democracy, the relative importance of these two forms of decision-making has been largely dependent on the contest between two different types of power resources: the (at least in principle) equally distributed political resources, and the highly unequally distributed power resources in the markets. By using their votes, wage-earners have been able to encroach upon and to limit the sphere of operations of the markets, where they are more often at a disadvantage. An example of the shift from markets towards politics is the decision-making determining levels of unemployment. Where Keynesian ideas have been accepted, the level of unemployment has come to be seen as a responsibility of the political authorities, and no longer to be left only to market processes. Also, distributive processes have been affected, e.g., through social policy and taxation.

A DEMOCRATIC CLASS STRUGGLE?

I have suggested above that, in the capitalist democracies, it is fruitful to view politics as an expression of a democratic class struggle, i.e., a struggle in which class, socio-economic cleavages and the distribution of power resources play central roles. In contemporary social science, this view will be challenged from different directions. From a pluralist point of view the primacy which this interpretation gives to class cleavages will be questioned. While accepting the importance of class, those who lean towards the Leninist interpretation of Marxism tend to argue that the major organized interest groups, which presently are the main actors in these conflicts, do not actually represent the interests of the working class. Many writers on neo-corporatism also share such a view. Let us look briefly at the concepts concerned and the counter-arguments made.

The class concept is of relevance, inter alia, in attempts to explain social conflict, the distribution of goods and social change. This concept should therefore sensitize us to the many fissures and rents in the social fabric, which may become cleavages delineating the bases upon which citizens will organize themselves into collective action in the conflicts of interest in society. According to my reading of Marx and Weber, the two dominant figures in the theory of class, they both view the class concept in this perspective.[22] Marx no less than Weber recognized a multitude of potential cleavages on the basis of which citizens can combine themselves for collective action. The two differ, however, in the relative importance which they ascribe to different types of bases of cleavages.

Marx assumed that, in the long run, the conflicts of interest rooted in the sphere of production and especially in the economic organization of production would come to dominate over the other potential cleavages, such as those based on market resources and status. Contrary to what is often assumed, the class theory of Marx is not a one-factor theory. Its basic hypothesis is instead that, among the multitude of lines of cleavage and conflicts of interest, the relative importance of those arising from the economic organization of production will increase in the long run.

Weber, however, places class, market resources and status on an equal footing as potential bases for cleavages and assumes that over time their importance will tend to oscillate. The class theory of Weber has also often been misinterpreted, not least by those who regard him as their intellectual standard-bearer. Weber explicitly argued that power must be seen as the generic concept of social stratification, the threefold expressions of which are class, status and party. Yet, pluralist writers have often conceived of power as a separate 'dimension' of social stratification, parallel to, but not included in, 'class' and 'status'.[23] In contrast to Weber's stress on power as the basic independent variable behind social stratification, pluralist writers have therefore tended to conceive of power as restricted to the realm of the political order. While Weber saw 'property' and 'the lack of property' as the basic characteristics of all class situations, the institution of property has received scant attention in pluralist and functionalist analyses of industrial societies.

In the following chapters I will use the class concept to refer to categories of individuals delineated on the bases of their relations to the means of production. The term 'social stratum' will be used to describe categories of individuals with reference to their market positions and status attributes.

The Marxian hypothesis that, in the development of capitalism, the relative importance of class will increase at the expense of other possible bases of cleavages has been attacked by generations of social scientists. A recent challenger, Frank Parkin, develops a self-professed bourgeois critique, based on a neo-Weberian approach to stratification which puts power and conflict in a central place. In contrast to the Marxian class theory, which he interprets to be a one-factor theory of distributive conflict, focused exclusively on the positions in the productive system, Parkin argues for a multi-dimensional approach where control over productive resources, race, ethnicity, religion, sex, etc., are viewed as equally importance bases for cleavages and the formation of conflict groups. Against the background of developments during the 1960s and 1970s, e.g., in Northern Ireland, Belgium and the United States, Parkin maintains that, in contrast to Marxian predictions, not class but rather 'racial, ethnic, and religious conflicts have moved towards the centre of the political stage in many industrial societies', and that therefore 'any general model of class and stratification that does not fully incorporate this fact must forfeit all credibility'.[24] Parkin thus explicitly denies the primary role of the sphere of production as a basis for conflict of interest.

Another challenge to the centrality of class in modern Western societies has been made by students of electoral behaviour, who have analysed the relative importance of different bases for party cleavages. While s[illegible] them stress the importance of socio-economic factors, [illegible]gue that religion and language are more important.[25] [illegible] study of party choice in Belgium, Canada, the Nether[illegible]outh Africa, Lijphart comes to the following conclu[illegible]ial class is clearly no more than a secondary and subsi[illegible]luence on party choice, and it can become a factor of impo[illegible]e only in the absence of potent rivals such as religion and language'.[26]

It goes without saying that language, religion and race are easily and frequently seen as introducing a communality of interests and therefore often become bases for collective action. In fact, language and religion are so important bases of cleavages that over the centuries they have helped to generate decision-making units, i.e., states, which tend to be more or less homogenous with respect to these characteristics. Class divisions, on the contrary, occur within decision-making units. In this sense, then, cleavages based on language, religion and ethnicity can be seen as primary to class.

However, a different picture emerges when we look at the cleavages within the present nation-states. Parkin's claim that race, language and religion are of equal or greater importance than the sphere of production in generating social cleavages in industrial society appears to be based on the extent to which different cleavages have generated open or violent conflicts. This, however, is a rather superficial reading of the evidence. While conflicts based on religion, race, ethnicity and also on environmental issues clearly have been the most violent ones during these decades, this fact tells us little about the importance of different cleavages as bases of collective action, which is what is here in question. The power distribution approach outlined above indicates that the extent of manifest conflicts primarily reflects changes in the distribution of power resources between groups or collectivities.

To evaluate the relative importance of different bases of cleavages, we must primarily look not only at the violent conflicts, dramatic as they may be, but also at the more institutionalized conflicts and, above all, at the extent to which these cleavages have served as bases for organizations of interest. In this perspective class organizations in the sphere of production, i.e., unions and employers' (or business) organizations, emerge in the central roles. These organizations have been the key participants in the societal bargaining which has emerged in the Western nations during the postwar period. Only rarely have religious or ethnic groups figured in such contexts. Socio-economic cleavages also remain central bases for the party structures in most Western nations.

As indicated above, many neo-corporatist writers have assumed a major 'goal-displacement' within the organizations purporting to represent the interests of the working class. In neo-corporatism these organizations are assumed to serve largely the interests of the organizational leaderships and to control their members on behalf of the dominant groups in society. Schmitter assumes that this holds for labour unions while, e.g., Panitch and Jessop acquit unions and place social democratic parties in the central controlling roles.

While 'goal displacement' within interest organizations is a clear possibility, it is an empirical question to what extent this has occurred in the wage-earner organizations. Assuming rational actors, a high level of voluntary union membership and party support can support the assumption that the union or party furthers the interests of the actors as perceived by them. The claim that unions in the Western nations have largely ceased to represent the interests of their members appears difficult to substantiate. In view of the fact that union members have daily opportunities to evaluate the consequences of leadership decisions at the place of work, such an assumption strikes me as rather absurd.

As far as the left parties are concerned, the variations between them would appear to be greater. Since they are rooted largely in the continuum of social stratification, political parties have a more flexible basis than unions, which reflect class divisions. Therefore goal displacements may occur more easily in left parties than in labour unions. The policy which a left party comes to represent when in government is affected by many factors, and such a party may come to choose a strategy which severely compromises working-class interests. The extent to which this has occurred probably varies considerably between countries. If we assume that unions tend to represent working-class interests more closely than the parties on the left, the closeness of the relationship between a left party and the union movement can be seen as one indicator of the type of policy which the party stands for.

My general hypothesis is that the presence of reformist socialist parties in the government can bring public policies closer to wage-earner interests. Also in this context, the distribution of power resources in society is of crucial importance. In the tripartite societal bargaining between the state, labour and capital, the distribution of power resources and the political composition of the government can affect the pattern of coalition formation in this triad and the outcomes of the bargaining. The smaller the disadvantage in power resources of the labour movement and the stronger the left party hold over the government, the more likely are state representatives to side with labour in the tripartite bargaining. Accordingly, the compromises resulting from societal bargaining can be expected to be more to the favour of wage-earners. There are considerable differences in the power position of the wage-earners between the Western nations. To these differences we shall now turn.

3 WORKING-CLASS MOBILIZATION

The theoretical perspective outlined in the preceding chapter indicates that the distribution of power resources between the main collectivities or classes in a society is of key importance for its distributive processes and institutional structures as well as for patterns of conflict and of change. The difference in power resources between wage-earners and business interests depends, of course, on changes affecting both these collectivities or parties. The power position of business is, for example, affected by the degree of concentration of private ownership in the economy and by the extent to which a country is dependent on its export industries. The extent and nature or organization of business interests are also of relevance here, as are the type of parties which forge political alliances between business interests and other groups in society. Viewed in a historical perspective, however, it would appear that the greatest changes have occurred with regard to the power resources of the wage-earners. For the present, therefore, we shall limit ourselves to an examination of changes in wage-earners' power resources over time and differences between countries.[1]

In a capitalist democracy the major power resources of the wage-earners are their organizations for collective action. Through these organizations the individually small power resources of the wage-earners can be combined and their significance increased. In this context, the organizations of primary interest are unions and political parties. This chapter examines the development of the political strength of left parties as well as of unions in eighteen OECD countries. The consequences of change in the distribution of power resources are then discussed with reference to the political developments in Sweden during the present century.

CONDITIONS FOR MOBILIZATION

The working class, created by the Industrial Revolution, came into being in distinctly different contexts in different countries. The contexts and conditions for the organization and mobilization of the workers had been shaped over the centuries through the patterns of cleavages found between different collectivities in society and the alliances or conflicts these groups had entered into.[2] The conflicts had occurred during different junctures in the histories of these countries: in the processes of nation-building, in the struggles for control over the church and the formation of community norms, as well as in the economic struggles between landed and urban interests. The residues of these conflicts, in the form of coalition of interest groups and political parties as well as in terms of traditions of cleavages and co-operation, of autocratic or representative rule, proved to be of significance for the extent and the ways in which the emergent working class came to organize and to mobilize.

Among the factors of significance for the mobilization of the working class in Western Europe, the timing of the struggles for nationhood and the linguistic and religious cleavages were of particular importance. Some of the European countries, including Britain, Denmark, France, the Netherlands, Sweden and Switzerland, have traditions as nation-states stretching back into history. In other European nations, however, the mobilization of the working class took place in the cross-currents generated by the struggles for nationhood, struggles which have lasted well into the twentieth century. In the nineteenth century, Belgium achieved nationhood and Germany as well as Italy were united. Norway, Finland, Ireland and Iceland, however, have achieved independence only in the present century. The Austrian republic developed out of the collapse of the Habsburg empire at the end of World War I.

The ethnic-territorial cleavages activated during the struggles for nationhood left most of the Western European countries relatively homogeneous in terms of languages spoken by the citizens. The main exceptions here are Belgium with two and Switzerland with three major language groups.

The conflicts between the state and the church taking place since the Reformation came to be very important for the formation of coalitions between classes in Western Europe. In the sixteenth and seventeenth centuries the Reformation and the Counter-Reformation concerned control over the church, whether it was to be a national church controlled by the state or a supranational one controlled from Rome. These struggles left a Europe split between a Protestant north (including the five Nordic countries and Britain), a Catholic southern and central Europe (including Italy, France, Spain, Belgium and Austria) and a central belt of religiously divided countries (the Netherlands, Germany and Switzerland).

The way in which the cleavages between the church and the state had been resolved during the Reformation and Counter-Reformation proved to be crucial for the form in which the liberal ideas connected with the French Revolution came to be implemented in the different countries. In the nineteenth century the cleavage between the church and the state was activated most clearly in the struggles for control over mass education.

In the Protestant countries, where the state controlled the church, the leaders of the church had become allies to the state elites. Without much conflict, the church was put in charge of mass education. In southern and central Europe, however, the

Roman Catholic church had become allied with the privileged groups of the 'ancien régime', primarily the landed interests. During the nineteenth century in these countries, a polarization tended to develop where a Catholic-traditionalist movement was set against a bourgeois opposition, forming a secular political movement with a liberal and national thrust. In the struggles since the nineteenth century over the control over mass education, political parties in defence of the Catholic church were formed in all of these countries with the exception of Ireland. After the breakthrough of general suffrage, these parties proved to be successful in winning mass support among the workers.

The contexts and conditions for the mobilization of the working class were also of significance for the shaping of the movements representing the interests of the upper and middle classes in these societies. Of particular importance was the way in which the conflicts between the landed interests and the interests of the urban bourgeoisie came to be resolved during the Industrial Revolution. In southern and central Europe, where the large landowners were important, the landed interests generally formed coalitions and parties with the urban and industrial powerholders. In the five Nordic countries, where farm units were smaller and feudal traditions weak or absent, special parties for the agrarian interests developed.

The way of resolving the conflict between the state and the church thus came to be of significance also for the organization of the dominant interests in the Western European countries. In some of these countries, notably Britain, Austria, Italy and Germany, the dominant interest groups became represented through one major party. In other countries the political representation of the upper and middle strata became more fragmented. The degree of fragmentation in the representation of the dominant interests was of importance for the structure of power and thus also for the relative position of the working class.

The 'new' nations - the United States, Canada, Australia and New Zealand - lacked some important factors which structured the cleavages in the Old World. They did not have a nobility or a landed gentry. There, the relations between state and church were settled without severe conflicts and led to a separation of the churches from the state and also largely from public education. In spite of their multi-religious character, therefore, these nations did not develop strong religious parties. The contexts and conditions for working-class mobilization in these countries thus came to differ from those in Europe. These differences have been discussed primarily in the context of efforts to explain why the United States has not developed any mass-based socialist labour movement of the European type.[3]

The explanations for the absence of a socialist labour movement in America have usually been phrased in terms of the lack of need for such a movement. In comparison with workers in Europe, the frustrations of American workers have been seen as limited by their greater affluence and the democratic tenor of American daily life. Greater prospects for social mobility, the frontier and the availability of free land have been assumed to form 'safety valves' and to have dissipated frustrations which otherwise could have been ignited into explosive radicalism. The fact that universal suffrage was granted well in advance of the expansion of the industrial working class avoided the overlapping of struggles for political and industrial citizenship which were important for the development of labour movements in Europe. In addition, the sheer size and complexity of the United States have been advanced as major explanations of 'American exceptionalism'.[4]

The argument that American workers did not 'need' a socialist labour movement must however be questioned. Thus, in the crucial half-century before World War I, real wages for workers appear to have increased less rapidly in the United States than in Sweden, France, Germany and Britain.[5] In any event, the conditions under which workers earn their living can be assumed to be of greater importance for their political views than their level of affluence. The importance of the frontier as a safety valve was probably limited in the latter part of the nineteenth century and later, when geographical and occupational mobility took place primarily from the countryside into the cities and from farming into industry. It also remains to be explained why American workers did not come to use their suffrage to block anti-labour legislation and to limit the anti-union use of state power.

Although the mainstream explanations of 'American exceptionalism' point to issues of relevance in this context, it appears to me that the major factors behind the absence of a socialist labour movement in America must be sought in the difficulties for organization which American workers have been confronted with. The major part of these difficulties are rooted in the fact that the American working class was created through slavery and through successive waves of ethnically very heterogeneous immigrants. The racial and ethnic heterogeneity of the American working class generated spontaneous social organization along ethnic lines and inhibited collective action on the basis of class. American employers also became skilled in exploiting the racial and ethnic cleavages among workers. In addition, immigrants generally tended to define their stay in the new country as a temporary one, and often for a long time retained the hope of returning to 'the old country', something which probably counteracted long-term commitments to collective organization.

The conditions for working-class mobilization in Australia and New Zealand appear to have been more favourable than in America. The main differences are related to the absence of slavery and the lesser heterogeneity of the immigrants. The Japanese working class came into being in a semi-feudal, authoritarian setting which lasted until the end of World War II.

UNIONS IN WESTERN NATIONS

The contexts and conditions for the organization of workers can be expected to have influenced their unionization as well as their political organization. The relevance of religion for unionization becomes apparent when we look at the patterns of splits within the union movements defined in terms of the existence of competing confederations for unions of manual workers (Table 3.1). In the Catholic countries (except Ireland) as well as in the religiously split countries of Europe, competing union confederations exist or have existed. However, the role of religion appears to be decreasing. When the union movements in Germany and Austria were re-established after the end of World War II, they were thus organized on a unified base. In the 1970s the Catholic and the socialist confederations in France, the Netherlands, and Italy have increased their co-operation.

Table 3.1 Unity and splits in manual union confederations in eighteen OECD countries by religion

Religion	Unified confederations	Split confederations
1 Catholic	Ireland	France, Italy, Austria (before World War II), Belgium
2 Mixed		
(a) Europe		Germany (before World War II), Netherlands, Switzerland
(b) 'New nations'	Australia, New Zealand	Canada, USA (craft-industrial, 1936-55)
3 Protestant	Denmark, Iceland, Norway, Sweden	Finland (political)
4 Other		Japan (political)

In the religiously split 'new' nations, religion has not been a very important factor for structuring cleavages and conflict groups. These countries, therefore, have had only minor splinter unions based on religion. American unions, however, were split between craft and industrial confederations from 1936 to 1955. Of the Protestant countries, only Finland has had significant splits within the union movement, based on conflicts between as well as among Social Democrats and Communists. Japan, however, has a political split union movement.

Since most Western nations are relatively homogeneous in terms of languages spoken, linguistic cleavages appear to have been of relatively small significance in this context. In Switzerland, where the three dominant languages are of relatively equal status, the language issue has not created major cleavages within the unions. In Belgium, however, where the two main languages also are associated with socio-economic differences, the linguistic cleavage has become intensified in the 1970s.

Table 3.2 Union densities in eighteen OECD countries, 1900-76, by religion

Religion		Before World War I	Interwar	1946-60	1961-76
		%			
1 Catholic	Austria	6	43	54	56
	Belgium	5	28	42	52
	France	7	12	28	19
	Ireland	-	15	33	40
	Italy	11	19	27	18
2 Split					
(a) Europe	Germany	16	46	36	34
	Netherlands	16	27	31	33
	Switzerland	6	15	25	22
(b) 'New nations'	Australia	30	37	52	48
	New Zealand	17	25	44	39
	Canada	8	12	25	27
	USA	8	10	27	26
3 Protestant	Denmark	16	34	48	50
	Finland	5	8	30	47
	Norway	6	19	47	44
	Sweden	11	30	65	76
	UK	15	29	43	44
4 Other	Japan	-	20	26	28

Table 3.2 shows the changes in the level of unionization in eighteen OECD countries during the present century. The table gives the number of union members as a percentage of the non-agricultural labour force according to census statistics for each country. The figures have been computed as averages for four different periods of time: from the turn of the century to the outbreak of World War I, the interwar period, the years 1946-60 and the years 1961-76.[6] The averages for the different periods of time bring out long-term trends more clearly; however, they conceal some sharp variations within each period, e.g., the drastic decreases in union membership after the unsuccessful general strikes in Sweden in 1909 and in Britain in 1926, as well as the trebling of union membership in Finland in 1917, the year before the Civil War.

In the period before World War I, the highest level of

unionization was found in Australia, where it had become very high already at the beginning of the century. This was probably due to the introduction of a compulsory arbitration system, which made it possible for low-paid workers to register their organizations under arbitration law and to compel employers to negotiate and to accept wages and employment conditions achieved by stronger groups.[7] Additionally, New Zealand, Germany, Denmark, the Netherlands and Britain had high levels of organization relatively early. At that time Sweden ranked about in the middle of the table, partly as a result of the defeat of the unions in the general strike of 1909. On the other hand, Belgium, Finland, Austria, Switzerland and Norway initially had low rankings.

In comparison with the period before World War I, the level of unionization doubled during the interwar years. The increase was especially marked in Austria, Belgium, Germany and Sweden. During this period Sweden moved into the upper third of the table.

The level of unionization also increased markedly during the period 1946-60; on average, roughly 50 per cent in these countries, although the trends vary. Thus, Germany did not reach the level of organization of the pre-Nazi period. The increases were also low in the Netherlands and in Japan. Other countries - Finland, Norway, Sweden, the United States, Canada, Ireland and France - more than doubled their level of unionization. In this period Sweden assumed the lead in the level of unionization.

During the 1960s and 1970s the growth in the level of unionization has stagnated in several countries. Although the number of union members generally has increased, this increase has often not kept pace with the increase in the non-agricultural labour force. A slight decline occurred in Germany, the United States and Switzerland, but there were sizeable decreases in France, Italy, New Zealand, Australia and Norway. In contrast, the percentage of union members has increased in Finland, Belgium and Sweden. The level of unionization in Finland has increased dramatically since the split within the union confederation was overcome in 1969. In terms of period averages, however, since the 1960s the distance between Sweden's level of unionization and its nearest competitors has clearly widened. In a comparative perspective, the growth of union organizations in Sweden stands out as exceptional.

Although religious cleavages have tended to generate splits in terms of union confederations, they do not appear to have been of major importance for the levels of unionization. The observed differences in union densities instead largely reflect the extent to which unions have been able to enrol salaried employees and women in their ranks. As white-collar employees and women have swelled the ranks of the labour force, the level of unionization has dropped in several countries, e.g., Norway. However, in the United States, Canada, West Germany, Switzerland, the Netherlands, Italy and France, significant portions of male workers also remain unorganized.

Can the level of union organization be taken as an indicator of the propensity of wage-earners to define their interests in collective rather than in individualistic terms and of their capability to enter into collective action? Many writers on corporatism would appear not to think so; they tend to assume that in the period of neo-corporatism union membership is compulsory. Such a view implies that union membership by and large is involuntary and enforced, and that members are objects more than subjects. However, these corporatist writers have produced little if any empirical justification for the assumption, crucial in their thought, that in Western nations unions have now changed from voluntary to compulsory organizations.

With the exception of the closed shop, unions in these countries have few if any means of compelling or forcing wage-earners to join their ranks. Unions are limited to convincing and inducing wage-earners to join, for example, through ideological persuasion, the provision of services and social pressures from workmates. It seems a safe hypothesis that variations in the level of unionization between the Western nations cannot be accounted for in terms of differences in the extent to which unions have been able to compel or to force workers to join.

As a case of special interest let us here look at Sweden, which often is presented as the paragon of neo-corporatism and at the same time is the most highly unionized country. Survey studies in Sweden indicate that the overwhelming majority of union members perceive their membership as voluntary and as motivated by the belief that they benefit from the membership, or want to be solidaristic with the labour movement.[8] In Sweden compulsory measures such as the union shop have never been utilized. However, social pressures from workmates to join the union are probably relatively strong.

As distinct from several other countries, social benefits in Sweden are largely the result of legislation rather than of union negotiations. Eligibility for benefits is therefore generally based on citizenship, not on employment. Union membership is practically never a requirement for eligibility for social benefits. Even unemployment insurance can be acquired without being a union member. The increasing level of unionization in Sweden thus probably reflects a growing propensity of wage-earners - both salaried employees and workers - to define their interests in relation to the employer collectively rather than individually. Also in other Western nations, the level and type of unionization probably largely reflects variations in the capacity of wage-earners to act collectively.

POLITICAL MOBILIZATION

In the area of politics the consequences of the contexts and conditions for the organization of workers can be traced in terms of the bases for the cleavages which structure the party systems as well as in terms of the share of the vote which the left parties have received. Political sociologists have attempted to quantify the relative importance of different bases of cleavages by using differences in voting patterns as their dependent variable.[9] A frequently used measure has been the well-known Alford index of 'class voting', in terms of which the percentage difference between manual and non-manual voters for the left parties have been compared, for example, with the percentage difference in votes for religiously based parties between frequent and less frequent churchgoers.[10]

Such comparisons, however, cannot easily be interpreted as indicators of the relative importance of different bases of cleavages. Since we cannot assume a linear relationship between the independent and the dependent variables, e.g., frequency of church attendance and probability of voting, the Alford index becomes sensitive to the choice of the point of dichotomization of the independent variable. If, for example, the probability of voting for a party increases most rapidly when we move from medium to frequent church attendance, a dichotomization at this point may yield a higher value on the Alford index than a dichotomization separating infrequent churchgoers from the others. The social and political significance of the religious cleavage, however, depends also on the relative number of frequent churchgoers, as well as on the size of the religious parties, something which this index does not inform us about. Since the manual-non-manual dichotomization generally produces something close to a 50-50 split on the independent variable, in this context the political significance of the Alford index tends to be greater. It can give an indication of the extent to which socio-economic cleavages structure the party system.

The main bases for cleavages in the party system of our eighteen OECD countries in the 1970s are crudely summarized in Table 3.3.[11] This summary is based on voting patterns as well as on the relative size of different types of parties. As can be expected, the religious factor, or more precisely Catholicism, has been important in structuring party cleavages. In the Catholic and religiously split European nations, religious-secular cleavages cross-cut those based on the socio-economic positions of voters. With one exception, the index of class voting receives low values in these countries. The party systems of the Netherlands, Switzerland and Belgium, however, are based primarily on religious cleavages. In Belgium socio-economic cleavages have also been pronounced and the linguistic ones have increased in the 1970s. The Irish party system was established in the struggles for nationhood, and socio-economic cleavages are very weak. In Austria, Italy and Germany, however, socio-economic cleavages largely overlap the religious ones. In France in recent years the religious-secular cleavage has tended to be overshadowed by the conflict between the socialist-bourgeois blocs. In these countries, therefore, socio-economic cleavages would appear to be almost as strong as the religious ones in forming the bases for party systems.

Table 3.3 Main basis for cleavages in party systems of eighteen OECD countries in the 1970s, by religion

Religion	Country	Major cleavages	Index of 'class voting'
Catholic	Austria	Religious/socio-economic	44
	Belgium	Religious/linguistic/socio-economic	27
	France	Religious/socio-economic	21
	Ireland	Nationhood	16
	Italy	Religious/socio-economic	17
Split			
(a) Europe	Germany	Religious/socio-economic	26 17
	Netherlands	Religious	21
	Switzerland	Religious	
(b) 'New nations'	Australia	Socio-economic	33
	Canada	Unclear	4
	USA	Unclear	18
	New Zealand	Socio-economic	43
Protestant	Denmark	Socio-economic	47
	Finland	Socio-economic	54
	Norway	Socio-economic	39
	Sweden	Socio-economic	45
	UK	Socio-economic	35
Other	Japan	Socio-economic	27

In the religiously mixed 'new' nations, the religious issue has not been decisive for the structuring of the party systems. In the North American countries, the bases for party systems are unclear. Socio-economic cleavages form the main basis for the parties in Australia and New Zealand. In the Protestant countries as well as in Japan, socio-economic cleavages are predominant.

The extent to which party choice is structured by socio-economic cleavages can be expected to depend on the resources for collective action achieved by wage-earners. While citizens in the middle and upper socio-economic strata generally vote for parties which represent their interests, workers are more dependent on mobilization through collective organizations. This is clearly reflected in the extent to which the levels of union densities in our eighteen OECD countries covary with the index of class voting. The coefficient of correlation between them is 0.71, which indicates that about one-half of the variance in class voting is related to the level of unionization.

DECLINING ROLE OF RELIGION?

Has religion maintained its position relative to the socio-economic cleavages as a basis for collective action and organization in the Western nations during the postwar period? To answer this question we would need empirical data which are not now available; for example, changes in church membership and activity during the postwar years. Changes in the size of votes for religious parties are also of interest in this context, although they are difficult to interpret. In countries where religious cleavages have been of minor importance, the establishment of religious parties (e.g., in Sweden and Finland during the 1960s) was a protest against the continuously declining role of religion rather than an indication of the increased importance of religion. The Norwegian religious party, however, has maintained a sizeable following during the postwar period.

Table 3.4 Percentage of votes for religious parties during the postwar period in six countries of Western Europe

	Percentage of votes for religious parties		
	Up to 1965	1966-80	Decline
	%	%	%
Austria (1945-62)	45.1	44.2	0.9
Belgium (1946-65)	42.8	33.3	9.5
Germany (1953-61)	46.9*	46.3	0.6
Italy (1948-63)	42.3†	38.7	3.6
Netherlands (1946-63)	53.8	40.0	13.8
Switzerland (1947-63)	23.9	23.3	0.6

*In 1949 = 31.0
†In 1946 = 35.2

The share of the vote for religious parties in the European countries, where religion has formed a major basis for the party systems is given in Table 3.4.[12] In Italy and Germany the Christian Democratic parties received a considerably lower proportion of votes in the first democratic elections after the demise of fascism than they have done later. If we disregard the first post-fascist elections in both these countries, when the new party systems were far from established, we find a considerable decline for the Christian Democrats in Italy but relative stability in Germany. The referendum on abortion in Italy in 1980, in which the alternative supported by the Catholic church was clearly defeated, is another indication of the declining role of religion in Italy. In Austria, however, the share of the vote of the middle-class-based religious party has declined very little. In Germany and Austria, where the Catholic church appears to play a politically less active role than in Italy and where religion and class cross-cut each other in what are largely two-party systems, changes in the vote for the middle-class and religiously based parties are difficult to interpret.

The clearest indication of the declining role of religion is found in the Netherlands, the country where religious cleavages in the party system traditionally have been most pronounced. Since the mid-1960s the share of the vote for the religious parties has declined by no less than 14 per cent. A similar decline has taken place in Belgium, where the importance of linguistic cleavages has increased. In Switzerland the decline of the religious parties has been relatively small. When combined with the observations above on the increasing co-operation between confessional and secular unions in some countries, the data would appear to indicate that in Western Europe religion is losing some of its previous influence as a basis for collective action.

LEFT VOTING, 1900-80

What patterns can be found in the development of the voting strength of the 'left' parties during the present century? As left, labour, socialist or social democratic parties, we shall here define the reformist socialist or social democratic parties and the parties to their left. Splinter parties from the social democrats towards the right (some of which label themselves 'Social Democrats') will be excluded. The proportions of the valid vote given to the left parties thus defined are given in Table 3.5 for four different time periods: from the turn of the century to the outbreak of World War I, the interwar period, 1946-60 and 1961-80.

In the years before World War I the relative strength of the socialist parties partly reflects the degree to which suffrage was extended to workers. At that time left parties were already relatively strong in several countries, notably Finland, Germany, Australia, Austria, Belgium and Denmark, where they received about one-fourth to one-third of the vote. Around the end of World War I universal and equal suffrage for men existed in all our countries except Japan.

Religious cleavages appear to have been of some importance for the relative strength of the left parties. During the interwar years, the strongest social parties were thus found in the Protestant countries, where they received about 40 per cent of the vote. Among the Catholic and religiously split countries in Europe, socialist parties were strong in Germany and Belgium with about 40 per cent of the vote. The French socialist parties were also relatively strong, while the left parties were considerably weaker in Italy, the Netherlands, Switzerland and Ireland. In the 'new nations', the Australian Labour Party remained

Table 3.5 Left percentage of valid votes in eighteen OECD countries, 1900-80, by religion

Religion		Before World War I	Interwar	1946-60	1961-80
Catholic	Austria	23	41	48	48
	Belgium	23	38	42	34
	France	13	32	43	41
	Ireland	–	10	12	15
	Italy	18	26	35	41
Split					
(a) Europe	Germany	31	40	34	41
	Netherlands	13	25	36	33
	Switzerland	16	28	30	28
(b) 'New nations'	Australia	37	45	50	47
	New Zealand	5	35	48	44
	Canada	0	3	13	17
	USA	4	5	1	0
Protestant	Denmark	26	39	45	46
	Finland	40	39	48	46
	Norway	15	36	52	50
	Sweden	13	46	52	51
	UK	5	33	48	45
Other	Japan	–	–	32	41

strong and the Labour Party in New Zealand increased its strength. On North American soil, however, the socialist parties did not achieve a foothold.

A year-by-year analysis of voting figures (not given in Table 3.5) indicates that around the end of World War II, the share of the vote for the socialist parties peaked in several countries. These peaks were generally followed by decreases in vote shares in the years up to 1960, decreases which generated discussions among social scientists of the 'embourgeoisement' of the working class and of the 'end of ideology'. The declines in left votes following this peak were marked in Australia, Britain, Denmark, France, Germany and Sweden. In Finland, the Netherlands, Norway, Italy and Japan, the left parties were able to maintain their relative strength in these years.

In comparison with the average for 1946-60, in the period 1961-80, the electoral fortunes of the left parties have improved in Italy, Ireland, and Germany. Sizeable decreases however took place in Belgium and some decrease occurred in the Netherlands and Switzerland. In France the socialist share has tended to increase since the late 1960s. The Labour parties in Australia and New Zealand have had slipping electoral support, while in Canada the weak social democratic party has become somewhat stronger. In the Protestant countries the socialist share of votes has to decrease slightly. Japan, finally, has seen an increasing strength of its left parties.

WORKING-CLASS POWER RESOURCES

Not only the level of unionization, but also the type of unions and their interrelationships, are of importance for the extent to which union organizations constitute power resources for wage-earners. Thus it is of significance whether workers are organized on the basis of craft or industry, and whether unions are united in one confederation or fragmented along religious or political lines. The extent of co-operation between the socialist parties and the union movement must also be assumed to influence working-class power resources. An interaction between union and political resources can be expected, so that changes in the resources on the one side can weaken or reinforce resources on the other side. In the political arena the power potential of the working class is reflected in the amount of support given to the socialist parties, in working-class participation in elections, and in the extent to which the left parties are divided among themselves.

Working-class power resources can be expected to be greatest where the labour movement is well integrated and has strong support from wage-earners. This implies a high degree of unionization in industrial rather than craft unions, close co-ordination between different unions in a strong union confederation, and a close collaboration between the trade union movement and a socialist party, which is clearly dominant on the left and which has strong support among the electorate. Where one or more of these conditions are lacking, the power resources of the working class are expected to be lower.

Thus, several of the organizational characteristics of unions often regarded as expressions of 'neo-corporatism' are here seen as factors contributing to the strength of working-class organizations. These characteristics are significant for the distribution of power resources in the capitalist democracies, the strategic independent variable in my approach outlined in Chapter 2.

The level of working-class power resources as manifested on the labour market and in politics in our eighteen countries is summed up in Table 3.6 as averages for the period 1946-76.[13] Since the extent of electoral participation in itself is an important aspect of the political mobilization of the working class, we have here chosen to look at the proportion of the electorate voting for socialist parties (i.e., not on the proportion of socialist votes of votes cast). On the basis of their combined ranks on the level of unionization and share of the electorate voting for left parties, we have divided the countries into three groups having low, medium and high levels of working-class mobilization.

Mobilization measured in this way is an important aspect of the entry of the working class into the political arena. But this measure does not reveal much about the extent to which the working class has actually been able to exercise political influence through parliamentary channels. To shed light on the working class's exercise of political power, we can examine two additional

Table 3.6 Patterns of working-class mobilization and political control in eighteen OECD countries, 1946-76

Pattern	Country	Percentage unionization	Left votes as percentage of electorate	Working-class mobilization	Weighted cabinet share	Proportion of time with left representation in cabinet	Splits within the labour movement: Parties	Splits within the labour movement: Unions
		%	%					
High mobilization, stable control	Sweden	71	43	High	High	High		
	Austria	55	45	High	Medium	High		
	Norway	46	41	High	High	High	Minor	
High mobilization, occasional control	Denmark	49	39	High	Medium	Medium		
	New Zealand	42	41	High	Medium	Medium		
	UK	44	35	High	Medium	Medium		
	Belgium	47	32	High	Medium	Medium	Minor	Political, religious
Medium-high mobilization, low control	Australia	50	44	High	Medium	Low		
	Finland	39	37	Medium	Medium	Medium	Major	Political, religious
	France	25	32	Medium	Low	Low	Major	Political, religious
	Italy	23	34	Medium	Low	Medium	Major	Political, religious
	Japan	27	28	Medium	Low	Low	Major	Major
Low mobilization, exclusion	Ireland	36	9	Low	Low	Medium		
	Canada	26	11	Low	Low	Low		
	USA	27	1	Low	Low	Low		
Low-medium mobilization, partial participation	Germany	35	31	Medium	Low	Medium		
	Netherlands	30	31	Medium	Low	Medium	Minor	Religious
	Switzerland	23	18	Low	Low	High		Religious

indicators. The first pertains to the representation of labour parties in government. We have measured this by an index of weighted cabinet share, where the proportion of seats in each cabinet held by socialist parties has been weighted by the socialist share of seats in parliament and by the duration of the cabinet. This weighted cabinet share can be interpreted as an indicator of the working class's ability to exercise political influence.

A second aspect, which is of importance for the strategies of class conflict, is the stability of socialist control over the government. Where the participation of labour parties in government is stable and of long duration, we can expect different types of conflict strategies than in countries where socialist representation in government has been irregular or sporadic. A qualitative aspect of the mobilization and power resources of the working class, which is not captured by the measures above, is the extent of religious and political cleavages in the labour movements of different countries. The major splits are noted in the table. The degree of co-operation between the dominant left party and the unions is also of importance for the power position of the wage-earners.

On the basis of the level of working-class mobilization and the pattern of socialist party participation in government, our eighteen countries can be grouped into five fairly distinct categories. Among the countries with a high level of mobilization, Sweden, Norway and Austria have had a pattern of strong and stable social democratic participation in government. In Sweden and in Norway the social democratic parties took control of the executive and enjoyed an electoral majority as early as the 1930s, and this control continued through most of the postwar period. In Austria the social democratic party was strong already during the early years of the interwar period and up to the fascist period. In the second Austrian republic, the social democrats have been one of the two major parties throughout the postwar period. They participated in coalition governments from 1945 to 1966, and since 1970 have formed a majority government. In these countries union confederations are strong and the co-operation between the political and unions wings of the labour movement has been close.

In a second category consisting of four countries - Denmark, New Zealand, Britain and Belgium - the level of working-class mobilization has been high but working-class parties have had only periodic control over the executive (ranging from one-fourth to three-fourths of the postwar period). In Britain and New Zealand the Labour Parties have formed majority governments at irregular intervals. In Denmark and Belgium, the Social Democratic and Socialist Parties have periodically entered into coalition governments or formed minority governments. Relations between unions and the political parties have been problematic.

In the next group of five countries, the mobilization of the working class has ranged from high to medium but socialist parties have been largely unsuccessful contenders for government control. Despite a strong union movement and a large share of the electorate, the Australian Labour Party has remained an opposition party except for two short periods. In the other four countries the labour movements have been internally divided. From time to time the socialist parties in Finland, Italy and France have participated in coalition cabinets or formed minority governments, which often have been unable to count on the support of the large communist parties in parliament. Only in Finland have the communists been represented in government to any appreciable extent. Italy's membership in NATO has contributed to the barring of communists from government. Japan, finally, has had minority left party representation in the government for only two years, in the late 1940s.

In a fourth group, comprising the United States, Canada and Ireland, the level of union organization has been relatively low and the socialist parties have generally been outsiders in the political decision-making processes. In the United States left parties in the European sense are insignificant. The Canadian social democratic parties have enjoyed some success at the regional level. In Ireland the party system emerged in the struggle for nationhood and its Labour Party has had only minority representation in government.

The fifth category of countries - the Netherlands, West Germany and Switzerland - constitute the religiously split part of Europe where Catholics and Protestants are of about equal strength. In these nations working-class mobilization has attained only low or medium levels but the social democratic parties have participated in governments on a fairly regular basis. In Switzerland the Social Democratic Party was admitted to the Federal Council, a non-parliamentary type of executive, in the 1940s and has remained there ever since except for a brief exodus in the 1960s. The Dutch social democrats have participated in coalition and minority governments during about half of the post-war period. In Germany, on the other hand, the Social Democratic Party was consigned to the opposition up until 1966 when it entered the 'grand coalition' with the Christian Democrats. From 1969 to 1982 it was the dominant party in a coalition government with the small Liberal Party.

The above grouping of the eighteen countries into five categories is based on three quantitative indicators (level of unionization, level of left electoral support, and the extent and pattern of left party participation in government), which all are seen as measures of the central independent variable in my theoretical approach, the distribution of power resources within a country. The three indicators tend to covary. In Germany, the Netherlands and Switzerland, however, in spite of relatively low levels of unionization and left voting, the parties of the left have participated in governments during long periods. From the point of view of my theoretical approach these three countries would thus appear to be the most problematic ones. This indicates that also other factors, such as religious cleavages, can be of significance for the pattern of interest mobilization and aggregation in a country. Empirical applications of this way of classifying countries will indicate to what extent and in which ways it should be revised.

It is of some interest to compare the classification of OECD countries arrived at here with the classifications suggested by the corporatist approach. Although corporatist writers have primarily been engaged in case studies of single countries, some efforts have recently been made to classify countries in terms of the degree of corporatism.[14] The bases for such classifications are, however, relatively vague and vary between authors. They include aspects which from the power distribution perspective appear as independent variables (such as level of unionization and position of union confederations) as well as those which appear as intervening variables (e.g., institutional structures for societal bargaining) and dependent variables (e.g., the level of industrial conflict).

Most corporatist writers, however, tend to view Austria, Sweden and Norway as strongly corporatist countries. The Netherlands, Switzerland and Japan are also often included in this category - countries which from the power resource perspective can be expected to differ significantly from the first mentioned ones. In the category of weak corporatism, countries are often included which from our perspective appear as very heterogeneous, such as on the one hand France, Italy and Britain and on the other hand the United States, Canada and Ireland.

POLITICAL BATTLE LINES

During the postwar period levels of unionization in our eighteen countries have generally tended to be higher than the levels of electoral support for the left parties. While in the 1980s in a few of these countries unionization has reached or surpassed 80 per cent of the non-agricultural labour force, not even in the countries where the left parties are strongest has their electoral support among wage-earners been more than temporarily above the 50 per cent mark. In countries with two-party systems or with blocs of parties arranged along the left-right continuum, in the long run the distribution of votes tends to oscillate around the 50-50 mark.

In explaining these differences in the 'success' of the mobilization of unions and of left parties it is instructive to use the distinction between classes and social strata. The class concept refers to categories or collectivities of citizens defined in terms of their positions in the sphere of production, whereas social strata are categories distinguished on the bases of market positions and or status attributes. Unions are an outgrowth of the class structure in the Western countries and consequently are based primarily on the clash of interests between labour and capital.

This is an enduring line of conflict. Unions can thus grow until they include all wage-earners - a situation which is becoming a reality in Sweden. In a capitalist democracy, however, a political party would be doomed to failure if it were solely based on entrepreneurs. Accordingly, all political parties in these countries try to appeal to a relatively wide spectrum of the socio-economic hierarchy.

In countries where socio-economic cleavages dominate the party system, the position of the parties and political blocs along the left-right continuum normally can be expected to correspond roughly to the relative position in the socio-economic hierarchy of the voters from where the party draws the bulk of its support. But in a democracy, the parties and blocs must in principle try to win at least 50 per cent of the votes, otherwise their activity is reduced to demonstrations. In order to win a majority of the electorate, the parties or blocs may find it necessary to modify their policies. The economic theories of democracy, pioneered by Anthony Downs, take similar observations as their starting points in the explanation of the dynamics of party politics.[15] The expected long-range outcome of such policy adjustments is the emergence of a fairly evenly divided distribution of voters between the blocs.

But where on the left-right continuum will the political line separating the two blocs be located? It appears obvious that in different countries the crucial line of party conflict around which the voters are currently formed into two blocs will be located at very different points. Economic theories of party competition cannot explain differences between countries in the location of the political battle line along the left-right continuum. In my theoretical perspective, however, the location of this dividing line appears largely as the result of the distribution of power resources within the society. Its location is reflected, for instance, in political struggles centred around distribution.

Structural preconditions undoubtedly are of significance for the distribution of power resources between collectivities and classes in a society, and thus for the issues that are in the focus for the political struggles. None the less, variations in structural factors can only partially explain the wide differences between Western nations in levels of unionization and in political resources and the social consciousness of wage-earners. Thus, for example, the dramatically different courses of development of the labour movements in Britain and in Sweden during the 1970s and early 1980s are difficult to interpret in structural terms. To explain such differences we also have to look at the strategies and policies pursued by the unions and left parties in the different countries.

It is possible, for example, that the degree of success in unionizing salaried employees is affected by the type of union confederations into which they are to be organized, whether in politically independent confederations or in confederations cooperating with socialist parties. The Swedish and Finnish salaried employees have been successfully organized in the former type of confederations. In Norway and Britain, on the contrary, salaried employers have been more or less reluctant to join confederations of the latter type. The nature of the compromises into which left parties enter when they participate in governments must also be assumed to have consequences for social and institutional structures as well as for the social consciousness of citizens - consequences which may facilitate or hamper the growth of left political support.

CLASS RELATIONS IN SWEDEN[16]

The discussion above indicates that by the early 1980s the Swedish wage-earners had attained levels of unionization and mobilization which were unsurpassed in any other Western country. During the postwar period, unionization among Swedish wage-earners has increased to a level unique among the Western countries. Moreover, Sweden is the country where the socialist parties have enjoyed the strongest and most stable electoral support, and the Social Democratic Party has had the longest tenure of executive power. Clearly, then, an analysis of Swedish politics, both in terms of historical and contemporary trends, is of interest as a test case for the development of class relations in the Western countries.

Let us now use the theoretical perspective outlined in Chapter 2 to examine briefly developments in Sweden during the past hundred years. In early industrialism, an enormous gap existed in the power resources of an upper class comprised of the newly emergent bourgeoisie and the traditional elite groups of society, on the one hand, and the still fragmented working class, on the other hand. But the workers began to organize into trade unions and to become politically activated. In 1889 Socialdemokratiska Arbetarepartiet (the Social Democratic Workers' Party) was formed and in 1898 Landsorganisationen, the LO (the Swedish Trade Union Confederation) came into being. The differences in power resources between labour and business interests decreased. This led to an increase in industrial disputes. The improved capacity of the workers to co-ordinate their actions induced the employers to organize. The employers' associations experienced a breakthrough in 1902 and formed confederations, the most important of which became Svenska Arbetsgivareföreningen, the SAF (the Swedish Confederation of Employers' Organizations). The employers countered union mobilization with massive lockouts. The general strike of 1909 was triggered by the threat of a lockout and, comparatively speaking, was the largest industrial dispute up to that time in the Western countries.

The decrease in the power resource disadvantage of the working class and the conflicts ensuing from this decrease generated institutional changes, which must be seen as important gains for the labour movement. The rights of unionization and collective bargaining were thus recognized in an agreement between the LO and the SAF in 1906. But the growing strength of the workers also increased their demands and aspirations. During the decades around the turn of the century the question of political citizenship became the most controversial social problem. Towards the end of World War I the propertyless workers, strengthened by an alliance with middle-class groups represented by the Liberals, were able to change significantly the institutions of society by forcing the adoption of political democracy. These settlements can be seen as the first 'historical compromise' between the classes in Swedish society, a compromise which significantly affected the conditions for class conflict in the years to come.

Despite the introduction of political democracy, the Swedish labour movement was largely excluded from executive power and consigned to fighting for a fairer distribution of the results of production through industrial action. The employers adopted a strategy of intransigence. Around the end of World War I, industrial disputes intensified. The employers continued to use industry-wide lockouts. At times conflicts on the labour market were of a political nature. Among these were the general strike for universal suffrage in 1902 and the nationwide strike protesting against the Collective Contracts Act of 1928.

Measured in terms of the number of working days per worker (used for industrial disputes) from the turn of the century up to the early 1930s, Sweden had the highest level of strikes and lockouts among the Western nations. Industrial conflicts in Sweden were long and relatively large. They reflected bitter conflicts of interest and the high degree of the organization of both workers and employers.

THE COMPROMISE OF THE 1930s

The Great Depression of the 1930s and the 1932 election to the Second Chamber of the Riksdag resulted in a change in the political situation. In the election for the first time the socialist bloc (Social Democrats and Communists) received a little over half of the votes. Because of the electoral system, the socialist majority among the voters was not immediately reflected in the composition of parliament. The bourgeois parties (Conservatives, Agrarians and Liberals) maintained their majority in the indirectly elected First Chamber of the Riksdag. Through a deal with the Agrarians, the Social Democrats were able to form a government under the leadership of Per Albin Hansson. During the subsequent elections in 1934, 1936 and 1938 the party increased its support among the voters. Yet, since the First Chamber of the Riksdag reflected an older electoral opinion, the Social Democrats were unable to achieve an overall parliamentary majority before World War II. However, in contrast to the ineffectual Social Democratic minority cabinets of the 1920s, the governments led by the party during the 1930s had the backing of an increasing proportion of the electorate.

This majority support for the socialist parties was something new in Swedish politics. Through the entrenchment of the Social Democrats as the dominant governmental party, the labour movement could mount a successful offensive in the class struggle in the political arena - through parliament and the government. Governmental power had now been separated from economic power. This crucial decrease in the power resource difference between the two main protagonists in Swedish society induced them to re-evaluate their earlier strategies of conflict.

For the labour movement, control of executive power offered great advantages. It could avoid costly industrial conflicts and rely on political instruments to redistribute the results of production and to strengthen the position of the wage-earners. The level of employment could be raised, reducing the spectre of unemployment. Social and fiscal policies could be used to influence the distributive processes in society. The labour movement had much to gain by attempting to reach a settlement with business interests in the industrial arena and to transfer its initiatives in distributive conflicts to the political arena.

For the employers, the Social Democrats' firm grip on governmental power was a major loss. The absence of a friendly government meant that the employers could no longer utilize their ultimate weapon, the general lockout, as successfully as before. They also had to fear possible political intercessions in the economy. Moreover, state intervention in industrial relations, which previously had generally benefited the employers, could now shift to the advantage of labour.

In this new situation, opinions diverged markedly among the employers on which strategy they should adopt. The directors of Sweden's multinational corporations advocated an aggressive stance towards the Social Democratic government. They urged industry to co-operate with the bourgeois parties, especially the Liberal Party, to unseat the Social Democratic government as quickly as possible. However, the leaders of the SAF, where enterprises dependent on the home market dominated, believed that the Social Democrats' control of the executive was likely to continue for a long time. For the employers the best course of action, therefore, was to maintain formal political neutrality and to act as a pressure group to influence the political process.

The pronounced reduction in the inferior position of power of the labour movement, resulting from the Social Democrats' firm control of the government, prompted the two major protagonists in society to enter what can be called the second 'historical compromise' between capital and labour. This second compromise emerged gradually. In 1936, for the first time since the general strike of 1909, LO and SAF initiated negotiations which two years later resulted in the so-called Saltsjöbaden Agreement. The actual content of the agreement was not as important as its symbolic significance. The 'Saltsjöbaden spirit' signified that the parties on the labour market and the main protagonists in society had adopted new strategies of action.

The preconditions and terms for the historical compromise were summed up by Ernst Wigforss, Minister of Finance in Per Albin Hansson's government and the foremost socialist theoretician within the party, in a speech to the Gothenburg Bourse Society in 1938. Wigforss's point of departure was that neither the labour movement nor business interests could realistically hope to resolve the conflict between them by suppressing the other party. For the foreseeable future both parties thus had to recognize the existence of a very powerful adversary. Wigforss argued that in this situation labour and capital had to examine the possibility of a compromise. He formulated the two legs of the second historical compromise in the following words:

> Expressed without euphemisms this means, on the one hand, that those who have power over larger or smaller sectors of the private economy do not base their actions on the assumption that the current tendencies in government are a transitory phenomenon, that a political change will take place within a future near enough that a discussion based on the possibility of concessions, accommodations and compromises becomes unnecessary.
>
> On the other hand, it also means that the representatives of political power admit the necessity of maintaining favourable conditions for private enterprise in all those areas where they are not prepared without further ado to replace private enterprise with some form of public operations.[17]

The major prerequisite for the historical compromise was thus a stable division of economic power and governmental power between opposing classes. Out of the compromise grew arrangements for handling societal problems which sometimes have been termed the 'Swedish model'. This model was based on the mutual contributions of the parties to increase economic growth. They would co-operate in 'making the pie larger in order that there would be more to divide'. Through control of the government, the labour movement could then influence the distribution of economic growth. Business enjoyed favourable conditions for investment and expansion.

Thus, the historical compromise did not abolish the clash of interests in society. Instead, the altered power relations changed the preconditions for conflict and induced the parties to revamp their strategies of conflict. A dramatic result of the new conflict strategies appeared on the labour market. From having the highest relative volume of industrial disputes in the world up to the mid-1930s, Sweden was transformed within a decade into a paragon of peaceful industrial relations. The foundation for industrial peace, however, was neither a change in values nor a basic consensus between labour and business interests. Industrial peace was the result of altered power relations inducing the parties to devise new conflict strategies.[18]

For the labour movement, the new strategy of conflict did not entail the abandonment of long-range political goals. The leadership within the Social Democratic Party, Per Albin Hansson, Ernst Wigforss and Gustav Möller, viewed the emphasis on economic growth embodied by the compromise as one element in a strategy to increase the electoral support of the party and to hasten the 'maturation' of the capitalist society.

In an interview in 1974, Wigforss summarized the development of the socialist strategy of the Social Democrats up to the 1930s in the following way:

> When I had written my little book on 'The Materialist Conception of History' (in 1906), I became acquainted with a group of younger Social Democrats, Per Albin Hansson, Gustav Möller and Richard Sandler. And what I definitely can say is that at that time the question of concentration in industry was still the big issue. This is because a concentration in economic life, with the victory of the big firms, etc., would facilitate socialization. Precisely the idea that socialism would come through capitalism in the way which Engels analysed in his at that time very influential book, 'Socialism: Utopian and Scientific', captured the interest of many of us. We saw the whole economic development as an example of the correctness of the Marxian description of capitalist development. This was a precondition for our political strategy.
>
> In the 1930s, when we had made the deal with the Agrarians, we were wondering what could be done right away. Per Albin Hansson and I agreed that we had to try to hasten the development towards big enterprises and thereby the need for economic planning which we had assumed in our programme. And when we now had state power in our hands in the form of a majority in the Riksdag I could only see one option, which was to go to private enterprise and say: 'Will you not help us to hasten this development?' Of course we did not express it in that way, but this was our motive. The idea was thus to urge on the Marxian concentration, to hasten the development which from the beginning we had seen as a condition for socialism.
>
> Then it had always been clear to me that the unions were to participate in this interaction with industry. This was to be a school for them, before we would be able to adopt the line which I advocated, namely to take over the role of the capitalists. . . . One can say that our strategy pre-supposed a development of the liberal welfare state. Welfare was to be the immediate result. But behind it were the greater possibilities for workers themselves to take over the production.[19]

The fact that the formula for the historical compromise was to endure for over thirty years indicates that the 'Swedish model' for handling the clash of interests between capital and labour was successful in several respects. In its spirit Sweden was transformed from one of the less developed European countries into an industrially and socially advanced society. Wage-earners as well as business interests derived significant benefits from the compromise. For wage-earners the single most important aspect of the compromise was probably the full employment policy; for business interest it was the favourable opportunities for investment and expansion of the most effective and profitable enterprises. Foreign observers - and even many Swedes - tended to see this welfare capitalism as the 'happy ending' to the conflicts which have beset Western countries ever since the Industrial Revolution.

BREAKING UP FROM THE COMPROMISE

The historical compromise of the 1930s was not however the final chapter, but only a long episode in the development of a capitalist democracy. Since it was worked out in a situation where the labour movement had reduced but far from eliminated its inferior position in terms of power resources vis-a-vis business interests, the seeds of change were contained in the compromise. The policies in the spirit of the compromise also had substantial negative consequences for wage-earners.

The 'necessity of maintaining favourable conditions for private enterprise' acknowledged by the Social Democrats eventually meant that economic growth occurred largely on the terms of capital. Company profits steered the development of the economy. The trade union movement had to accept a more intensive utilization of labour. The development of technology was determined by company profits - not by the needs of the wage-earners. In accordance with the demands of business, the labour force was increasingly concentrated to urban communities, resulting in a migration of labour and rural depopulation. Company calculations of profits did not include the costs of environmental degradation and the misuse of human resources which followed in the wake of economic growth. During the postwar period the concentration of ownership and power in the economy, which was already high, continued to increase.

The leadership of the labour movement found it difficult to keep alive the idea of a fundamental transformation of society. The requirements of day-to-day politics, focusing on the efficient functioning of the economy and on winning marginal improvements, took time and energy from the long-range plans for social change. The trends toward centralization of decision-making in the labour movement and larger units of local government made contacts between the leadership and the rank-and-file membership more difficult. When the bourgeois parties eventually endorsed the main features of the social reform policies, the differences between the political blocs seemed to dwindle. The leaders of the labour movement appeared to be administrators of the mixed economy rather than the potential creators of a new society. They often defended the compromise policies even when these were to the detriment of their members and voters.

The bourgeois parties were not successful in opposing the social reforms, which for the members of the labour movement were the positive feature of the compromise policy. They came to be much more successful in criticizing the disadvantages of the compromise policies and in mobilizing the electorate against their negative effects. The Agrarians, who changed their name to the Centre Party in 1957 and subsequently adopted a new party programme, eventually enjoyed the greatest success. In its attempts to gain a foothold among new groups of voters to compensate for its rapidly shrinking electoral base in rural areas, the Centre Party could concentrate its criticism on unsatisfactory conditions for which the Social Democrats appeared to share responsibility: rapid urbanization, regional imbalances, the establishment of larger decision-making units creating more distance between citizens and their elected representatives, environmental destruction and, finally, nuclear energy.

Since the development of the expansionary economic policies in the 1930s to combat unemployment, the co-operation between the political and the union wings of the Swedish labour movement have been close. It should be noted, however, that this co-operation has been based on a relative equality between the parties. Corporatist writers have assumed that under neo-corporatism, which is supposed to be especially well developed in Sweden, the state induces organizations like unions to observe 'certain controls on their selection of leaders and articulation of demands and supports'.[20] In the context of the Swedish labour movement, however, this assumption appears ridiculous. If anything, the Social Democratic government has been the 'transmission belt' for union demands rather than the other way around. Traditionally, union leaders have been represented on the executive board of Social Democratic Party and in the Riksdag. On the local level, also, union activists have been frequently represented in local party organs and in local government.[21] The unions have thus exerted a major influence on the internal processes of the party. The Social Democratic Party, however, has conspicuously refrained from attempting to influence leadership selection within the unions.

The relations between the LO and the Social Democratic government have at times been strained, however.[22] This was the case especially in the late 1940s, when the Social Democratic government managed to convince union leaders about the necessity of a wage freeze. After two years, however, the wage freeze was abandoned. In the 1950s the government adopted a new economic policy, the key to which was the 'active manpower policy' developed by the LO. In the 1970s it was primarily demands from the LO which made the Social Democratic government depart from the policies of the 'historical compromise' of the 1930s.

Beginning in the late 1960s, the combination of pressures from other parties and protests from its own rank and file against unsatisfactory conditions, for example through a series of unofficial strikes,[23] forced the leadership of the labour movement to reappraise its earlier policy. This rethinking started within the unions. It took place in a situation where the inferior position of the labour movement vis-a-vis the representatives of capital and allied groups had further decreased since entering the historical compromise in the 1930s. As a result, the labour movement now started to question conditions which had previously appeared unrealistic to change. The initiative for the departure from the compromise of the 1930s thus came from the labour movement, especially from the unions.

Through a programme of labour legislation initiated by the LO, in the first years of the 1970s an offensive was launched to limit managerial prerogatives and to increase the influence of the employees at the place of work. The offensive was also manifested in the LO proposal for 'löntagarfonder', wage-earners' funds, which questioned the distribution of economic power in the private sector. Simultaneously, the employers' organizations and the bourgeois parties mobilized their forces. The clash of interests intensified. In the first half of the 1970s, even before the international economic crises had seriously affected Sweden, the strategies and policies based on the historical compromise of the 1930s thus ceased to work. The symbol of the compromise, the Saltsjöbaden Agreement between the LO and the SAF, was terminated by the LO when the new law on joint consultation at the place of work came into effect in 1976. In the final chapter we shall return to this discussion. The following four chapters analyse voting and politics in our 'test case', Sweden. The focus here will be on the conditions for mobilization and collective action of the wage-earners.

4 ELECTORAL PARTICIPATION

To influence the political process, citizens must participate in it. Obviously, an individual can participate in politics in a variety of forms: she can vote, discuss politics at home and on the job, keep informed about politics through the media, join political organizations, participate in demonstrations, serve in office, etc. These various forms of participation differ, inter alia, in terms of the amount of initiative and mutual co-operation required as well as in their effects.[1]

Elections afford an opportunity for every citizen to influence the political process in a simple but perhaps decisive way. Electoral participation is therefore a traditional area of interest in the social sciences. In recent decades, however, the significance of participation has often been overlooked. Students of electoral behaviour have thus focused on party choice and have tended to neglect the substantial variations found in electoral participation within as well as between countries. In this chapter we will begin by discussing factors affecting electoral participation and will review turnout differences during the postwar period in our eighteen OECD countries. Thereafter we will focus on changes in participation in Swedish elections since the introduction of universal suffrage and variations in turnout among different groups. Finally, we shall examine some additional aspects of political involvement.

FACTORS INFLUENCING PARTICIPATION

Electoral participation varies between countries and over time. In every country it also varies between communities and regions and between different categories of the population. Among the factors which can be assumed to affect electoral participation, the following are of special interest.

Administrative and Practical Circumstances

Electoral participation is affected by various administrative and practical circumstances. Some countries have attempted to encourage voting through legislation making voting compulsory. Also, the administrative arrangements surrounding elections vary considerably between countries in ways which affect turnout. Of relevance here is whether voters are registered automatically or on their own initiative; the number of days during which one can vote; whether voting takes place on work or rest days, and whether postal, advance and proxy voting is permitted. Definitions of eligible voters also vary between countries, as does the accuracy of voter registers, the bases on which turnout is computed. Turnout computed on the basis of total population in the eligible age-groups tends to yield lower figures compared with those computed on the basis of persons officially defined as eligible.

Among the practical circumstances, transport facilities and the distance to polling places previously played a significant role. Such factors have been particularly decisive for certain occupational groups and for the elderly.

The Relevance of Government Policies

Voting usually presupposes that citizens believe that their welfare is affected by political decisions. Generally, electoral participation can be expected to increase when the resolution of highly relevant issues is at stake. But voting turnout is also influenced by the extent to which the electorate is aware and informed of the consequences of political decisions. Differences between categories of citizens in levels of awareness about the consequences of government policies are probably more important for variations in electoral participation than are the differences in the actual effects of policies for these categories.

Individual and Collective Resources

Voting is encouraged if the individual believes that he and those with similar backgrounds and interests are able to influence political outcomes. In this context individual and collective power resources of voters are of importance. It can be expected that the larger the resources at the disposal of an individual or group, the higher the voting turnout.

As a rule, individuals in the upper socio-economic strata possess sufficient resources to ensure that their electoral participation will be high. Individually based resources, especially education, have been proposed as the key variable in electoral research and in voting.[2] However, such an individualistic approach is often accompanied by a neglect of the role of collective resources. Among citizens in the lower socio-economic strata with individually small resources, the availability of collective resources in the form of organizations - primarily trade unions and working-class parties - is of prime importance for political participation. Differences in the availability of collective resources is probably a major explanation for the variations between the Western countries in working-class electoral participation.

The voters' perceptions of their ability to influence political outcomes is also affected by their experiences regarding the effectiveness of the political system. If the voters' expectations are repeatedly disappointed, they may become disillusioned and abstain from voting.

The Collective Nature of an Individual's Problems

The degree of relevance of government policies for an individual depends not only on the nature of policy decisions but also on the nature of the problems which are central to an individual. Some types of problems, such as those concerning livelihood and standard of living, are shared by the vast majority of people. But some persons' most pressing problems are of a personal nature, having no direct connection with politics. The lower electoral participation of certain groups of the population can be partially understood in these terms.

Social Environment

Social scientists have long postulated that the increasing numerical dominance of a particular social group in a community will lead to growing pressures of the group not only on its members but also on others in the community.[3] These assumptions have been based on observations that left parties have been stronger in communities where manual workers have comprised a clear majority of the population than in more 'mixed' areas.

The explanations of such 'contextual effects' rest on the assumption that the individual's social relationships occur mainly in the residential area. The larger the proportion of workers in a residential area, the greater the frequency of social contacts between workers. This may create social pressures which reinforce the influence of working-class organizations and culture. At the same time, competing influences from bourgeois quarters are weakened, and cross-pressures are thus reduced. Accordingly, this produces what might be termed a 'hot-house effect', which nurtures and reinforces working-class influences. Changes in housing patterns and community structures are thus of potential significance for the possibility to mobilize working-class voters.

In practice, however, it is difficult to isolate contextual effects of this type in empirical social research. The effects of concentration of a specific group in a community are compounded by the effects of the composition of the group. For example, workers living in middle-class areas often have jobs in the service sector, whereas those in working-class areas tend to be employed in large manufacturing industries or mining.

CROSS-NATIONAL DIFFERENCES IN PARTICIPATION

With some significant exceptions, electoral participation in the Western countries has tended to increase since the breakthrough of political democracy, which occurred around World War I for many of these countries. However, there are still sizeable variations in electoral participation between them.[4]

The average electoral participation in our eighteen countries during the period 1965-80 and the trend in participation from

1945 to 1959 are presented in Table 4.1.[5] Of the four countries with the highest participation rates, three have legislation pressuring citizens to vote: Australia, and Belgium have compulsory voting; in Italy non-voting is registered on official identification documents and is therefore easily perceived as a stigma. When compulsory voting was abolished in the Netherlands in the late 1960s, in the following three elections the turnout dropped on the average by 11.2 per cent. Also, differences in administrative arrangements discussed above are of significance here.

Table 4.1 Average turnout in parliamentary elections, 1965-80, and postwar trend (difference in turnout between 1945-59 and 1965-80) in eighteen Western countries

Country	Turnout	Trend
	%	%
Australia[a]	95.1	-0.3
Austria[b]	92.6	-2.8
Italy[a]	92.4	+0.2
Belgium[a]	92.3	-0.5
Sweden	90.2	+10.5
West Germany	88.8	+4.8
Denmark	87.9	+4.7
New Zealand	83.7	-9.4
Netherlands[c]	83.5	-11.2
Norway	83.1	+4.1
France	81.2	+1.3
Finland	79.5	+3.0
Ireland	76.2	+1.9
Great Britain	75.6	-3.1
Canada[d]	74.8	-0.1
Japan	71.7	-2.2
United States	56.2	-1.1
Switzerland[b]	55.3	-14.4

a Compulsory voting or equivalent.
b Compulsory voting only in provinces with less than 10 per cent of the electorate.
c Turnout refers to the period 1970-80 when voting was voluntary. The trend measures the difference from the period 1945-67 when voting was compulsory.
d Data not available for 1974 election.

Among countries without compulsory voting Austria has the highest turnout (although in Austria and Switzerland voting is compulsory in provinces with less than 10 per cent of the population). As early as the 1920s and early 1930s, electoral participation in Austria was very high - roughly 20 per cent higher than in Sweden during the same period. During these years women in Austria voted nearly as frequently as men, while in Sweden there were sharp differences in voting participation between the sexes. The postwar trend in turnout in Austria has however been a decreasing one. Austria is now followed by Sweden, West Germany and Denmark with turnout figures ranging between 87 and 90 per cent. Next come New Zealand, the Netherlands, Norway, Finland and France - all having a turnout of over 80 per cent or higher. On the other hand, the turnout in Ireland, Great Britain, Canada and Japan is considerably lower.

The United States and Switzerland stand out, however, as having the lowest electoral participation. In the past both of these countries had much higher participation in elections.[6] In the United States the decline in the mobilization of the electorate occurred after the turn of the century and was partially a result of changes in voting procedures and requirements which discriminated against the participation of blacks and the large immigrant groups in industrial areas.[7] The decline in participation in Swiss elections has taken place during the postwar period. This would appear to reflect declining interest in the elections resulting from the fact that the composition of the federal coalition government has not been affected by the outcome of the elections.

The postwar trend in turnout, from the period 1945-59 to the period 1965-80, has however been an increasing one in all the Nordic countries and in West Germany. This increase has been most dramatic in Sweden; 11 per cent. The background to the drastic decrease in turnout in the Netherlands and Switzerland has already been mentioned. In New Zealand and Britain also the decrease has been considerable. If we exclude the 1948 election, the United States too has experienced a considerable downturn in electoral participation. The same holds true for Japan.

In the Western countries the upper social strata consistently have a higher voter turnout than workers. The difference in electoral participation between workers and the higher occupational strata, however, varies substantially between the countries. In the United States the difference is great, whereas for example in Austria it is fairly small.[8] Similarly, in Sweden the difference is now relatively narrow. Generally in countries where socio-economic cleavages form the basis for the party system, we can expect that the lower the voter turnout, the larger the differences in the electoral participation between workers and the upper socio-economic strata.[9] Until now, however, such 'class differences' in electoral participation have received scant attention in political sociology.

We have assumed above that the availability of collective resources in the form of working-class-based organizations is of relevance for the electoral participation of workers. In the absence of comparative data on voting in different socio-economic groups, we will here take the national participation level as a proxy. Union density and the percentage of votes for the left parties (as defined in Chapter 3) can be taken as indicators of the organizational resources of workers. From this analysis we shall exclude Australia, Belgium and Italy, where legislation plays an important role in increasing participation.

In the remaining fifteen OECD countries, the correlation between union density in 1946-76, and turnout in 1965-80 is 0.63, whereas the correlation between the left vote in 1946-80 and turnout is 0.70. If we combine union density and left voting by taking the average of the two figures for each country, the correlation with turnout increases to 0.75. While an individual resource such as education is related to turnout only on the individual level, a collective resource like unionization thus affects participation also cross-nationally.

MOBILIZING ELECTIONS

In the first two general elections in Sweden after the introduction of universal and equal suffrage (1921 and 1924), the voting turnout was low (Figure 4.1 and Table A1 in the Appendix). Nearly every second eligible voter failed to go to the polls. Since then electoral participation has risen. To some extent, the increase in turnout rates simply reflects the fact that it has become easier to vote; for example, in recent years improved communications as well as the extension of proxy voting and postal voting has made participation more convenient.

Nevertheless, increasing electoral participation primarily represents the gradual incorporation and mobilization of the Swedish people in the democratic class struggle. This mobilization of the people has not been a steady, smooth process. Instead, it has been characterized by abrupt spurts in turnout during elections where important political issues have stirred the feelings of the electorate and where control of the government was at stake. During the intervening elections, the voting turnout subsequently has often fallen but has remained at a higher level than before the mobilizing election. This pattern can be clearly observed in the turnout statistics for the Swedish general elections.

The first major mobilization of voters occurred in the so-called Cossack election in 1928,[10] when the Social Democrats campaigned on radical demands and the bourgeois parties feared that the Social Democrats might win a sufficient number of seats to form a strong government. In particular, better-off citizens were mobilized in large numbers, and the Social Democrats' challenge was successfully countered. After a slight rise in voter turnout during the 1932 election, the next major mobilizing election came in 1936. The Social Democratic government resigned in June 1936 over the issue of raising the national pension and was replaced by an Agrarian cabinet - the so-called 'vacation government'. Three months later Social Democrats succeeded in securing their largest number of seats in parliament so far.

The first general election after World War II, in 1948, was also

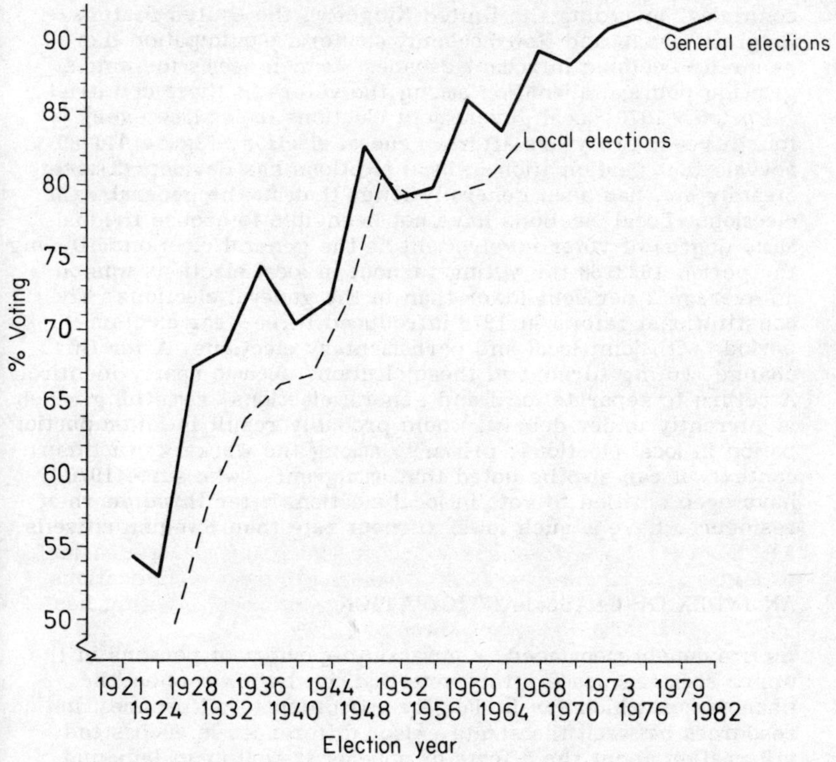

Figure 4.1 Voting turnout in local and general elections, 1921–82

a major mobilizing election. The bourgeois parties attempted to rally the voters against what they portrayed as the threat of a planned economy. The 1960 campaign, another mobilizing election, occurred in the aftermath of the struggle over the supplementary pension scheme and concerned the expansion of the public sector. In the 1968 election the Social Democrats were predicted to lose, but they managed to mobilize the voters and win their largest victory under the banners of 'more equality' and 'full employment'. The struggles for the control of government in the 1973 and 1976 elections spurred the voting turnout to new record levels. In the 1979 election, however, voter participation dropped slightly, but it increased somewhat in the 1982 elections.

The stable increase in electoral participation in Sweden indicates that the citizens view elections as meaningful acts significantly affecting their living conditions. It further indicates that the electorate feels that through voting it can influence the direction of politics in a fairly meaningful way. In several countries, including the United Kingdom, the United States, Belgium, Japan and New Zealand, electoral participation has generally declined in recent decades - which seems to suggest growing political alienation among the voters in these countries.

Up until 1970, local government elections took place every fourth year, two years after a general election. Figure 4.1 reveals that participation in local elections has developed more steadily and has been generally lower than in the general elections. Local elections have not been able to arouse the same degree of voter involvement as the general elections. During the period 1928-68 the voting turnout in local elections was on an average 2 per cent lower than in the general elections. The constitutional reform in 1970 introduced three-year election periods with joint local and parliamentary elections. After this change, voting turnout in these elections became nearly identical. A return to separate local and general elections, something which is currently under debate, would probably result in lower participation in local elections, primarily among the workers. In this context, it can also be noted that immigrants, who since 1976 have been entitled to vote in local elections after three years of residence, have a much lower turnout rate than Swedish citizens.

AN INDEX OF CLASS PARTICIPATION

As previously mentioned, a greater proportion of persons in the upper socio-economic strata vote than in the lower ones, a phenomenon which can be largely attributed to differences in resources between the strata. Also, differences in access to information about the effects of policies as well as in levels of aspiration are important here. Some interesting variations in the main pattern, however, can be pointed out. Thus, voting turnout among male elementary schoolteachers has been very high - as high as among categories listed in the election statistics as 'landed proprietors, wholesale merchants, industrialists and rentiers'. Generally, public employees have had relatively high participation figures. This is also true of categories of workers in public employment (e.g., postmen, stationhands and municipal workers). In the middle strata, independent farmers have had a high voting turnout. Among seamen and the nomadic Lapps electoral participation has been very low, for understandable reasons.

In the working class, agricultural and forestry labourers as well as tenant farmers - sizable categories until World War II - have had a low voting turnout. Among working-class women, the formerly large category of domestic servants had by far the lowest voting turnout, 15-20 per cent below the average for working-class women.

To describe changes over time in the electoral participation of socio-economic strata, we can examine differences in the voting turnout between socio-economic categories traditionally distinguished in Swedish electoral statistics. On the basis of occupation, the electorate has been divided into three 'social groups': an 'upper middle class' category (social group I), a 'middle class' category (social group II), and the working class (social group III). An index of 'class participation' can be constructed by simply taking the percentage difference in turnout between, on the one hand, the working class and, on the other hand, the two combined middle strata.[11]

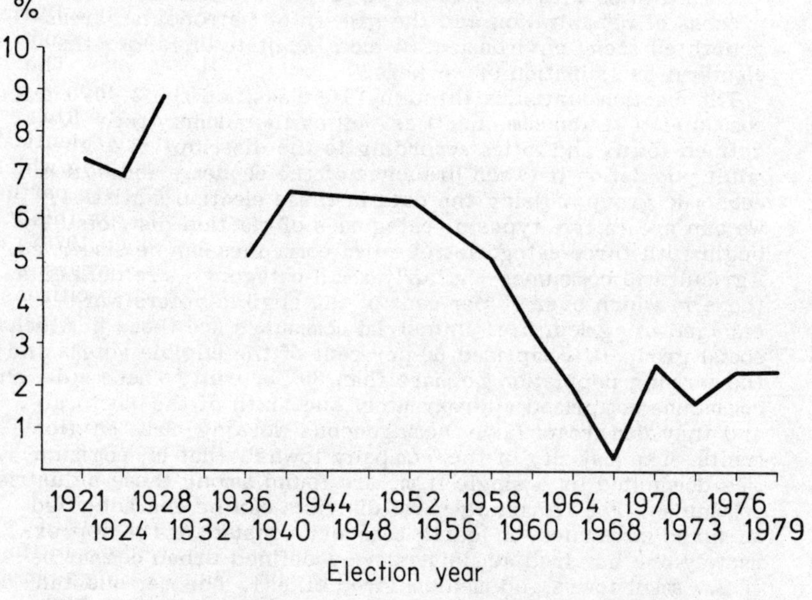

Figure 4.2 Class difference in voting turnout in general elections, 1921-79: difference between social groups I and II and social group III

The index of class participation shows that until the beginning of the 1950s social groups I-II had a substantially higher voting turnout than the workers (Figure 4.2). The differences were most pronounced - roughly 9 per cent - in the 1928 election and remained around 6 per cent until the 1956 election. Subsequently the class differential in electoral participation has markedly declined - reaching a record low level, less than 1 per cent, in the mobilizing election of 1968. Since then, the differential has been slightly higher, approximately 2 per cent. The decline in class differences in participation since 1956 coincides in time with the breakthrough of television in the electoral campaigns, something which may have contributed to increasing interest in the campaigns among working-class groups.

MOBILIZATION OF THE WORKING CLASS

Figures on the general elections compiled by the Swedish Central Bureau of Statistics (SCB) up to the elections of the 1950s enable us to trace in more detail the mobilization of the working class at the ballot box. It is of particular interest to elucidate the importance of the residential environment for the electoral participation in various social strata by analysing the turnout rates in communities with different types of social structure. Has the process of urbanization and the growth of metropolitan areas generated social environments which facilitate or hinder the electoral participation of workers?

The election statistics through 1948 classified the 2,400 rural communes ('landskommuner') as well as the administratively defined towns and cities according to the distribution of the adult population between branches of the economy and socio-economic groups. Using the data in these election statistics, we can create five types or categories of election districts. To begin with three categories of rural communes can be discerned.[12] Agricultural communes - a fairly small category - are defined as those in which over 60 per cent of the eligible voters were engaged in agriculture. Industrial communes are those in which social group III comprised 60 per cent of the eligible voters and the farming population no more than 30 per cent. These industrial communes comprised approximately one-sixth of the electorate, and they demarcate fairly homogeneous working-class environments. The majority of the 'company towns', that is, communities dominated by a single firm, are found among these industrial communes. The remaining rural districts can be characterized as mixed communes. A fourth category consists of the approximately one hundred administratively defined urban communes (i.e., small towns and medium sized cities). The metropolitan centres of Stockholm and Gothenburg as well as the Malmö constituency (which also includes the cities of Helsingborg, Landskrona and Lund) make up a fifth category.

The electoral participation in social groups I and II has not varied markedly between these five types of communes. In contrast, substantial differences have existed between communes in terms of mobilization of the working class in the parliamentary elections. This is evident in the 1928, 1936 and 1948 elections (Table 4.2). The voting turnout for both working-class men and women has been lowest in the agricultural communes, followed by the mixed communes. The industrial and the urban communes have consistently exhibited the highest working-class turnouts. Among men electoral participation has been slightly higher in industrial communes than in the towns and cities. Workers in the metropolitan centres, however, have had only 1-2 per cent lower turnout rate than workers in industrial communes in the countryside. Working-class women have had at least an equally high turnout in the metropolitan centres as in the rural industrial districts.

Table 4.2 Percentage turnout of working-class voters (social group III) by sex in various types of communes in the 1928, 1936 and 1948 general elections

Type of commune	Men 1928	Men 1936	Men 1948	Women 1928	Women 1936	Women 1948
	%	%	%	%	%	%
Agricultural communes	62	73	78	48	60	69
Mixed communes	67	75	80	55	65	74
Small and Medium-size towns	71	78	83	60	69	79
Industrial communes	74	80	84	64	73	80
Stockholm, Gothenburg, Malmö Constituency	73	78	83	65	72	81

It is possible that the figures in Table 4.2 somewhat underestimate the mobilization of workers in company towns and industrial communities, since, in addition to the densely populated areas where industry is located, the commune may also include varying proportions of rural population. In an attempt to identify purely industrial communities we have utilized the descriptions of densely populated areas (excluding cities, boroughs and municipalities) contained in the 1930 census, where the distinctive character of densely populated communities in the countryside was specified. Among these, approximately 160 industrial communities or company towns with over 400 inhabitants were listed. In 1928 the average voter turnout of the working class in the communes or election districts containing these communities was not however higher than the figure noted above for all industrial communes.[13] We have also examined the approximately 110 boroughs and municipalities which were classified as industrial communities (where 50 per cent or more of the economically active population was engaged in industry). Again, the working-class turnout here in 1928 was not higher than the average for industrial communes.[14]

Among a total of approximately 270 industrial communities and company towns, however, we find nearly 110 communes or election districts where the voting turnout in the working class was higher than in social group II. And in seventeen of these industrial communities the working class attained an exceptionally high degree of mobilization in 1928 - a turnout rate of over 85 per cent. But electoral participation in industrial communities and company towns has varied rather sharply. In the 1928 election there were also a number of communes and election districts with industrial communities where the working-class turnout was exceptionally low - below 60 per cent.

Of the metropolitan centres, the Malmö constituency has traditionally had an extremely high working-class turnout. In Stockholm and Gothenburg, however, electoral participation among the workers has not been higher than in other urban areas. Even in the working-class-dominated districts of the South Side (Söder) of Stockholm, the worker turnout was lower than the average worker turnout in Malmö. The working class has also had a remarkably high rate of electoral participation in the agricultural districts surrounding Malmö.

The high working-class mobilization in the Malmö area probably has a historical explanation. The socialist labour movement came to Sweden via Denmark and was first established in this area. It managed even to create a foothold among farm labourers in the large estates common in this part of Sweden. Rural workers migrating to Malmö were therefore socialist to a larger extent than rural migrants to other metropolitan areas.

In Swedish discussions, the electoral setbacks for the Social Democrats since 1968 have often been explained in terms of the decline of the 'red company towns', which once constituted a unique 'hot-house' environment for working-class culture. Especially the metropolitan areas have been seen as providing an unfavourable social environment for working-class mobilization. The findings here, however, suggest that urban environments, and especially the metropolitan centres have generally provided as favourable conditions for the growth of the labour movement as did the industrial communities in the countryside. On the other hand, agricultural and rural environments seem to have clearly inhibited the mobilization of the working class. Similarly, in the mixed rural districts the voting turnout of the workers was considerably lower than in the urban areas. On the whole, then, the process of urbanization may have favoured rather than hampered the development of the labour movement.

INCORPORATION INTO THE POLITICAL PROCESS

An analysis of electoral participation by sex and age offers interesting insights into the process by which individuals and categories of citizens have been incorporated into political life. Women were long excluded from the political process. Whereas the franchise was extended to the majority of men by 1911, women were not enfranchised until 1921. During the first elections with universal and equal suffrage, the voting turnout of women was nearly 15 per cent lower than the turnout rate of men (Figure 4.3). Subsequently, however, the sex differential in electoral participation has gradually declined. Sex differences in voting turnout have been smaller in the cities than in the countryside.

In the 1973 and 1976 elections the male lead in electoral participation vanished. The 1979 election was historical inasmuch as the voting turnout among women for the first time was higher than among men. In all Western countries, women have traditionally had lower turnout than men. In other countries also, for example Finland, the differences have diminished.[15] Sweden, however, is among the first countries where the traditional sex pattern in electoral participation has been reversed.

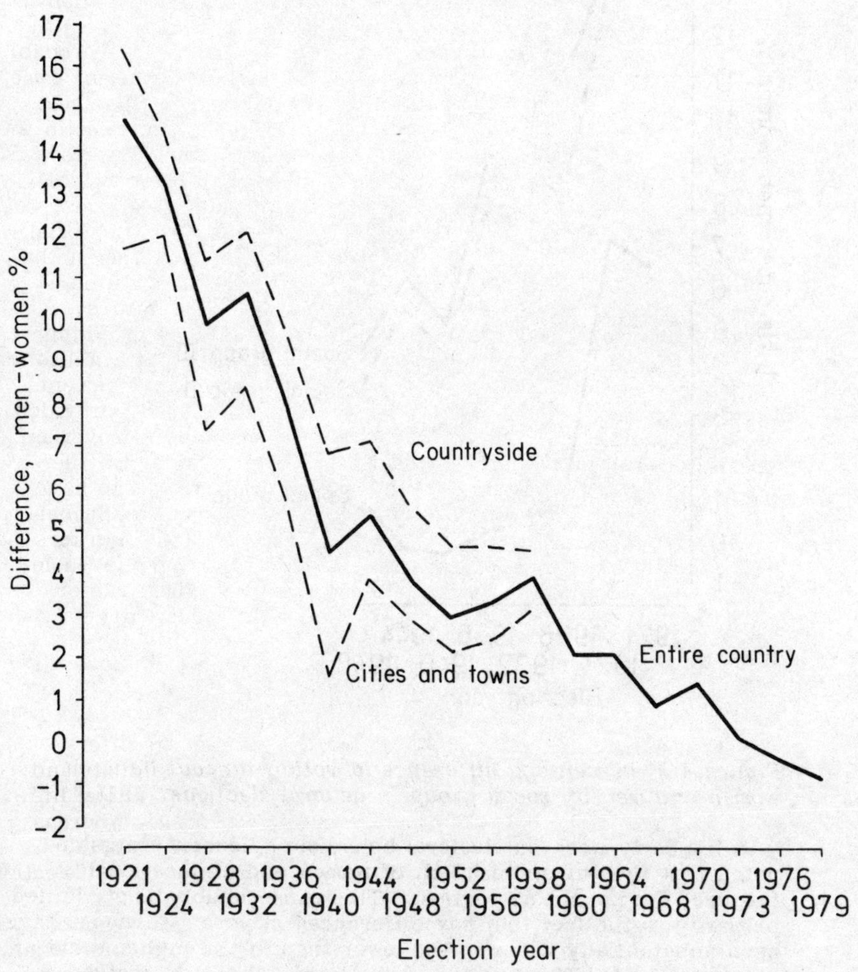

Figure 4.3 Percentage difference in voting turnout between women and men in general elections during 1921–79 for the entire country, cities and the countryside

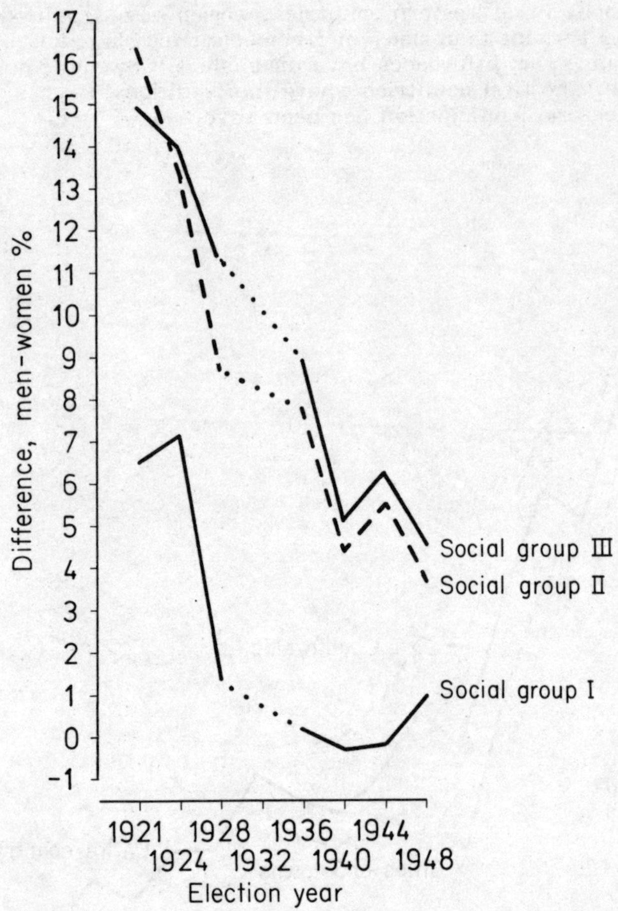

Figure 4.4 Percentage difference in voting turnout between women and men by social group in general elections, 1921-48.

In his early work on electoral behaviour, Herbert Tingsten noted that the enfranchisement of women had unquestionably favoured the bourgeois parties.[16] This can probably be attributed primarily to the fact that sex differences in voting turnouts have been substantially wider in the lower than in the higher socio-economic strata. Through the 1948 election, Swedish election statistics contained data on the electoral participation among men and women by socio-economic group. As is evident in Figure 4.4, variations in voting turnout between the sexes have been relatively small in social group I. They have been considerably larger in social group II and especially large in social group III.

In the 'Cossack election' of 1928 the voting turnout among men increased in similar proportions in all socio-economic strata. The socialist parties, however, lost the election largely because of the increased mobilization of women in the higher socio-economic strata. Bourgeois campaign posters in the 1928 election were directed particularly to women, and warned: 'Women of Sweden! Whoever votes for the "labour party" is voting for the dissolution of family bonds, the demoralization of children, and the downfall of morals.' These exhortations seem to have been effective. In this election women in social group I for the first time turned out to vote in nearly the same proportions as men, something they have continued to do ever since. Likewise in social group II there was a sizable mobilization among women, while the voting turnout of working-class women did not increase to the same extent. In the subsequent mobilizing elections of 1936 and 1948, however, the participation rate of working-class women increased as much as those of other groups. The voting turnout in 1940 dropped more sharply among men than among women, probably because military service made it more difficult for men to vote.

This gradual but, in terms of content, dramatic change in women's political involvement as mirrored in their electoral participation has primarily been the result of a generational shift. The inter-generational change can be traced in election statistics (Figure 4.5). In the 1932 election men in all age categories still voted much more frequently than women. Subsequently the differences between men and women, however, decreased in the youngest age categories. In the local elections of 1942 women in the youngest age category, for the first time, voted as frequently as men. The differences between men and women in electoral participation in the 1948 election had shrunk considerably in age groups under 30, while the differences were still substantial among voters over 45 years of age. As the older generations have successively passed away, the differences between the sexes in electoral participation have dwindled. In the 1979 election the new edge for women in turnout rates was especially pronounced among younger and middle-aged voters.

Figure 4.5 also shows that in the 1930s and 1940s there were major differences in the voting turnout between age groups. Young people's incorporation into the political process proceeded slowly. Electoral participation subsequently began to fall off even among voters who were in their fifties. Thus, among both men and women electoral participation peaked at around 40 years of age.

With the increase in electoral turnout to the record high level in 1976, Sweden has approached the ceiling of maximum feasible participation. This increase has not only obliterated differences between men and women, it has also straightened out the age curves in Swedish voting. In the 1979 election, first-time voters went to the polls nearly as frequently as their parents. Pensioners up to the age of 75 voted almost as often as middle-aged voters.

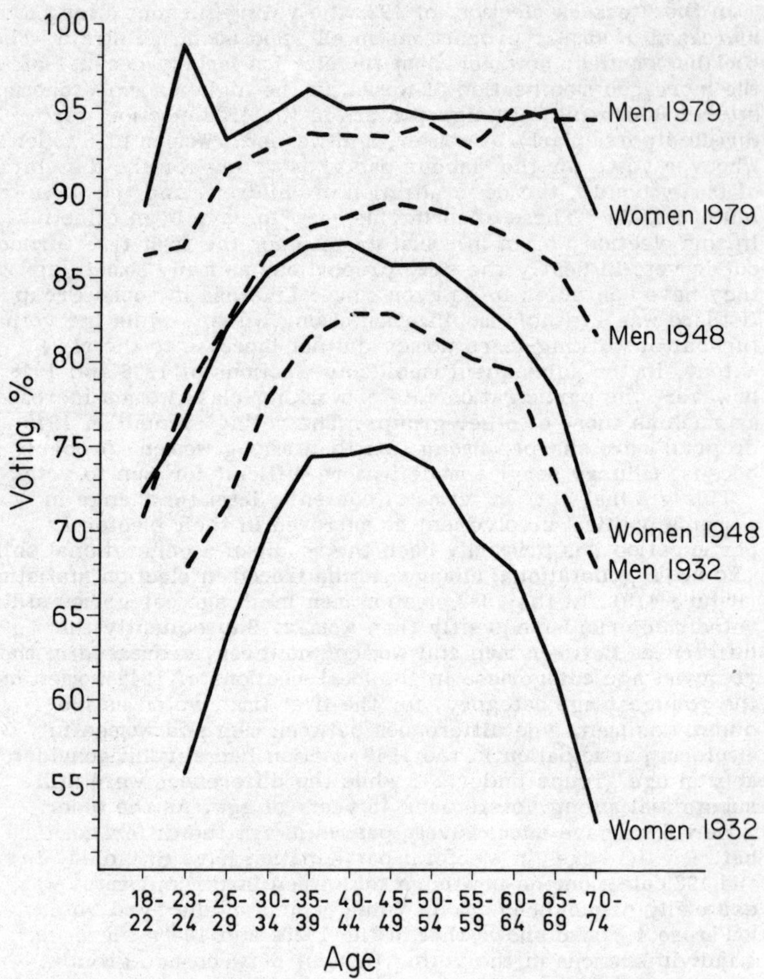

Figure 4.5 Percentage voting in the general elections of 1932, 1948 and 1979 by sex and age

ON THE FRINGES OF SOCIETY

The individual's family life, social relations and position in the job market can be assumed to affect the extent to which his or her pressing problems coincide with issues on the political agenda. These factors therefore can be expected to be reflected in electoral participation. Unfortunately, the official statistics on voter turnout, compiled by SCB in recent years, are of meagre value for this and other purposes. These statistics probably do not include a large portion of non-voters and furnish unsatisfactory data about voters.[17]

Table 4.3 Electoral participation in 1979 by sex, age and marital status

Age	Marital status	Turnout	
		Men	Women
		%	%
18-34	Married	90.5	93.4
	Unmarried	90.0	93.1
34-75	Married	96.8	97.0
	Unmarried	86.4	87.4
	Previously married	83.2	91.6

To acquire data on election participation according to sex and marital status, I have re-analysed data from a study conducted by SCB in connection with the Party Preference Survey during the 1979 election. Table 4.3 reveals that the variations between categories of different marital status are small in the age groups between 18 and 34 years. Among persons between the ages of 34 and 75, however, voting turnout was highest among married people and considerably lower among unmarried individuals. The lowest turnout occurred among previously married men, i.e., among divorced men and widowers. Previously married women had a substantially higher turnout rate than previously married men.

These categories based on marital status are interesting because they can be expected to indicate the degree of integration in social life and the extent to which the major problems of individuals coincide with current political issues. Men and women in the 'normal' state - matrimony - thus vote very frequently. For this group, problems of making a living and economic issues can be assumed to be paramount, while social relations in general are less problematic.

On the other hand, among older unmarried and previously married persons considerable numbers of individuals are in various ways less integrated into society and their personal problems may sometimes overshadow the economic issues which are central in the political process. This is particularly the case for middle-aged and older men who are divorced or unmarried. In the major metropolitan areas especially, they run greater risks of being rejected by the labour market and society. For example, divorced men are less often gainfully employed, and they must rely on means-tested social assistance much more frequently than married men of the same age.[18]

Among women, gainful employment is a rather important factor in determining electoral participation. Table 4.4 indicates that among housewives the voting turnout in 1973 and 1976 was lower than employed women.[19]

Table 4.4 Percentage voting among housewives and employed women by age groups (averages for the 1973 and 1976 elections)

	Turnout by age groups			
	18-22	23-29	30-49	50-59
	%	%	%	%
Employed women	88.7	93.0	95.5	96.0
Housewives	86.1	91.4	94.0	94.3
Difference	2.6	1.6	1.5	1.7

Unemployed persons can be expected to display rather weak involvement in politics. Among men who were unemployed during the month of the election, turnout was lower than among employed persons by 10 per cent in 1973 and by 15 per cent in 1976. The comparable differences among women were smaller; 5 and 10 per cent respectively.

REGIONAL DIFFERENCES

Regional variations in electoral participation can be elucidated through analysis of voting patterns in the different constituencies. The current apportionment of the electorate into 28 constituencies dates from the 1921 election. Generally, the constituencies correspond to the counties. The cities of Stockholm, Gothenburg and Malmö (also including Helsingborg, Landskrona and Lund) are the most important exceptions to this generalization.

During the 1920s there were sizeable differences in electoral participation between the constituencies. For example, Norrbotten in the far north had the lowest voting turnout, with only 45 per cent, while the Malmö constituency had the highest one, with a turnout of 62 per cent - a difference of 17 per cent. In the 1979 election the range of variation between the constituencies had shrunk to 4 per cent.

Figure 4.6 provides a picture of the differences in voting participation by presenting the variation between the constituencies from 1921 to 1979. In order to make the category of metropolitan centres more uniform, the figures we present here and in the following tables in this chapter are for the city of Malmö, not for the constituency of which Malmö is a part. Over time, the differences between constituencies have declined. In elections where the turnout has risen, constituency differences have decreased; while they have increased when electoral participation has dropped.

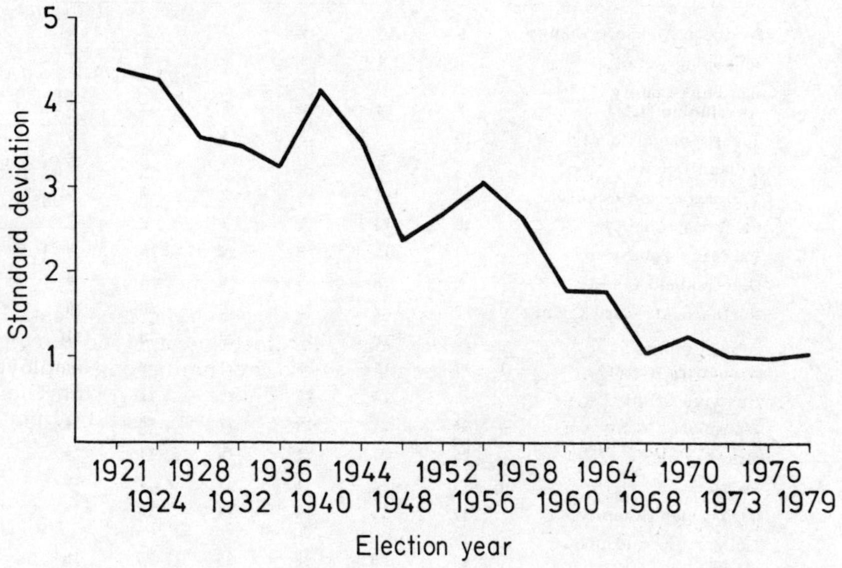

Figure 4.6 Standard deviation in percentage voting between constituencies in general elections, 1921–79

Since the introduction of universal suffrage, electoral participation in the different constituencies has changed at fairly dissimilar rates. In Table 4.5 we have taken the average turnout of the individual constituencies for each decade and have then ranked the constituencies from the highest to the lowest electoral participation. Hence in the table we can follow the ranking of each constituency in terms of voting turnout during six decades.

Certain constituencies display a relatively high electoral participation during the entire period. Among these constituencies are the counties of Jönköping, Malmöhus and Södermanland. The constituency of Southern Älvsborg has also ranked relatively high during the entire period and in the 1970s has had the highest turnout. Turnout has tended to increase more quickly in the constituencies of Västernorrland, Stockholm and Kalmar counties and Northern Älvsborg than in the remaining constituencies. Constituencies with traditionally low participation include Norrbotten, Jämtland, Gävleborg and Kopparberg - all located in the northern half of the country.

Table 4.5 The rank order of constituencies in electoral participation, 1921-79 (average turnout per decade)

Constituency	Elections during the years 1921-8	1932-6	1940-8	1952-8	1960-8	1970-9
Southern Älvsborg County	6	13	10	3	2	1
Jönköping County	5	4	4	5	5	2
Malmöhus County (excluding Malmö)	2	2	2	2	3	3
Södermanland County	10	7	3	4	4	4
Halland County	3	5	8	13	10	5
Västernorrland County	13	9	14	8	7	6
Stockholm County	19	13	11	7	8	7
Värmland County	14	16	19	20	14	8
Östergötland County	8	8	5	6	6	9
Northern Älvsborg County	23	22	22	16	20	10
Kalmar County	26	18	17	22	18	11
Kronoberg County	11	17	20	21	19	12
Blekinge County	17	24	25	26	23	13
Skaraborg County	24	11	18	17	15	14
Örebro County	25	21	21	19	11	15
Malmö	1	1	1	1	1	16
Västmanland County	12	13	12	14	13	17
Gothenburg and Bohus County	27	25	23	25	25	18
Kristianstad County	18	19	13	15	16	19
Uppsala County	9	20	16	18	12	20
Västerbotten County	21	15	15	11	17	21
Gotland County	22	3	9	9	9	22
Kopparberg County	15	26	24	28	28	23
Gävleborg County	20	27	27	27	27	24
Norrbotten County	28	28	26	23	26	25
Jämtland County	16	23	28	24	24	26
Stockholm	4	6	7	10	22	27
Gothenburg	7	10	6	12	21	28

Perhaps the most interesting changes in voting participation, however, have occurred in the three metropolitan centres. Malmö, which had the highest turnout in the country for five decades, dropped to a middle position in the 1970s. Stockholm and Gothenburg ranked in the upper third through the 1950s, dropped to the lower third during the 1960s, and have the two lowest rankings in electoral participation during the 1970s.

THE METROPOLITAN ENIGMA

The question of why electoral participation in the metropolitan centres has not increased as rapidly as in the rest of the country has attracted much attention in the Swedish debate.[20] This is an interesting question but it should not be blown out of proportion. Since constituency differences in electoral participation have fallen sharply during the period, the metropolitan centres now are not much below the average national turnout. In the 1979 election an additional 10,300 votes in Stockholm, 7,500 votes in Gothenburg and 1,600 votes in Malmö would have enabled these cities to reach the average turnout in the other constituencies.

Part of the explanation for the relative slippage in electoral participation of the metropolitan centres is probably that previous advantages of these areas have been gradually wiped out during the postwar period. Among these advantages were multiple channels of communication facilitating the spread of political information and the convenient location of polling places.

An interesting question in this context is whether the lower rate of electoral participation in the metropolitan centres is disproportionately greater among the working class. We can shed light on this question by re-analysing data from the 1976 election survey, which gives information on participation in the elections of 1970, 1973 and 1976, and the earlier mentioned study in connection with the 1979 election. In both surveys, data on participation was collected via electoral registers. Among persons eligible to vote in these three elections (n = 2,272 persons), we find that the difference between social group III and social groups I+II (i.e., manual-non-manual persons) in the proportion

Table 4.6 Electoral participation in 1970-6 and in 1979 by social strata in the three metropolitan centres and remaining constituencies

Constituency	Voted in all elections 1970, 1973 and 1976		1979 election	
	Social group III	Others	Social group III	Others
	%	%	%	%
Stockholm, Gothenburg, and Malmö	74	85	87	94
Remaining constituencies	85	90	93	94
Entire country	84	89	92	94

voting in all three elections is higher in the three metropolitan areas than in the rest of the country (Table 4.6). The same pattern also emerges in the 1979 election ($\underline{n}$ = 2,454 persons). These data thus indicate that the relatively low voting participation in the big cities is more pronounced in the lower than in the middle and upper strata.

Two types of explanations for the lower turnout in the big city areas can be suggested. One possibility is that the urban structure is associated with a higher incidence of social problems in the population than are other types of community structures. Voters with these problems subsequently go to the polls in fewer numbers than other categories of the population. This type of explanation assumes that categories of citizens with a low turnout rate are over-represented in the populations of the metropolitan centres.

Another frequently offered explanation is that lower electoral participation in the metropolitan centres is due to the effects of the social environment. The social structure of the metropolitan areas purportedly weakens the class consciousness and class culture of the workers, making it more difficult to mobilize working-class voters in these areas. These negative cultural influences are assumed to be mediated by the residential environment. It is argued that the labour organizations have greater difficulties in reaching voters in the residential environment of the metropolitan centres than in other types of communities. As a result, workers in the metropolitan centres are influenced more by bourgeois values and culture. In effect, this is the reverse of the argument concerning the 'hot-house effects' which supposedly arise in the company-town environment.[21]

Let us begin by examining the merits of the simpler of these two models - the one based on the assumption that there is now

Table 4.7 Differences in marital status of the population of metropolitan centres and the rest of the country in 1950, 1960 and 1975

	Men			Women		
	Married	Widower	Divorced	Married	Widow	Divorced
	%	%	%	%	%	%
Stockholm						
1950	4.2	-1.1	1.9	-2.5	0.4	2.9
1960	1.4	-0.8	2.5	-4.3	1.0	3.5
1975	-1.1	0.3	3.6	-6.4	3.0	4.6
Gothenburg						
1950	3.2	-0.8	1.2	0.5	-0.6	1.3
1960	2.2	-0.7	1.7	0.0	-0.4	1.8
1975	1.0	-0.2	2.5	-2.4	0.1	2.7
Malmö						
1950	4.9	-0.5	0.9	0.5	-0.3	1.3
1960	3.7	-0.6	1.1	0.1	-0.1	1.5
1975	1.7	-0.1	2.5	-1.3	1.1	3.0

a greater incidence of categories with low turnouts in the metropolitan centres than in the rest of the country. In comparison with the nation as a whole, the composition of the population in the three principal cities during the postwar period has become increasingly unfavourable in terms of the likelihood of voting. Differences between the population of metropolitan centres and the rest of the country with regard to marital status are presented for the years 1950, 1960 and 1975 in Table 4.7. Among men, an earlier metropolitan surplus of married men, who have a higher turnout, has shrunk during the years and in Stockholm has been replaced by a deficit. Similarly, the proportion of married women in the metropolitan areas during this period has developed in an unfavourable direction; in 1975 the proportion of married women in the three major cities was lower than in the rest of the country. The figures on the proportion of married persons, however, can be partly affected by the higher incidence of cohabitation without marriage in the metropolitan areas.

With regard to widows and widowers who have a relatively low rate of electoral participation, previous 'shortages' in the three cities have decreased or been transformed into 'surpluses'. Since 1950 the proportion of divorced persons has been larger in the metropolitan areas than in the rest of the country, but the differences have grown, to the disadvantage of the cities.

Table 4.8 Actual and predicted electoral participation in 1976 on the age structure and marital status of the adult population of the metropolitan centres

Constituency	Actual	Predicted	Difference
	%	%	%
Stockholm	90.3	90.7	-0.4
Gothenburg	90.1	91.2	-1.1
Malmö	91.5	91.3	-0.2

On the basis of reasonable assumptions about the voting probability of various groups of electors, we can calculate the expected turnout in the metropolitan centres, assuming that various sub-categories of the population vote with the same probability in these areas and in the rest of the country.[22] Our calculations are based on the composition of the population in the three cities according to the 1975 census. The predicted electoral participation can be compared with the actual voting turnout.

We find that the actual metropolitan turnout in the 1976 election is slightly under the predicted rate, mainly in Gothenburg (Table 4.8). It ought to be recalled here that traditionally Gothenburg has had relatively low electoral participation. However, the differences between the actual and the expected turnouts are now marginal. To close the gap between the actual and expected levels of voting, electoral participation would have had to increase by 2,000-4,000 votes in Stockholm and Gothenburg and by a few hundred votes in Malmö. The relatively greater frequency of drug addicts, etc., in the metropolitan areas is probably sufficient to account for these remaining differences.

In this context it can also be noted that white-collar groups and members of the upper socio-economic strata with relatively high turnout rates have been traditionally over-represented in the metropolitan centres, especially in Stockholm. However, since class differences in electoral participation also have dwindled, these differences affect the voting turnout only marginally to the advantage of the metropolitan centres. This slight advantage is probably offset by the likelihood that the metropolitan centres have a disproportionately large share of immigrants, who have become Swedish citizens but whose electoral participation probably remains somewhat lower than the turnout rate of Swedish-born voters.

A sociological study has mapped out the characteristics of a sample of election districts, including several in Stockholm and Gothenburg, which had either extremely low or high turnout rates in the 1976 election.[23] In the metropolitan centres the election districts with extremely low voting turnouts consisted of areas with high-rise housing built during the 1960s and 1970s or run-down areas in the centre of the city. To some extent these areas are characterized by multiple social problems, such as low incomes, social assistance cases and alcoholism. A relatively large percentage of the residents of these areas are divorced men, single mothers, early retirement pensioners, widows, widowers and immigrants. Areas with co-operative multi-family housing with occupant-owned flats have a higher voting turnout and demographic features which are conducive to electoral participation. Without exception, the highest turnout rates are found in residential areas with single-family dwellings, where the upper socio-economic strata are well represented and the more visible forms of social problems are rare.

Obviously, the types of problem areas mentioned above are not a favourable environment for the organizations of the labour movement to operate in. But even in the major metropolitan areas these environments constitute an exception rather than the rule. It is possible that in recent decades residential segregation has increased in Sweden, and individuals with poor resources and multiple social problems have congregated in certain housing areas. In the metropolitan regions the differences between the most attractive and the least desirable residential areas can be great. With the massive housing construction of the 1960s and early 1970s, when one million new flats were built during a ten-year period, many new residential areas sprang up and groups with social problems have been concentrated to some of these new areas. After some years, however, the new residential areas with rented housing often seem to have stabilized and thus usually have not become permanent slum areas.

It appears therefore unwarranted to interpret the relative lag in the increase in voting participation in the three major cities as a result of their producing a cultural environment which adversely affects the labour movement's efforts to mobilize its voters. The major part of the relatively lower turnout in these cities can evidently be explained in demographic terms. Categories of voters with relatively lower turnout rates have become more numerous in the metropolitan areas during the post-war period, something which is also witnessed by the relatively high occurrences of social deviation, drug abuse, etc. The causal mechanisms operating here can function in two ways. The metropolitan areas may attract socially maladjusted individuals, but the urban environment may also impede the development of stable social relations.

Finally, a fourth type of explanation should not be entirely neglected in this context. The lag in the increase in electoral participation in the big cities may also reflect a silent protest by certain groups of voters against trends of development which they feel have worsened their situation. In the 1979 election, for example, the percentage of blank ballots cast in Stockholm and Gothenburg was somewhat higher than the national average.[24]

ELECTION DAY v. EVERYDAY

The survey above reveals that on election day the Swedish people now, by and large, act in the same way. We have seen how the marked differences in the electoral participation between socio-economic strata, men and women, and age groups have gradually diminished. The rule of thumb now is: nearly everyone votes. Does this mean that other aspects of political involvement of these various categories are also fairly similar?

As distinct from election day, however, the differences between people in terms of political interest and activities, seem to be fairly large in everyday life. This becomes apparent when we analyse data from the interview survey carried out by SCB in connection with the 1976 election. One question was: 'How much political news and articles in the newspapers do you usually read?' and another: 'How interested are you generally in politics?' Respondents stating that they often read political material in the newspaper and that they are either very interested or fairly interested in politics can be combined into a category of high political interest.

There are substantial differences in the degree of political interest, measured as indicated above, between socio-economic strata, sex and age groups (Table 4.9).[25] Political interest is highest in the upper socio-economic stratum (social group I) and lowest among the workers (social group III) and farmers. In all socio-economic strata political interest is considerably higher among men than women. With one exception, political interest as here measured is higher among older persons.

Another aspect of political involvement is discussing politics

Table 4.9 Percentage with high political interest by sex, age and social group

Social group	Men 18-34	Men 35-64	Men 65-80	Women 18-34	Women 35-64	Women 65-80
	%	%	%	%	%	%
I	68	74	77	44	48	80
II	43	58	59	29	44	31
III	25	40	52	14	22	33
Farmers	-	38	41	-	-	-

with friends and acquaintances. The interview survey also asked: 'What do you usually do if you are in a group where the conversation gets on to the topic of politics?' Looking at those who answered: 'I usually take part in the discussion and state my opinion', we find that this kind of political activism is much more common in the upper socio-economic strata than in the lower - and is also more common among men than women (Table 4.10). With one exception, however, it declines with age. The younger age group therefore is most active in discussing politics with friends and acquaintances.

Table 4.10 Percentage discussing politics often by sex, age and social group

Social group	Men 18-34	Men 35-64	Men 65-80	Women 18-34	Women 35-64	Women 65-80
	%	%	%	%	%	%
I	43	49	18	52	38	33
II	36	31	17	34	30	14
III	27	25	13	22	13	9
Farmers	-	16	14	-	-	-

One would expect that working women would be politically more interested and active than women who are housewives. However, among women who are married or cohabitate we do not find any clear differences between employed women in terms of political interest as defined here. On the other hand, the data reveal that married women who are employed take part in political discussions and state their views somewhat more often than housewives (Table 4.11). It seems plausible that work experiences provide women with the substance and perhaps also the self-confidence to participate more often in political discussions.

Voting for a party can be the result of a temporary choice, but it can also be anchored in a strong sense of party attachment. The extent of party identification was tapped by the following question: 'Some people are strongly convinced supporters of their party. Other people are not so strongly convinced. Do you belong to the strongly convinced supporters of your party?'

Table 4.11 Percentage discussing politics often among married and cohabiting women by husband's social group and by own employment

Husband's social group	Housewives	Working women
	%	%
I	31	35
II	14	25
III	12	24

The responses disclose that party identification increases with age, something which reflects the process by which people become involved in politics (Table 4.12). Among men, the largest proportion with a strong party identification is found among workers (social group III) and farmers. Voters in the upper socio-economic strata are much less frequently strong adherents of the party they currently prefer.

Table 4.12 Percentage with strong party identification by sex, age and social group

Social group	Men			Women		
	18–34	35–64	65–80	18–34	35–64	65–80
	%	%	%	%	%	%
I	12	21	45	39	43	53
II	19	30	38	20	30	33
III	29	44	64	29	34	49
Farmers	–	47	54	–	–	–

These differences in party identification reflect the number of parties among which individuals in the various socio-economic strata usually choose. Among workers the Social Democrats are clearly the dominant party, while the Centre Party has the same position among the farmers. In social groups I and II, in contrast, votes are split more evenly between the parties. The comparatively sizeable circulation between the bourgeois parties is reflected in the weaker party identification among voters in the upper socio-economic strata.

POLITICAL PARTICIPATION

In the classical democratic tradition originating in Rousseau and J.S. Mill, the participation by all citizens in political decision making was seen as the essence of democracy.[26] According to Mill, political participation contributes to the making of good citizens, who through participation learn to take responsibility not only for themselves but also for the whole society. Participation also trains citizens to defend their interests. Only universal participation in decision-making can assure that the interests of all citizens will be taken into account. In the classical tradition, democracy was thus government *by* the people.

Since the observations in the 1930s that the downfall of democracy in countries like Germany and Austria was preceded by exceptionally high political activity and voting turnouts, many social scientists have viewed high electoral participation with considerable suspicion. The classical democratic theory has been revised to a focus on the institutions through which party elites compete for the votes of the citizens. Democracy has thus increasingly come to be seen as government *for* the people.[27]

With such a revision of the democratic theory, the participation of citizens in political decision making fades into the background. This view appears to have spilled over into an unfortunate neglect among social scientists of electoral participation and its variations within as well as between countries. In the perspective of classical democratic theory, however, a low level of electoral participation and differences in participation between various collectivities or groups appear as problematic and constitute indications of the malfunctioning of democracy. This perspective problematizes, for example, the extremely low levels of electoral participation in the United States and Switzerland, of which the former country now is often described as a great democracy and the latter one as the best governed democracy.[28] In this perspective also the decreasing trend in electoral participation in several Western nations in recent decades appears alarming, and mirrors disillusionment with the capacity of the political system to solve major problems confronting society.

The focus on individual resources like education in studies on political participation has inhibited attention to the roots of the differences in electoral participation in the structure of society and in the functioning of the political system. By now we have a number of studies on 'class voting' but very few data on what I have here called 'class participation'.

The correlation which we have noted between electoral participation and the extent of working-class-based political resources in the form of union density is of interest also for the discussion of the theses of neo-corporatist writers. It puts into an odd light the assumptions by many of them that, with the development of neo-corporatism, political parties fade into the background and unions become largely instruments for the social control of wage-earners on behalf of the interests of the economically dominant groups. If we exclude the countries where legislation pressurizes citizens to vote, both electoral participation and union densities are in fact highest in the two countries generally regarded as the most typical cases of well developed neo-corporatism, Austria and Sweden. It is difficult to reconcile the neo-corporatist hypotheses with a model of rational voters.

In the perspective of classical democratic theory, the increasing electoral participation and very high voter turnout in Sweden are clearly indications of the vitality of democracy and the meaningfulness of politics in this country. Talk of growing distrust of politicians must not obscure the fact that the electorate has viewed voting and the alternatives provided by the parties as meaningful and important opportunities of choice.

During the postwar period, the Swedish people have become 'politicized' in the positive sense of the word. Nearly everyone has been incorporated into the political life - at least to the degree that he or she votes in elections. This means that the earlier pronounced differences in electoral participation between socio-economic strata, regions and age groups have been drastically reduced. With regard to sex differences in voting participation, the traditional pattern has been reversed. As a result of the high voting turnout, the Swedish political system now more closely approximates the democratic ideal where the principle of one person, one vote prevails not merely formally but also in practice. However, fairly important differences in electoral participation between the socio-economic strata remain. Joint parliamentary and local elections tend to decrease the effects of the class differential. Suffrage tied to citizenship has widened class differences in politics inasmuch as immigrants in Sweden, the bulk of whom have working-class occupation, do not have the right to vote in parliamentary elections.

On the whole, the structural transformation of the economy and the urbanization process have probably facilitated the mobilization of the working class in the democratic class struggle. Agricultural districts and small rural communities have traditionally presented the greatest difficulties in attempts to get out the working-class vote. In contrast, the metropolitan areas have offered relatively good opportunities for the mobilization of the working class, nearly as favourable conditions as in the highly industrialized communities. During the postwar period, however, the rate of increase in voting participation has been slower in the metropolitan centres than the rest of Sweden. This lag is due at least partly to urban environments, which are associated with higher incidence of individuals with social problems of various kinds.

Class differences in electoral participation have declined since the breakthrough of democracy. However, this process was accelerated from the mid-1950s through the end of the 1960s. The labour parties and trade unions have played a vital role in getting working-class voters to go to the polls. The sharpest decline in class differences in voting turnout coincides with the advent of televised election campaigns.

The lessening of differences between the sexes in electoral participation has also proceeded since the introduction of universal suffrage. The differences decreased most rapidly up to World War II and subsequently have continued at a more modest rate. The growing voting turnout among women has been the result primarily of inter-generational political change. Women in working-class and rural areas had to overcome the widest gaps in participation. Consequently, urbanization has contributed to the reduction of sex differences in electoral participation. Additional important factors are probably the increasing rate of women's participation on the labour market, and perhaps also the decrease in the size of families. With the main exceptions of the women's associations of the Social Democratic and Centre Parties, during most of this period few organizations have effectively attempted to mobilize women on a broad basis. That women's voting turnout exceeded men's in the 1979 election can to some extent reflect the fact that during the 1970s labour force participation has dropped among men.

However, even if equality in terms of electoral participation has clearly increased in Sweden, the influences of social position persist with regard to other forms of political participation. On a day-to-day basis the upper socio-economic strata display higher political interest and involvement than workers. This pattern also recurs in other countries.[29] The labour movement's organizations have been able to bring about an equalization in voting participation but, at least so far, have not been able to eliminate other aspects of political inequality. Since changes over time in the variations between socio-economic strata with respect to, say, political interest and informal political activity cannot be traced in the same fashion as for voting turnout, it is impossible to say whether the equalization in electoral participation has been accompanied by growing equality in these other areas.

The traditional differences between the sexes concerning political involvement and interest continue to exist. This pattern also prevails in other Western countries. One attempt to explain the lower political participation of women emphasizes the effects of a distinctive female culture, shaped by women's roles in reproduction and child care.[30]

5 SOCIAL ROOTS OF PARTY PREFERENCES

A voter's party choice is influenced by many circumstances. Childhood experiences can leave an imprint in the form of vague sympathies or a strong sense of attachment to a party or a political tendency. Other decisive factors are related to the individual's life situation as an adult. Still other factors may be of a temporary nature, such as influences during an election campaign.

In this chapter we will discuss how the positions of the voters in the division of labour combine with political socialization to produce differing patterns of party allegiances. We shall also examine the effects of structural changes in Swedish society during the postwar period as well as changes in the platforms of the parties on the political preferences of voters in different socio-economic strata. Factors which make voters conform to or deviate from the political influences dominant in their environment are analysed. Further, we discuss how party preferences are affected by the current life situation of the voter, including experiences on the labour market and in housing.

SOCIAL BACKGROUND

In most Western countries in varying degrees the party systems reflect cleavages based on the social stratification of society and also sometimes on religion and ethnicity. In Sweden, as in the other Nordic countries, religious and ethnic cleavages are of relatively limited significance; it is primarily the individual's social origin and current socio-economic position which determine party preferences.[1] To some extent, however, the influence of religion does persist. Thus, religiously active individuals sympathize more frequently with the bourgeois parties than do the rest of the population.[2]

As is well-known the party preferences of parents and children often coincide. This correlation occurs partly because both parents and their offspring are affected by influences from the same social environment. Also, the social position of the parents is important in determining children's education and their social position in adult life.[3] In addition, party preferences may be directly influenced by parents.

The effects of childhood environment and present socio-economic position on party preferences can be summarized by the relationships between party choice and the 'social groups' of the voter and his or her father. A path analysis of interview data from the 1976 election indicates that the social group of the voter is of greater importance than the father's social group in determining party choice on the left-right axis (Figure 5.1).[4] However, the father's social group also influences party preferences indirectly, inasmuch as it affects the voter's socio-economic position.

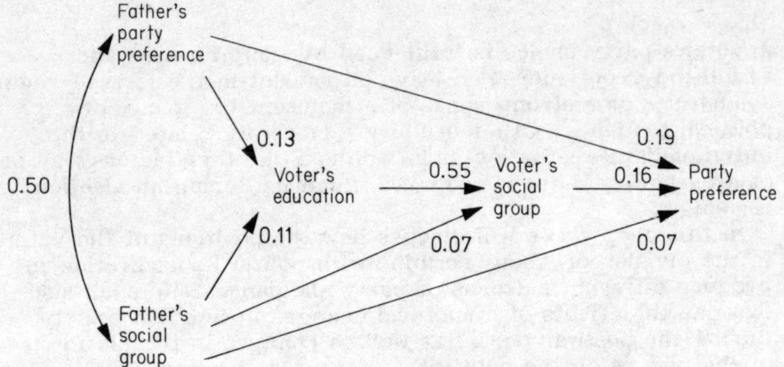

Figure 5.1 The effects of social background factors on party preference

Table 5.1 Party choice by party preference of father

Party choice	Party preference of father					
	Communist	Social Democrat	Centre	Liberal	Conservative	Unknown
	%	%	%	%	%	%
Communist Party	31	4	2	3	5	3
Social Democratic Party	55	70	23	20	15	43
Centre Party	10	11	55	24	18	27
Liberal Party		8	8	32	10	14
Conservative Party	2	5	10	17	51	12
Christian Democratic Union*	2	1	2	2	1	1
	100	100	100	100	100	100

*This party, which puts special emphasis on Christian values, has attempted to gain parliamentary representation since 1964 but without success.

There is also a fairly large degree of congruence between the party preference of the voter and the recalled party choice of the voter's father. Part of this correlation reflects a 'political legacy' from the family environment. The correlation is of course also magnified, since in borderline cases children may perceive the similarity between generations as greater than it actually is (Table 5.1).

The political legacy is strongest among persons with Social Democratic fathers. More than two-thirds of those who report having a Social Democratic father are Social Democrats themselves. Among Liberals and Communists, on the other hand, the political inheritance has more frequently dissipated. Only one-third of those whose father was a Liberal or a Communist reported that they shared their father's party preference. The stability of the political legacy from Centre Party and Conservative fathers appears to lie somewhere in between. Among the children of Communist parents it has been quite common to become a Social Democrat. The children of Liberals have often switched to other bourgeois parties.

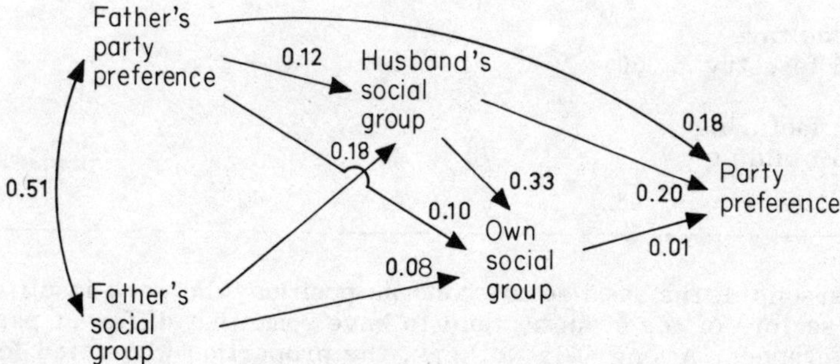

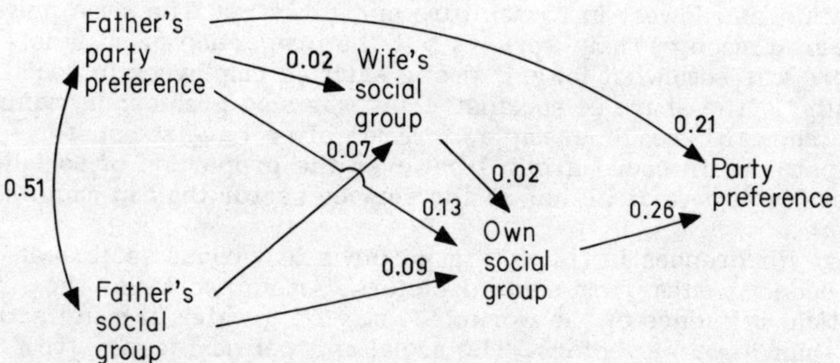

Figure 5.2 The effects of social background factors and husband's and wife's social group on the party preferences among working married women and married men

Despite some advances in equality between the sexes and increased female employment, the husband's occupation still plays a larger role in determining the socio-economic position of the family than does the wife's occupation. This is manifested among working married women inasmuch as her party preference is influenced by her husband's social group to at least the same extent as by the social group of her own occupation (Figure 5.2).[5]

Table 5.2 Percentage voting for the socialist bloc by social group, sector of the economy and sex (economically active only)

	Social group III		Social group II (salaried employees)		Social group I
	Men	Women	Men	Women	Men
	%	%	%	%	%
Agriculture and forestry	60	-	-	-	-
Manufacturing and building	75	70	49	-	22
Services	66	62	41	42	27

Persons in the same socio-economic position who work in different sectors of the economy tend to have somewhat different party preferences. Among male workers, the proportion who voted for the socialist bloc in the 1970 election was 83 per cent in the metal-working industry, 75 per cent in the service sector and 66 per cent in agriculture and forestry.[6] The 1976 election reveals a similar pattern (Table 5.2). Among male workers, the proportion voting for the socialist parties was largest in manufacturing and building and lowest in agriculture and forestry. The same pattern occurred among female workers but the proportion of socialist voters was somewhat lower. Among salaried employees in social group II, the share of socialist votes was also greatest in manufacturing, where for example, foremen often have socialist sympathies. In social group I however the proportion of socialist voters is somewhat higher in the service sector than in manufacturing.

The differences in the voting patterns in various sectors of the economy stem from several factors. Among workers, the political influence of the workplace may be greater in manufacturing than in other sectors. The social and political legacy from the childhood environment is probably also important; the proportion of workers who have grown up in socialist homes is probably larger in manufacturing than in other sectors of the economy. In social group II a large proportion of foremen are recruited from the workers. In social group I the stronger socialist element in the service sector is especially pronounced among public employees.

'CLASS VOTING'

Where party preferences are rooted in the social stratification of society, the pattern of party preferences will vary between different socio-economic strata. A simple procedure for summarizing these differences is to dichotomize the social stratification continuum by placing workers in one category and remaining occupational groups in a second category. The percentage point difference between the workers and the other occupational groups in support of the socialist parties gives the well-known Alford index of 'class voting'.[7]

The use of this measure as an expression of class voting is, however, easily misleading. According to some definition of the class concept, salaried employees and workers belong to the same class by virtue of their position as wage-earners and should not be assigned to different classes as this measure does. The term also implies that somehow it is natural for white-collar groups and manual workers to vote for different parties. None the less, the percentage difference in socialist preferences between workers and other occupational groups is still pertinent as a crude indicator of the voting patterns in different socio-economic strata.

The election surveys conducted by the Central Bureau of Statistics (SCB) in connection with the general elections since 1956 make it possible to trace changes in the voting patterns of occupational groups and socio-economic strata through the years. Comparable data for the 1979 election have been taken from the Party Sympathy Survey carried out by SCB two months after the election.

In the subsequent analysis of the voting patterns in various occupational groups, the terms 'workers', 'working class' and 'social group III' are used interchangeably to designate workers in manufacturing as well as agriculture and forestry and low-level non-manual workers in private or public employment (e.g., postmen, firemen, hospital workers and child care workers). For the sake of simplicity, the terms 'middle strata' or 'middle class' apply to occupations in both social group I (e.g., teachers in secondary schools, professors, bank officials, judges, military officers, big businessmen) and social group II (e.g., office workers, draughtsmen, nursery and elementary school-teachers, foremen, nurses) as well as small businessmen and farmers.[8]

Figure 5.3 presents the proportions of votes for the socialist parties among workers and in the other occupational groups during the regular general elections between 1956 and 1979.[9] The major trends can be briefly summarized as follows. Among the workers, the socialist proportion has been fairly stable during the period 1956-68, reaching its highest point in 1960. Since 1968 the percentage of socialist voters among the workers has fallen. It reached its nadir in the 1976 election and rose in the 1979 election. In the middle strata, where the salaried employees obviously dominate, the socialist proportion increased from 1956 to 1968, and subsequently slightly decreased through the 1973 election but has risen somewhat since then.

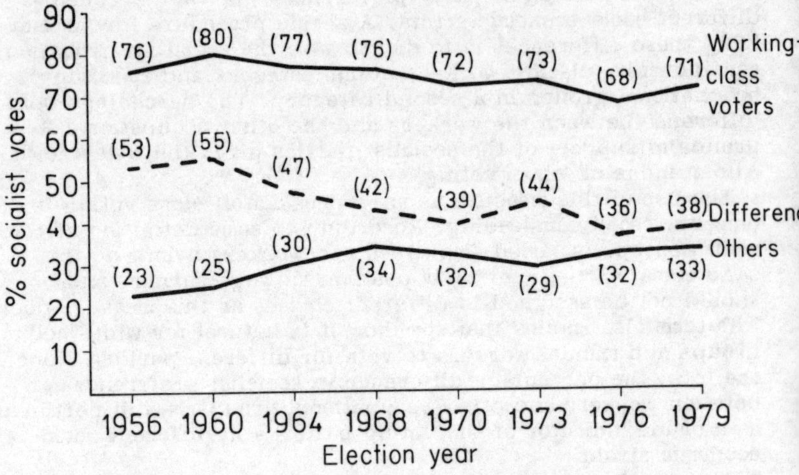

Figure 5.3 Percentage of votes for the socialist parties among working-class voters and other voters in elections 1956-79

The index of class voting was 53 percentage points in the 1956 election but only 38 percentage points in 1979. The reduction of this difference results primarily from the increase in the proportion of salaried employees and others in the middle strata voting for the socialist bloc, an increase of 10 percentage points. However, it is due also to a decline in socialist voting among workers, a decrease of 5 percentage points.[10]

During the postwar period the Social Democrats and the Communists thus have generally strengthened their position among white-collar groups. On the other hand, the bourgeois parties, especially since the 1968 election, have succeeded in making inroads among the workers. The Social Democrats' loss of power as a result of the 1976 election was due primarily to the bourgeois parties' gaining the support of a growing number of working-class voters. In the 1979 election the Social Democrats managed to recoup part of this loss.

In Finland, also, salaried employees have increasingly come to vote for the socialist parties.[11] This is not the case in Norway, however. There, the working-class support for the socialist parties has been decreasing since the late 1940s, especially among young workers, but the socialist support in the middle strata has remained stable.[12]

YOUNG VOTERS

The extent of the socialist vote in various socio-economic strata is related to age. This is particularly the case for voters in social groups I and II. In the category of salaried employees, businessmen and farmers, twice as many voters in the youngest age group voted for the socialist parties in the 1979 election as did those in the oldest age group (Table 5.3). Among working-class voters the relationship between the share of the socialist vote and age has been weaker and has fluctuated: in the 1960 election young workers voted socialist more often than older workers; the situation was the reverse in the 1976 election, and during the 1968 and 1979 elections no correlation existed between age and voting for the socialist parties among working-class voters.

Table 5.3 Percentage of votes for the socialist bloc in the 1979 election by age and social group

Social group position	Age 18-29	30-9	40-9	50-9	60-9	70-80	Total
	%	%	%	%	%	%	%
Workers	73	75	76	78	74	75	71
Businessmen, salaried employees farmers	54	43	38	36	27	23	33
Difference	19	32	38	42	47	52	38

Since the 1960 election, changes in the proportions voting for the socialist bloc among voters under 30 years of age have been more dramatic than for the electorate as a whole (Figure 5.4).[13] In the 1968 election the socialist bloc made very sizeable gains in its share of the young middle-class voters. Its share of votes in this group decreased in the 1973 election but increased markedly again in the 1979 election, when more than 50 per cent of the young middle-class voters supported the socialist parties. The proportion of young working-class voters supporting the socialist parties dropped in the 1964 and 1970 elections but clearly increased in the 1979 election. Hence, among the young voters the difference between workers and the middle strata in the proportion voting socialist has markedly decreased. This decline in class voting has been due largely to a growing proportion in the young middle-class section of the electorate voting for the socialist parties.

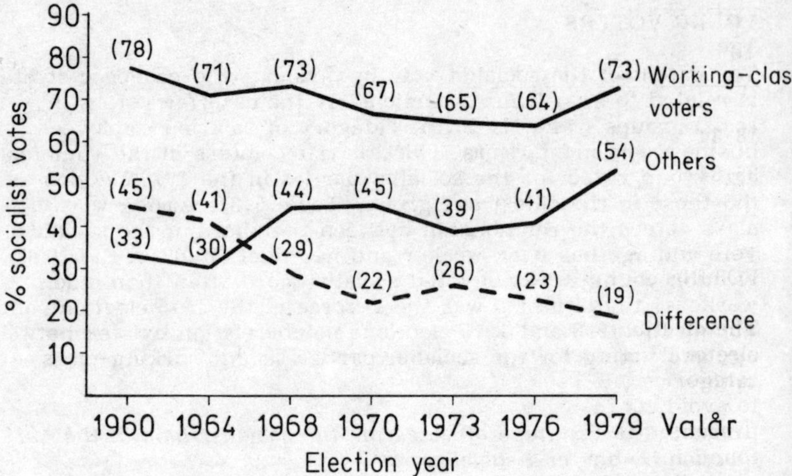

Figure 5.4 Percentage of votes for the socialist parties among working-class voters and other voters in the age group of thirty years and under in elections 1960–79

The radicalization in the younger white-collar stratum noted above is also clearly reflected among the members of the white-collar unions. In the Central Organization for Salaried Employees (TCO), organizing the great majority of the white-collar employees, the Social Democrats and Communists are supported by roughly half of the members under thirty-five years but by only about a third of the older members (Table 5.4). In the smaller Swedish Confederation of Professional Associations (SACO/SR), where members usually have academic degrees, a comparable trend recurs but the proportion of socialist voters is consistently lower. Unorganized white-collar employees seemed to be politically more conservative than white-collar employees in general.

Among the various parties, we find few generational differences in their electoral support. The only exception is the Communist Party, which is supported more strongly by the generation of voters born since the end of the 1940s, who were influenced by the leftist wave during the late 1960s and early 1970s. The Communists have also a relatively strong backing among voters born in the 1920s or earlier. In contrast, they have been extremely weak in the intervening generation, whose political beliefs were formed during the cold war of the 1950s.

Table 5.4 Percentage voting for the socialist bloc among white-collar employees in social groups I and II by union membership and age

Age	Membership in: TCO	SACO/SR	Non-member
	%	%	%
18-34	49	23	26
35-64	37	15	20

VOTING PATTERNS OF SOCIO-ECONOMIC STRATA

The election surveys enable us to analyse the changes in the electoral support of the parties among different occupational categories and social groups during the years 1956-79. In order to avoid confusing detail, only the trends for three parties are presented in the following figures. (A complete presentation is found in Table A4 in the Appendix.) Among workers (social group III) the Social Democrats are clearly the dominant party (Figure 5.5). However, the working-class support for the Social Democrats has been 8 to 9 per cent lower in the 1970s than it was in the elections between 1956 and 1968. On the whole, working-class support for the Communists has been stable, with perhaps a slight increase among younger workers during the 1970s.

In the 1950s the Liberal Party had substantial backing among working-class voters. However, during its period of expansion during the 1960s the Centre Party gradually gained a footing among many of the Liberals' core groups of supporters, including the bourgeois working-class voters. As can be observed in Figure 5.5, the Centre Party's gains among working-class voters have probably largely occurred at the expense of the Liberals. The Social Democrats, however, also lost working-class voters to the Centre Party. The Conservatives have had roughly the same proportion of workers' votes as the Communists. The Centre Party's losses among working-class voters in the 1979 election were accompanied by slight gains for the Conservatives.

In social group II the pattern of party preferences is much more fragmented. Among middle-level salaried employees, however, the Social Democrats have been the largest party since the 1960s - a position which the Liberals seem to have held previously (Figure 5.6). Again, among this category it is apparent that during the period 1956-73 the Centre Party strengthened its support at the Liberals' expense. The Conservatives' electoral support in this group seems to have been fairly stable, with however a pronounced increase in the 1979 election. The Communists have experienced a slight increase among this category of salaried employees since the end of the 1960s.

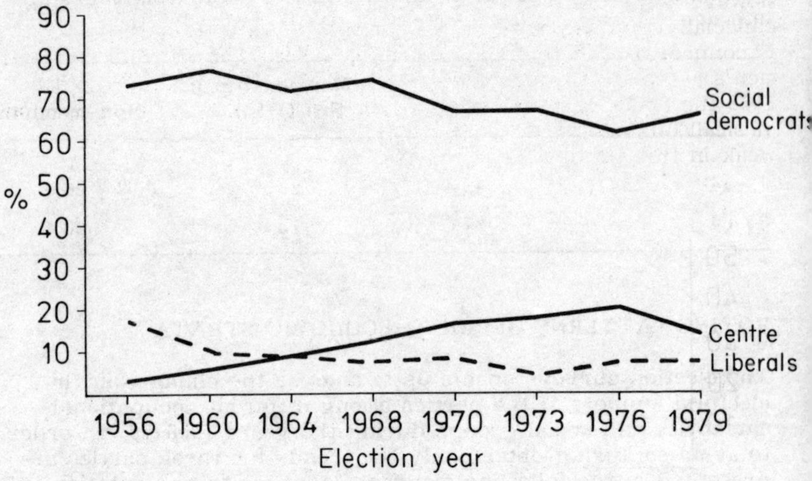

Figure 5.5 Percentage of votes for different parties among workers (social group III) in elections 1956–79

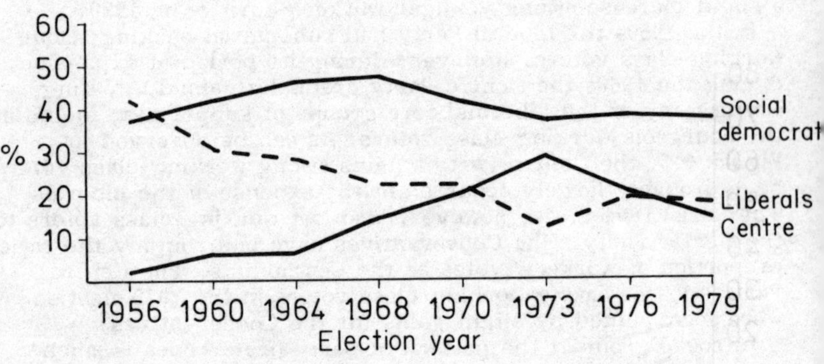

Figure 5.6 Percentage of votes for different parties among middle-level salaried employees in elections 1956–79

The party preferences of small businessmen and entrepreneurs are now fairly evenly divided among four of the parties (Figure 5.7). The Liberals' firm footing among small businessmen during the 1950s has been gradually undermined by the Centre Party, which became stronger than the Liberals also in this category of voters during the 1960s. The Conservatives too lost votes among small businessmen to the Centre Party during this period. However, the Conservative upswing in the 1979 election was especially pronounced among small businessmen, which perhaps is connected with the special political campaigns of small businessmen's associations during the elections in 1976 and 1979. Since 1968 the Social Democrats have received a diminishing proportion of small businessmen's votes. The Communists are extremely weak in this group.

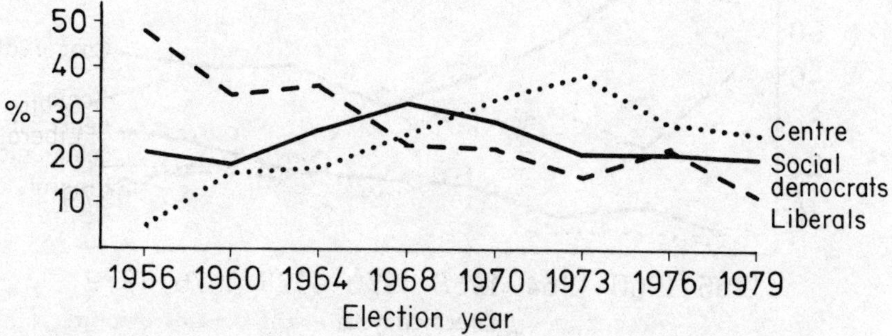

Figure 5.7 Percentage of votes for different parties among small businessmen and entrepreneurs in elections 1956-79

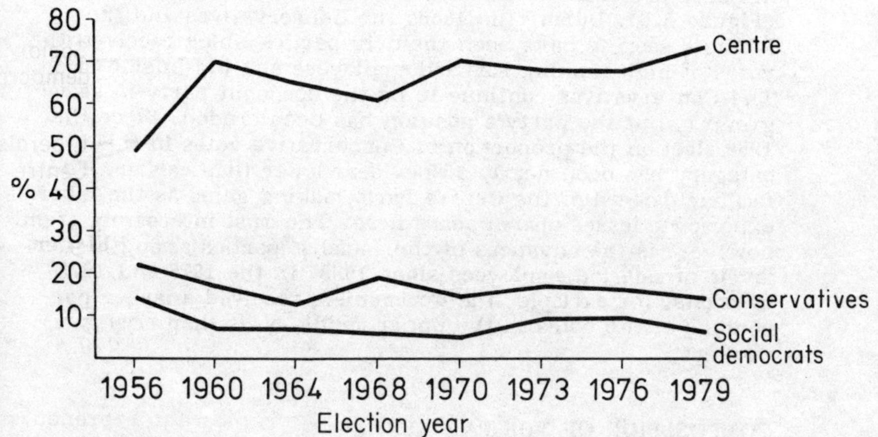

Figure 5.8 Percentage of votes for different parties among farmers in elections 1956-79

Among the farmers, the Centre Party is clearly the major party

(Figure 5.8). This dominance has grown as the small farmers have gradually declined in numbers. The Centre Party's main rival for the farm vote are the Conservatives. In the 1979 election, however, the Centre Party managed to strengthen its support among the farmers.

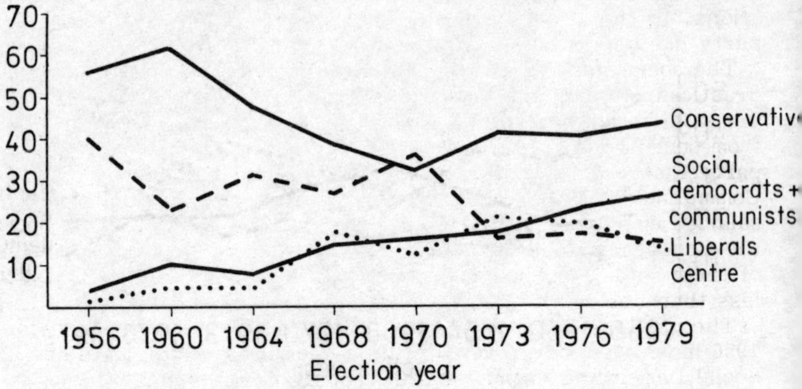

Figure 5.9 Percentage of votes for different parties cast in social group I in elections 1956–79

In the upper middle class (social group I) substantial changes in party preferences have occurred since the 1956 election (Figure 5.9). During the 1950s the Conservatives and the Liberals seem to have been the only parties which received the votes of high ranking salaried employees and big businessmen. The Conservatives continue to be the dominant party in social group I, but the party's position has been eroded. Since the 1968 election the proportion of Conservative votes in this category has been nearly 15 per cent lower than earlier. The familiar pattern of the Centre Party making gains as the Liberals experience losses also appears here. The most interesting trend, however, is the advances of the socialist parties among higher levels of salaried employees since 1968. In the 1976 and 1979 elections, for example, the Communists received a larger percentage of the votes in the upper middle class than among workers.

COMPOSITION OF THE PARTIES

These changes in the voting patterns of various occupational categories during the period between 1956 and 1979 have markedly altered the social base of two parties (Table A5 in the Appendix). The most striking change has occurred in the social composition of the Centre Party. Until the 1950s the Centre Party, then the Agrarians, was almost exclusively a party of farmers. In the 1956 election, three out of four votes for the party were cast by farmers. After changing its name and adopting a new programme in the late 1950s, the party successfully broadened its electoral base. Subsequently the Centre Party has become a middle-of-the-road bourgeois party, but it has also retained its strong ties with the farmers and their associations. In the 1970s, however, only every fifth vote for the party has been cast by a farmer.

The social base of the Communist Party has also changed drastically during the 1970s. Until the 1964 election the Communists, who received nearly 90 per cent of their votes from social group III, were a more homogeneous working-class party than the Social Democrats. The major gains of the Communist Party, however, have occurred among younger salaried employees and students. In the 1979 election both the Conservatives and the Communists received a quarter of their votes from social group I and students, while a little less than half of the Communist votes came from workers.

The changes in the social base of the remaining parties since 1956 have been marginal. Despite a decline, two-thirds of the Social Democratic votes are still cast by workers.

SOCIAL AND POLITICAL MOBILITY

The occupations of most people are in roughly the same socio-economic stratum as their parents. Thus there is a marked stability in social positions among generations. However, because of the decline in agricultural employment and the growth of white-collar groups, the present occupational structure of society differs markedly from that which existed merely a generation ago. These structural changes result in many persons having occupations in different socio-economic categories than their parents. Apart from this 'involuntary' mobility, there is also in most societies a 'pure' social mobility which would occur even if the occupational structure of society remained unaltered. Comparing the occupations of parents and children, one thus finds that a sizeable group of individuals, nearly 40 per cent of the population, has experienced upward or downward mobility. In Sweden during the postwar period this intergenerational mobility has increased somewhat.[14]

Among all persons belonging to a particular social stratum, significant numbers therefore have had parents in a different social stratum. Dissimilar social backgrounds, perhaps somewhat unexpectedly, are most widespread in the upper middle class (social group I): only about a quarter of those whose occupations are now in social group I have parents who also belonged to this social group. Approximately every other person in social group II has parents in the same social group. Persons now belonging to social group III however, have the most uniform social background: three-quarters of them have parents who also belonged to social group III.[15] During the early stages of industrialization a major portion of the working class was recruited from agriculture. In contrast, the working class is now recruited from its own ranks, and the proportion of first-generation workers is quite small. This pattern of social backgrounds contributes to a situation where one bloc of parties has a very strong dominance in social group III, while party preferences are more evenly distributed in social groups I and II.

Table 5.5 Party choice by social mobility and party preference of father

	Party choice 1976	Father's party preference Bourgeois	Socialist	Unknown	Total
		%	%	%	%
Stable working class	Bourgeois	49	9	29	19
	Socialist	51	91	71	81
		100	100	100	100
Stable middle-class	Bourgeois	86	40	76	76
	Socialist	14	60	24	24
		100	100	100	100
Upwardly mobile	Bourgeois	90	41	66	54
	Socialist	10	59	34	46
		100	100	100	100
Downwardly mobile	Bourgeois	59	26	52	49
	Socialist	41	74	48	51
		100	100	100	100

The 1976 election survey furnishes data for an analysis of the effects of social mobility and the political legacy on the voting behaviour of the electorate. Since the analysis is based on the voter's recollections of his or her father's occupation and party preference, the results must be viewed with caution. However, the results can offer valuable insights into long-term social processes affecting party choice. As is well-known, socialist party preferences are clearly dominant in the working class, whereas bourgeois party preferences predominate in the middle-class strata. Thus the analysis here focuses on persons whose political and social inheritance deviates from the main pattern and explores the extent to which they have adopted the predominant party allegiances of the strata to which they presently belong.

A comparison of the stable middle strata (both voter and father belonging to the middle strata) and the stable working class (both voter and father being working class) indicates that the social environment of the working class may be somewhat more effective than that of the middle class in 'converting' persons whose political legacy deviates from the overall pattern (Table 5.5). In the stable working class 51 per cent of the children of bourgeois fathers have become socialists, while in the stable middle-class strata 40 per cent with socialist fathers are now adherents of the bourgeois parties. The social environment of the working class also seems to be as effective as that of the middle class in maintaining the dominating bloc pattern in the class or inducing persons with no knowledge of their father's party preference to conform with the dominant bloc pattern.

Furthermore, the social milieu of the working class appears to be nearly as effective as the middle-class environment in converting persons whose heritage deviates both socially and politically. Among downwardly mobile persons (father middle class, voter working class) whose fathers had bourgeois sympathies, 41 per cent became socialists. The same percentage of upwardly mobile persons (father working class, voter middle class) with socialist fathers had bourgeois party preferences. Among those who do not know their father's party preference, a smaller proportion of the downwardly than the upwardly mobile persons have accepted the prevalent bloc pattern of the class.

The working class environment also appears less effective in stabilizing the party preferences of socially downwardly mobile individuals whose fathers were socialists than the middle-class environment is in stabilizing the bourgeois preferences of upwardly mobile persons whose fathers supported bourgeois parties.

On the whole, however, the social environment of the working class in Sweden appears to be nearly as effective as the middle-class milieu in inducing voters with divergent social and political backgrounds to adopt the prevalent party preferences in the stratum. In this respect Sweden probably differs from, say, Britain, where the social environment of the working class exerts less political influence than the middle-class environment. For example, in Britain downwardly mobile persons more frequently retain bourgeois party allegiances than they do in Sweden.[16]

The effects of childhood environment and current social position vary among different age groups (Figure 5.10). In the stable working class, approximately 80 per cent in all age groups voted for the socialist parties. If the bourgeois parties had succeeded in making inroads in the hard core of the working class, it would have been apparent among the younger age groups in this category. However there is no indication of this even in the 1976 election, which was the Social Democrats' worst showing in a general election during the postwar period.

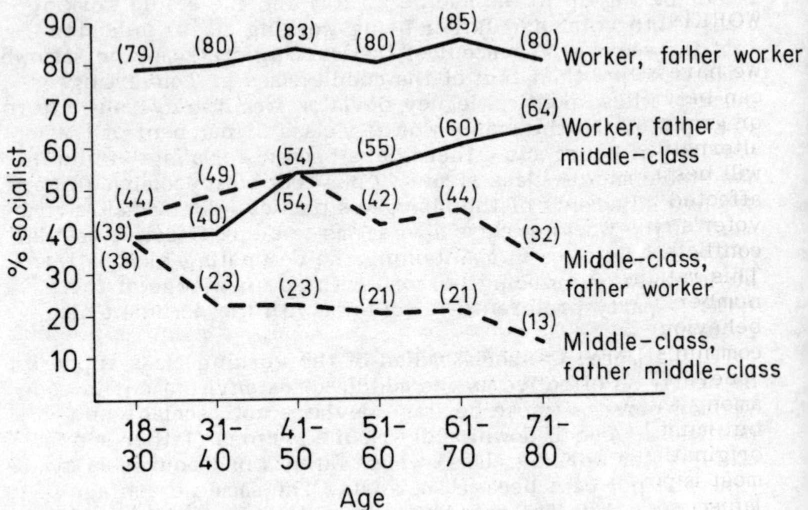

Figure 5.10 Percentage voting for the socialist parties by current social position, father's social position, and age

Among downwardly mobile persons, however, the proportion voting socialist was much lower among the younger voters than among the older age groups. This may indicate that the bourgeois parties have gained a footing among first-generation workers. But in this context a couple of alternative or complementary factors should be taken into account. Some of the younger downwardly mobile workers will eventually move up the social ladder again. Among those who remain in the working class, a part of the bourgeois political legacy which these downwardly mobile workers have brought along from their childhood environment will gradually be eroded as they are assimilated into their new social environment. A study of Swedish metal-workers, for example, suggests that the bourgeois political legacy begins to weaken after about ten to fifteen years in the metal-working industry.[17]

Among upwardly mobile individuals the older age groups vote for the socialist parties less often than younger and middle-aged voters. Again, socializing effects from the current environment can be eventually expected, so that the predominantly bourgeois political environment of the middle class will gradually erode the socialist legacy of the upwardly mobile individuals. But in the white-collar strata there is also a general swing to the left, which becomes evident when we examine the stable middle-class voters. Among the youngest persons in this category, the percentage voting socialist is substantial.

WORKING-CLASS COMMUNISM

We have assumed here that essentially the voter's party choice can be viewed as rational behaviour. On the bases of individual or group interests, material or otherwise, and knowledge about alternatives, the voter decides on the party he or she believes will best serve these interests. Admittedly, party choice is also affected by, among other things, childhood influences and the voter's current surroundings - influences which at times may conflict but often reinforce what appear to be rational choices. This rational model of voting has been called into question by a number of social scientists, especially in cases when political behaviour has been considered as somehow deviant, such as communist voting among the workers.[18]

Several influential theories have claimed that communist voting among the workers cannot be understood as rational behaviour but must be entirely or partially explained in terms of aberrations originating from personality traits or environmental factors. The most important has been the theory of working-class authoritarianism advanced by Seymour M. Lipset.[19] According to Lipset, workers are more predisposed to be authoritarian in their values and personality than are the middle class, since a low level of education and patterns of family life among workers produce fairly high levels of psychological and economic insecurity. The authoritarian personality is characterized by intolerance towards dissenters, prejudices, a lack of appreciation of nuances, emphasis on the immediate, emotional thinking, hero worship, etc. Lipset further argues that the workers are radical on economic issues but are conservative and reactionary in cultural matters. He concludes that authoritarian personality traits must be viewed as the most important explanation for workers supporting undemocratic movements, above all communism but also, for example, Peronism in Argentina.

Lipset notes that, since the labour movement's early struggle for economic improvements also encompassed the introduction of civil liberties and rights such as universal suffrage, democratic norms and procedures were infused in working-class organizations. But he maintains that in these organizations it is primarily the leaders who are the defenders and carriers of these institutionalized norms, and who thus prevent the worst instincts of the masses from coming to the surface.

Lipset goes on to argue that authoritarian personality traits make workers prone to choose the simplest, or least complex, solution when deciding between parties. In countries with large communist parties, the most authoritarian workers vote for the communists and consequently the bulk of communist support therefore can be expected to come from low-income groups. On the other hand, in countries with small communist parties, such as Sweden, the decision to vote for the communists instead of the large social democratic party necessitates a fairly complex intellectual process emphasizing long-range results. Such complex reasoning cannot be expected of the poorest-off workers. Thus in countries with small communist parties, according to Lipset, it is mainly the better-off workers who support the communists.

The Finnish sociologist, Erik Allardt, has long been interested in communist voting. In the same fashion as Emile Durkheim at the turn of the century constructed his theory of society based on the study of suicide, Allardt has devised a theory of social structure and tensions in society derived from his studies on the sources of communist support in Finland.[20] Allardt views communist voting as an expression of legitimacy conflicts in society; i.e., such voters do not support the existing political system or view it as illegitimate. Following Durkheim, Allardt seeks to explain variations in solidarity with reference to the strength of social norms and the division of labour in society.

Allardt distinguishes between two types of communism with different social bases. The first type is 'traditional communism', which exists in the industrial centres in southern and western Finland. The second type is 'emerging communism' or 'backwoods communism', principally found in the rural areas of northern and eastern Finland, where it has grown in strength during the postwar period. The background of emerging communism, according to Allardt, is the rapid social change in these areas which has weakened traditional norms and values. Emerging communism is not a rational phenomenon but should be seen as a result of anomie, i.e., a sense of disorientation and a lack of relatedness in society as well as the absence of fixed rules and norms. In this situation people turn to communism for emotional support and steadfast leadership. As distinct from traditional communism, this emerging communism, in Allardt's view, is an emotional protest rather than an instrumental act oriented towards political goals.

Both Lipset's and Allardt's theories of the irrational sources of working-class communism must be challenged. In another context I have shown the inadequacies in the data used by these authors to support their theories.[21] For example, the much higher level of unemployment in the north-eastern parts of Finland is a sufficient factor to explain the higher proportion of communists in that part of the country as compared with the south-west. Nor is there any clear-cut empirical evidence supporting the assumptions about the authoritarian views of the working class. Even if economic and other hardships are obviously more common among the workers than among middle-class employees and these difficulties can be expected to affect children as they grow up, it is doubtful that such influences assume the authoritarian form hypothesized by Lipset and others. In certain respects the workers' views on cultural issues are more conservative and traditional than those of middle-class groups, but in other respects they are not. In Sweden, for instance, the middle class more often than the workers seems to have favoured imposing severe sanctions on criminals and corporal punishment of children.

Two earlier studies which I have conducted provide data on the sources of communist voting among workers. The first is a nationwide study of the metal-workers, and the second deals with miners in northern-most Sweden.[22] Among the metal-workers we would expect to find what Allardt calls traditional communism. The miners, however, live in an area adjacent to and very similar to the parts of Finland where Allardt expects communism of an irrational type to emerge. Although at the time of the study they were living in mining communities, close to half of the miners had grown up in villages and small towns where according to Allardt backwoods communism can be expected to flourish.

Table 5.6 Differences between Communists and Social Democrats with respect to various kinds of deprivation among Swedish metal-workers and miners in northern Sweden (standardization for age and residence)

	Metal-workers			Miners		
	Communists	Social Democrats	Difference	Communists	Social Democrats	Difference
	%	%	%	%	%	%
Long-term unemployment of father	41	32	9	56	45	11
Early economic hardship	73	60	13	69	53	14
Has experienced long periods of unemployment	48	40	8	49	40	9
Does not own a car	55	43	12	31	17	14
Does not own home	86	74	12	78	66	12
Low wages	45	41	4	52	43	9
Unskilled work	41	41	0	43	31	12
(N)	(372)	(2,446)		(171)	(378)	

The differences among Social Democratic and Communist workers in terms of experiences and life situation indicate, however, that communist voting among both the miners and metal-workers can be given a rational explanation related to their experiences and present life situation (Table 5.6). The percentage reporting experiences of long-term unemployment, the unemployment of their father for long periods, and economic distress during their childhood, is higher among the Communists than the Social Democrats. Also, the proportions who do not own a car or a home are higher among Communists than among Social Democrats. Among the miners, the Communists are unskilled workers with low pay more often than the Social Democrats. The latter differences did not recur among the metal-workers. In general, however, these findings fail to support Lipset's and Allardt's hypotheses. Communist voting among the workers in Sweden can thus be given a rational explanation in the sense that the Communist workers have experienced greater deprivations than the Social Democrats.

THE BOURGEOIS WORKERS

Why do some workers vote for the bourgeois parties? A very important explanatory factor here seems to be the political and social legacy of their childhood environment (Table 5.7). Among workers voting for the Social Democratic and Communist Parties, six out of ten reported that their fathers sympathized with one of the socialist parties. Among bourgeois workers, only two out of ten have socialist fathers, while twice as many had bourgeois fathers or did not know their father's party preference.

Table 5.7 Political and social legacy among workers by party choice

	Respondent's party choice		
	Bourgeois party	Social Democrats	Communists
	%	%	%
Party preference of father			
Socialist	19	58	59
Unknown	42	29	27
Bourgeois	39	13	14
	100	100	100
Social position of father			
Worker	34	69	60
Middle class	66	31	40
	100	100	100

The bourgeois workers have also experienced downward social mobility to a striking degree. While nearly two-thirds of the fathers of Social Democratic and Communist workers belonged to the working class, the same proportion of bourgeois workers had fathers in social group I or II. The bourgeois workers therefore seem primarily to carry on the traditions of a bourgeois political and social heritage. Less frequently, they are workers who have rejected socialist traditions from a working-class childhood environment.[23]

MIDDLE-CLASS COMMUNISM

In contrast to what is the case among workers, in the middle strata it is instead the bourgeois and Communist voters who have similar social and political backgrounds.[24] Only slightly under one-third of the bourgeois and communist sympathizers come from working-class homes (Table 5.8). On the other hand, among social democrats in the middle strata, over half are of working-class origin. Moreover, two-thirds of the social democrats in the middle strata had socialist fathers, while this is the case for only half of the communists and one-fifth of the bourgeois voters.

Table 5.8 Political and social legacy among salaried employees and businessmen by party choice

	Respondent's party choice		
	Bourgeois party	Social Democrats	Communists
	%	%	%
Party preference of father			
Socialist	22	62	49
Unknown	30	25	11
Bourgeois	48	13	41
	100	100	100
Social position of father			
Worker	28	55	31
Middle class	72	45	69
	100	100	100

The swing to the left which is observable among white-collar groups thus appears to have an interesting social background. The social democrats in the middle strata frequently have roots in the working class and in socialist homes, while the Communist sympathizers in these strata largely come from the middle class and have often broken with their father's bourgeois convictions. Since the Communist Party is perceived as being to the left of the Social Democrats on the political spectrum, one would expect that a party defector coming from the bourgeois parties would more frequently switch to the Social Democrats instead of moving even farther to the left. But the data here indicate that many of those with bourgeois backgrounds who have been radicalized since the late 1960s have not regarded the Social Democrats as a veritable alternative to the bourgeois parties. Instead, they have sought alternatives farther to the left, in the Communist Party and its offshoots.

WORKING WOMEN AND PUBLIC EMPLOYEES

In the postwar period, employment among married women has become increasingly common. A very large portion of this growth in female employment has occurred in the public sector and through part-time jobs. An interesting question here is whether employment among married women has influenced their political beliefs.

For married or cohabitating women, the proportion who voted Social Democratic and Communist was higher among working women than among housewives (Table 5.9). The differences however are small. Among women whose husbands belong to social group II or III, the difference is only 3-4 per cent. In social group I there is an opposite trend, but the number of women in the sample is here very small. Even if the differences in party preferences among working married women and those who are housewives may also reflect the economic needs of the family, the data appear to provide some, admittedly slender, evidence for the assumption that women's job experiences can result in increased support for the socialist parties.

Table 5.9 Percentage voting for the socialist bloc among married or cohabitating women, by employment and husband's social group

	Husband's social group		
	I	II	III
	%	%	%
Employed women	33	39	68
Housewives	(41)	35	65

It is often assumed that public employees are politically more radical than private employees.[25] Government employees purportedly realize their dependency upon the growth of the public sector and accordingly support parties advocating relatively high public expenditures. Comparing the share of the socialist vote among public and private employees, we find some support for this assumption (Table 5.10). The differences however are substantial only in social group I. Among high-level salaried employees, those in the public sector thus vote considerably more often for the socialist bloc than do their counterparts in the private sector. In Norway, the differences in socialist support between salaried employees in the public and in the private sector appear to be somewhat greater.[26]

It is necessary to point out here that the values of the individual may have influenced both the choice of occupation and party sympathies. Among university graduates who seek employment in the public sector, we might expect less of a bourgeois dominance than among those who choose the private sector.[27] In the public sector, the high-level salaried employees who vote for the socialist parties appear to be mainly working in the areas of human services and culture.[28]

Table 5.10 Percentage voting for the socialist bloc among employees, by social group and public or private employment

Sector	Occupation in social group I	II	III
	%	%	%
Public	35	43	71
Private	22	41	68

HOME OWNERS

In Swedish politics home owners are a group extensively courted by the political parties in a variety of ways. An importance aspect here is the role of housing policy for party preferences in the short and long run. Various studies show that home owners sympathize with the bourgeois parties more often than do persons living in flats. In the 1976 election the difference between house dwellers and flat dwellers in terms of the percentage voting socialist can be estimated to be around 13-14 per cent both among workers and in the middle strata. Various types of explanations for this phenomenon can be offered.

One common hypothesis is that the social milieu in residential areas with single-family dwellings encourage the 'embourgeoisement' of voters. Admittedly, this type of social influence may occur, but it is probably not the most important explanation for the differences in party preferences between house owners and flat dwellers.[29] Of greater significance is that home ownership affects the economic interests of the individual. Inasmuch as tax provisions concerning the deductibility of mortgage interest, and to some degree real estate taxes, are important items in the family budget, home owners are especially sensitive to party proposals in these areas. Wage-earners who own their homes therefore may have special economic interests which set them apart from other wage-earners.

Table 5.11 Percentage voting for the socialist bloc by social position, type of housing, and father's party preference

Type of Housing	Workers: Party preference of father: Bourgeois	Unknown	Socialist	Total	Salaried employees, small businessmen: Party preference of father: Bourgeois	Unknown	Socialist	Total
	%	%	%	%	%	%	%	%
Renters	48	69	88	75	23	40	64	45
Owners	38	53	84	61	10	23	57	31
Difference	10	16	4	14	13	17	7	14

Both of these explanatory models presuppose that the voter's party preference changes upon becoming a home owner. But it is likely that the bulk of the differences in party preferences between home owners and flat dwellers has arisen through self-selection. To purchase a house requires substantial financial resources, which fairly frequently are passed on from one generation to another. In each social group, therefore, we can probably expect persons possessing the financial wherewithal to buy a house to have bourgeois party preferences more often than others.

Few studies have attempted to examine whether party preferences actually change in connection with home ownership.[30] In studies based on representative samples it is impossible to isolate different processes of influence resulting in a lower proportion of socialist voters among home owners. In Table 5.11 however I have tried to gauge the importance of the political legacy in this context. As an indicator of political legacy I have taken the father's party allegiance, which can be expected to reflect not only political influences but also to some degree financial resources.

Among voters whose father was bourgeois or whose party preference is unknown, the differences in party choice between home owners and flat dwellers are considerable. The proportion voting socialist is 10-17 per cent lower among home owners than among people living in flats. This pattern recurs among both workers and middle-class groups. Among voters with socialist fathers, however, the differences between home owners and flat dwellers in terms of socialist voting are less; 4 per cent among the workers and 7 per cent among salaried employees and small businessmen. Thus, home ownership may have its greatest influence on party preferences in those groups where the political legacy is diffuse or bourgeois.

THE SOCIAL ROOTS OF PARTY PREFERENCES

The relationship between social position and party preference is generated by the fact that the social structure gives various groups in society partially divergent interests, which the political parties then may attempt to promote and safeguard. Therefore modifications in this relationship can be caused both by changes in the social structure and by the parties altering their policies. Frequently differences in class voting between countries and its changes over time are interpreted in terms of changes in the class structure. Too often the possibility has been overlooked that blurred differences between the policies of the parties can also reduce class voting.

In Sweden, as in the other Nordic countries, social position has been a major force shaping electoral choice. The shrinking difference between workers and other groups in the proportion voting for the socialist bloc in the postwar period has frequently been interpreted as evidence that this relationship has attenuated. This shrinkage has also been viewed as an effect of the development of industrial society and consequently as ominous for socialist parties.[31] The analysis here indicates that this interpretation must be revised.

The major changes in Swedish social structure in the postwar period, primarily the growth of white-collar groups, have obviously had important repercussions for the political parties. But these changes have involved patterns of social stratification rather than class interests. This is underlined by the fact that during the postwar years the Social Democratic Party has succeeded in strengthening its electoral support among white-collar groups without having to abandon its basic ideological course to achieve this. On the contrary, it can be argued that a radicalization of the party has occurred during the 1970s. The common class interests of workers and salaried employees as wage-earners thus seem to have been more important than the divergences created by social stratification. The rapid increase in the level of unionization among white-collar groups during the 1970s also points in the same direction. Probably increasing levels of union organization have been important in 'radicalizing' the salaried employees. This is indicated by a comparison with Norway, where unionization among salaried employees is very weak and the socialist proportion among salaried employees has remained stable. Also, in Finland salaried employees have increased their levels of unionization as well as of left support.

The decline in socialist voting among workers during the 1970s may reflect the workers' dissatisfaction with some elements of the Social Democratic government's policy but need not be an inevitable trend of development. If the proportion of industrial workers in the electorate continues to decrease, however, this will constitute a problem for the socialist bloc, since workers in manufacturing have voted socialist to a greater extent than those in the service sector. Trends of development operating in the opposite direction include the reduction of workers in agriculture, the increasing female participation of the labour market and the growing number of employees in the public sector.

That a party can successfully appeal to new groups of voters through a major overhaul of its programme is demonstrated by the Centre Party. From having been purely a party of farmers and rural groups, it has transformed itself into a bourgeois party in the middle of the political spectrum and has successfully competed, primarily with the Liberals, for the middle-class vote. During its upsurge through the mid-1970s the Centre Party also won working-class votes from both the Liberals and the Social Democrats

Similarly, the social base of the Communist Party has changed drastically since the first half of the 1960s. From being the most clearly working-class-based party, the Communists now have a larger proportion of votes from the middle strata than the Social Democrats. The leftist wave which swept across many countries at the end of the 1960s played an important role in this development; however, changes in the party programme also aided the Communists in appealing to new groups. In the 1970s the Swedish Communist Party rather successfully presented itself as an 'environmentalist' party and sided with the Centre Party against the expansion of nuclear energy.

In the long-term perspective, the fairly extensive social mobility in Sweden, which has increased somewhat during the postwar period, may play a significant part in the development of party preferences. As distinct from what is the case in several other countries, however, the Swedish working class appears to have produced social environments which are perhaps as effective as middle-class milieux in politically socializing young people and in shaping the party preferences of the socially mobile. The unions and political organizations can be assumed to be of central importance in this connection. In Sweden social mobility thus does not siphon off the socialist allegiances of the working class in the same way as it does in some other countries.

The social stratification in the working class influences the worker's party choice. The workers who have voted for the Communist Party appear to have grown up in somewhat harsher economic conditions and in adult life to have had a lower material standard than the Social Democrats. The bourgeois workers are often carriers of a bourgeois political and social legacy and have more seldom broken with socialist traditions from their childhood environment. In the middle strata, on the other hand, the Communists have often broken with a bourgeois family environment; while the Social Democrats are bearers of a Social Democratic political legacy.

The increase in single-family dwellings during the 1970s may prove a boon to the bourgeois parties, primarily by conferring on wage-earners an ownership interest, which in some instances may conflict with their interests as wage-earners. Experiences from Denmark, for example, show that conflicts between owner-occupiers and the tenant population can undermine the electoral support for the Social Democrats.[32] So far in Sweden, however, home ownership seems to have been of importance primarily for fairly sizeable groups which do not possess a socialist legacy from their childhood environment.

6 ELECTORAL GEOGRAPHY

The decision-making units in Swedish politics - communes, counties, constituencies - are geographically defined. Political action therefore occurs in an arena where geography is an important dimension. This is of course no haphazard phenomenon. Neighbourhoods and physically demarcated areas form crucial reference points in people's lives. The frequency of social contacts usually increases with decreasing distance between residential areas. Geographical regions and districts thus also tend to become social units.

Nature has endowed various parts of the country with different physical conditions shaping people's livelihood, conditions based, among other things, on the fertility of the soil, mineral resources, sources of energy, transport routes and climate. Accordingly, the economy in different districts and regions has developed from dissimilar conditions. In varying degrees these differences between districts and regions have persisted through the centuries.

Superimposed on these given geographical conditions are layers of personal experiences of an area's inhabitants in the form of traditions and organizations, customs and values, which also can operate for generations. Regional differences in the degree of religiosity and the strength of popular movements are interesting examples of dissimilarities based on such experiences. For these reasons the political geography of Sweden has long attracted the interest of scholars and the general public.[1] This chapter examines the political colouring of different parts of the country, changes in regional strength of the parties over the years, and the relationship between partisan strength and the social structure of different regions. We shall also analyse the classic questions of how the social environment influences voting and how electoral choice varies between different types of communities. In the Swedish debate the political changes in the metropolitan areas have been the focus of major attention. Here we shall attempt to shed light on the background of these changes.

DECREASING GEOGRAPHICAL DIFFERENCES

An overall picture of the political geography of Sweden can be obtained by examining the percentages of the votes cast for the two political blocs in the parliamentary constituencies. In the 1921 election there were sizeable differences between the constituencies not only in electoral participation but also in the distribution of votes between the blocs. The socialist bloc received only 15 per cent of the votes on Gotland and 16 per cent in Västerbotten - in contrast to 60 per cent in Gävleborg and 62 per cent in the Malmö constituency (Malmö, Helsingborg, Landskrona and Lund).

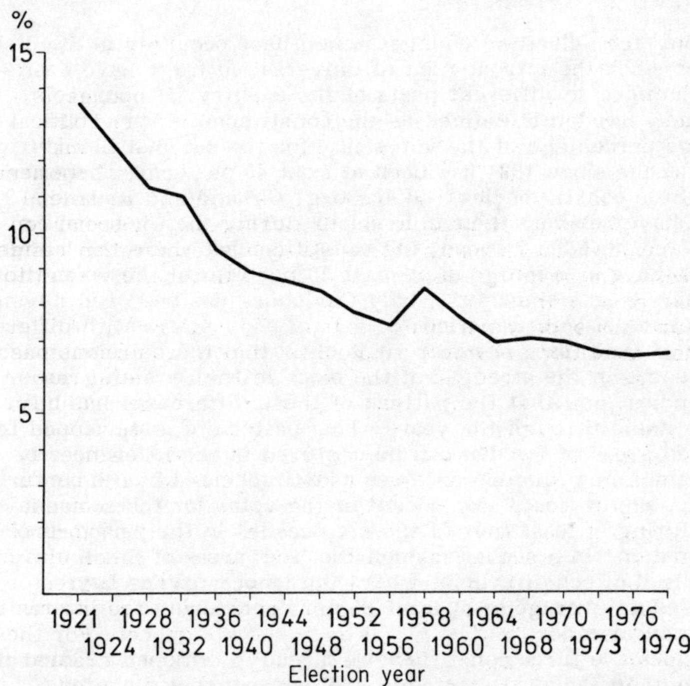

Figure 6.1 Standard deviation of socialist voting percentage in the constituencies in general elections, 1921–79

The trends in the differences between the constituencies in the percentage of votes for the socialist bloc in the general elections from 1921 to 1979 are summarized in Figure 6.1. The dispersion between the constituencies has continuously declined over the years. The extra election in 1958, called at the height of the supplementary pension conflict, constitutes a major exception. In that election dissimilarities in voting trends between different parts of the country increased. The fact that Communist candidates did not run in several constituencies contributed to this increase.

In the elections since 1970 the range of variation between the constituencies seems to have stabilized. In the 1979 election the widest differences were between, on the one hand, Halland and Skaraborg, where the socialist bloc received 39 and 40 per cent of the votes respectively, and, on the other hand, Norrbotten and Gävleborg, where 68 and 59 per cent respectively voted for the Social Democrats and the Communists.

BLUE, GREY AND RED AREAS

The long-term electoral changes which have occurred in Swedish politics since the introduction of universal suffrage have been fairly uniform in different parts of the country. If bourgeois, or 'blue', Sweden is defined as the constituencies where the average percentage of the votes cast for the socialist bloc during each decade since 1921 has been at most 45 per cent, there are only three constituencies - Skaraborg, Gotland and Halland - which have retained their blue colour during the whole period. If by 'red' Sweden is meant the constituencies where the labour parties have an average of at least 55 per cent of the votes during each decade since 1921, only Gävleborg has been red during the entire democratic period.

At the same time, however, it is clear that there are important differences in the strength of the blocs in the remaining constituencies, and that the pattern of these differences has been fairly stable through the years. This pattern of distinctively blue and red areas of Sweden can be captured in the following way. We define 'blue' Sweden as those constituencies which have an average of, at most, 45 per cent of the votes for the socialist bloc during at least four of the six decades in the period under examination. In a similar fashion the 'red' areas of Sweden are comprised of constituencies where the labour parties have received an average of at least 55 per cent during four or more of the six decades.

Besides the three constituencies already mentioned (Skaraborg, Gotland and Halland), six additional constituencies can be classified as blue areas using the above criterion. They are Jönköping, Kronoberg, Bohus, Kristianstad and both the Southern and Northern constituencies of Älvsborg. Table 6.1 lists the constituencies so that the voting percentages for the socialist bloc in the 1960s and 1970s generally increase as one reads down the table. Accordingly, the red constituencies, besides Gävleborg, include Norrbotten, Västernorrland, Västmanland, Örebro, Södermanland, Värmland, Kopparberg and the Malmö constituency. These criteria leave ten constituencies in a 'grey' or twilight zone: the cities of Stockholm and Gothenburg, Stockholm county, Kalmar, Malmöhus, Västerbotten, Uppsala Östergötland, Jämtland and Blekinge.

The political map of Sweden, arrived at in this way, is shown in Figure 6.2. Besides Gotland, the blue constituencies are found in the south-western regions of the country. In addition to the Malmö constituency, red Sweden consists of much of central and northern Sweden. This map seems to reflect not only economic but perhaps to some degree cultural differences between various sections of the country. If, for example, we juxtapose the political map with a map of the frequency of church attendance in different regions, we find certain similarities.[2] Church attendance appears to have been higher in the blue regions than in the red ones.

Table 6.1 Political colour of the constituencies (counties) based on the average percentage of votes cast for the socialist bloc in general elections, 1921–79

Constituency	1920s	1930s	1940s	1950s	1960s	1970s
	%	%	%	%	%	%
Blue						
Skaraborg	27	36	41	37	40	39
Gotland	16	29	37	35	39	41
Halland	30	37	43	39	42	39
Jönköping	28	38	46	42	44	41
Kronoberg	31	39	46	42	45	43
Bohus	37	45	47	44	46	42
Kristianstad	38	43	48	41	45	43
Southern Älvsborg	26	37	46	42	46	43
Northern Älvsborg	37	43	48	44	47	44
Grey						
Malmöhus	51	52	54	48	50	45
Stockholm city	52	53	59	49	51	46
Kalmar	30	42	49	47	50	48
Gothenburg	57	60	62	48	52	48
Stockholm county	52	57	55	46	51	49
Västerbotten	21	37	48	48	50	50
Uppsala	46	52	54	50	52	49
Östergötland	47	54	60	54	56	52
Jämtland	36	50	57	53	55	53
Blekinge	43	48	55	50	55	54
Red						
Malmö constituency	60	63	66	54	57	52
Kopparberg	52	60	61	56	57	53
Värmland	51	59	62	57	60	53
Södermanland	52	60	61	56	58	55
Örebro	49	57	62	56	58	55
Västmanland	54	60	63	59	61	57
Västernorrland	52	62	64	60	61	57
Gävleborg	60	64	66	61	63	59
Norrbotten	47	60	70	68	69	66

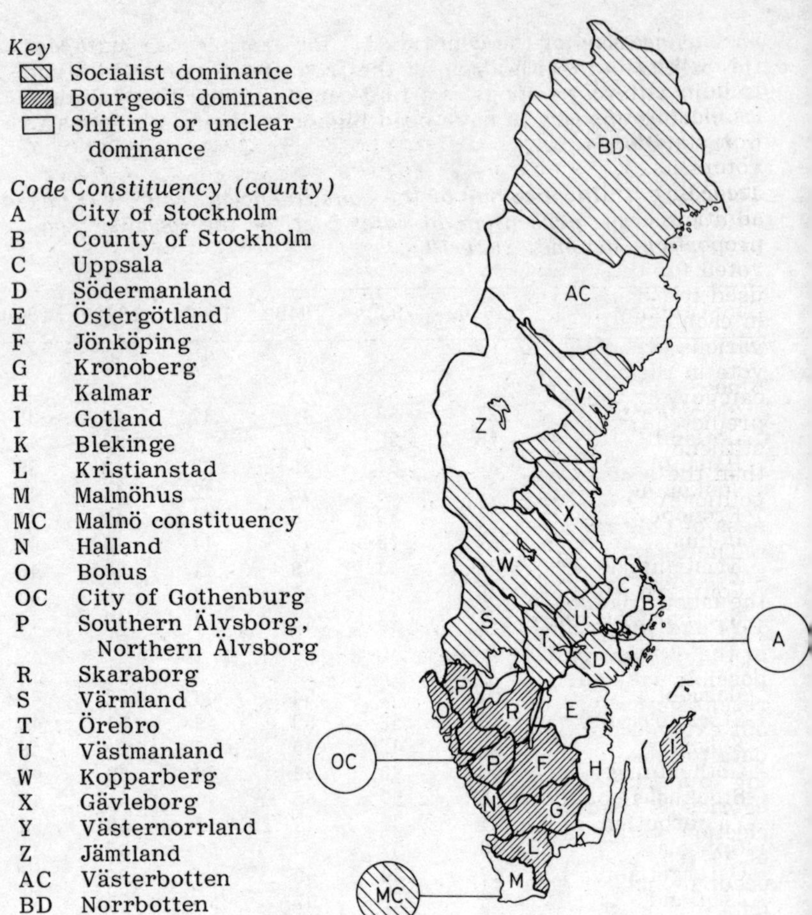

Figure 6.2 Political colour of constituencies based on distribution of votes for bourgeois and socialist blocs in elections, 1921-79

SOCIAL STRUCTURE

A partial explanation of constituency differences in the voting strength of the socialist parties is that the occupational structure and class complexion of the constituencies differ. For example, the proportion of occupations in agriculture varies between constituencies, as does the proportion of working-class occupations (social group III). Thus there would be differences in the election results of the constituencies even if voters in the same occupational category voted in the same way irrespective of which constituency they live in.

Now we can estimate the distribution of votes in a constituency to be expected on the basis of the occupational composition of its electorate.[3] One basis of such estimates are the official election statistics where, through the 1948 election, the eligible voters in each constituency were classified by social group according to the occupation listed in the electoral register. In addition, nationwide surveys make it possible to estimate what proportions of the voters in each occupational category have voted for the different blocs. These two sets of data can be used to calculate the expected voting percentage for the blocs in each constituency under the condition that the voters in the various occupational categories in the respective constituencies vote in the same way as the voters in the same occupational category in the country as a whole. The differences between the predicted and actual voting percentages for a bloc in the constituency can be assumed to depend primarily upon factors other than the occupational composition of the electorate, such as political or other traditions in the constituency and the effectiveness of political organizations.

The Swedish sociologist, Gösta Carlsson, has computed differences between the estimated and actual voting percentages for the labour parties in each constituency for the elections of 1911, 1924 and 1940.[4] Since the classification of voters by social group in the election statistics ceased in the 1950s, it has not been possible subsequently to make similar calculations. However, in recent years the Central Bureau of Statistics (SCB) has carried out extensive sample surveys which also included occupational data for the respondents. Occupations have been grouped according to a scheme which can be broken down into the same categories as the classification into social groups used in earlier election statistics.[5] With the aid of these surveys from the years of 1977-9, we can estimate the distribution of voters in different occupational categories for each constituency. At the same time, data on how the electors in different occupational categories voted in the 1979 election can be obtained from SCB's Party Sympathy Surveys.

The dispersion between the constituencies with respect to expected votes for the socialist bloc remains fairly constant in the 1911, 1925 and 1940 elections but decreases subsequently up to the 1979 election. This suggests that differences in the distribution of occupations have become more similar during the post-war period. Figures given above indicate that the dispersion in the proportion of votes cast for the socialist bloc between constituencies has decreased during the entire period. The dispersion of the differences between the actual and estimated voting percentages for the socialist parties in the constituencies diminishes until 1940 but then remains at the same level through 1979. Up to 1940 the distribution of votes therefore appears to have increasingly approximated the occupational structure of the constituencies.[6]

Table 6.2 Differences between actual and predicted socialist voting percentages in the constituencies in the 1911, 1924, 1940 and 1979 elections

Constituency	Election			
	1911	1924	1940	1979
	%	%	%	%
Blue				
Skaraborg	-10.6	- 8.9	- 4.3	- 7.9
Gotland	- 7.9	-13.8	- 7.5	- 2.8
Halland	- 3.5	- 8.4	- 4.7	- 8.8
Jönköping	- 9.1	-11.1	- 4.4	- 7.9
Kronoberg	- 3.1	- 3.7	+ 1.3	- 7.0
Bohus	- 9.9	-11.6	- 7.4	- 6.6
Kristianstad	+ 0.9	+ 0.3	+ 0.8	- 5.6
Southern Älvsborg	-18.3	-12.8	- 9.7	- 8.0
Northern Älvsborg	+ 0.2	- 2.6	- 2.7	- 4.0
Grey				
Stockholm county	+ 4.5	+ 3.9	+ 0.9	- 1.0
Kalmar	-11.1	- 6.8	- 4.5	- 1.9
Gothenburg	-10.1	- 5.1	- 1.6	- 2.9
Malmöhus	+14.0	+ 9.9	+ 2.7	- 4.3
Stockholm	+ 6.9	+ 0.2	- 2.9	+ 1.7
Västerbotten	-18.3	-11.4	+ 1.0	+ 3.6
Uppsala	- 1.9	+ 3.8	+ 0.6	+ 0.2
Östergötland	+ 1.1	+ 1.9	+ 2.3	+ 0.7
Jämtland	-11.2	- 1.9	+ 9.1	+ 5.9
Blekinge	- 1.5	- 3.9	- 2.6	+ 2.2
Red				
Malmö constituency	+18.4	+ 2.2	+ 2.5	+ 0.2
Kopparberg	+11.9	+ 5.2	+ 7.2	- 0.9
Värmland	+ 2.8	+ 8.4	+ 8.4	+ 1.5
Södermanland	+ 6.4	+ 6.5	+ 4.5	+ 5.1
Örebro	+ 1.8	+ 1.5	+ 2.4	+ 3.9
Västmanland	+ 7.8	+ 6.6	+ 2.6	+ 5.8
Västernorrland	- 8.0	+ 5.0	+ 4.9	+ 6.9
Gävleborg	+10.7	+ 9.4	+ 7.3	+ 6.8
Norrbotten	+12.5	+ 7.0	+14.8	+16.4

In comparison with the expected values, we find in the blue constituencies several cases of persistent and fairly large deficits in the actual votes cast for the socialist bloc (Table 6.2). This applies to Skaraborg, Halland, Jönköping, Bohus and the constituency of Southern Älvsborg. But in Kronoberg and Kristianstad as well as the constituency of Northern Älvsborg, it appears that, at least through 1940, the occupational structure mainly explains the blue colouring of these constituencies. At present, the occupational structure appears to account primarily for the strong position of the bourgeois parties on Gotland. It can also be noted that the initially very large deficit in the percentage of socialist votes in the constituency of Southern Älvsborg has declined through 1979.

Similarly, in the red constituencies we find several cases of substantial surpluses when we compare the actual and expected voting percentages for the socialist bloc. This is true, for example, of the northernmost counties and Södermanland. In the county of Örebro, however, the occupational composition seems primarily responsible for the colouring of the constituency. The large excess of Social Democratic votes in the Malmö constituency in the 1911 election has shrunk. Since the 1920s the distribution of votes in this constituency seems mainly to have reflected its occupational structure. In Kopparberg the initially large surplus in the percentage of socialist votes has dwindled and been displaced by a slight deficit in the 1979 election.

Among the grey constituencies, a sizeable surplus of socialist votes in Malmöhus county in the 1911 election has gradually shrivelled up and was converted into a shortfall in the 1979 election. Stockholm county reveals a similar but not quite so pronounced trend. From the 1940 election onwards, however, the voting support for the labour parties in this constituency, as in the other metropolitan areas, has on the whole reflected the occupational composition of the electorate. On the other hand, in the county of Kalmar the previous large deficit for the socialist bloc has markedly declined during these years. In Jämtland and Västerbotten earlier deficiencies for the socialist bloc have been replaced by surpluses in the 1940 and 1979 elections.

A comparison of the seemingly rather similar two northernmost constituencies of Norrbotten and Västerbotten can illustrate the influence of occupational structure, tradition and politics on electoral choice. Through the years the socialist vote has been approximately 20 per cent higher in Norrbotten than in Västerbotten. Much of this difference stems from the larger number of independent farmers in the electorate until the postwar period in Västerbotten. Of the eligible voters in the two constituencies in the 1928 election, 33 per cent in Norrbotten as compared with 46 per cent in Västerbotten were farmers. The strong dissenter church tradition in Västerbotten, along with the relative sparseness of large industry, have also contributed to the fact that this county, in contrast to the other northern ones, does not now have a surplus of socialist votes.

The exceedingly large surplus of socialist votes in Norrbotten during the past four decades is based not only on political traditions but probably above all on the combined effect of economic problems and party policies. Irrespective of occupation and social position, the bulk of the electorate in Norrbotten has come to view a Social Democratic government as perhaps the only hope of overcoming unemployment problems resulting from the semi-colonial economic position of the county in relation to the rest of Sweden.

COMMUNITY STRUCTURE AND SOCIALIST VOTING

Political sociologists and public commentators have frequently dwelt on the question of the influence of the social milieu on the political behaviour of the individual. The problem crops up in the discussion on the social preconditions for the political mobilization of the working class.

The gist of the problem, as formulated in the political discussions in Sweden during the 1970s, has been: does the political mobilization of the working class require that the workers live in homogeneous working-class environments, which isolate them from bourgeois influences and reinforce the influences of their own class and its organizations? In the debate on the causes of Social Democratic losses in the elections of the 1970s, it has been argued that a fundamental prerequisite for a strong Social Democratic party has been social milieux which created a 'hot-house climate' for the labour movement, i.e., 'the red company towns'. With the disappearance of these social milieux through structural changes in the economy, it is claimed, the long-term preconditions for a powerful Social Democratic party and labour movement have vanished. In particular, the Social Democrats' decline in the metropolitan centres has been interpreted in these terms.[7]

Empirical evidence supporting this type of argument, however, has been meagre. This is due, inter alia, to difficulties of establishing the effects of the social environment on political behaviour on the basis of the type of data which usually are accessible in social science research. To do this requires comparisons of the same type of voters in different types of social milieux. In practice, however, we cannot examine identical types of voters in different social environments. To be sure, we can identify voters with occupations in the same social group in different types of communes. However, workers for example living in different types of communes differ in a variety of ways. In industrial districts they are usually employed in manufacturing; in rural districts, they are generally farm labourers or forestry workers; while in the major cities they often work in the service sector. Our data base therefore is not adequate to eliminate this type of differences between workers in different districts, which are of relevance for their political behaviour. In addition, there are also statistical difficulties concerning the reliability of the classifications used and the risks of incorrect conclusions.[8]

A standard point of departure for speculations about the effect of social environment on political behaviour has been Herbert Tingsten's theory of 'the social centre of gravity'. This hypothesis was derived, in part, from a study of the relationship between social composition of voters and the distribution of votes in Stockholm. For the 1932 election, Tingsten selected five parishes in Stockholm representing extreme poles in class composition. He then ranked the fifty-five election districts in these parishes according to the strength of the labour parties and found that socialist voting in the election districts increased more rapidly than the proportion of eligible voters in the working class.[9]

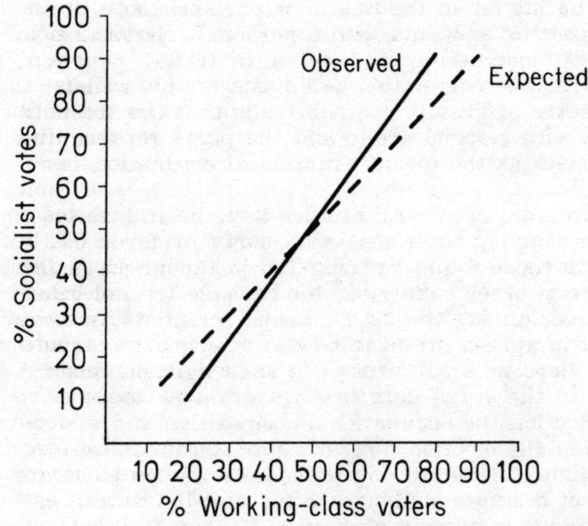

Figure 6.3 The relationship between the percentage of working-class voters and the percentage of votes cast for the socialist parties in fifty-five election districts in the city of Stockholm in the 1932 election

Tingsten's primitive analysis of his figures can be summarized by a regression line adjusted to the data from the fifty-five election districts showing how the percentage of socialist votes changes with the percentage of working-class voters in the district (Figure 6.3). The figure includes a broken line indicating the expected percentage of votes on the basis of the rather unrealistic assumption that the percentage of votes for the socialist parties will increase in equal proportion to the number of working-class voters in the district. A more realistic assumption ought to take into account that not all of the working-class electors vote for the socialist parties and that these parties also receive votes from other social groups; this assumption would lead to a slower expected increase in socialist voting than the one contained in the figure. Despite this, the observed socialist percentage increases more rapidly than the expected vote as the proportion of working-class voters rises in these election districts.

Tingsten was cautious in interpreting this relationship. To some extent it could be due to the influence of the social environment on voters, but it could also depend upon additional factors.

Among other things, he pointed out that the parties probably campaigned more intensively in their core areas of support. The composition of the voters in social group III also varied in the different election districts. The workers' level of income could be expected to be higher in the wealthier parishes, and the proportion of domestic servants with a personal relationship to their employer differed among the election districts. Tingsten, however, employed the correlation as a basis for his well-known 'law of social centre of gravity', which holds that the strength of identification with a social group and the party representing the group increases as the group's numerical domination in an area increases.[10]

Since Tingsten's days, several studies have been done on the effects of the community environment on party preferences. Similar results to those found by Tingsten in Stockholm have been reported from other countries, for example from election districts in Britain during the 1960s. Social scientists, however, are not entirely in agreement as to how to interpret the observed relationships.[11] Here we shall attempt to shed light on this complex problem with the aid of data from different periods.

In the 1928 election the occupational composition and distribution of votes in the election districts and communes were described in unusual detail. Using these data we can elucidate the importance of community structure for socialist voting in Sweden's first major mobilizing election.

Table 6.3 Working-class mobilization ratio in different types of communes in the 1928 election

	% votes for the labour parties	% working-class voters	Working-class mobilization ratio
	%	%	
Agricultural communes	19.2	34.3	0.56
Mixed communes	42.1	52.7	0.80
Stockholm, Gothenburg and Malmö constituencies	52.4	55.6	0.94
Other towns and cities	49.1	58.6	0.84
Industrial communes	67.0	72.5	0.92

On the basis of the percentage of eligible voters in the working class (social group III) and in agriculture, the communes in the countryside have been classified, as in Chapter 4, into three types: agricultural, mixed and industrial communes (see pp. 62-3). Among the administratively defined towns and cities, we have separated out the three metropolitan centres; Stockholm, Gothenburg and the Malmö constituency. As expected, the percentage of votes for the Social Democrats and Communists is extremely low in the agricultural communes and very high in the industrial communes, while the other types of units fall between these two extremes (Table 6.3). The table also shows that these types of units differ markedly with respect to the proportion of working-class voters. In the agricultural communes only one-third of the voters are in the working class, while in the industrial communes three out of four voters are workers. In the remaining types roughly half of the electorate have working-class occupations. The percentage of socialist votes increases more rapidly between the five types of communes than does the proportion of working-class voters.

For each type of commune we can compute the ratio between the percentage of socialist votes and the percentage of the working-class voters. This 'mobilization ratio' for the working class in the different types of communes indicates that, in relation to the proportion of workers, the three metropolitan centres had as high a percentage of socialist votes as the industrial communes. The remaining cities and towns were next in order. The next lowest mobilization ratio was in the mixed communes, and by far the lowest ratio was found in the agricultural communes.

This pattern largely coincides with the earlier picture of electoral participation of the working class in these different types of communes (pp. 62-4). The turnout rate of the working class was low in the agricultural and mixed communes but, on the other hand, about equally high in the metropolitan areas and the industrial communes. The workers in smaller towns and cities also had a relatively high turnout.

The labour movement was thus confronted with many difficulties in mobilizing the workers in agricultural and mixed communes in the countryside. In contrast, during this period towns and cities, and especially the three metropolitan areas, seem to have provided preconditions for mobilizing the working class which were roughly as favourable as those in the industrial communes, where working-class voters constituted the dominant element in the electorate.

The difficulties in mobilizing the rural proletariat posed a serious strategic problem for the labour parties. In a May Day speech in 1930 the Social Democratic party leader, Per Albin Hansson, dealt with the necessity of creating unity among 'the poor in the agricultural population, on the one hand, and the industrial workers and socially allied groups, on the other hand'. He declared:

> More than ever before, the central question is this: How shall we be able, first and foremost, to rally all oppressed people to a common endeavour of liberation, to create a people's policy which irresistibly unites the masses in agriculture with the

masses in the cities and industrial communities, despite differences in conditions, mentality and seemingly to some degree also in interest?

Hansson spoke of 'the proletariat in farming and forestry . . . , the people in the gloomy farm-hands' quarters, the miserable cottages and small tenant farms . . .', which the Social Democrats had to draw into the struggle for 'folkhemmet' (the 'People's Home'), where not only political democracy but also social and economic democracy were to be achieved and the 'economic dictatorship' of the few was to be abolished.[12]

The parties to the left of the Social Democrats faced the same strategic problem, which they also tried to solve by forging an alliance between the urban and rural poor. This effort was marked, for example, when one of the Communist factions in 1934 adopted the name 'the Swedish Socialist Party, the Alliance of Workers and the People of the Soil'.

We can speculate about the causal mechanisms underlying the differences in the mobilization of the workers in the various types of communes. The low mobilization of the working class in the countryside, chiefly workers in agriculture, forestry and services may perhaps reflect the difficulties in fairly traditionalist environments where the workers (e.g., farm labourers and tenant farmers and a more personal relationship with the employer and the workplaces were small. The industrial communes and company towns can perhaps be taken as examples of the 'hot-house environments' envisioned in the current political debate. However, the company towns have also presented mobilization hurdles, such as the worke complete dependency on a single employer in the area and the patriarchal traditions which often developed in these communities.

A larger labour market with many different employers and consequently less dependency on a single employer was probably important in giving urban workers a comparative freedom of actic vis-a-vis the employer. The urban workers were also an accessib target of the labour movement's efforts in spreading ideologies and establishing organizations. The relatively favourable milieu of the towns, and in particular the metropolitan centres, for mobilizing the working class, however, can be interpreted only partially as a result of socially isolated communities such as the working-class districts in the cities.

TYPE OF COMMUNITY AND VOTING

Using more recent data, we can attempt to detect influences of the surrounding environment on the party choice of persons in the same occupational category. Two Party Sympathy Surveys - the first concerning voting intentions in November 1978 and the second voting in the 1979 election - provide data on an adequate number of individuals (over 11,000 respondents) to make the endeavour possible.

In this context communes (which at present number approximately 270) have been classified according to the distribution of economically active persons in industry and the service sector respectively. This classification procedure results in five categories of communes: (a) metropolitan communes (with high percentages in the service sector); (b) service communes (at least 55 per cent in the service sector and at most 41 per cent in industrial employment); (c) partly industrialized communes (42–9 per cent in industrial employment); (d) industrial communes (at least 50 per cent in industrial employment); and (e) mixed communes (at most 54 per cent in services and at most 41 per cent in industrial employment).[13]

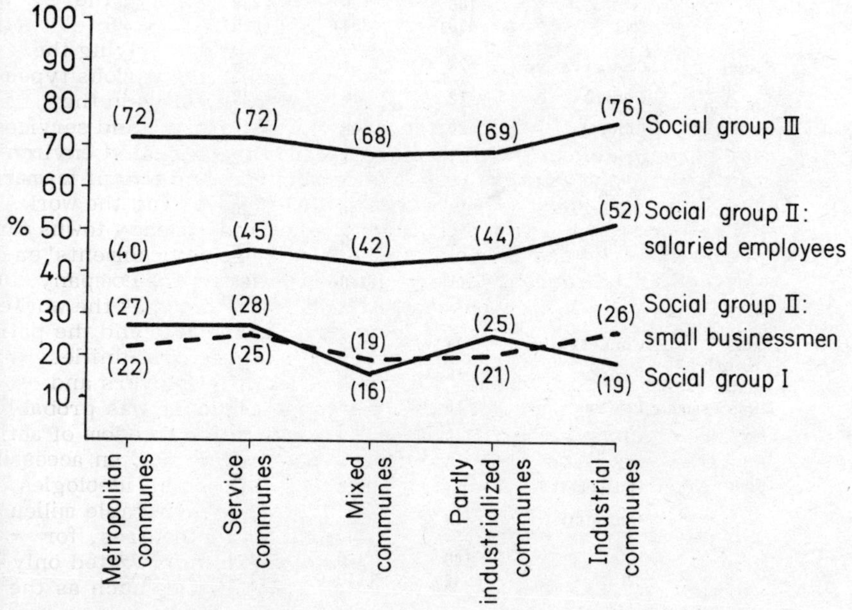

Figure 6.4 Percentage of socialist party sympathizers by social group and type of commune, 1978–9

Among the working-class categories (social group III) socialist party sympathizers were roughly 70 per cent in all types of communes with the exception of the industrial communes, where the proportion was about 76 per cent (Figure 6.4). Thus the percentage of workers voting socialist in the metropolitan areas was not lower than in most of the other types of communes.

Table 6.4 Party preference by social group and type of commune, 1978–9

Social group	Party preference	Metro-politan communes	Service communes	Mixed communes	Partly industrialized communes	Indust[illegible] commu[illegible]
		%	%	%	%	%
Social group I	Conservative	46	39	39	42	39
	Centre	16	16	20	18	1[illegible]
	Liberal	10	16	23	13	2[illegible]
	CDU*	0	0	3	2	[illegible]
	Social Democrat	19	22	14	22	1[illegible]
	Communist	9	6	3	3	[illegible]
		100	100	100	100	10[illegible]
	(N)	(469)	(294)	(80)	(169)	(11[illegible]
Social group II: salaried employees	Conservative	28	21	18	18	1[illegible]
	Centre	12	16	22	21	1[illegible]
	Liberal	20	18	17	16	1[illegible]
	CDU*	1	1	2	1	[illegible]
	Social Democrat	35	40	40	41	4[illegible]
	Communist	5	5	2	3	[illegible]
		100	100	100	100	10[illegible]
	(N)	(1,277)	(931)	(260)	(660)	(53[illegible]
Social group II: small businessmen	Conservative	44	29	25	32	2[illegible]
	Centre	16	30	35	32	3[illegible]
	Liberal	15	16	20	13	1[illegible]
	CDU*	0	0	1	2	[illegible]
	Social Democrat	21	22	17	20	2[illegible]
	Communist	3	3	2	1	[illegible]
		100	100	100	100	1[illegible]
	(N)	(242)	(219)	(122)	(193)	(14[illegible]
Social group III	Conservative	9	6	5	6	[illegible]
	Centre	9	15	19	16	[illegible]
	Liberal	9	7	7	7	[illegible]
	CDU*	1	1	1	1	[illegible]
	Social Democrat	66	69	65	67	[illegible]
	Communist	6	3	3	3	[illegible]
		100	100	100	100	1[illegible]
	(N)	(1,412)	(1,114)	(686)	(993)	(1,3[illegible]

* CDU = Christian Democratic Union

Among middle-level salaried employees (social group II), however, the percentage voting for the socialist parties was somewhat lower in the metropolitan areas than in the other communes. The socialist voting percentage of this category in the purely industrial communes was considerably higher than in other types of communes. This may be due partly to the effects of the political legacy, since the salaried employees in the industrial communes have been largely recruited from the working class.[14]

Among small businessmen and voters in social group I, the number of interviews is fairly small and the estimates concerning party choice are therefore unreliable. However, no clear-cut trends in difference between the various types of communes regarding socialist party preferences are apparent.

On the basis of these interview data, variations in the strength of the individual parties by type of commune can also be examined (Table 6.4). In social group I the Conservatives are very strong in the metropolitan areas, while the Liberals are relatively weak. The Communists also have a fairly strong support in social group I in the metropolitan centres.

Among the middle-level salaried employees and small businessmen, the Conservatives again are strongest in the metropolitan areas. The Social Democrats have relatively weak support among middle-level salaried employees in the three principal cities but have a very strong position among comparable groups in the industrial communes. The Centre Party appears to have a relatively weak support among these white-collar employees and small businessmen in the metropolitan centres as well as among salaried employees in the purely industrial communes.

In the working class the Social Democrats are strongest in the industrial communes. The party's strength does not however vary much between the remaining types of communes. The Communists are again relatively strong among workers in the metropolitan areas. The Centre Party conversely seems to have had difficulty in gaining a footing among workers in the metropolitan regions.

A frequent assumption in the debate on the erosion of Social Democratic support in the metropolitan centres during the 1970s has been that the party has encountered difficulties especially among working-class groups. The data here indicate that it is rather among middle-level salaried employees in the metropolitan areas that the Social Democrats are particularly weak.

STRUCTURAL CHANGES IN CITIES

A very important part of the background to the altered distribution of votes in the three major urban centres during the 1970s is found in the rapid structural changes in the economy of these areas. Table 6.5 presents the proportion of economically active persons employed in manufacturing and construction in the three metropolitan centres and the entire country during the period 1945-79.[15] For all of Sweden, the proportion of employed persons in manufacturing and construction increased until about 1965 but dropped to the level of the 1940s in 1979.

Table 6.5 Percentage of economically active persons in manufacturing and construction in the three principal cities and in Sweden, 1945-79

	Stockholm	Gothenburg	Malmö	Sweden
	%	%	%	%
1945	36	45	50	38
1950	36	44	49	41
1960	38	46	49	41
1965	31	42	43	43
1970	26	38	38	40
1975	22	34	34	38
1979	21	28	30	33

In Stockholm the percentage of persons employed in manufacturing and construction has been lower than the rest of the country since 1945. On the other hand, the percentage of industrial employment in Gothenburg and Malmö until 1960 was actually larger than in the rest of the country. After 1960, however, there has been a drastic drop in industrial employment in the three metropolitan areas. The decline is around 17-19 per cent, nearly twice as large as for the whole country. It seems to have hit Malmö harder than the other two cities. Moreover, since the industrial companies have increasingly located their administrative and research-and-development offices in the metropolitan regions, a growing number of persons employed in manufacturing and construction in these communes are salaried employees.

An examination of the class complexion of the electorate casts additional light on changes in the social structure of the cities (Table 6.6). Ever since the 1920s the percentage of voters with occupations in social group III has been fairly constant for the entire country, approximately 55 per cent. In the city of Stockholm, however, the proportion of working-class voters began to slip as long ago as the early 1940s, and this trend has continued ever since. Stockholm county and the two other metropolitan constituencies had a slightly larger proportion of working-class voters to the end of the 1940s; since then a very sharp decline in working-class voters has occurred in Stockholm county. Furthermore, both the city and county of Stockholm have unusually large proportions of voters in the upper middle class (social group I), roughly 14-15 per cent at the close of the

1970s. Similarly, in Gothenburg and the Malmö constituency the percentage of working-class voters has markedly decreased during the postwar period.[16]

Table 6.6 Percentage of working-class voters in metropolitan constituencies, 1924-79

	Stockholm	Stockholm County	Gothenburg	Malmö constituency	Entire country
	%	%	%	%	%
1924	55	58	65	57	55
1936	55	61	61	61	56
1944	52	61	60	61	56
1948	46	60	57	57	55
1952	43	-	57	55	-
1979	36	37	50	46	50

SWEDISH ELECTORAL GEOGRAPHY

Since the first democratic election in Sweden in 1921, the regional contrasts in the strength of the two political blocs have narrowed considerably. During the postwar period the diminishing differences between the parliamentary constituencies seem primarily to reflect structural changes which have made the economy and occupational structure of the constituencies more similar. At the outset of the 1980s, however, substantial constituency differences in partisan strength remain, differences which stem, among other things, from dissimilar economic bases, political traditions and cultural differences. Norrbotten, the constituency where the actual distribution of votes deviates most sharply from the pattern expected on the basis of occupational structure, also demonstrates that the actions and programmes of the political parties in combination with serious problems affecting most of the population can contribute to massive support for one of the blocs among voters in most socio-economic strata.

The political map contains 'blue' tones chiefly in the south-western parts of the country and 'red' ones primarily in central and northern Sweden. In relation to the occupational composition of the electorate, the socialist bloc appears to have strengthened its position during the past fifty years in the counties of Kalmar, Jämtland, and Västerbotten; while the bourgeois bloc has made gains in the Malmö constituency, Malmöhus and Kopparberg.

The classic question of the social influences of the community environment on the voter's political convictions is difficult to answer conclusively on the basis of the data available to social science research. The observed increases in turnout and socialist voting of the working class in election districts and communes with increasing proportions of working-class voters in the electorate have sometimes been misinterpreted as being solely the result of the effects of the social environment on the voters. Several other factors, perhaps primarily differences in the composition of the working class itself, also contribute to these increases. The social contacts between individuals in a neighbourhood or a larger community no doubt affect political consciousness and actions; in my opinion, however, the effects of differences in such social environments between different types of communities has often been overestimated.

Contrary to the common assumption that the predominantly working-class industrial communities have constituted a fundamental prerequisite for the strength of the labour movement, our analyses here indicate that towns, and in particular the major urban centres, have offered approximately as good opportunities as the industrial districts for the electoral mobilization of the working class. Historically, the labour movement has had most difficulty in mobilizing workers in agricultural areas and in small communities in the countryside. The growing density of population resulting from urbanization can therefore be expected to have improved the preconditions for the mobilization of the working class.

The discussion on the preconditions for working-class mobilization has also focused on changes in urban housing patterns, especially in the metropolitan areas, and on how these changes have affected the mobilizing potential of the labour movement. In the metropolitan centres social segregation decreased somewhat during the first decades of the postwar period.[17] This is reflected, inter alia, in a housing shortage, the decreasing numbers of workers living in the city centres, and the planned mixture of flats of different sizes in the new housing areas. During the 1970s housing segregation has probably increased somewhat. The changes in social segregation, however, have scarcely been of a scale which could have decisively influenced changes in the electoral strength of the political blocs.

Our data indicate that the pattern of voting in the three principal cities since the 1940s is in accord with what would be expected on the basis of the socio-economic composition of the electorate in these constituencies. The choice between the blocs by voters with different social positions during the years 1978-9 does not differ by type of commune sufficiently to substantiate the assumption that the community environment strongly influences current party preferences. Socialist voting among working-class voters is higher, however, in industrial communes than in other types of communes, including the metropolitan centres. This may indicate that the three major cities have lost some of their earlier structural advantages in terms of mobilizing the working class, advantages which once put them on a par with the industrial communes in this respect. But probably the difference between the metropolitan areas and the industrial communes largely reflects differences in the composition of the working class with regard to employment in sectors of the economy. The socialist parties may however have met increasing difficulties in reaching the growing stratum of middle-level salaried employees in the metropolitan areas.

The declining election returns of the Social Democrats in the metropolitan regions during the 1970s must therefore be viewed above all as a result of the rapid changes in the composition of the electorate in terms of occupation and sector of employment. During the last two decades the proportion of workers has dipped sharply in the metropolitan regions, and industrial employment has plummeted. In the big cities an increasing proportion of workers are immigrants who are not permitted to vote in parliamentary elections. In addition, increasing portions of those employed in manufacturing and construction in the three principal cities consist of administrative personnel and technicians rather than manual workers. Since the distribution of votes between the blocs has traditionally reflected occupational affiliation and the sector of employment among the voters, the changes in the composition of the electorate have had direct consequences for the strength of the parties in the metropolitan constituencies.

7 VOTERS ON THE MOVE

Compared with many other countries, the party system and voting pattern in Sweden have been relatively stable over a long period. But beneath the calm surface, we find interesting shifts in the allegiances of the electorate, fluctuations which have gathered momentum in the 1960s and 1970s. As a backdrop to the analysis of recent changes, we shall first outline the long-range shifts in the electoral support of the parties. The changes in the 1970s raise the question of whether the basic left-right dimension in Swedish party politics is now complemented by a new conflict dimension, in which economic growth, advanced technology and large-scale production are pitted against ecology, small-scale organization and opposition to nuclear power. We shall also analyse the opposition to nuclear energy as reflected in the 1980 referendum and the extent of support for the women's movement in various sections of the population.

THE SWEDISH ELECTORATE, 1921-79

In the 1930s the Swedish party system assumed its current form with basically five parties represented in the Riksdag. During the postwar period, despite several attempts, no new party has succeeded in achieving parliamentary representation.[1] The relative strength of the parties was also established at a fairly early date. As early as 1917 the Social Democrats had become the largest party, and since the 1930s it has been a party with a majority bent, i.e., capable of winning an absolute majority - a position none of the other parties has approached (Figure 7.1 and Table A1 in the Appendix). In the local elections of 1938 and 1942 as well as the 1940 general election the Social Democratic Party won over 50 per cent of the votes cast. In the 1962 and 1968 elections the party again gained a majority. During the 1950s and 1970s, on the other hand, the Social Democrats suffered serious setbacks.

The Communist Party, which emerged after the split in the Social Democratic Party in 1917, has had the smallest parliamentar representation during the entire period. The electoral backing of the party, however, has fluctuated a good deal, owing among other things to internal schisms and changes in the international political situation related to the role of the Soviet Union. In the 1944 and 1946 elections the Communists obtained their largest victories at the polls, winning 10-11 per cent of the vote. Their poorest showing – a mere 3 per cent – occurred in the 1968 election, a few weeks after the Soviet invasion of Czechoslovakia.

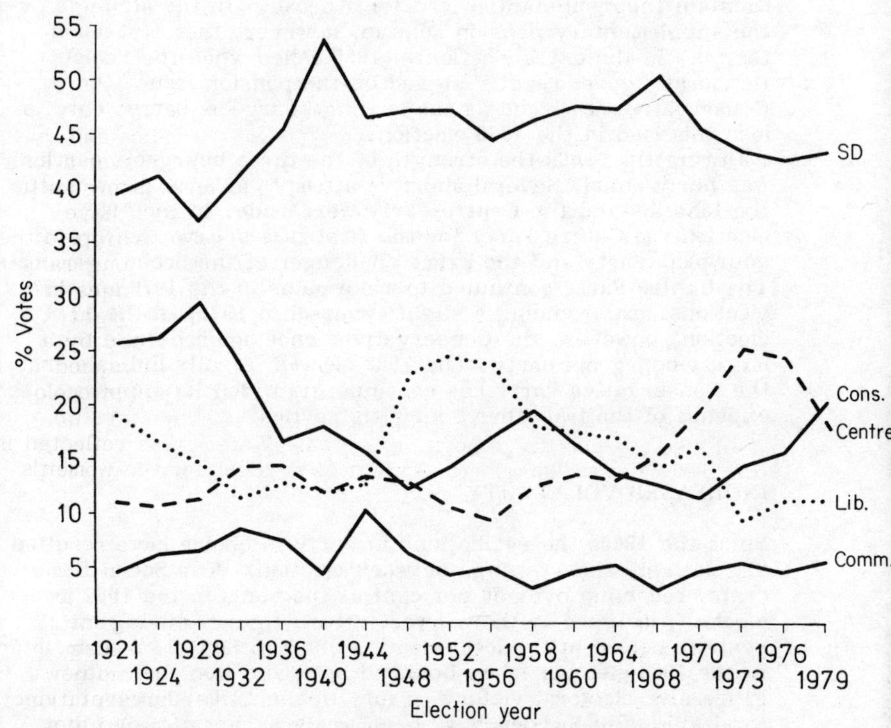

Figure 7.1 Percentage of votes cast for the parliamentary parties in elections, 1921–79

In a long-term perspective, the three bourgeois parties have been of roughly similar size. Their electoral fortunes, however, have varied through the years and each has experienced a nadir in electoral support at around 10 per cent and a zenith of between 20 and 25 per cent. In large measure, one party's victories have been won at the expense of the other two parties. In the early 1980s none of the three bourgeois parties has thus been able to establish itself as a more permanent major rival of the Social Democrats.

The Conservatives remained the largest bourgeois party until after World War II. Influenced by the massive support of the Social Democrats in the elections from 1938 to 1942, the bourgeois parties moved to the left. In the 1948 election the Liberals – with a new party leader, Bertil Ohlin, at the helm and a revised party programme stressing 'social liberalism' - clearly out-distanced the other two bourgeois parties. In this election the Conservatives and Agrarians each received 12 per cent of the votes, while the Liberals won 23 per cent. The Liberals were able to maintain their substantial lead for a decade. In the struggle over the supplementary pension scheme, however, they lost much terrain. In the extra election in 1958 called when the Social Democratic government resigned on the pension issue, the Conservatives emerged as the leading bourgeois party, only to lose this lead in the 1960 election.

During the 1960s the strength of the three bourgeois parties was fairly equal. Several abortive attempts at a merger between the Liberals and the Centre Party were made. In the 1968 election the Centre Party for the first time became the largest bourgeois party and the prime challenger of the Social Democrats. The Centre Party continued to make gains in the 1970 and 1973 elections, experiencing a slight reversal in 1976. In the 1979 election, however, the Conservatives once again became the largest bourgeois party. The 1982 election results indicate that the Conservative Party has continued to widen its support at the expense of the two other bourgeois parties.

INCREASED VOLATILITY

Since the 1960s the vacillations in partisan choice have resulted in relatively sharp swings between elections. The Social Democrats, receiving over 50 per cent of the votes in the 1962 local election, dropped to their lowest return figures during the postwar period in the local election of 1966. Only two years later, in the 1968 election, they bounced back and won their most impressive electoral victory so far. In the 1970s, however, electoral swings in Sweden have been smaller than in many other European countries.[2]

Elections, however, register only a portion of the shifts in voter preferences. Public opinion surveys, which have been carried out since the late 1940s, reveal that voters' sympathies can also change dramatically between elections. In examining the increasing volatility of the electorate, we shall utilize data for secondary analyses from three different interview surveys. The most important here is the Party Sympathy Surveys which were conducted by the Central Bureau of Statistics (SCB) two to three times a year from 1972 to 1981. The second source is data from SCB's Election Surveys, which have been carried out since 1956 in connection with the parliamentary elections. To some extent we shall also draw upon the polls which the private Swedish Institute for Public Opinion Research (Sifo) at present publishes ten times a year.[3]

Figure 7.2 describes the shifts in electoral support between the socialist and the bourgeois blocs during the period 1972-82 as estimated by SCB's Party Sympathy Surveys and Sifo's voter

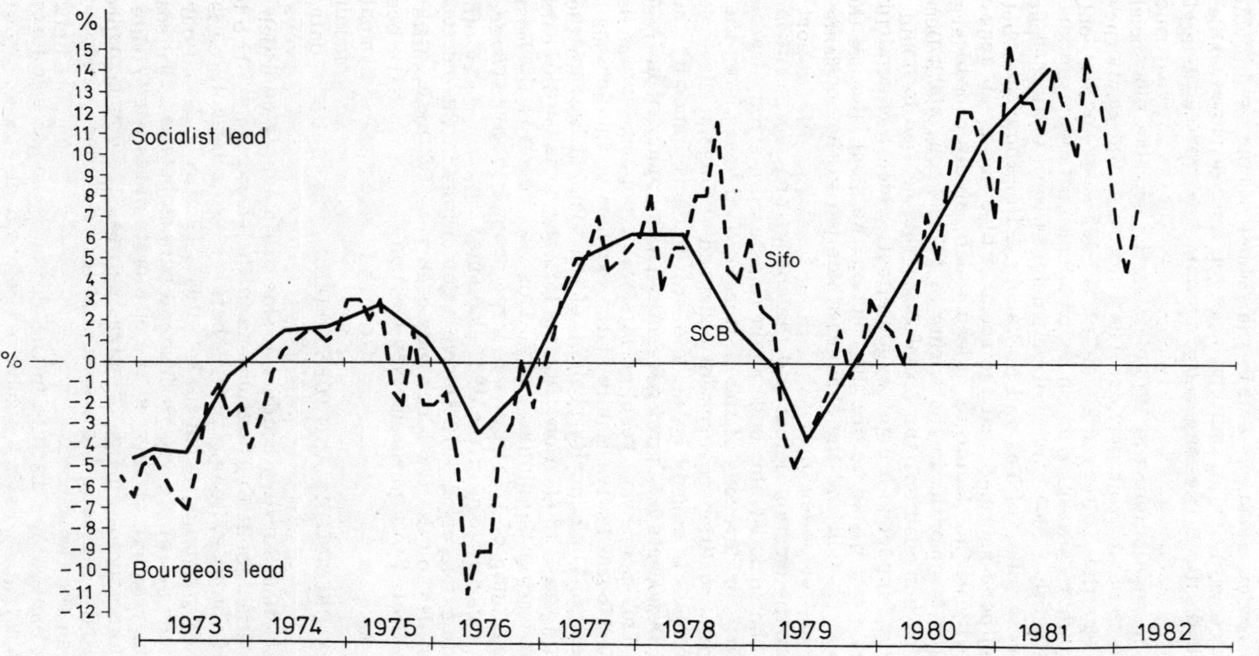

Figure 7.2 Changes in bloc lead in SCB party sympathy surveys and Sifo's voting polls, 1972–82

polls. The data series of Sifo's polls reveal sharper fluctuations than SCB's. This is due among other things to dissimilarities in the interview questions and to the smaller sample used by Sifo as compared with SCB, resulting in larger random variations in their estimates.[4] The long-range trends, however, largely coincide.

In the polls before the 1973 election the socialist bloc trailed behind the bourgeois parties. The outcome of the election, however, was the 'Lottery Riksdag' of 175-175 seats for the two blocs, where a number of issues on which sufficient support from the other bloc could not be mustered were settled through random sampling of Yes and No ballots. After the election, opinion polls revealed that the socialist bloc had again acquired a majority in the electorate, a lead which rapidly crumbled during a few months in the spring of 1976. Then, starting from a record low position, the Social Democrats seemed to have built up support in a band-wagon effect, which was suddenly broken a few weeks before the election. We shall later discuss this phenomenon and the changes which led to the Social Democratic loss of power in 1976.

After the election defeat and the change of government in 1976, the socialist bloc once again registered a strong lead in the party preferences of the electorate. Two years later the bourgeois coalition government collapsed because of disagreement on the nuclear energy issue, and with the acceptance by the Social Democrats a Liberal government was appointed in October 1978. This manoeuvre resulted in sizeable popular opinion gains for the Liberal Party, mainly at the expense of the Social Democrats. The minority position of the socialist bloc persisted through the 1979 election. During 1980 the socialist bloc resumed a clear lead in the opinion polls. This lead began to shrink in the beginning of 1982, but was large enough to give the socialist bloc a clear victory in the 1982 elections.

During the period 1972-80 five major swings in the electorate's sympathies for the two blocs thus occurred. Of these, only one was reflected in a parliamentary election.

PARTY DEFECTORS AND IDENTIFIERS

The Election Surveys conducted since 1956 supply additional information about the fluctuations in the electorate.[5] The proportion of voters switching parties between two consecutive elections has nearly doubled since the late 1950s (Figure 7.3).[6] During the 1970s one out of six voters changed parties between elections. This increasing volatility in the electorate stems partly from a more extensive exchange of voters between the bourgeois parties and partly - although to a somewhat lesser extent - from switches between the two blocs.

The increasing volatility in the electorate is also manifested in the fact that a growing number of voters decide how they are going to vote fairly late. Since 1964 the election interview surveys have inquired: 'When did you make up your mind how you would vote this year? Was it the last week before election day, earlier in the autumn and summer, or did you know how you were going to vote for a long time?' The proportion answering that their party choice had been decided 'for a long time' has fallen from 81 per cent in 1964 to 76 per cent in 1968, 73 per cent in 1970, 72 per cent in 1973 and 70 per cent in 1976 and 1979.[7]

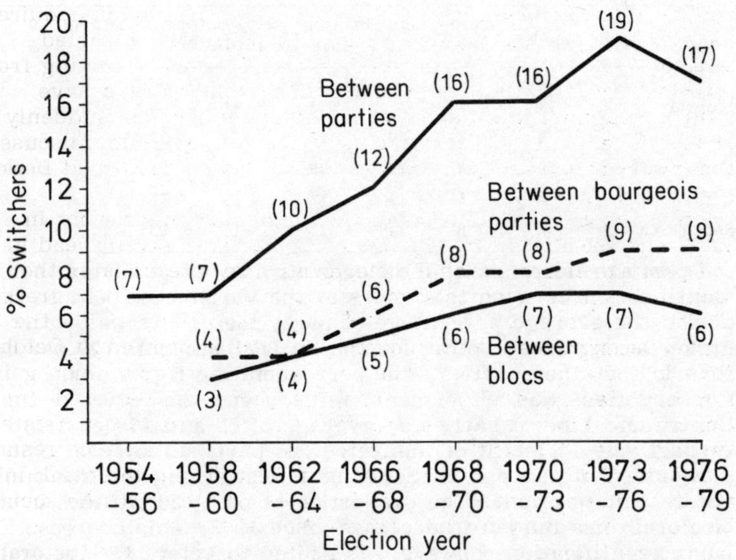

Figure 7.3 Percentage of voters switching party or bloc between two consecutive elections, 1954-79

Of the individual parties, the Liberals and the Communists have experienced the largest drain of their voters away to other parties (Table 7.1).[8] In their worst elections they both have lost nearly half of their voters from the preceding election. The Centre Party and the Conservatives possess more stable electoral backing but during their worst setbacks have lost every fourth voter. The Social Democrats have clearly had the most stable electoral support during this period but in the elections of the 1970s have lost every tenth voter. Similar differences between the parties also emerge in terms of losses due to non-voting.[9]

The differences in the volatility among the various parties' voters are also reflected in differing strengths of party identification. The concept of party identification describes the degree to which a voter views him- or herself as an adherent of a party or has a sense of personal attachment to the party. The election surveys during 1968-79 make it possible to estimate the average levels of party identification for the parties' voters during these years. The proportion of party identifiers in the electorate has decreased somewhat, from 65 per cent in 1968 to 59 per cent in 1979. This decrease, however, is evident only among voters for the bourgeois parties.

Table 7.1 Percentage of party defectors, by party, 1958-79

Party	Percentage changing party between elections							
	1958-60	1962-4	1966-8	1968-70	1970-3	1973-6	1976-9	Average
	%	%	%	%	%	%	%	%
Liberal	13	16	27	23	41	28	32	26
Communist	8	18	50	22	14	37	15	23
Conservative	20	20	17	29	12	13	7	17
Centre	5	6	11	13	13	27	28	15
Social Democrat	2	6	4	11	11	12	7	8

There are fairly sizeable differences in average levels of party identification between the voters of the various parties. In this period the average percentage of party identifiers was much higher among those voting for the Social Democrats (77 per cent) than in the other parties. The corresponding figure for the Conservatives was 59 per cent; while among the voters of the Centre and Liberal Parties an average of 52 and 47 per cent, respectively, thought of themselves as party adherents. The percentage of party identifiers was lowest among the Communist voters - 45 per cent. The proportion of party identifiers in the electorate has tended to decrease since 1968. This decrease in party identification, however, is limited to voters for the bourgeois parties. A similar pattern emerges in the changes of party choice in the elections from 1968 to 1976. Among the voters who had participated in all four elections, the percentage voting for the same party in all the elections was clearly highest among the Social Democrats and lowest for the Communists.[10]

The low proportion of party identifiers among Communist voters may be partially explained by the fact that the party has attracted large numbers of young voters whose party identification, as a rule, is weaker. But the Communists, perhaps more than any other party, also seem to have been a protest party or a party of dissatisfied voters. In the elections between 1968 and 1976 dissatisfaction with the parties and politicians was highest among the Communist voters.[11] On election day the strongly convinced adherents of the Communist Party, for example those who turn out to demonstrate on the first of May, are joined by many lukewarm voters who perhaps want to display their dissatisfaction with another party, usually the Social Democrats.

For several years, the Communist Party's electoral support has hovered precariously close to the 4 per cent threshold for representation in the Riksdag, which was introduced in 1970. In the 1962 local elections and the 1968 general election the party's share of the vote was below it. A critical question for the Communists, therefore, is whether the party identification of the young voters won by the party in the 1970s will eventually stabilize.

SHIFTS IN VOTING, 1964-80

The gross changes between the parties and blocs described above include moves in opposite directions and consequently to some extent cancel out one another. Their net effect on the voting strength of the parties is therefore smaller. The strength of the parties is also influenced by shifts between non-voting and voting as well as by changes in the electorate due to mortality and the inflow of first-time voters.

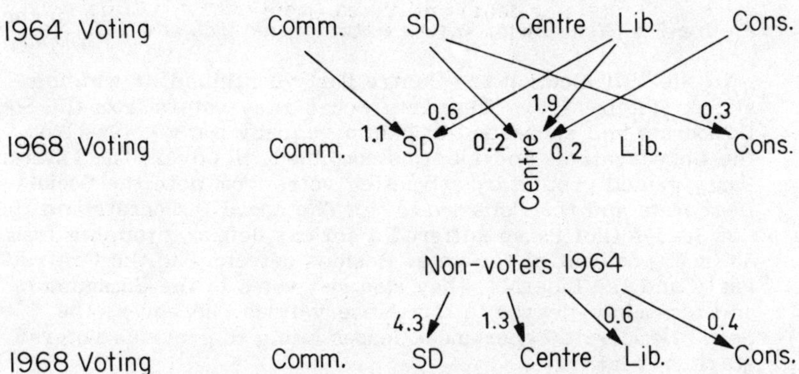

Figure 7.4 Net Flow of Voters between the 1964 and 1968 Elections

The Election Surveys and Party Sympathy Surveys enable us to cast light on the net effects of partisan change in the electorate since 1964.[12] Only the net flow of voters between the parties and, in some cases when of special interest, the shifts between voting and non-voting are described here (Figure 7.4). The arrows indicate the direction of the flow and the figure beside each arrow the size of the flow as a percentage of all eligible voters in both elections.

The figures on the shifts in voting obtained in this way show that the Social Democrats' major election victory in 1968 was only to a small degree the result of net gains from the other parties. The Social Democratic triumph was achieved primarily by mobilizing the non-voters in the 1964 election: the party's gains among the non-voters amounted to no less than 4.3 per cent of the electorate. These gains were supplemented by voters switching, primarily from the Communists to the Social Democrats and secondarily from the Liberal Party. Simultaneously, the Social Democrats lost voters to the Conservatives and the Centre Party.

In the 1968 election the Centre Party succeeded in winning voters chiefly from the Liberals but also a small portion from the Conservatives. Additionally, the Centre Party made substantial gains among former non-voters. The combined effect was that the Centre Party became the largest bourgeois party. The Communists lost approximately half of their previous voters, and roughly every fifth voter deserted the Liberals and the Conservatives.

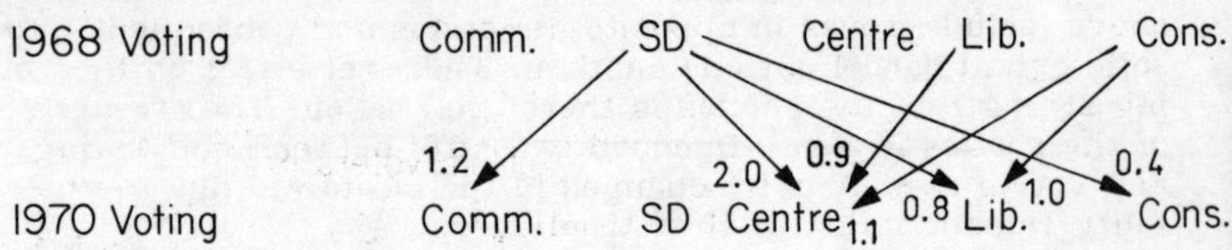

Figure 7.5 Net flow of voters between the 1968 and 1970 elections

In the 1970 election the Centre Party continued its winning streak (Figure 7.5). The party wooed away voters from the Social Democrats and succeeded in gaining equally many voters from the Conservatives and Liberals combined. However, the Liberal Party gained ground by attracting votes from both the Social Democrats and the Conservatives. The Social Democrats and their new leader Olof Palme suffered a serious defeat, dropping from 50 to 45 per cent of the vote. Besides defectors to the Centre Party and the Liberals, they also lost votes to the Communists and to a minor degree to the Conservatives. Moreover, the Social Democrats experienced losses owing to previous voters staying at home.

The continued success of the Centre Party in the 1973 election, which was Torbjörn Fälldin's first campaign as party leader, stemmed largely from winning votes from the Social Democrats and the Liberals (Figure 7.6). The party also benefited from substantial gains among former non-voters. The Liberals suffered a devastating defeat, losing nearly half of their previous voters to the Centre Party and the Conservatives. The Conservatives' gains were further strengthened by attracting votes from both the Social Democrats and the Centre Party as well as from previous non-voters. The Communists also succeeded in winning a fairly large amount of votes from the Social Democrats, who were aided however by a rise in voter turnout.

The outcome of the fluctuations in the party preferences of the voters between the 1973 and 1976 elections was a marked shift to the bourgeois bloc and a change in government. The flow of voters between the bourgeois parties was also considerable (Figure 7.7). The Social Democrats lost voters mainly to the

Liberals and the Centre Party but they also experienced modest losses to the Conservatives. The Centre Party, however, lost heavily to the Conservatives and Liberals. The record high mobilization of the electorate operated primarily to the advantage of the Social Democrats. Finally, the Communists lost votes to the Social Democrats.

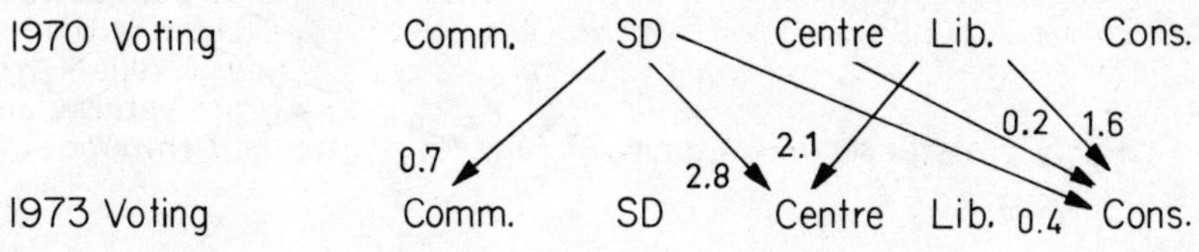

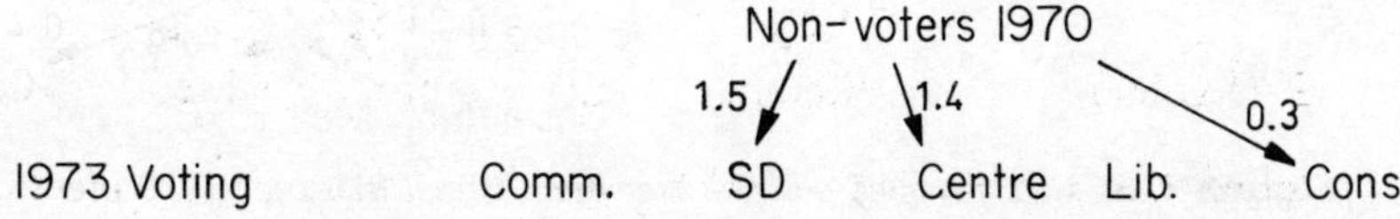

Figure 7.6 Net flow of voters between the 1970 and 1973 elections

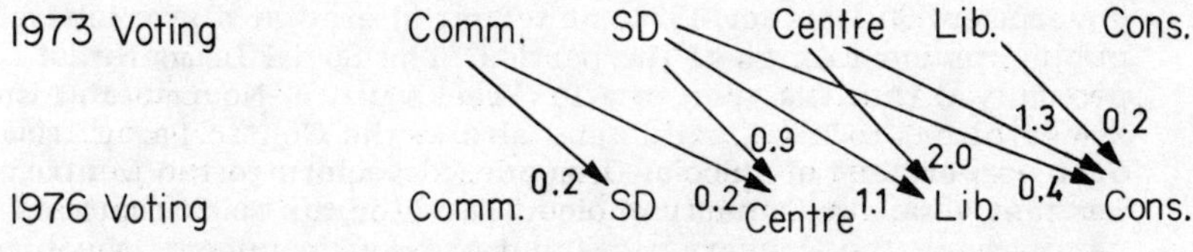

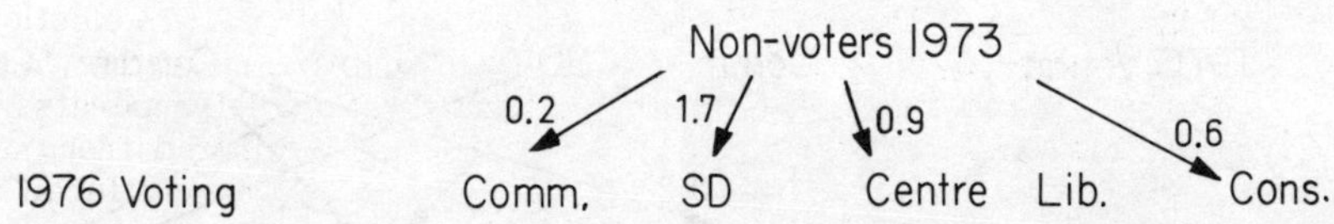

Figure 7.7 Net flow of voters between the 1973 and 1976 elections

The resurgence of the socialist bloc in the opinion polls during the first two years of the bourgeois coalition government until May 1978 was the result of net gains for the Social Democrats from principally the Centre Party but also the Liberals and to a minor degree from the Conservatives (Figure 7.8). The centre Party also experienced minor losses to the Communists and moderate losses to the Conservatives and the Liberals. In addition, fairly substantial numbers who had voted bourgeois in the 1976 election had become uncertain as to their party choice in May 1978. Those who were hesitant had mainly voted for the Centre Party in 1976, but even some former Conservative and Liberal voters were uncertain. Simultaneously, the Social Democrats made some headway among non-voters in the 1976 election.

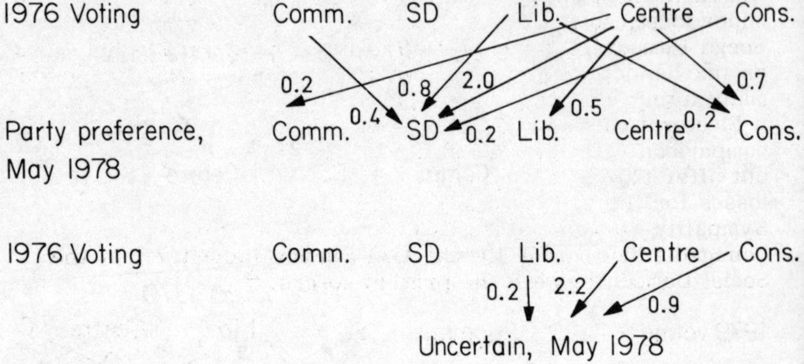

Figure 7.8 Net flow of voters between the 1976 election and May 1978

The dissolution of the three-party bourgeois coalition and the Social Democrats' acceptance that the Liberals form a minority government in October 1978, however, altered at a stroke the public opinion ratings of the parties. The Social Democrats, probably within the span of a few weeks up till November, lost sympathizers to the Liberals and also to the Centre Party. Moreover, several former Social Democratic sympathizers now became hesitant about their party choice. The Liberals made further gains among the Conservatives and previously uncertain voters. The Liberal Party's popularity continued to rise through the winter but turned downward in the late spring of 1979.

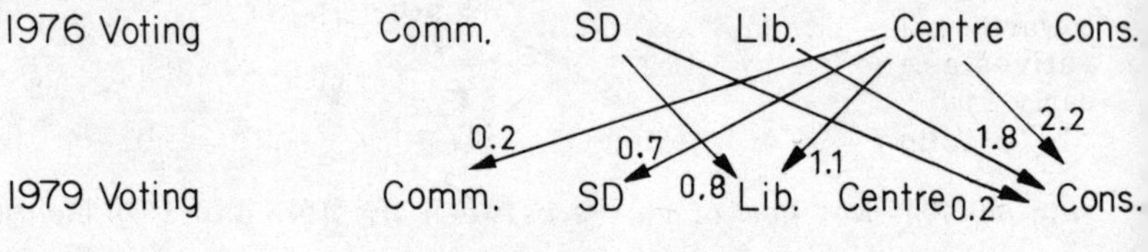

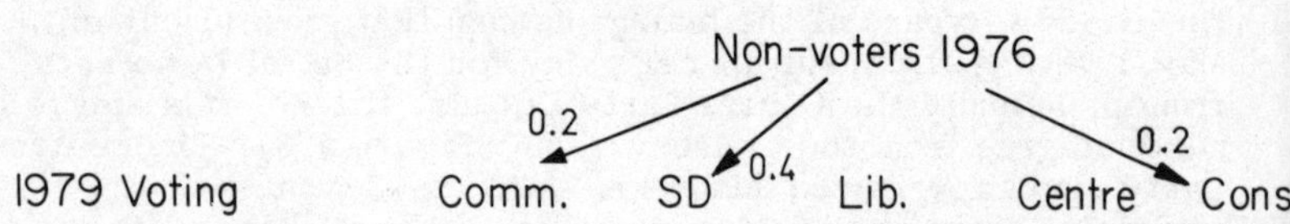

Figure 7.9 The net flow of voters between the 1976 and 1979 elections

The upshot of the shifts in the electorate between the 1976 and 1979 elections was a major victory for the Conservatives (Figure 7.9). Their success stemmed from voters switching from the Centre Party and the Liberals. The Centre Party also suffered fairly large losses to the Liberals and the Social Democrats. In the final phases of the campaign the Social Democrats incurred minor losses to the Communists, probably as a result of the Social Democrats being pressured into a very favourable stand on tax deductions for home owners, a proposal which irritated many living in rented accommodation.

Electoral participation in the 1979 election declined slightly in comparison with the 1976 election. The two voter surveys carried out after the election give different estimates of the relative losses for the two blocs since 1976. According to the Party Sympathy Survey the losses were somewhat greater for the bourgeois bloc, while the Election Survey indicates that the Social Democrats were the primary losers.[13]

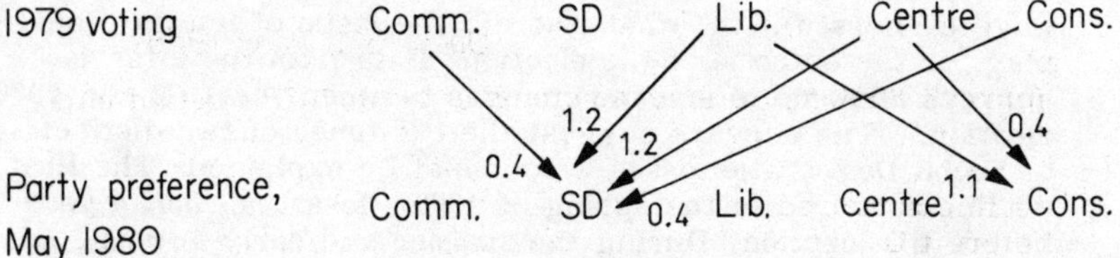

Figure 7.10 The net flow of voters between the 1979 election and May 1980

The upswing in the popularity of the socialist bloc from the 1979 election to November 1980 resulted from net gains by the Social Democratic Party from the Liberals and the Centre Party but also from the Communists and Conservatives (Figure 7.10). At the same time the Conservatives received net gains from the Liberals and the Centre Party. Thus there was a tendency towards polarization, with the Social Democrats and the Conservatives as the leading parties. This tendency continued up to early 1982.

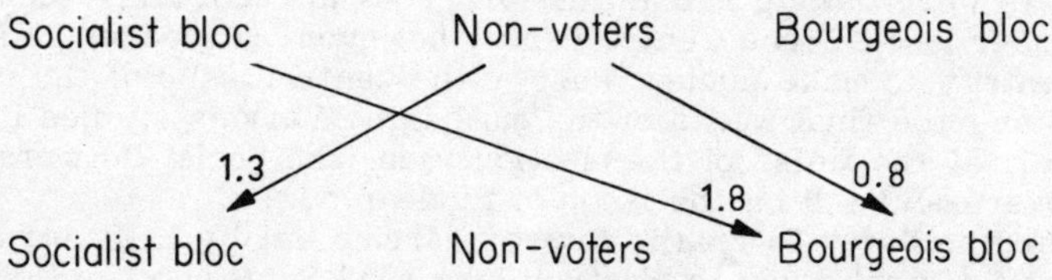

Figure 7.11 Average net flow of voters between the blocs and non-voters to blocs, 1964-79

The average net flows of the voters in the parliamentary elections between 1964 and 1979 show that the socialist bloc on the whole experienced appreciable net losses to the bourgeois bloc (Figure 7.11). These losses occurred in the elections between 1970 and 1976. The total losses of the socialist bloc, however, have been reduced by the socialist parties having a large reserve of non-voters, which they have been able to mobilize, most dramatically in the 1968 election.

THE SOCIAL DEMOCRATIC DEFEATS IN 1976 AND 1979

Since the 1976 election resulted in an historical change of government, it is of particular interest to attempt to illuminate the background to the Social Democratic losses in this election. Did the voters turn their backs on the Social Democrats because they were fed up with the welfare state? Were the Social Democrats perceived as too radical because of the discussion about wage-earners' funds? What role did the issue of nuclear energy play for the outcome of the election? Data from the interview surveys allow us to analyse changes between the 1973 and 1976 elections. The surveys suggest the existence of two distinct sets of Social Democratic losses which must be explained. The first decline occurred in the spring of 1976 - less than half a year before the election. During the summer and early autumn, however, the Social Democrats managed to recoup most of these losses, only to face a new decline a few weeks prior to the election.[14]

The setbacks for the Social Democrats during the spring of 1976 must be seen in the context of the prolonged and intensive treatment in the mass media of a series of incidents or 'affairs'. These incidents created an image of the Social Democrats as secretive, autocratic, and growing more distant from the people.[15] As we shall demonstrate later, there is little indication that the electorate had grown weary of welfare policies and deserted the Social Democrats on this count. On the other hand, the debate on the wage-earners' funds during the spring and summer of 1976 led to some popular opinion losses for the Social Democrats.

During the months before the 1976 election the Social Democrats were making substantial progress in recovering their earlier losses. The Centre Party, however, succeeded in its strategy to make nuclear energy the central issue of the election during the final weeks of the campaign. Various studies indicate that, at the finish of the election race, the Social Democratic government fell on the issue of nuclear power.

In the Party Sympathy Survey carried out by SCB during the last two weeks before election day on 19 September, we can follow the day-by-day developments by comparing the estimates based on interviews conducted up to a particular day with the total estimate based on all of the interviews for the two-week period. The results show that the Social Democrats from the

7th through the 16th of September lost a significant proportion of votes (Figure 7.12). During the same period the Centre Party increased its strength markedly. The support of the remaining parties, in contrast, did not change notably. That the observed changes might be the result of methodological artefacts seems unlikely, since similar changes in party sympathies did not recur during the interview period of the three other Party Sympathy Surveys completed during 1976.[16]

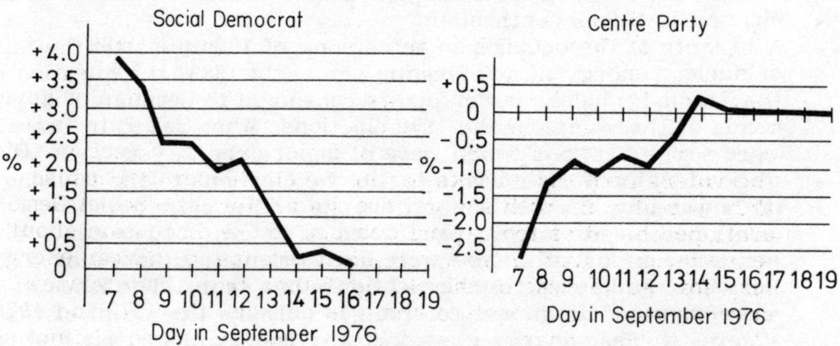

Figure 7.12 Change in the proportion intending to vote for the Social Democrats and the Centre Party respectively among persons interviewed up to a particular day during the period 7-17 September 1976

The Election Survey of the 1976 election also indicates that a major portion of the Social Democrats' losses between 1973 and 1976 occurred in the weeks before election day while the Centre Party simultaneously won votes. The issues of nuclear power and state intervention in the economy were the two attitude dimensions most clearly associated with changes in party choice between 1973 and 1976. The negative evaluations of the Social Democrats' energy policy increased sharply during the weeks before the election. This was the most important question for voters who switched from the Social Democrats to the Centre Party. On the other hand, the issues of state intervention and equality were significant for voters who changed from the Social Democrats to the Liberals.[17]

An interview survey done by the Swedish Broadcasting Corporation after the election suggests that the nuclear energy issue was more important than the wage-earners' funds in influencing the party choice of the voters. Nine per cent of the respondents stated that nuclear energy was the issue which determined how they had voted, whereas 4 per cent declared that the wage-earners' funds was the most important issue. Moreover, the nuclear power issue became increasingly important as election day grew near. The proportion reporting that the nuclear issue had been of 'very great importance' for their party choice was

23 per cent among the voters who had made up their minds before the summer of 1976, 30 per cent among those who decided during the summer and early autumn, but 39 per cent among those who decided during the final week of the campaign.[18]

Changes in electoral choice are admittedly a long process involving many factors where earlier influences determine the effects of later factors. The 1976 election was unusual inasmuch as a single issue - nuclear energy - came to completely dominate the final spurt of the campaign and determine the outcome of the election at the eleventh hour.

In spite of the decision in the spring of 1979 to settle the issue of nuclear energy in a referendum in early 1980, the question of the Swedish nuclear power plants continued to dominate the minds of the voters in the 1979 elections. When asked if 'there were some questions which were of importance to you when you decided which party to vote for in the elections to the Riksdag on September 16', the issue of energy and nuclear power was mentioned by the largest proportion of voters, 24 per cent. The next most important issues were employment (mentioned by 17 per cent) and taxes (mentioned by 15 per cent). The issue of wage-earners' funds was referred to only by 4 per cent of the voters. Nuclear energy was especially important for those who opposed the expansion of nuclear energy.[19]

CONFLICT DIMENSIONS

In analysing voting social scientists have traditionally used a model which assumes that the voters, on the basis of their values, needs and desires, assess the policy of the different parties. They then choose the party which best meets their demands. Such an 'economic' model of democracy has been formalized by Anthony Downs.[20] In discussions of changes in party choice, however, it is frequently forgotten that voters can switch parties not only because their demands on the parties change but also because the policy of the parties is altered or is assessed differently than earlier.

The values, needs and desires of the electorate, traditionally decisive in Swedish party politics, have been related to what is usually called the left-right dimension of politics. This left-right dimension concerns the organization of production and the distribution of the results of production. It is reflected, among other things, in the issues of taxation, social benefits, employment, the public sector, equality and the scope of private enterprises. As distinct from several other countries, moral and cultural issues, including for example religion, abortion and divorce laws, have been of minor importance in shaping the party choice of the voters in Sweden. Even if Sweden is now perhaps the most secularized society among the Western countries, however, religion still plays some role for the voters and encourages bourgeois voting, also among the workers.[21]

During the 1970s the issues of the environment, conservation of natural resources and the energy supply coupled to the expansion of nuclear power have come to the forefront in Swedish politics. Also fused to these issues is a debate on the quality of life in industrial society, the pros and cons of advanced technology, large production units and centralization of decision-making. All labels attempting neatly to summarize this complex of new issues, which have thus been drawn into Swedish politics, are more or less misleading. Nevertheless, in this context it is perhaps possible to talk of a 'technology-ecology' dimension as a potential new line of cleavage in Swedish politics.

The prime issue around which the technology-ecology dimension has revolved during the late 1970s, has been the utilization of nuclear power for the production of energy. Both the Centre Party and the Communists have opposed the expansion of nuclear power; while the Social Democrats, the Liberals and the Conservatives in varying degrees have advocated its use. When the Centre Party accepted the continued use of nuclear reactors rather than refraining from participation in bourgeois governments, an 'Environmentalist Party' was formed in 1981. These questions have also become major political issues in other Western countries during the 1970s.

Social scientists have argued that, inter alia, environmental issues and nuclear power are the beginnings of the 'new politics' in the post-industrial society where politics will be increasingly divorced from the class structure of society. It is also claimed that a 'silent revolution' is transpiring among the voters of the Western countries, where the earlier materialistic issues of the left-right dimension, because of an unprecedented degree of economic security, will be eclipsed by 'post-materialist' issues concerning the quality of life.[22] Since Sweden is among the richest of the Western countries and environmental issues have assumed new prominence in Swedish politics, it is an interesting country to examine also from this perspective.

In Sweden many observers maintain that the new technology-ecology dimension in the late 1970s is virtually on a comparable footing with the left-right dimension in influencing the voters' decisions concerning the parties and their policies.[23] They argue that the voters and parties are now distributed within a two-dimensional space of politics. Along the left-right axis the parties retain their traditional positions. However, we would find the Centre Party and the Communists located near the ecology pole of the new axis, while the Social Democrats, Liberals and Conservatives would be located towards the technology pole.

In recent years social scientists have empirically analysed the conflict dimensions of party politics in several Western countries, using a variety of methods.[24] One approach has been to study how voters perceive the stands of parties on different issues. Another and more interesting approach is to examine how the dimensions are reflected in the actual movements of voters between parties. This approach assumes that in switching parties the voters more frequently change over to a neighbouring party rather than to parties located at greater distance from their earlier party.

If the electorate and the parties were solely arrayed along the left-right dimension, the probability, for example, that Centre Party voters will switch to one of the other bourgeois parties is higher than the probability that they will switch to the Social Democrats, which in turn is higher than the probability that they will switch to the Communists. Similarly, voters switching from the Communist Party would much more frequently choose the Social Democrats than a bourgeois party. The opposite ought to apply to voters defecting from the Conservatives.

If the technology-ecology dimension were to approach the importance of the left-right dimension in party politics, this would affect the pattern of partisan change in the electorate. One would expect, among other things that, since both the Centre Party and the Communists are located near the ecology pole, the exchange of voters between these two parties would increase. Likewise, Conservative voters changing parties would find it easier to switch to the Liberals than to the Centre Party.

Using data on partisan change between the elections of 1958-60, 1962-4 and 1964-8, we shall first describe the 'traditional' situation in Swedish party politics. The question of nuclear power became an issue generating party controversy in Swedish politics when in the spring of 1973 the Centre Party reversed its previously positive view on nuclear energy. In the 1976 election nuclear energy was a central campaign issue. If as a consequence the technology-ecology dimension had established itself as a new and fundamental cleavage in Swedish politics, this ought to show up in the pattern of partisan change in the electorate after 1976. We shall therefore examine the changes in party preferences after the 1976 election up to November 1979, as registered in the eight Party Sympathy Surveys conducted by SCB during the period.

To get an indicator of the distance between the parties, we have compared the number of actual changes between parties with the expected number of changes, under the assumption that the probability of choosing a new party was not influenced by the voter's earlier party preference. The difference between the actual and expected frequencies of changes between the parties thus reflects the distance between the parties. Through statistical methods we can then identify the fewest number of dimensions describing the political space and plot the locations of the parties in this space.[25]

The analysis of partisan changes during the period 1958-68 shows, as expected, that the political space contains primarily a left-right dimension (Figure 7.13). The distance between the parties along this axis depends quite a bit on the methods used to obtain the empirical data for the analysis. Therefore it is the ordering of the parties which is of prime interest here. The Communist Party, which is located farthest to the left on the continuum, is arbitrarily assigned the value of 0, whereas the Conservatives, located farthest to the right, are given the value of 100. Between these poles, moving from left to right, are the Social Democrats followed by the Centre Party and then the Liberals.

When the analysis is repeated, using data on changes in party preferences during the period 1976-9, the results show that the left-right dimension still, and to the same extent as earlier, explains changes between the parties. The most important difference is that on the left-right axis the Centre Party has now moved to the right of the Liberals. This finding thus confirms dimensional analyses based on voters' perceptions which also indicate that a shift of this type has taken place during the 1970s.[26]

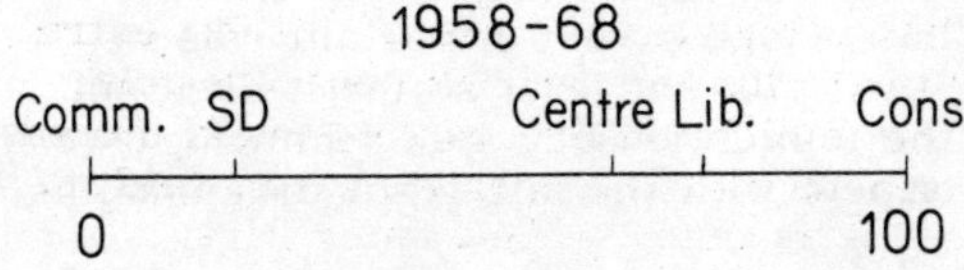

Figure 7.13 Party positions on the left-right axis based on party switches 1958-68 and 1976-9

The altered position of the Centre Party is reflected in modifications in the pattern of changes in partisan choice. Previously Conservative sympathizers more frequently changed to the Liberal Party, but during the years 1976-9 they have more often switched to the Centre Party than to the Liberals. Similarly, the pattern among Social Democratic defectors has also changed. Previously Social Democratic defectors clearly went over to the Centre Party rather than to the Liberals, but now Social Democratic sympathizers more often change to the Liberals. During 1976-9 the Centre Party sympathizers themselves switched to the Social Democrats less frequently than earlier.

On the other hand, the analysis does not provide support for the assumption of the emergence of a new technology-ecology dimension in party politics of sufficient strength that it can rival the left-right dimension in influencing the voters when they switch parties. To be sure, the flow of voters between the Centre Party and the Communists increased slightly during the period

1976-9, but it was still marginal.[27] Nor do the modifications in the pattern of changes in partisan choice described above fit the assumption of a new technology-ecology dimension in Swedish politics.

This analysis of patterns of shifts between parties contradicts dimensional analyses based on voters' perceptions of the stands of the parties on different types of issues. Such analyses indicate that voters clearly have learned that on the issue of nuclear energy the Centre Party and the Communists are opposed by the Conservatives, the Social Democrats and the Liberals.[28] In terms of making inferences to the underlying dimensions of party choice, however, the analysis based on shifts between parties appears to be more telling. These results suggest that the groups of voters for whom nuclear power and ecological questions are the decisive issues have remained relatively small. Even if the issue of nuclear power has played a very important role in Swedish politics during the 1970s, at least so far it does not appear to have formed the foundation of a new technology-ecology dimension, which can compete with the left-right dimension as a basis of electoral choice.

THE NUCLEAR REFERENDUM

That the technology-ecology dimension has not become a fully fledged rival of the left-right dimension does not of course mean that the issues associated with it have been insignificant in Swedish politics during the 1970s. Among these issues, the debate on the expansion of nuclear energy has been central. We have seen what key role this issue played for the outcomes of the 1976 and 1979 elections. Moreover, the issue led to the unusual step of a consultative referendum in March 1980.

As the controversy took shape, many other issues related to the technology-ecology dimension were also incorporated in the fight against nuclear power. The opposition, 'The People's Campaign against Nuclear Power', which was formed with great enthusiasm several months before the referendum, was based on the Centre Party and the Communists with the additional support of religious groups, women's organizations and environmentalist groups. Besides its anti-nuclear stance, the People's Campaign emphasized as its positive aspirations zero economic growth, alternative technology, small-scale production and decentralization. In the referendum the People's Campaign sponsored 'Alternative 3', which opposed the starting of new reactors and called for phasing out reactors in operation within a ten-year period. An analysis of the backing given to Alternative 3 in the referendum can provide a picture of the support for the notion of 'the good society' related to the technology-ecology dimension as it has figured in the political discussion of the 1970s.

In the referendum the Social Democrats, the Liberal Party,

LO and TCO endorsed 'Alternative 2', advocating the utilization of existing nuclear power reactors, along with those under construction, for a maximum period of twenty-five years, a halt to further expansion of nuclear energy, and the nationalization of nuclear power plants. The Conservatives, stressing the positive aspects of nuclear energy and of its continued utilization, campaigned for 'Alternative 1', which however also advocated a maximum period of twenty-five years for the use of nuclear energy.

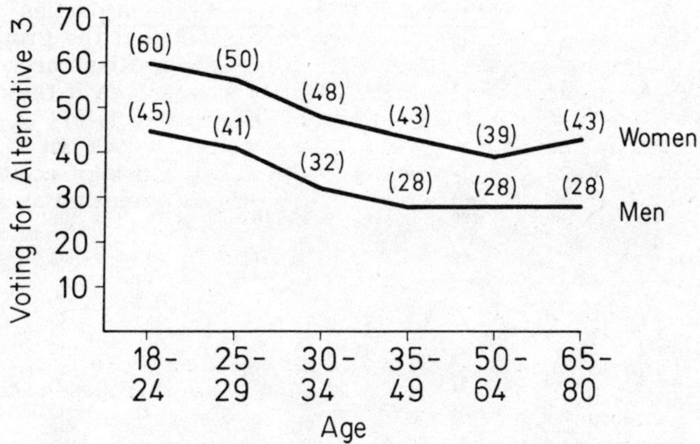

Figure 7.14 Percentage voting for Alternative 3 in 1980 referendum, by sex and age

Data from SCB's Party Sympathy Survey after the referendum (March 1980) revealed a 15 per cent higher endorsement of Alternative 3 among women than men. It was also the younger generation, mainly people under thirty, who voted for Alternative 3 (Figure 7.14). The debates on nuclear power therefore seem to have shattered the political unity of many families. Husbands and wives took opposite sides; teenagers and parents had conflicting views.

Alternative 3 received the largest number of votes from women in all occupational categories except workers, where Alternative 2 had a slight edge (Table 7.2). Male workers and lower-level salaried employees most often supported Alternative 2, the so-called 'wage-earners' alternative'. The clash of views on nuclear power appears, however, to have been most intense in the families of higher-level salaried employees. In this category, most men backed Alternative 1, while a majority of women favoured Alternative 3. Among the women in these families, blank voting was not unusual. In the families of farmers, the core group of the Centre Party„ the overwhelming majority of women supported Alternative 3 but a little over one-fourth of the men voted for Alternative 1 or 2. Alternative 3 was definitely the most popular among students of both sexes; however, they also cast a substantial proportion of blank votes.

Table 7.2 Percentage voting for the alternatives in the 1980 nuclear referendum, and voting turnout, by sex and occupational category

	Workers	Low-level salaried employees	High-level salaried employees	Farmers	Business-men	Students
	%	%	%	%	%	%
Men						
Alternative 1	10	29	47	18	41	26
Alternative 2	59	42	23	10	21	22
Alternative 3	28	26	28	72	36	45
Blank	3	2	3	1	2	7
	100	100	100	100	100	100
Voting turnout	79	89	91	74	81	83
Women						
Alternative 1	9	22	26	5	28	14
Alternative 2	47	31	15	4	21	18
Alternative 3	42	42	53	90	51	57
Blank	2	5	7	1	1	11
	100	100	100	100	100	100
Voting turnout	79	88	93	76	77	89

Voting participation in the referendum was considerably lower than in recent parliamentary elections. The earlier class differences in electoral participation partly reappeared in the referendum. The turnout among workers was approximately 10 per cent lower than in the higher socio-economic strata. Also the participation among farmers was rather low.

It has been suggested that the opposition to nuclear power was disproportionately strong among persons employed in the public sector. In contrast to industrial employees, those in the public sector are assumed not to view their jobs as being directly dependent upon the supply and costs of energy. However, a reanalysis of the data on preferences for the referendum alternatives, collected by Sifo during the period of January - March 1980, furnishes a rather mixed picture of the situation (Table 7.3).[29] Among men it is actually only in the relatively small category of workers in the public sector that Alternative 3 seems to have been favoured by a majority. In contrast, this alternative enjoyed a clear majority among middle-class women in public employment, i.e., among those who ordinarily work in the areas of education and human services.

Table 7.3 Percentage favouring alternative 3 in January-March 1980 among men and women in public and private employment

Occupational group	Men		Women	
	Public	Private	Public	Private
	%	%	%	%
Worker	38	26	50	48
Lower middle class	27	40	54	39
Upper middle class	23	20	63	(37)

A comparison of the combined share of the vote for the Centre Party and the Communists in the 1979 county council election and the percentage of votes cast for Alternative 3 in the referendum by various types of communes indicates that Alternative 3 won support from adherents of other parties most easily in the Greater Stockholm region and in Gothenburg (Table 7.4).[30] In these areas Alternative 3 received a voting percentage which was roughly 20 per cent higher than the combined vote for the Centre Party and the Communists in the election six months earlier. In the other types of communes the percentage of votes for Alternative 3 exceeded the two parties' share of the vote by 13-15 per cent. An exception was the city of Malmö, where the excess of votes for Alternative 3 was only 10 per cent.

Table 7.4 Surplus of votes for Alternative 3 compared with combined share of vote for the Centre Party and Communists in the county council election 1979 in different types of communes

Type of commune	% votes for Alternative 3, 1980	% votes for Centre and Communists, 1979	Surplus
	%	%	%
Greater Stockholm	38.3	18.6	19.7
Gothenburg	41.5	19.5	22.0
Malmö	19.8	10.8	9.8
Service communes	38.4	23.3	15.0
Mixed communes	44.2	30.9	13.3
Substantially industrialized communes	39.9	26.0	13.9
Industrial communes	37.9	24.7	13.2

The greater receptivity of Alternative 3 in Stockholm and Gothenburg can perhaps be interpreted to the effect that issues such as nuclear power, like many other innovations and currents of thought, gain acceptance in the urban centres and spread from there. The fact that Malmö clearly deviates from the picture suggests, however, that other factors are also operating here. In Malmö the Centre Party and the Communists have been traditionally weak. Nor did the daily press back Alternative 3 to the same extent in Malmö as in the other metropolitan areas.

PARTY LOYALTY

Sex differences in the support for Alternative 3 become apparent when we look at the degree of congruity between party choice in the 1979 parliamentary election and voting for the referendum alternatives advocated by the various parties (Table 7.5).[31]

Table 7.5 Support for alternatives and voting turnout in the nuclear referendum in 1980, by party choice in the 1979 parliamentary election and sex

	Party choice in the 1979 election				
	Cons.	Centre	Lib.	SD	Comm.
	%	%	%	%	%
Men					
Alternative 1	75	8	31	6	5
Alternative 2	8	11	43	76	17
Alternative 3	14	79	22	16	76
Blank	2	2	4	3	3
	100	100	100	100	100
Voting turnout	89	86	87	85	85
Women					
Alternative 1	61	4	13	5	1
Alternative 2	11	8	38	63	6
Alternative 3	24	88	40	28	90
Blank	4	1	6	4	3
	100	100	100	100	100
Voting turnout	87	89	89	84	92

Party loyalty was definitely strongest among voters for the Centre Party and the Communists, especially among women, of whom 90 per cent supported Alternative 3. Among the Social Democratic voters, three-fourths of the men but only two-thirds of the women favoured Alternative 2. Roughly the same pattern recurs among Conservative voters in supporting Alternative 1. The Liberals, however, did not succeed in getting even half of their voters to support Alternative 2.

Table 7.6 Percentage voting for the referendum alternative recommended by the party, by sex, age, social group and party choice in the 1979 election*

	Socio-economic strata	Party choice in the 1979 election Cons.	Centre	Lib.	SD	Comm.
		%	%	%	%	%
Men						
18-34 years	Workers	66	77	(50)	71	71
	Salaried employees, farmers, businessmen, etc.	77	89	43	64	93
35-75	Workers	61	77	53	83	65
	Salaried employees, farmers, businessmen, etc.	79	80	44	79	(82)
Women						
18-34 years	Workers	50	83	(39)	55	(92)
	Salaried employees, farmers, businessmen, etc.	57	88	39	50	97
35-75 years	Workers	52	89	38	73	(84)
	Salaried employees, farmers, businessmen, etc.	70	91	43	65	(86)

*Conservatives, Alternative 1; Social Democrats and Liberals, Alternative 2; Centre Party and Communists, Alternative 3.

The relationship between party loyalty and sex, age and social group demonstrates how conflicting forces influenced the choice of alternatives in the referendum (Table 7.6). Young people and women were attracted to Alternative 3, while workers, men and middle-aged and elderly groups tended to favour Alternative 2. Among Social Democratic voters in the 1979 election, workers displayed greater party loyalty than middle-class groups. Of the younger workers who voted for the Social Democrats in the 1979 election, however, nearly one-third of the men and nearly one-half of the women deviated from the party's alternative in the referendum; the most loyal Social Democrats were elderly male workers.

Voters for the Conservatives, the Centre Party and the Communists in the 1979 election exhibited the opposite tendency. Party loyalty was greater among middle-class voters than among working-class voters, who in significant numbers voted for Alternative 2. The disarray of the Liberals in their choice of alternatives was reflected in women and young people voting for Alternative 3 and middle-aged and elderly men backing Alternative 1.

THE WOMEN'S MOVEMENT

The demands for equality and equal opportunities between the sexes have grown during the 1960s and 1970s in Sweden, as in several other Western countries. These demands for equality were a continuation of the long historical struggle for the equal rights of women, which in the early stages focused on inheritance rights, the right of employment in the civil service and women's suffrage. The sharp increase in employment among married women in the postwar period, and the problems resulting for families where both parents work and from the double workload for women, form the background to the current discussion of equality between the sexes.

Table 7.7 Percentage disagreeing with the statement: 'Men should go out to work while women stay at home and take care of the house' among youth between the ages of eighteen and twenty four in various countries

	%
Sweden	86
USA	71
UK	67
France	64
Australia	64
West Germany	59
Japan	32

At least among the younger generation, the perceptions of sex roles seem to be less traditional in Sweden than in most Western countries. In a comparative study from 1977-8, young people between the ages of eighteen and twenty-four years were asked whether they agreed with the statement: 'Men should go out to work, while women stay at home and take care of the house.' The percentage disagreeing with the statement was considerably higher in Sweden than in the other Western countries (Table 7.7).[32]

The demands for equality between the sexes have assumed a variety of forms in different countries. In Sweden care of pre-school children became an important political issue during the 1970s. Party differences have concerned support to mothers in their homes or expansion of public day-care facilities and other forms of child care to enable women to go out to work. This discussion led to large public investments in the construction of municipal day-care facilities. Women's representation in political assemblies was also among the issues discussed. Quotas to ensure women's representation in political bodies have been one of the alternatives advocated.

In this context it is of interest to examine the extent of support in various socio-economic strata for the pursuit of equality between the sexes. One assertion sometimes voiced in this discussion is that a conservative outlook on these issues is especially prevalent in the working class.[33] Accordingly, the issue of equality between the sexes could possibly clash with the longstanding working-class aspiration for equality.

The election survey in 1976 provides some data which can be utilized in examining the extent of support in various socio-economic strata for efforts to achieve equality between the sexes. The interview survey posed two questions of relevance here. Respondents were asked whether they agreed or disagreed with, first, the proposal 'to build more municipal day-care homes' and, second, the proposal 'that half of the members of the Riksdag must be women'. An analysis of the responses shows that the proportion of men favouring the construction of more day-care centres was somewhat higher among workers than in the middle strata (Table 7.8). Among women there were no differences between social groups. More women than men favoured a quota for women in the Riksdag. Among men the proposal received greater support from the workers than from the middle strata.

The idea that opposition to equality between the sexes is stronger among workers than in the middle strata is based on a fairly common notion in sections of the middle class that the workers are more conservative than the middle strata on cultural issues and more authoritarian in their values. In Sweden the empirical evidence for these assumptions has been very meagre. It is possible that the general orientation concerning sex roles is more conservative among the workers than other groups.[34] The figures here, however, indicate that this need not be the case with regard to adopting a position on concrete reforms to increase equality between the sexes.

Table 7.8 Percentage supporting the proposals to build more day-care centres and to introduce a quota to ensure that half of the members of the Riksdag are women, by socio-economic strata, sex and age

Proposal	Men, age 18-34	35-64	65+	Total	Women, age 18-34	35-64	65+	Total
	%	%	%	%	%	%	%	%
Build more day-care-centres								
Workers	83	72	66	73	85	69	57	70
Middle Strata	78	68	59	67	89	64	54	69
Introduce sex quota to the Riksdag								
Workers	43	47	58	46	62	53	43	57
Middle Strata	26	39	46	33	56	27	45	50

SHIFTING ALLEGIANCES

What are the explanations behind the increased volatility of the electorate in the 1960s and 1970s? One often suggested explanation is an increasing distrust of politicians. The available data on changes in the voters' confidence in parties and politicians during the years 1968-80 indicate that distrust has grown, especially after 1976.[35] The high and increasing electoral participation during the 1970s, however, must be interpreted as an indication that the electorate still believes that it can influence the course of politics through voting.

The confidence of the voters in politicians is ultimately based on what the politicians do or fail to do, what they promise, and how they keep their promises. During the 1970s there have been cases of prominent politicians making personal pledges which they subsequently could not keep. These instances of course fuel distrust of politicians.

But if voters are dissatisfied with the outcome of politics, this can also result from the increasing complexity of the problems facing political decision-makers. During the 1960s the electorate grew more aware of the drawbacks of the existing policy of rapid economic growth, the cornerstones of which had been laid through the historical compromise of the 1930s. During the 1970s it also became more difficult to attain the basic goals of this policy, specifically, full employment and a rising standard of living.

The difficulties and failures of political decision-makers in solving fundamental societal problems, rather than some general distrust of politicians, provide a more plausible explanation of the voters' quest for new political alternatives and solutions. The increased volatility of the voters is probably mainly the result of the mounting complexity of problems and the attempts to solve them having often ended in failure. The recurrent shifts in a majority opinion for the two blocs during the 1970s suggest that the electorate has repeatedly encountered disappointments, and that voters perhaps have shifted blocs in protest rather than because of belief in the other bloc.

A large part of the exchange of voters between the parties consists of switches among the bourgeois parties. The profiles and the policy priorities of the bourgeois parties are of course significant in bringing about these changes. However, the changes in party choice among the bourgeois voters probably cannot be solely ascribed to party differences in policy positions. The personalities of the party leaders, together with appraisals of the parties' possibilities of achieving perhaps the most urgent goal in the eyes of their voters - a bourgeois government - are probably also important factors here.

That the positions of the parties on the political spectrum are not permanently fixed is revealed by the fact that during the latter half of the 1970s the Centre Party has moved to the Liberals' previous location adjacent to the Conservatives on the left-right axis. In this instance the altered policy of the Centre Party, from its days as a coalition partner of the Social Democrats in the 1950s to its becoming the party of the Prime Minister in the bourgeois coalition government, has left its mark on the pattern of changes in partisan choice. In the early 1980s, however, the Liberal Party made changes in its programme and leadership which moved it towards the right on the political spectrum.

Changes in partisan choice, however, explain only a portion of the parties' electoral fortunes. Especially for the Social Democrats, the mobilization of non-voters has been of major significance for the outcome of the elections. The Social Democrats' increased share of the vote in the 1968 election was mainly the result of greater success, as compared with the bourgeois parties, in getting their voters to the polls. In a society where both party choice and electoral participation are correlated with social class, a high voting turnout in general can be expected to favour the labour parties.[36]

Yet in comparison with other European countries and especially its Scandinavian neighbours, Norway and Denmark, the Swedish voters have been relatively stable, something which partly reflects the continuing centrality of the left-right dimension in Swedish politics. Sweden has thus not experienced basically 're-aligning' elections of the type which were fought in Norway and Denmark in connection with the question of entry to the European Economic Community. In Norway and Denmark this cross-class issue has severely weakened the Social Democratic parties' support among the voters.[37] Although the issue of nuclear energy has had important consequences for the Swedish Social Democrats, it appears to have been handled in a way which gives it a smaller long-term significance. The severe splits in the labour movements caused by the EEC issue in Norway and Denmark were avoided in Sweden.

The debate on how to economize in the utilization of natural resources and the environment, including the issue of nuclear energy, which has been carried on since the 1960s, deals with concrete and serious problems confronting society. It is not surprising that primarily young people were aroused by the debate. Problems of resource management and the survival of mankind are issues which have come to concern the youth in all Western countries. The postwar generations, who have grown up during a period of prosperity and economic security, have raised greater demands for increased influence at the workplace and in society, along with opportunities to pursue a freer life style. It has been claimed that we have experienced a 'silent revolution' which has ushered the young into a world of 'post-materialist' politics.[38] The worldwide and deep economic crises starting in the 1970s has made the talk about the 'post-materialist revolution' appear dated. Yet it is of interest to discuss briefly the implications of the renewed stress on quality of life and the environment.

It is far from certain that the problems of resource management, the environment and the quality of life will form a new dimension in party politics, detached from the left-right dimension. One strong reason for questioning this development is that the traditional left-right dimension focusing on the organization of production is also probably vital for resource management and protection of the environment. The principle of maximizing profits in the private enterprise economy can easily come into conflict with resource management and protection of the environment. The economic interests associated with production are so powerful that they exert a strong influence on government policy irrespective of the party composition of the executive.

Many of the issues involving the quality of life, which seem to strike a chord of increasing approval with young and well-educated voters in the Western countries, are also more or less clearly related to the problem of the economic organization of production and the distribution of power in the economy and society. Among these issues are greater employee influence at the workplace and in society and the extension of the sphere of influence for people's ideas and desires at the expense of corporate power. A meaningful definition of the concept of the quality of life can scarcely ignore its dependence on the distribution of power in society and the role of work in people's lives. It is therefore not unrelated to the curse of unemployment which in the 1980s plagues the Western nations.

8 THE POLITICS OF INDUSTRIAL CONFLICT

In the beginning of May 1980 Sweden was brought close to a standstill by a nationwide lockout. This conflict became the largest one in Swedish history. In terms of the proportion of the labour force involved, it was perhaps the largest industrial conflict ever to have taken place in a Western nation. Lockouts and strikes are classical expressions of conflicts of interest generated by the class structure of the capitalist democracies. In this chapter we shall analyse the long-term changes in the patterns of industrial conflict in eighteen Western nations. We begin by discussing the prevailing theoretical interpretations of industrial conflict as a background to an analysis of factors affecting the paths which the development of industrial strife has taken in these countries.[1]

THEORIES OF INDUSTRIAL CONFLICT

The approach to the development of industrial conflict, dominant in the social sciences during the postwar years, has been based on the pluralist industrial model of society (see Chapter 2). This body of thought asserts that the extent and importance of labour disputes in the highly developed, industrial societies will gradually decline. One of the foremost scholars in this tradition, Clark Kerr, has summarized the pluralist hypothesis and its background in the following way:

> Worker protest in the course of industrialization tends to peak relatively early and to decline in intensity thereafter. . . . As time passes, formal organizations of workers emerge, and . . . the forms of overt protest become more disciplined and less spontaneous. The organizations gradually become centralized, formalized, and viable. The industrializing elite develops its strategies and means of controlling, limiting or directing worker protest. . . .[2]

> Contrary to Marx, . . . industrializing societies face more and more peace once the early period of industrial unrest has passed.[3]

Besides the general increase in standards of living, which improve the possibilities to satisfy needs, the pluralist industrial model sees the relative decline in industrial conflict largely as an outcome of institutional development. Through the building of secure unions and employer acceptance of collective bargaining, the need to balance the power of workers against the power of employers has been largely accomplished. The development of institutions on the labour market allows industrial conflict to be isolated and disengaged from political conflicts.[4] Although conflicts of interest remain in industry, they are far from irreconcilable and their expressions can be strongly limited. Two other American students of industrial relations, Arthur Ross and John Dunlop, have formulated similar expectations on 'the withering away of the strike' in the advanced industrial societies.[5]

On the European scene the pluralist hypothesis, that industrial conflict reflects the malfunctioning of social institutions, has emerged most clearly and most forcefully in what has become known as 'the Oxford school' of industrial relations. Two of the leading exponents of this 'school', Hugh Clegg and the late Allen Flanders, have stressed the importance of the fit between institutions of industrial relations and the problems these institutions have to solve for the degree of industrial conflict.[6] While they see a modicum of industrial conflict as inevitable in any industrial relations system, a high level of conflict is a sign of severe dysfunction. Such dysfunctions are created when the adaption of the industrial relations system cannot keep pace with changes in technology and their consequent effects on industrial employment.

Clegg argues that there is a high degree of correspondence between, on the one hand, arrangements concerning the structure and scope of collective bargaining, the legal status of contracts and other organizational or procedural variables and, on the other hand, the level and forms of strike activity. Thus 'the number of strikes . . . is likely to be high where disputes procedures are absent or are defective'.[7]

The views of the 'Oxford school' have shaped official British attempts to deal with industrial conflict.[8] The increasing strike level since the 1960s was seen as reflecting a combination of full employment and other factors which had increased the power of the workers at the shopfloor level. The formal industrial relations system had not been able to adapt to this change. An increasingly important part of negotiations thus came to take place at the shopfloor, outside the formal industrial relations system. If the level of strike activity was to be brought down, the system of industrial relations had to be reformed to encompass and to formalize also the shopfloor negotiations.

During the 1970s this dominant theoretical approach has encountered competition from two different quarters, which however have followed partly similar lines. Sociologists who had begun to interest themselves in comparative and historical studies of social conflict asserted that industrial strife must be seen as a form of collective action, where collectivities of citizens come into conflict over the distribution of scarce resources. Industrial conflict must therefore be placed in a political context and be regarded as part of a wider political context between different social collectives.[9] Since the 1960s some industrial relations researchers have also relied on the Marxist tradition of ideas, wherein industrial strife is conceived of as a conflict of interests between classes and is assumed to be closely related to political conflict.[10]

From corporatist writings it is difficult to deduce a unanimous hypothesis on the relationship between neo-corporatist patterns of interest intermediation and industrial conflict. Some writers view a low level of industrial conflict as a defining characteristic of neo-corporatism. Lehmbruch assumes that neo-corporatism tends to produce low levels of conflict. On the other hand Panitch, for example, maintains that neo-corporatism is continuously destabilized from below by worker militancy.[11]

A CENTURY OF INDUSTRIAL CONFLICT

In order to illuminate the adequacy of the pluralist industrial model in describing the development of industrial conflict in the West, let us now examine available facts. Almost all Western countries have collected data on their industrial conflicts in time series which go back as far as the turn of the century or earlier. Although deficient in many ways, these data can nevertheless be used in making comparisons between different countries and periods of time. We shall here analyse data on industrial conflict in eighteen Western countries from 1870 to 1976. Figures on strikes and lockouts will be combined and we shall follow the partly misleading tradition of using the word 'strikes' as a summary term in this context.

The available statistics from the different countries contain annual aggregates of three kinds of data. These are: the number or frequency of industrial conflicts (F), the number of workers involved in the conflicts (I) and the number of man-days idle or the volume of conflict (V). On the basis of these data we can derive measures of the size of conflict, i.e., the average number of workers per conflict ($S=I/F$). We can also calculate the duration of strikes, i.e., the number of man-days of idleness per strike ($D=V/I$). It is important to distinguish between these different aspects of industrial conflict, since their variations reflect different types of labour disputes. The statistical correlations between them are also moderate. The three dimensions - duration, size and frequency - can be used to describe the profile or shape of industrial conflict in a country during a period of time.

The volume of a conflict is the product of the three dimensions of duration, size and frequency. It is of interest as a summary measure but ought not to be used as a single indicator, since it can be influenced by different types of changes in the profile of conflicts. In addition to this measurement we shall here use data on involvement, i.e., the number of workers affected. This measure reflects the degree to which workers have been drawn into conflicts and is thereby of manifest political and social importance. In comparing countries, our data on industrial conflict have been put in relation to the number of persons in the non-agricultural labour force. Thus, for example, relative involvement refers to the number of employees involved in strikes and lockouts during a year relative to the non-agricultural labour force.

Among the Western nations changes in strikes over time show great variation from year to year, and occasional 'peak years' when industrial disputes soar to exceptional heights. To discern the trends in the development of disputes in the different countries two approaches will here be utilized. The development of relative involvement in our eighteen Western nations is presented in Figure 8.1 in terms of weighted, five-year moving averages based on logged data.[12] Arithmetic averages for three periods (1900-13, 1919-38, 1946-76) are given in Table 8.1.[13]

During the first third of this century the pattern of industrial conflict evolved in a fairly parallel way in the different countries. With the exception of the United States and Canada, the secular trend in relative involvement was an upward one until about 1920 in all the countries for which data are available. The years at the end of World War I saw the outbreak of an international strike wave which peaked around 1920. In many of the Western nations this period was also marked by deep-going institutional changes, related to the introduction of universal suffrage; with the exception of Japan, legislation concerning universal manhood suffrage had been enacted by the end of World War I in all countries under study.

In all of our countries the strike waves culminating around 1920 were followed by a decrease in the 1920s. During the latter part of the 1930s, however, our countries begin to diverge. In about half of them strikes tend to decrease, a decrease which partly coincided with political changes like the emergence of fascism in Germany and Austria or the coming to power of social democratic governments in Norway and Sweden; in the latter two countries industrial conflict declined sharply from record high levels of relative volume during the first third of the century. In the other half of the countries, once the depths of the Great Depression had been passed, strikes again tended to increase.

World War II was again followed by an international strike wave. During the postwar period, however, great differences in the development of relative involvement and volume become apparent between our countries. In six cases - Sweden, Norway, Austria, Germany, Netherlands and Switzerland - involvement in industrial conflict has fallen to very low levels. In the Netherlands and Switzerland, however, involvement was already relatively low in the period between the wars, having begun to decrease after the post-World War I peaks. Austria and Germany, which had high levels of industrial conflict before the emergence of fascism, have

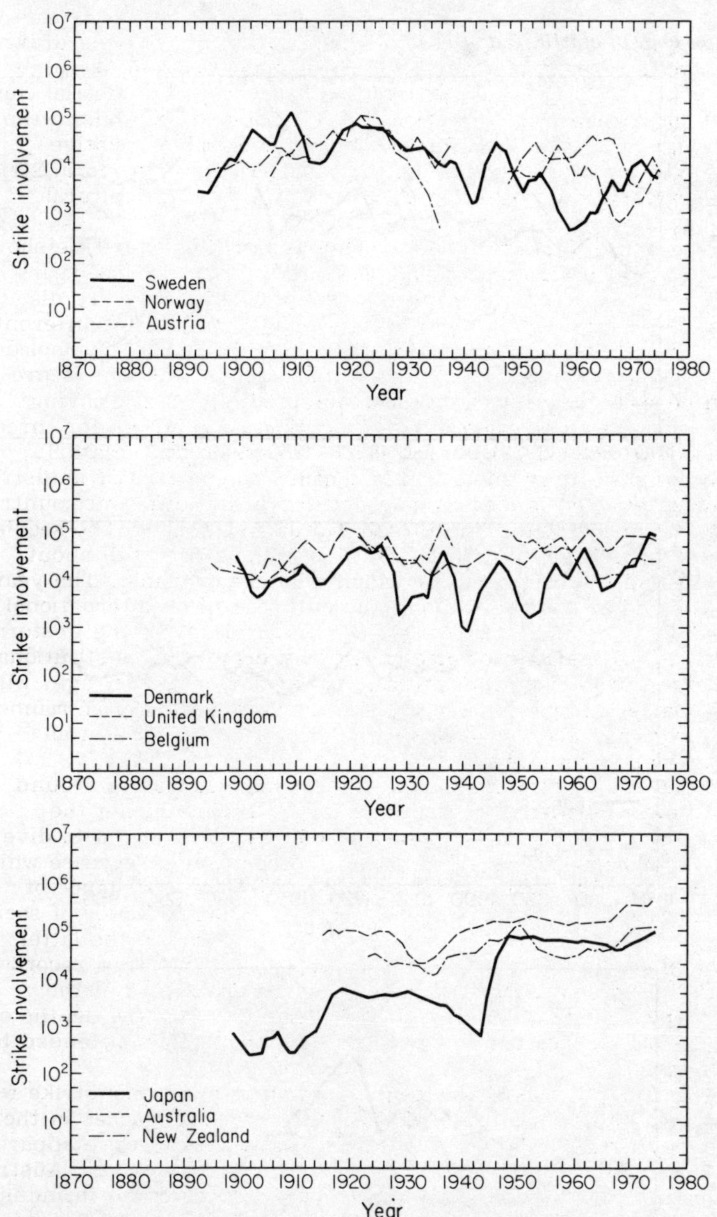

Figure 8.1 Relative strike involvement in eighteen capitalist democracies 1870–1976: weighted, five-year moving averages based on logged data

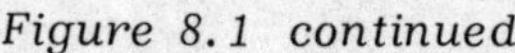

Figure 8.1 continued

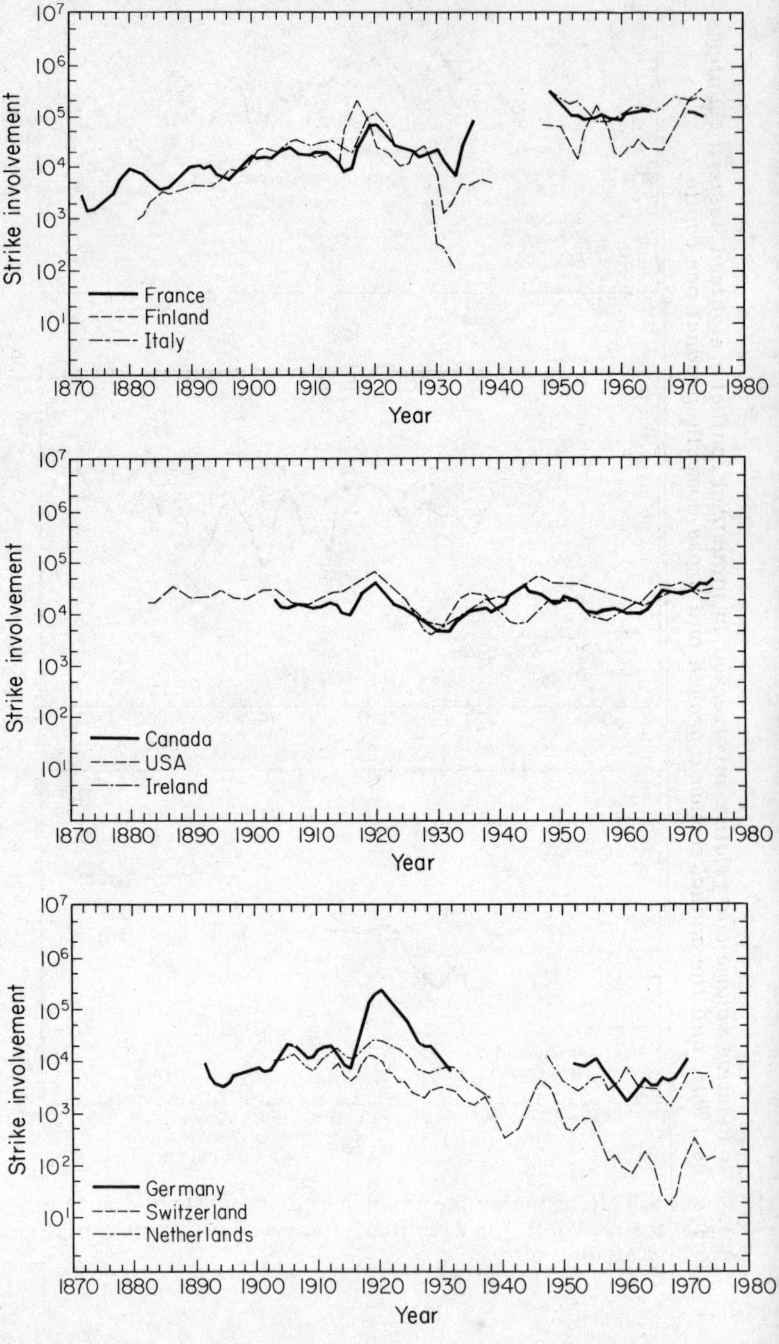

Table 8.1 Relative volume and relative involvement in industrial conflict in eighteen Western countries during the 1900s, and the annual economic growth and gross domestic product per capita

Working-class mobilization and political control	Country	Relative volume*			Relative involvement†			Economic growth per capita 1950-75‡	Gross domestic product per capita 1965 ($US)§
		1900-13	1919-38	1946-76	1900-13	1919-38	1946-76		
High mobilization, stable control	Sweden	1,286	1,440	43	397	295	36	3,3	2,549
	Norway	491	1,853	90	165	384	64	4,0	1,890
	Austria	280	325	44	177	343	145	4,8	1,287
High mobilization, temporary or partial control	Denmark	272	681	173	94	203	184	3,3	2,120
	UK	460	1,066	213	237	396	432	2,5	1,818
	Belgium	722	665	255	168	468	331	3,8	1,804
	New Zealand	-	146	191	-	180	523	4,1	1,980
Average-high mobilization, low control	Australia	399	684	381	323	517	1,589	3,8	2,002
	Finland	834	399	630	233	120	835	4,8	1,749
	France	309	404	566	184	388	1,367	4,5	1,924
	Italy	293	126	631	270	394	2,313	4,6	1,104
	Japan	-	40	241	3	32	450	8,4	861
Low mobilization, exclusion	Ireland	-	508	443	-	140	293	2,8	980
	Canada	471	296	509	173	151	314	4,0	2,473
	USA	-	356	585	259	277	354	3,0	3,575
Low-average mobilization, partial control	W. Germany	489	875	31	151	775	92	5,2	1,901
	Netherlands	251	379	34	122	116	57	4,3	1,554
	Switzerland	-	55	11	79	42	7	3,4	2,333
Mean		504	572	282	189	290	521		
Dispersion		282	470	221	93	184	610		

* Number of man-days of idleness per 1,000 workers.
† Number of persons involved in industrial conflict per 10,000 workers.
‡ Sources: United Nations, 'Yearbook . . . 1966', pp. 707-10, and 'Yearbook . . . 1978', pp. 182-299. Data for Australia cover 1950-73 and for New Zealand, 1950-65.
§ Source: C.L. Taylor and M.C. Hudson, 'World Handbook of Political and Social Indicators', pp. 515ff.

had very low levels in the postwar period. In Norway the level of involvement was much lower when the collection of statistics was resumed after the Nazi occupation. Sweden, however, exhibits an even more remarkable pattern of change. From having had the highest average volume of all Western nations up to the mid-1930s, it moved to one of the lowest levels after World War II. Moreover, strikes did not decline in a gradual fashion, as the 'withering-away' thesis suggests: instead, the strike experienced a rather sudden death in the late 1930s.

In six of our countries - Italy, Australia, France, Finland, New Zealand and Japan - strike involvement has increased markedly from the interwar to the postwar period. In the first three of these countries, involvement was already at rather high levels in the period between the wars. However, in both Finland and Japan authoritarian forces had held down involvement in strikes during the 1930s. This group of six countries has had the highest levels of relative involvement of all the Western nations during the postwar period. In another group - the United Kingdom, Belgium, Denmark, the United States, Canada and Ireland - the level of involvement has been relatively stable and at middling levels since the period between the wars.

Our data thus do not support one of the central ideas in the pluralist industrial model, that the Western countries will converge in a development where industrial conflict is of only marginal importance. The two summarizing lines at the bottom of Table 8.1 show the mean values during the three time periods for relative volume and relative involvement. The dispersion between countries during these periods is also indicated here. These figures reveal that the shape of industrial conflict has changed but that their social and political importance remains.

The shape of industrial conflict has changed in that the average duration of conflict has diminished, which has in turn led to a decline in volume. The average duration of conflict has decreased from approximately twenty-two days per conflict before World War II to approximately nine days per conflict during the postwar period. Up until World War II labour disputes consumed over 500 workdays per 1,000 workers per year. During the postwar years this figure sank to approximately half the interwar level. The difference between the countries has also decreased.

On the other hand, there is nothing which suggests that the social and political importance of industrial conflict has decreased. On the contrary, relative involvement in industrial conflict has quite clearly increased during the postwar period. Before World War I an average of barely 200 of 10,000 workers were drawn into industrial conflict per year. This figure rose to slightly over 300 in the period between the wars and to slightly over 500 in the postwar period. The differences between the countries also became much greater during the postwar years than they had previously been. The number of industrial conflicts shows a similar trend.[14]

In summary, we find that the pattern of development of industrial conflict in these countries contradicts the expectations derived from the theory of pluralistic industrialism. Involvement in industrial conflict has increased rather than decreased. Instead of a convergence of countries, we find a greater diversity of development between them during the postwar period. However, in the majority of countries the long, drawn-out type of conflict has tended to disappear.

THE EFFECTS OF ECONOMIC GROWTH

The theory of the pluralistic industrialism fails to receive support when we consider the importance of economic growth and the high standard of living for the pattern and level of conflict. Average economic growth during the period 1950-75 in our eighteen countries (see Table 8.1) shows no correlation with involvement in and volume of industrial conflict.[15] Average growth during the years 1950-75 was as high in the twelve countries which had a high or increasing level of conflict in the postwar years as in the six countries where industrial conflicts have been very few. Japan, with the outstandingly highest economic growth, had a conflict level slightly above that of England, which had the lowest average growth. Sweden's average economic growth during these years was also relatively low.

Neither is there any clear correlation during the postwar period in these countries between the conflict level and the average standard of living in the country (measured as GNP per inhabitant in 1965 - see Table 8.1). Two of the richest countries, the United States and Canada, had very high conflict volumes, while two of the poorer countries, Austria and the Netherlands, enjoyed industrial peace.[16]

We have not here been able to make any detailed survey of the institutions for the settling of industrial disputes in these different countries. Nearly all of the countries, however, have developed the basic institutions for conflict resolution on the labour market. It is therefore hardly likely that such differences exist between them regarding institutions of industrial relations that they can explain the differences in their patterns of industrial conflict.

In the case of Sweden it can be shown that, historically, institutions of industrial relations have not developed in a manner which can explain the change and decrease in the frequency of conflict. At an early stage the trade union movement became strong, stable and centralized. The right of unionization and collective bargaining was acknowledged as early as 1906 in the so-called 'December Compromise' between the LO and SAF. Nationwide collective agreements had been made even before the outbreak of World War I. A law providing for the mediation of labour disputes was enacted in 1906, one providing for voluntary arbitration in 1920, and one providing for a labour court and making collective agreements legally binding in 1928. In spite of this institutional development, industrial strife continued up to the middle of the 1930s on an internationally very high level.[17]

A MODEL OF INDUSTRIAL CONFLICT

In order to understand the differences in the pattern of industrial conflict among the Western countries and the changes in these patterns which have occurred, we must look for explanations elsewhere than in the theory of pluralist industrialism. The theoretical outline developed in Chapter 2 concerning conflicts of interests in capitalist democracies may offer an alternative. It will here be taken as a starting-point for a model of how structural conditions and the distribution of power resources influence the probability of industrial disputes.

This model starts out with the assumption that the manner in which production is organized creates conflicts of interest between various groups of citizens and lays the foundation for the emergence of collectivities or classes. The distribution of power resources between two of the most important classes - wage-earners and capital - is assumed to vary over time and between countries. This distribution of power resources is also assumed to be of importance for, among other things, the distribution of goods as well as for the form and functioning of social institutions. It is, furthermore, assumed to affect the type of conflict strategies chosen by the collectivities and therefore the pattern of conflict in the society. Since the conflicts of interest between the collectivities based on the organization of production is assumed to be of crucial importance for the structure of society, economic and political conflicts become closely interrelated. These conflicting interests are the bases for the formation of trade unions and political organizations.

The central variable in this model, the difference in power resources between wage-earners and business interests, is naturally dependent on how the resources of both these parties vary in relation to each other. Mainly for practical reasons, we have been forced to limit ourselves to an attempt to chart the power resources of wage-earners. Among these, organizations for collective action in politics and on the labour market are of key importance. Figure 8.2 gives an outline of the factors which we assume to influence the distribution of power resources within a country and of the ways in which this distribution can be expected to influence industrial conflict.

The preconditions for the organization of the working class discussed in Chapter 3 may be expected to influence both the level of unionization and the political organization of wage-earners. As stated there, we expect a strong working-class organization to include a high degree of unionization, unions organized according to industry rather than craft, a powerful leadership for a strongly united trade union movement, and a

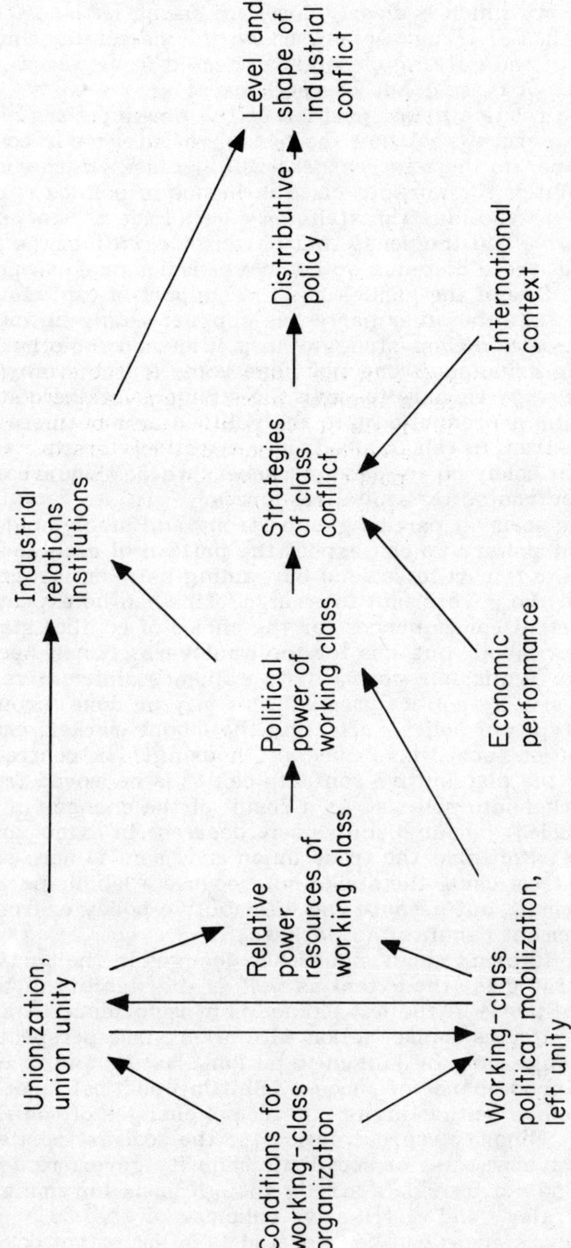

Figure 8.2 Schematic summary of major variables assumed to affect national patterns of industrial conflict

close collaboration between the trade union movement and a socialist party which is clearly dominant among leftist parties and which has a strong support among the electorate. The power resources of the working class are expected to be weaker where one or more of these conditions are absent.

When the relative power position of the working class is improved we can expect that the number of alternative courses of action open to the wage-earners will increase. In this context the possibilities for working-class influence in politics is of special interest. Industrial strife may be termed a 'non-democratic class struggle', in the sense that citizens drawn into the opposing sides in these disputes do not have similar or equal power resources. One of the parties has the support of capital resources while the other party has support mainly in numbers. In the 'democratic class struggle' in politics, on the other hand, the guiding principle is one man, one vote. It is therefore in the interest of wage-earners to move the struggle for the distribution of the fruits of production into the political arena, where their numerical strength can be used more effectively, rather than to carry it out solely on the labour market, where they are more directly confronted by capital resources.

When the socialist parties gain a strong and stable hold on government power, we can expect the pattern of coalition formation in the tripartite societal bargaining between labour, capital and the government to change. This can be expected to have important consequences for the choice of conflict strategies, not only for labour but also for the employers. It now becomes possible for the labour movement to influence distributive processes also by political means. This may be done through different types of policies affecting the labour market, employment, taxation, social insurance and housing. The centre of gravity of the distributive conflicts can thus be moved from the labour market into politics. As a result of the changes in distributive policies, labour disputes may decrease in extent and importance. Note that the trade union movement is here expected to refrain from using the strike not because a labour party is in government, but because the distributive policy exercised by the government benefits the workers.[18]

In order to bring about significant changes in the parties' conflict strategies, the extent as well as the stability of the political influence of the left parties is of importance. A shift in conflict strategies implies action with a long time perspective. Such a change must be judged to be long-lasting and to have a relatively good chance of success. Shifting political majorities need therefore neither invite nor compel changes of conflict strategies. Minority representation for the socialist parties in coalition governments, or socialistic minority governments, generally do not provide a strong enough basis for changes in conflict strategy and distributive policies.

Two circumstances can be expected to be important conditions of the manner in which conflict strategies are affected by the political power of the socialist parties. One is the degree of economic growth in the country. Periods of strong expansion facilitate the development of strategies where both parties can benefit from co-operation with each other. Low economic growth, on the contrary, tends to generate 'zero sum conflicts', where one party's gain is the other party's loss, and where conflict strategies therefore are more difficult to change. In this model the rate of economic growth thus becomes one of the conditions determining how conflicts between the parties develop rather than one of the most important determinants of conflict patterns.

A second important circumstance affecting choice of conflict strategies is the international situation of the country. This concerns the external political situation of the country and possible threats to its independence, but also the dependence of its economy on imports and exports and on multinational companies. In these respects, international relations may therefore influence the internal power struggles in a country.

As indicated above, writers in the tradition of pluralist industrialism view the institutions of industrial relations as central for the preservation of industrial peace. Our hypothesis is that these institutions play much less of a strategic role and are of importance primarily as variables intervening between the distribution of power resources and the patterns of conflict. Institutions and regulations on the labour market, whether arrived at by enacting laws or through bargaining, thus can be expected to reflect the relative extent of working-class power resources and the political power of the labour movement. However, once these institutions are established, they may be expected to have some influence on patterns of industrial conflict.

Among the writers on corporatism, the systems of interest mediation regarded as typically corporatist assume a role similar to those of institutions for conflict resolution in the pluralist industrial model. Neo-corporatist institutions too are thus seen by some writers as key stabilizing factors of modern societies which, once established, function relatively independently from the power structure of society. Our hypothesis, however, is that these neo-corporatist arrangements must be seen as intervening variables, mediating the influences from the distribution of power in society to the pattern of conflicts centred around distribution.

PATTERNS OF CHANGE

Let us now examine how conflict patterns and their changes during the present century fit into the theoretical model outlined above. We expect that the degree of working-class mobilization and control of government power will have an effect on the pattern of industrial conflict in the country. In Chapter 3, we have described the relative power of the working class during the postwar years in eighteen Western countries. Table 8.1 above shows the relative volumes of and involvement in industrial conflict during the present century in five groups of countries, defined on the bases of the degree of political and union mobilization of the working class as well as the extent and stability of left party participation in government.[19] For each category of countries, average relative volumes and involvements are given in Table 8.2.

Table 8.2 Relative strike volume and involvement in industrial conflict, 1946-76, in groups of countries with different degree of working-class mobilization and of left control of government

Group	Relative volume*	Relative involvement†
High mobilization, stable control		
Sweden, Norway, Austria	50	82
High mobilization, temporary or partial control		
Denmark, UK, Belgium, New Zealand	208	368
Average-high mobilization, low control		
Finland, Australia, France, Italy, Japan	612	1,311
Low mobilization, exclusion		
Ireland, USA, Canada	512	320
Low-average mobilization, partial control		
West Germany, Netherlands, Switzerland	25	75

* Number of man-days idleness per 1,000 workers.
† Number of workers involved in industrial conflict per 10,000 workers.

In Sweden, Norway and Austria the working classes are well mobilized and since World War II have had long and stable control of government power. By comparison with the period between the wars, the volume and involvement of industrial strife has clearly decreased in these countries. The development in Sweden is here of particular interest. As indicated above, up until the middle of the 1930s, Sweden was the leading country in the world with respect to the relative volume of industrial conflict. Its labour disputes were large and drawn-out. The dramatic decline of industrial conflict in Sweden during the period 1936-46 must be seen as the result of the 'historical compromise' between capital and labour made in the latter part of the 1930s (see Chapter 3).

This historical compromise became possible when, after the elections in 1932, the Social Democrats entrenched their position as the leading party in government. It evolved out of the realization on both sides that in the foreseeable future they would have to live with a division of power, where the labour movement had control over the government while the owners of capital retained their control over the economy. A co-operation between labour and business interests to increase economic growth, therefore, came to be seen as possible and desirable to both parties.

Against this background, new conflict strategies were developed. On the basis of strong unions and gradually full employment the labour movement was able to provide workers with reasonable wage increases at the same time as it could employ political instruments to influence the distributive processes. Although co-operation between the LO and the Social Democratic government was not without friction, it nevertheless functioned relatively well. Business interests, however, were able - often with great success - to make the Social Democratic government remember the acknowledgement made by Ernst Wigforss in 1938 of 'the necessity of maintaining favourable conditions for private enterprise' (cf. Chapter 3).

As a result of these new conflict strategies, strikes and lockouts soon lost their previously central role in the distributive struggle. Instead, they came to present a threat to the new co-operative strategies. The new political situation also affected the motives of the parties for the use of industrial conflict. The employers' most potent weapon, the general lockout, became more risky to use under a Social Democratic government. The Social Democrats, on their side, recognized that extended labour disputes were a threat to their attempts to reactivate the economy during the depression. During the negotiations between SAF and LO leading to the Saltsjöbaden Agreement in 1938, the LO intervened in the bargaining procedures of its member unions to prevent the outbreak of strikes. The most extensive strike in the following decades, the metal-workers' strike in 1945, was initiated contrary to the wishes of the union leadership.[20]

The new conflict strategies made industrial conflict in Sweden 'wither away' within a decade. The centre of gravity of the distributive struggles was moved to the political arena. Economic growth contributed to this development, as did the threats from abroad during the 1930s and 1940s.

In the Swedish case, the hypothesis that left party control over the government is of crucial importance for the level of industrial disputes can be illustrated by a regression equation, where we also bring in a couple of other variables often offered as explanations of the level of industrial conflict. The data consist of annual observation from 1894 to 1980. As our dependent variable we take relative involvement, which is logarithmically transformed because of its skewness. The independent variables are (1) S, strong Social Democratic dominance of government (this variable is set to 0 in the years 1894-1932 and 1977-80 and to 1 in 1933-76); (2) ΔU, change in unemployment from the previous year; and (3) M, union membership (in logged form).

The regression equation then is:

$$\text{Ln}\ (\textit{relative involvement}) = a + b_1 S + b_2 \Delta U + b_3 M + u.$$

An estimation of the regression coefficients gives the following results:

$S = -0.657$ no. of observations = 86
$\Delta U = 0.006$ $R^2 = 0.60$
$M = 0.091$ Durbin-Watson statistic = 1.46

Of the regression coefficients, only that for strong Social Democratic government dominance is significant and large.[21] This is clearly congruent with our hypothesis.

The Norwegian development in this area was somewhat less dramatic but followed similar lines. In Norway also the sharp decline in industrial conflict from a previously very high level came when the Social Democrats achieved stable control over the government after World War II.

To a rather large extent, the development in Austria duplicated the experiences in Sweden and Norway. One important difference, however, was that Austria's international position after World War II seems to have played a significant role in the shaping of its internal strategies of conflict. In the first elections after the war the Social Democrats were defeated by a slight bourgeois majority. But Austria was at this time an occupied country - divided between the Western powers and the Soviet Union. The desire to avoid a permanent division of the country according to the patterns in Germany or Korea was probably a crucial inducement for the establishment of a coalition government after the war. This government was led by a bourgeois prime minister but had a strong Social Democratic representation. It was recognized by both the Soviet Union and the Western powers. The Social Democrats were furthermore accorded proportional representation in the many new public and semi-public organs connected with the economy and public administration which were established after the war.

The pressures exerted by Austria's international situation towards national unity, the strong positions of the trade unions and the working class in its politics, and the disrepute of large sections of the bourgeoisie because of their alliances with the Nazis contributed to the development of conflict strategies on both sides focused on co-operation. In comparison with the period of independence between the wars, industrial conflict declined sharply. These co-operative strategies lasted through a short period of bourgeois government in 1966-70, after which a Social Democratic majority government came into power.

In a category of four countries comprising Denmark, the United Kingdom, Belgium and New Zealand, mobilization of the working class in postwar years has also been high. However, the social democratic parties in these countries, have had only a periodic and relatively weak control of government. In Denmark, Belgium and the United Kingdom, involvement in industrial conflict has been on an internationally high level and has remained roughly the same as during the period between the wars.[22] But since the duration of conflicts has decreased, the volume of conflict has also diminished. In New Zealand, however, both involvement and volume of industrial conflict have increased during the postwar period. My interpretation is that the control over the government by the labour parties in these countries has not been stable or strong enough for the actors on the labour market to be induced or able to change their conflict strategies.

In five countries - Finland, France, Italy, Japan and Australia - the working classes in postwar years have had a middling to high degree of mobilization and have competed for government power, but without any major success. The importance of the relatively long periods of social democratic and socialist government participation in Finland and Italy is considerably reduced by the political splits in their labour movements. In this category of countries involvement in industrial conflict has increased markedly. With the exception of Australia, the volume of conflict in these countries has also clearly increased. This indicates that the relatively well mobilized working classes in these countries have been forced to wage their struggle mainly in the labour market while government power has on the whole been pro-employer. Iceland, although not included in this study, actually also belongs to this category of countries and has had a similar increase in industrial conflict.[23]

In a fourth category of countries - the United States, Canada and Ireland - the working classes have had a low degree of mobilization and have in the main been excluded from government. Involvement in industrial disputes has increased only moderately in these countries. On the other hand, their conflicts have been of relatively long duration and have therefore added up to volumes of internationally record levels. Also in these countries the working classes have had to attempt to secure a reasonable share of the results of production through conflicts on the labour market.

In this category of countries the United States is of special interest simply in sheer quantitative terms. During the postwar period something in the order of one-half of all recorded man-days used for industrial conflict have affected American workers. Industrial conflict and industrial relations in the United States have retained key features common also in other Western nations during the early decades of the century, but which in the postwar period have disappeared in most other countries. Strikes in the United States thus continue to have a long average duration, about three weeks. The same average duration was found in other Western nations up to World War II but has since then been more than halved. Employers in the United States have also retained the strong, sometimes vehement, resistance to unions common in most countries in earlier decades. In the 1960s and 1970s, on average about one-sixth of all strikes in the United States were still being fought in the absence of a collective agreement or for the right to have an agreement. Furthermore, in the United States collective bargaining and wage agreements continue to take place primarily on the level of the firm or plant, while in most other countries they have been supplemented with industry-wide or even economy-wide agreements.

In a largely descriptive study of the development of industrial conflict in the United States, P.K. Edwards suggests that the continued long duration of strikes and employers' opposition to unions primarily reflects 'the intensity of struggle for job control'. In the United States 'the struggles which have occurred have assumed a particularly extreme form, because crucial interests of the parties have been at stake. These interests have gone beyond "economic" matters to include the basic rights of the parties.'[24] Edwards objects to what he describes as 'political' interpretations of 'American exceptionalism' as tending to be dogmatic and superficial. However, Edwards's own explanation of the persistence in the United States of patterns of industrial conflict and industrial relations, which have become 'outmoded' in most other Western nations, amounts to little beyond renaming the phenomena that are to be explained.

From a power distribution perspective, we would expect that, where the disadvantage of power resources between management and wage-earners is great, industrial conflict will be intense, will concern the basic rights of collective bargaining, and will take place primarily on the level of the workplace. However, when the gap in power resources decreases owing to the increasing organizational strength of wage-earners, employers will gradually be forced to accept the basic rights of workers for collective bargaining. Employer opposition to collective bargaining therefore tends to disappear. When the organizational strength of workers increases they will be able to act on a wider basis than on the level of the plant. If wage-earners are able to act in a co-ordinated fashion on the industry or economy level, this tends to necessitate organization also among employers.[25] Therefore collective agreements covering industries or the whole economy tend to become common. This approach suggests that the primary explanation of 'American exceptionalism' is probably that working-class organizations - unions and left parties - have remained weak and have not been able to achieve the changes which have taken place in many other countries.[26]

The final group of countries - West Germany, the Netherlands and Switzerland - do not easily fit into our suggested scheme of interpretation. In spite of the fact that the working classes in these countries are relatively weakly mobilized, they have nevertheless had very low levels of industrial conflict. During the postwar period this group has actually had a lower volume of and involvement in conflict than the group comprising Sweden, Norway and Austria (Table 8.2). The social democratic parties in West Germany, the Netherlands and Switzerland have participated extensively in coalition governments.

The decrease in industrial conflict does not, however, coincide in time with the inclusion of the social democratic parties into the government. Apart from a wave of strikes at the end of World War I, Switzerland has never had industrial conflict to any major degree. The conflict level in the Netherlands has also remained one of the lowest among the Western nations; the period of industrial peace during the reconstruction after World War II, however, started out with quite a long period of Democratic Socialist participation in government. While Germany during the Weimar Republic had very high conflict levels, the Federal Republic has had industrial peace during the major part of the postwar period, up to 1966 under a bourgeois government.

Thus, at least at a first glance, West Germany, the Netherlands and Switzerland are difficult to fit into the theoretical model of industrial conflict we have suggested here. Several unusual features can be assumed to have influenced the pattern of development in these three countries. They are the only countries in Europe which are genuinely divided by the cleavage between Catholics and Protestants. Religious opposition between these groups has undoubtedly made the mobilization of the working class more difficult. Especially in the Netherlands, but even in the other two countries, religion has provided an important basis for union and political organization. This split among workers along religious lines may have led to some part of their demands having been satisfied through the religiously based political parties.

In Switzerland, the picture is further complicated by fragmentation based on language and region. An additional basis for disintegration of the working class is provided by the large stratum of 'guest workers' from southern Europe, who constitute a sub-proletariat among workers. In Switzerland these factors have contributed to the creation of the perhaps weakest and least militant trade union organizations in Western Europe. During the postwar period, the majority of Swiss unions apparently have not even maintained strike funds.[27] In spite of the fact that a large proportion of Swiss workers are found in manufacturing, unions have not fought for their members' interests in ways which have provoked open conflict. The perilous position of the country between two fascist states in the north and south during the period between the wars may have contributed to this restrictive attitude. The Swiss working class thus appears to be incorporated into a social structure where inequality is relatively high. In the Netherlands, however, income inequality has been relatively low.

How are we to explain the low level of industrial conflict in

West Germany during the postwar period? Contrary to the situation in Austria, the Social Democrats were excluded from government power for a long time in West Germany. At the end of the war West Germany was in roughly the same position as Japan. The most important differences between Austria and Germany would appear to have been that the West German labour movement was considerably weaker and that the division of the country between East and West soon became a reality. There was thus not the same pressure as in Austria to include the Social Democrats in a national coalition government.

The experiences of the bitter internal struggles during the Weimar Republic, in combination with the proximity to Soviet-controlled East Germany, probably deterred the West German working class from engaging in a militant strategy, something which could be expected to place the Social Democrats in a permanent role as opposition. In Japan, on the other hand, the labour movement developed only after the fall of the former authoritarian government at the end of the war. Neither did Japan have any external political pressures which might have induced the relatively weak union movement towards a co-operative strategy.

DISTRIBUTIVE POLICIES

The model discussed above thus suggests that industrial conflict can be reduced if, under favourable political conditions, the centre of gravity of the distributive struggles can be shifted from the labour market to the political arena. This implies that the distributive policies in their wide sense must change character and be given such a content that they can partly replace strife on the labour market as a means of redistributing goods in society. Do, then, distributive policies differ among Western countries in such a manner as to reasonably explain the observed differences between them in patterns of industrial conflict? In the following chapter we shall discuss different aspects of distributive or social policies in these countries. Here we shall only attempt to illustrate briefly one important stage in the model of industrial conflict outlined in Figure 8.2, namely, the role of distributive policy in the linkage of the political power of the working class and the strategies of conflict to the extent and form of industrial conflict.

There is a shortage of comparable data on different aspects of distributive policies in the Western nations. One area of crucial importance for distributive policy is the level of unemployment in the country. The level of unemployment is influenced by many factors. It may be presumed, however, that government policy is one of its important determinants. In the choice between inflation and unemployment which most Western governments have faced in postwar years, the socialist parties can be expected to have tried to protect employment more often than the bourgeois parties, which can be expected to have given priority to anti-inflationary measures.[28]

A hypothesis in our model is thus that social democratic government power should decrease unemployment and thereby contribute to a long-term decrease in the level of industrial conflict. This 'political' hypothesis on the long-term relationship between unemployment and strikes is contrary to the results of studies on the short-term correlation between industrial conflict and economic fluctuations in different countries, where a general finding has been that the level of conflict rises when unemployment falls but falls when unemployment rises.[29]

The redistributive effects of social and taxation policies in different countries are difficult to establish. One indicator which is often used to describe social policy is the proportion of the government budget spent on social security. This indicator is however very unsatisfactory, since it does not capture many of the redistributive effects which social policy can have. It becomes somewhat less unsatisfactory if we weight it with the proportion of national tax revenue exacted by direct rather than by indirect taxation, since direct taxes can be assumed to be more progressive than the indirect ones. A primitive measure of the redistributive effects of the government budget can thus be arrived at by weighting the proportion of social security expenditure of the government budget with the proportion of national tax income derived from direct taxation.[30]

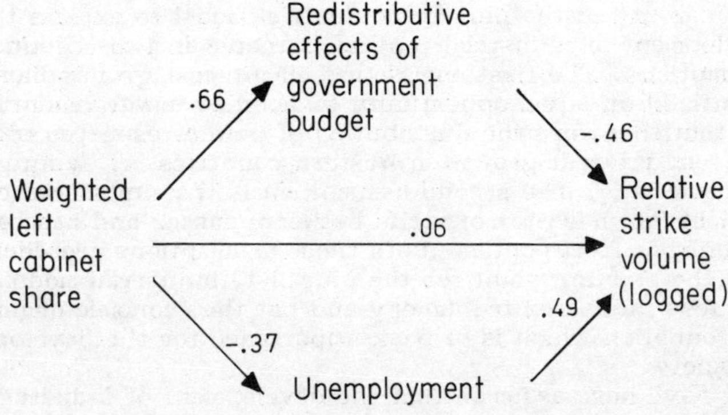

Figure 8.3 Path coefficients indicating relationships between political power of the labour movement, economic outcomes and relative strike volume in eighteen capitalist democracies, 1949-76

A path-analysis with data for our eighteen countries during the postwar years to illustrate the effects of socialist control of government power on unemployment, redistribution via the government budget and on industrial conflict gives some support to the model outlined above (Figure 8.3).[31] It would appear that the extent of left government control (i.e. their proportion of government posts multiplied by their proportion of seats in parliament and by the proportion of time with left representation in government) increases the redistributive effects of the government budget and reduces the level of unemployment. Redistribution via the government budget then reduces the relative volume of industrial conflict, while rising unemployment figures increase the volume of conflict. Socialist party control of government has, on the other hand, little direct effect on the volume of conflict.

These data thus suggest that it is not social democratic participation in government in itself which is of importance for the volume of conflict. When in government the social democrats must be able to influence the distributive policy in the country in order to change the conflict pattern on the labour market.

This statistical analysis based on available cross-sectional data for different countries cannot, of course, prove that the model of politics and industrial conflict outlined here actually has been working in the Western nations during the postwar period. There are too many uncertainties and possible sources of error in the analysis. Yet the analysis gives an illustration of what developments might have taken place.

THE POLITICS OF INDUSTRIAL CONFLICT

The inability of the pluralist industrial model to explain the development of industrial conflict is rooted in two unfounded assumptions. The first one is that all interest groups have potentially an equal opportunity to mobilize power resources, and that therefore the distribution of power resources between different interest groups in Western countries is, by and large, unproblematic. The second assumption is that industrial conflict has lost its character of strife between classes and has been disengaged from politics. Both these assumptions are derived from the starting point for the pluralist, industrial model, i.e., that it is industrial technology and not the economic organization of production which is of basic importance for the development of society.

We have here assumed that the development of industrial conflict in the West must be understood in relation to the distribution of power resources between employers and wage-earners. When the unions and political organizations grow, the power resources of the working class increase. This leads to an increase in industrial conflict, a development which is observed in the majority of the Western countries from the end of the past century up to the period between the wars.

But the strike must be seen primarily as a weapon in self-defence, which workers are forced to use for want of better alternatives. I do not share the view which has been common among many on the left that the level of strikes is an indicator of the radicalism and class-consciousness of the workers. Those who have based this interpretation on observations of Italy and France have forgotten that the volume of industrial conflict is as high in the United States, Canada and Ireland, where the workers hardly can be described as spearheads of the international proletariat. Strikes are taxing and costly, primarily for the strikers. For the labour movement it must therefore be strategically important to move the struggle from the labour market, where men are pitted against capital, to the democratic class struggle in politics, where each person in principle has one and only one vote.

In the democratic countries the conflicts of interest between the classes find expression not only in industrial relations but also in politics. A marked shift of the expressions of these conflicts from the labour market to the political arena can take place in countries where socialist parties gain a strong and stable hold over government power and can begin to employ political means to influence the distributive processes in society. Contrary to the Leninist interpretation of Marxism, I assume that it is then possible to advance the interests of the working class through the government and the parliament. In contrast to some writers on neo-corporatism, I assume that the institutional arrangements which are developed in this process need not be seen as means of social control over the workers, but can, under certain circumstances, be used to translate the organizational power of the wage-earners into the formation of economic and social policies favourable to working-class interests.

To understand the correlation between the political colour of governments and the extent of industrial conflict, we must assume that the distributive policies which bourgeois governments advocate tend to differ from those of socialist parties. The differences in distributive policies between bourgeois and socialist governments are of course not absolute but rather a matter of degree. It is sufficient to assume that the differences are important to the voters.

In the tripartite societal bargaining between workers, employers and governments the pattern of coalition formation - two against one - can be affected by the party composition of the government. It is likely that bourgeois governments find it easier to come to terms with the employers, and tend to favour the demands of the middle and upper social strata rather than those of the workers. The opposite tends to apply to left governments. With bourgeois governments the workers' foremost recourse in the distributive struggles is therefore action in the industrial arena. Under certain conditions, however, the distributive policies of left governments can be expected to further workers' interests.

We must keep in mind, however, that this discussion concerns the content of the distributive policies in a country, not the party composition of the government. In countries where social democrats in government have not been able or willing to carry out distributive policies to the benefit of the workers, industrial conflict will continue to rear its head.

Since we are here concerned with many countries, each with a unique background, a long time span and a phenomenon - industrial conflict - which is obviously influenced by a multitude of different factors and conditions, we cannot expect to find a complete fit between our model and the empirical data. It is therefore surprising that fifteen of the eighteen countries discussed here - Austria, Australia, Belgium, the United Kingdom, Canada, Denmark, Finland, France, Ireland, Italy, Japan, New Zealand, Norway, Sweden and the United States - fit fairly well into the scheme of interpretation we have developed here. Iceland, which was not included in our study, also appears to conform to the expected pattern.

Developments in the three religiously divided European countries - West Germany, Switzerland and the Netherlands - indicate, however, that there also are other ways of reducing industrial conflict than by a division of governmental and economic powers between labour and capital. The situation in these countries would appear to be the result of a long historical development, where conflicts based on religion and class have crossed each other.

Since the beginning of the 1970s the developments in the Western nations have underlined the error in the pluralistic assumption concerning the separation of economic and political conflict. The rapid rate of inflation in the West during these years has often been seen as a result of wage-earners and their organizations having grown so strong that they have been able to extract too large wage increases. The cure for this, in the views of many governments, has been the implementation of a policy of economic restraint, generating increasingly high unemployment levels which weaken the bargaining position of wage-earners. In other words, governments have attempted to influence developments on the labour market by the use of political means. The efforts to develop incomes policies in many countries is another expression of the correlation between political and economic conflicts.

Economists in the neo-classical mould have tended to look upon the rapid inflation since the beginning of the 1970s as largely the result of a series of unfortunate coincidence, such as the war in Vietnam and the rise in oil prices, which have affected the world economy. Even if such factors naturally are of importance, it appears to me more fruitful to see the rising inflation in the perspective of the distributive conflicts between the large collectivities or classes in the Western countries.[32] In this distributive conflict involving societal bargaining, economics and politics become more and more interwoven with each other. The distribution of power resources within the Western countries is thus of importance for the form which these distributive struggles will assume.

By comparison with the period between the wars, the degree of unionization among wage-earners has markedly increased after

World War II. This can be expected to have consequences for the form of the distributive conflict. The marked decline in the duration of industrial conflicts is here of interest. It indicates that in several countries the long and severe type of labour dispute has tended to disappear. This suggests that industrial conflict has lost its previous key role in the struggles concerning the distribution of the results of production.

The decrease in the duration of strikes since the 1930s has coincided with the long-term increase in the rate of inflation. This correlation may have been caused by a third factor, the increasing strength of unions. Stronger unions have made it more costly for employers to fight the decisive battles concerning the distribution of the results of production on the labour market. Various factors may have made it easier for companies to raise their prices instead, and thereby wholly or partly to recoup losses sustained at the bargaining table.

9 SOCIAL POLICY

What factors influence the development of the welfare state? Is the political composition of governments of significance in this process? These questions are of political as well as of scientific interest. During the postwar period social scientists have explored them using various theoretical perspectives. Most of these studies have come in the mainstream of the social sciences, where the ideas of the pluralist industrial model dominate.[1] Some have also represented varieties of Marxian theory.[2] Despite this theoretical diversity, however, their conclusions have been strikingly similar.

According to these studies, the political composition of parliaments and governments, and especially the relative strength of social democratic parties, have been of little or no significance for the development of the welfare state. The emergence and growth of the welfare state instead appears primarily as a functional necessity of industrialization and as a reflection of, among other things, economic growth, population structure and historical experiences. Some studies, however, have questioned or qualified such interpretations.[3]

Obviously, the question of the causes behind the development of the welfare state is an area where the theoretical perspectives of the pluralist industrial model clash with the approach departing from the organization of production and distribution of power resources outlined in Chapter 2. But my approach leads also to hypotheses about the development of the welfare state other than those inspired by the Leninist interpretation of Marxism. This chapter discusses the conceptual problems encountered in analysing the development of the welfare state and presents statistical data which illustrate the problems involved here.[4] Since social policy has constituted an essential component in the political programmes and platforms of the Swedish Social Democrats, we shall also examine its role in shaping the electoral choice of voters in the 1970s.

THE WELFARE STATE AND EQUALITY

The concept of the welfare state is a vague one. It has been applied to societies as diverse as Bismarck's Germany and contemporary United States and Sweden. Most of the Western industrial countries are usually characterized as welfare states. Definitions of the welfare state are generally based on the average standard of living, political democracy and the role of the state in the distribution of welfare in society.[5] A relatively high standard of living and a reasonably well functioning democracy, however, should be seen as prerequisites for the welfare state rather than as its definitional properties. In specifying the characteristics of the welfare state, the degree of equality or inequality in terms of the standards and conditions of living among citizens stands out as a basic variable. Even if we focus on what appears to be a more limited aspect - the absence of poverty among the citizens - we are implying a definition in terms of equality. This is because most Western governments in practice apply relative rather than absolute definitions of poverty.

In the area of social policy a distinction has long been made between absolute and relative definitions of poverty. The absolute definition was used at the turn of the century by Seebohm Rowntree. On the basis of nutritional requirements and other criteria of minimum needs, which have to be satisfied to maintain a worker's physical capacity, Rowntree established minimum levels in terms of food, clothing, housing, etc. Using these requirements he could then calculate a minimum income required to acquire these necessities and used it to draw a 'poverty line' among citizens.[6]

During the postwar period in most countries this absolute approach has been abandoned for a relative definition of poverty. Instead of comparing the standard of living with minimum requirements based on allegedly objective criteria, poverty is now defined in terms of the position of the worst-off categories in relation to the average conditions of the population. Consequently, this procedure involves the extent of equality or inequality among the citizens, even if it pertains only to the lower portion of the income distribution. Among the Western countries in the beginning of the 1980s, only the United States seems to use an official definition of poverty in terms of an absolute level of income, in principle based on nutritional requirements. However, American social scientists also admit that the relative definition is to be preferred to the absolute one. The poverty definitions used, for example, in Sweden and Great Britain to specify the need of social assistance are in practice relative definitions.[7]

Taking political democracy and a relatively high standard of living as prerequisites, we can thus adopt the extent of equality-inequality in basic living conditions among the citizens as the major criterion in determining the extent to which a country is a welfare state. A definition based on the degree of inequality in society is of course controversial. A somewhat 'milder' definition can instead be formulated as the absence of poverty among the citizens, in other words, in terms of the distance between the worst-off citizens and the average conditions of the population.

PROCESSES OF DISTRIBUTION

Viewing the welfare state in terms of equality-inequality leads to the question of how the distributive processes in society function and how they are influenced by political and other factors. The concept of social policy is used here in a comprehensive way to include public policy aiming to influence the distribution of welfare in society in an equalizing direction, where equalization can occur between groups of citizens or between various periods of an individual's life.

The distributive processes in the Western countries can be analysed in a variety of ways. One possibility is to examine their outcomes, that is, the variation in the degree and kind of inequality which is the assumed result of the distributive process. The distributive processes can also be analysed in terms of the conditions within which they take place, as well as in terms of the characteristics of the government measures which intervene in these processes, and therefore are of significance for inequality.

Within the social sciences there are a number of partly competing, partly overlapping theoretical approaches in the analysis of distribution and inequality in Western societies. These theoretical approaches appear to differ primarily in the way in which power resources[8] are seen as influencing the degree of inequality. In the pluralistic industrial model, power resources in advanced industrial societies tend to be viewed as being relatively equally distributed among a multitude of interest groups. Power resources therefore are not seen as being of major relevance for inequality and changes in the patterns of inequality. In economics the two dominant theoretical approaches, the marginal productivity theory and human capital theory, pay little attention to power differences. Some of the recent attempts to modify and to find alternatives to marginal productivity theory, however, accord a somewhat larger role to power.[9] In sociology the dominant structural-functional theory of stratification has been based on ideas similar to those that later were incorporated into human capital theory.[10] Some mainstream sociological theories, however, have given power a central place in the explanation of inequality.[11]

Approaches to distribution inspired by a Leninist interpretation of Marxism assume, on the contrary, that power resources in capitalist societies are basically distributed in a dichotomous pattern, so that the capitalist class controls practically all resources while the working class commands virtually none of them. Because of this highly uneven but stable distribution of power resources, in this approach also the distribution of power resources is seen as being of little significance in explaining cross-national variations in the development of the welfare state.

Contrary to both the pluralist and Marxist-Leninist approaches my point of departure for the study of the welfare state is the hypothesis that the extent of the disadvantage in power resource of the working class in the capitalist democracies can show important differences between countries and can also change over time (cf. Chapter 2). The variations in the difference between the two basic types of power resources - control over the means of production and the organization of wage-earners into unions and political parties - are thus assumed to be of major importance for the distributive process in capitalist democracies and for their final result; the extent of inequality (Figure 9.1). The distribution of power resources are assumed to have direct effects on the distributive processes. But power resources also affect the distributive processes indirectly, via politics, inasmuch as the scope and direction of state interventions in the distributive processes are dependent upon the variations of power resources in society. However other factors, such as economic growth, the composition of the population and historical factors, are also of significance in this context. The outcomes of the distributive processes can be seen as a multi-dimensional pattern of inequality in the distribution of welfare or levels of living including, for example, income, health, education and housing.[12]

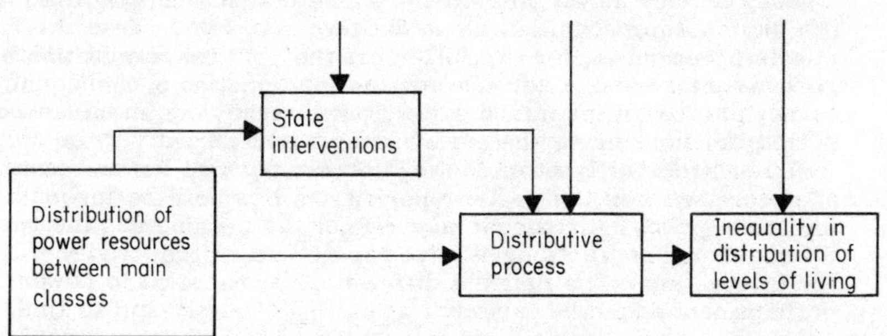

Figure 9.1 Rough sketch of hypothesized distributive processes in capitalist democracies

SOCIAL INSURANCE SYSTEMS

How are we to characterize the policies and actions by the state which affect the distribution of welfare among the citizens? In research on social policy the answer to this question has often been assumed as given. Studies of the welfare state thus have most frequently examined the development of social insurance systems and the relative importance of transfer payments through social insurance in various countries.[13] The ILO figures on social security expenditures as a proportion of GNP are an easily available and often-used indicator of the level of ambition of social policy.[14]

However, as indicators of the development of social policy, the

ILO figures are entirely too narrow. According to such an indicator, for example, a country is a better welfare state the more it spends on unemployment benefits. Efforts to combat unemployment through an active labour market policy and Keynesian economic policy are however not registered by this indicator. In many countries, substantial amounts of social policy spending also fall outside the ILO definition.[15] Furthermore, variations in this indicator are strongly influenced by expenditures for old-age pensions, which often are the single most costly item among the traditional social insurance systems.

In comparative studies of social policy, one must keep in mind the possibility that the frontiers of distributional conflicts may change over time. Thus, if we focus on a specific set of public measures, for example the major social insurance programmes, we must be aware of what might be called 'saturation effects'. At one particular period in a country, the set of social insurance programmes studied can be at the centre of the political struggles over distribution. Once these programmes have been implemented, however, distributional conflict can move to new frontiers. A focus on the specific set of programmes need thus no longer be a good 'dependent variable' in the sense that it sheds light on the distributional conflicts in a country.

Jens Alber finds, for example, that the political composition of governments was of relevance for the introduction of legislation concerning social insurance programmes during the interwar period but not during the period after World War II.[16] This does not necessarily mean, however, that the political composition of governments in the postwar period has had no importance for social policy. Instead, it may reflect the possibility that the distributional conflicts have moved to new frontiers. At present the interesting cross-national differences in social policy are perhaps found in other areas.

DIMENSIONS OF SOCIAL POLICY

This leads us to the question of how to define social policy measures in a way which is of relevance for distribution. This question, of course, is by no means new. Even in the 1950s, Richard M. Titmuss was calling attention to the redistributional effects of the tax system and benefits tied to employment which were of much the same nature as the traditional social policy measures.[17] The intervention of the state in the distributive processes in society is thus not limited to measures directed towards persons with publicly acknowledged needs.

Although earlier studies provide few leads for the specification of the dimensions or criteria in terms of which we can analyse public interventions into the distributive processes, researchers in these areas have undoubtedly had some dimensions or typologies in mind when writing on social policy. Thus, for instance, Titmuss assures us: 'Socialist social policies are, in my view, totally different in their purposes, philosophy and attitudes to people from Conservative social policies. They are (or should be) pre-eminently about equality, freedom and social integration.'[18] The closest that Titmuss appears to have come to a systematic discussion of different dimensions or typologies of social policy, however, is in his posthumously published lecture notes, where he briefly outlines different types of social policies.

In attempting to characterize various aspects of public interventions in the distributive processes in the Western countries, we can choose differing points of departure. One possibility, close at hand, appears to be an examination of different sectors of public policy. Another possibility is to characterize state intervention in terms of the stages in the distributive processes where they enter. We can also try to develop more comprehensive typologies of social policies.

State interventions into the distributive processes are structured in terms of policy areas which generally are institutionalized through governmental departments and agencies. Such policy areas provide a natural starting point in social policy research. Yet they do not provide much more than a check-list for increasing our awareness of possible variations in state interventions.

They thus remind us that, in addition to social insurance and other welfare programmes, there are also public policies related to housing, education, health, the labour market, employment, taxation, the economy, production, consumption, etc. However, although such institutionalized policy divisions are related in various ways to theoretical issues, they appear insufficient if we are searching for more basic dimensions of state interventions in the distributive processes.

One aspect of importance in characterizing public measures is the stage of the distributive processes at which they intervene. From this perspective we can describe the extent to which various measures prevent problems and needs from arising or if the measures alleviate problems and needs once they are manifest. This can be illustrated by examining how wages are converted into income and subsequently into buying power (Figure 9.2).[19]

The end result of a person's participation on the labour market in terms of buying power is affected by state interventions at several stages. In exchange for their labour, employees receive wages or salaries. Wages may have been modified by state interventions, for instance, in terms of minimum-wage laws or legislation affecting the bargaining power of unions. The conversion of wages to income is affected by the level of employment and extent of working time. Labour market policy, industrial policy and general economic policies shape employment opportunities. Consequently they are of central importance in determining the distribution of income. Of course, income is also affected by, among other things, returns from capital.

State interventions are also of importance in the conversion of income into buying power. This conversion is thus affected by taxation and inflation, which are related to fiscal and economic policies. It is also affected by public transfers, the traditional focus of studies in social policy. To a large extent also these interventions can be characterized in terms of their timing in the distributive process. Public goods and services available free of charge or at nominal rates for all citizens can be said to enter at an early stage in this part of the conversion process. Other types of public pricing policies, such as rent controls and subsidized foodstuffs, have a similar status. General transfer programmes available to citizens in terms of largely universal criteria, such as age, also come in at a relatively early stage of the distributive process.

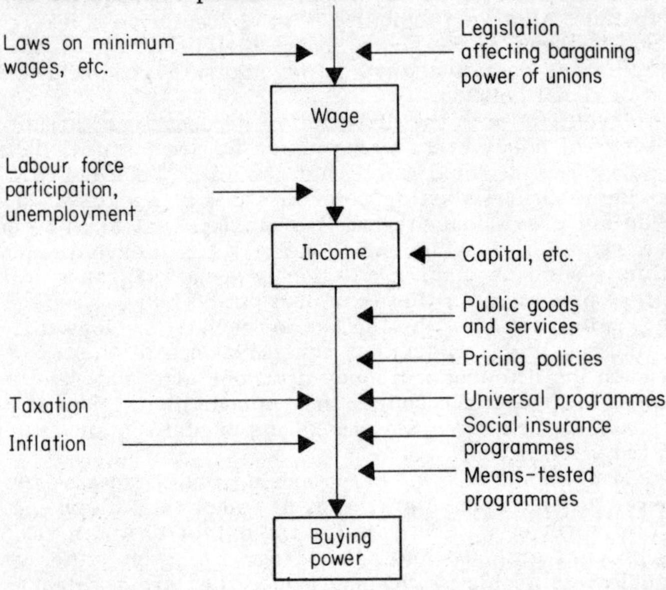

Figure 9.2 Public interventions at different stages of distribution of buying power

Social insurance programmes, however, which come into effect as soon as the earnings capacity of the individual has decreased, come in fairly late in the process. This is even more true of means-tested programmes, which are based on a schematic test of income according to established criteria. Measures based on individual means tests, e.g., social assistance, can be said to enter at the final stage of the distributive process, only when an unacceptable decrease in buying power has already occurred.

MARGINAL AND INSTITUTIONAL POLICY MODELS

In the social policy literature, for example in the writings of Titmuss, we find references to two polar types of social policy models. The first can be called a 'marginal' type of social policy, and the second an 'institutional' type of social policy.[20] These policy models, however, have not been spelled out in any detail. Titmuss talks about a 'residual welfare mode of social policy', which is based on the assumption that private markets and the family constitute the natural channels through which the needs of citizens are to be met; social policy is to enter only when these natural mechanisms do not function and then only as a temporary substitute. According to the 'institutional redistributive model of social policy', however, social policy is an integrated part of society and offers citizens public services outside the market on criteria of needs. In this latter model, social policy thus has an important function for redistributing resources in society.

Table 9.1 Preliminary outline of subdimensions of marginal and institutional ideal types

Subdimension	Social policy model	
	Marginal	Institutional
Proportion of GNP for social purposes	Small	Large
Proportion of population affected	Small	Large
Importance of full employment and labour force participation programmes	Small	Large
Importance of programmes preventing needs	Small	Large
Dominant types of programmes	Selective	Universal
Standards of benefits	Minimum	Normal
Dominant type of financing	Fees	Taxation
Progressivity of taxation	Low	High
Importance of social control	Large	Small
Importance of private organizations	Large	Small

These two models can be seen as ideal types representing opposite poles on a number of sub-dimensions, which ought to capture several relevant aspects of the social policy systems in various countries. Tentatively the following sub-dimensions can be assumed to be implied by these polar types (see Table 9.1). In the first place, we can expect that social policy has a quantitatively larger role in the institutional than in the marginal policy models. This is indicated by the proportion of GNP used for social purposes as well as by the proportion of the population affected by social policies. An institutional type of social policy can be assumed to enter and to affect the distributive processes at earlier stages than the marginal types of policies. This means that we can expect policies directed towards increasing labour force participation and decreasing unemployment to be more important in the institutional than in the marginal policy models.

Generally, we can expect that, in comparison with the marginal model, the institutional types of social policies will attempt to prevent needs from arising rather than being limited to alleviating needs which already have become manifest.

Further, we would expect universalistic measures, directed towards large sections of the population, to be important in the institutional model of social policy. Selective policies directed towards subgroups of the population with specific needs will be relatively more important in the marginal model. In this model the goal of most policies can be expected to be to provide for a minimum standard of living, whereas in the institutional model we would expect to find a greater stress on achieving a normal or average standard of living. Fees and actuarial principles can be expected to play a greater role in financing programmes in the marginal model, whereas taxation can be assumed to be more important in the institutional model. Generally, we would expect the progressivity of taxation to be higher in the institutional model than in the marginal model. Furthermore, social control, indicated for instance by the extent of stigmatizing individually means-tested programmes and aid in kind, is assumed to be more important in the marginal than in the institutional model. Private welfare organizations can be expected to play a greater role in marginal than in institutional policy contexts.

REDISTRIBUTION IN SOCIAL POLICY

As indicated above, Titmuss saw redistribution as one of the key goals of social policy. However, the issue of redistribution in social policy is a complicated one. A limited set of transfer programmes, constructed according to the marginal model and thus geared to alleviating the needs of the worst-off citizens, may have greater redistributive effects per unit of money spent than institutional types of programmes. On the other hand, the ultimate result of a social policy based on the institutional model can be assumed to be a society with less inequality than can be expected in the case of a marginal social policy.

In the long run, an institutional social policy will decrease inequality more than a marginal type of policy because it tends to have redistributive and political consequences which differ from the marginal type. In areas where universal programmes exist, an institutional social policy decreases inequality by making it possible for the lower socio-economic strata to enjoy roughly the same standard as other groups. For example, medical services for all citizens, based on a national health insurance, public hospitals and publicly employed physicians, can obviously reduce inequality in terms of access and quality of medical care without redistributing money income to the poorest section of the population. In the marginal model, a medical care system with special clinics and hospitals for the poor, for example of the types attempted in the United States, may mean, in relative terms, greater redistribution measured in money but can result in stigmatization and poorer medical treatment for the worst-off citizens.

It is also possible that redistribution of income in well developed welfare states does not occur primarily through welfare benefits but, among other things, through the system of taxation and labour market policy. Variations in the level of employment have been found to affect the distribution of income strongly.[21] Thus a policy creating a high level of employment and a low unemployment rate has important redistributive effects.

THE 'WELFARE BACKLASH'

Different social policy strategies can also have differing consequences in terms of the political support generated for the development of the welfare state. The topical discussion during the 1970s concerning the tax revolts in Denmark and the United States and other expressions of what has been called the 'welfare backlash' seems frequently to be based on the assumption that citizens do not want to pay high taxes, irrespective of what they receive in return for taxes paid. For example, Harold Wilensky argues that the welfare backlash has been avoided only in countries with centralistic, corporative patterns of governments where taxes are not highly visible.[22]

Wilensky's analysis can be criticized on several grounds. His dependent variable, the indicator of the extent of the welfare backlash, is so heterogeneous that practically all conceivable protests and deviations from the 'normal' political pattern are taken as expressions of opposition to welfare policies.[23] The empirical base of his conclusion is very weak.

If we view political actions as rational behaviour, it is not self-evident that a redistributional welfare policy should encounter opposition among the citizens. In the Western countries the distribution of income is negatively skewed so that a majority of the population shares less than half of the total income. At least theoretically, there ought to be a basis for coalition formations which strive to redistribute income in society. This raises the question of what factors impede and facilitate the formation of such coalitions.

The nature of social policy is probably of importance for the extent of support it can generate, the types of coalitions within the electorate which can be created, and thus for the future of the welfare state. Generally we would expect that a marginal type of social policy would have much fewer possibilities than an institutional type of social policy in generating coalitions in its defence. A marginal type of social policy, predominant for example in the United States, explicitly or implicitly draws a poverty line in the population and thus separates the poor and relatively small minority from the better-off majority of the population. A very large part of social policy measures, such as in the War on Poverty in the 1960s, was directed only to those below the poverty line. The negative income tax is another example of this kind of strategy.

But the marginal policy strategy results in a very large portion of the population receiving few direct benefits from social policy measures. Thus a rational base is not given for coalition formation between those above and below the poverty line for a redistributive policy. The poverty line, in effect, splits the working class and tends to generate coalitions between the better-off workers and the middle class against the lower sections of the working class. Marginalistic social policies thus create a large constituency for a welfare backlash (Figure 9.3).

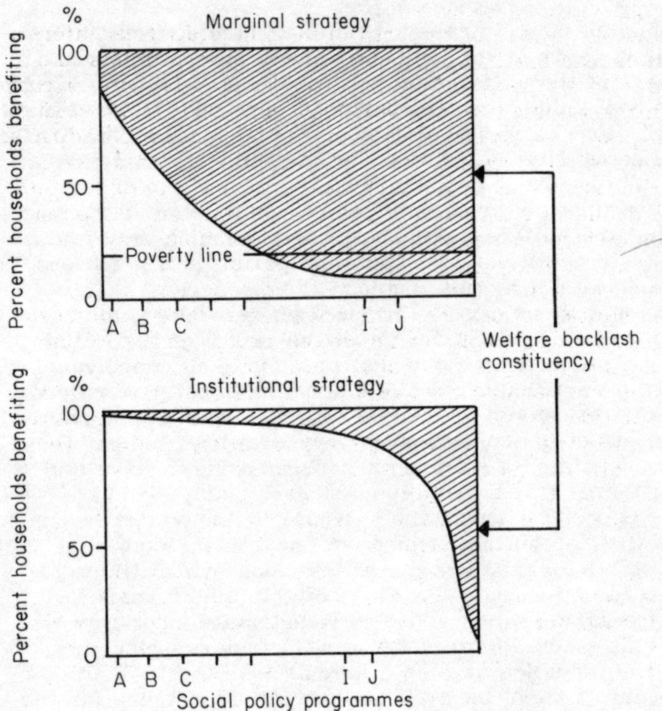

Figure 9.3 Size of welfare backlash constituencies created by marginal and institutional social policy strategies: (a) marginal, (b) institutional

An institutional type of social policy, where universal programmes tend to dominate, benefits most households in one way or another. Thus an institutional type of policy leaves a much smaller constituency for a potential welfare backlash. Instead, it can create rational motives for coalition formation between the working class and the middle class in support for continued welfare state policies. The poor and weak need not therefore stand alone.

POWER DISTRIBUTION AND INEQUALITY

According to our hypothesis, the distribution of power resources between the main collectivities or classes in a country affects the form and direction of public interventions in the distributive processes and thereby the extent of inequality in a country. Here we can only test this hypothesis in a very preliminary fashion in relation to available data on inequality and social policy in our eighteen OECD countries.

Unfortunately, there is a dearth of reliable statistical information which can be used in comparing income distributions in various countries. The best comparative figures available for the OECD countries pertain to the late 1960s and early 1970s and have been published by Malcolm Sawyer.[24] We will here use three of his measures on income inequality pertaining to post-tax household income. The first is the percentage of income going to the top decile in the income distribution. Sawyer also presents two indices of income inequality 'standardized' for size of households. One is the traditional Gini index, which tends to be sensitive primarily to differences in the central part of the income distribution; the other is the variance of logs, which is more sensitive to variations in the proportion of income going to the poorer section of the population. For some countries the OECD has also assembled data from the 1970s on the proportion of the population living in poverty. Here we will use a measure which indicates the percentage of the population living in relative poverty, where the 'poverty line' is 'standardized' according to household size.[25]

Indicators of the redistributive effects of taxation and social policy are difficult to find. On the basis of Sawyer's data, Toshiaki Tachibanaki has computed indices on the impact of taxation on income redistribution.[26] One of his measures of tax redistribution simply takes the difference between pre-tax and post-tax Gini coefficients and divides it by the pre-tax Gini coefficient. We will also use the index of redistributive effects of government budgets during the early 1960s suggested by Christopher Hewitt.[27] This index is based on the ILO measure of the proportion of public expenditures going to social security. On the assumption that direct taxes are more progressive than indirect taxes, this proportion is weighted by the proportion of total taxation which is based on direct taxes. The idea is that redistribution occurs not only on the expenditure side but also on the revenue side.

The level of unemployment in a country depends on many factors, of which the politically determined ones are only one part. Generally, however, we would expect that the choices made by

Table 9.2 Inequality of post-tax income, income redistribution by tax policy, percentage living in relative poverty, and redistributive effects of government budgets by level of working-class mobilization and government control in capitalist democracies

Working-class mobilization and government control		Income inequality: Percentage to top decile	'Standardized' household size: Gini	'Standardized' household size: Variance of logs	Tax re-distri-bution	Percentage poor	Redistributive effect of government budget	Percentage unemployment, 1959-78
		%				%		%
High	Sweden	21.3	0.271	0.060	0.127	3.5	9.5	1.8
mobilization,	Austria						9.3	(1.7)
stable control	Norway	22.2	0.301	0.072	0.133	5.0	6.9	(2.0)
High	Denmark						6.5	(3.9)
mobilization,	New Zealand						6.8	(0.2)
periodic	UK	23.5	0.327	0.080	0.076	7.5	6.8	3.3
control	Belgium							(2.6)
Average-high	Australia	23.7	0.354	0.109	0.003	8.0	4.2	2.1
mobilization,	Finland						5.2	(2.1)
low control	France	30.4	0.417	0.136	0.005	16.0	4.2	2.5
	Italy	30.9						3.8
	Japan	27.2	0.336	0.071	0.057		2.2	1.4
Low	Ireland						2.2	5.7
mobilization,	Canada	25.1	0.348	0.105	0.073	11.0	3.6	5.6
political	USA	26.6	0.369	0.111	0.057	13.0	4.5	5.4
exclusion								
Low-medium	West Germany	30.3	0.386	0.087	0.033	3.0	8.3	1.2
mobilization,	Netherlands	27.7	0.264	0.047	0.081		8.8	(1.8)
partial							5.1	(0.1)
participation								

governments in the inflation-unemployment dilemma, which many Western governments have perceived during the postwar period, have been affected by the political composition of the government. Social democratic governments can be expected to have opted for lower levels of unemployment whereas bourgeois governments more easily may have given priority to fighting inflation.[28] Unemployment figures are difficult to use in cross-national comparisons, because the figures are based on different definitions. For ten countries, however, there are fairly good comparable figures.[29]

The data available on these different categories for our eighteen countries are shown in Table 9.2. The figures indicate that our hypothesis of the consequences of differences in working-class mobilization and control over the government for the distributional processes in these countries receives quite a bit of support.

The countries with highly mobilized working classes and long-term control over governmental power, Sweden and Norway, appear to have less income inequality than most of the other countries for which we have data. They also have relatively small proportions of persons living in poverty. The redistributive effects of taxation are highest for these countries, and they would also appear to have relatively high redistributive effects of government budgets. Their unemployment levels appear to have been relatively low.

Among countries having highly mobilized working classes with only sporadic government control, we lack data on income distribution except for the United Kingdom, which has fairly low levels of income inequality and relative poverty. Its tax system appears redistributive. Also, government budgets appear to be relatively highly distributive in this category of countries. The levels of unemployment, however, have been relatively high in Britain and Denmark although very low in New Zealand.

In the two categories of countries where socialist parties have been more or less excluded from participation in government, inequalities in income distribution are relatively high. France, Italy and the United States have especially high income inequalities. The proportions living in relative poverty are also fairly high in these countries, and their government budgets do not appear to be markedly redistributive. Especially in Australia and France the tax systems have little redistributive effects. Japan is perhaps an exception here, since it appears to have a relatively low income inequality.[30] While the level of unemployment has been very high in the United States, Canada, Ireland and Italy, it has been very low in Japan.

In the category of countries where the working class has a medium or low mobilization but where socialist parties have a tradition of participating in governments, several interesting observations can be made. The Netherlands has a relatively high proportion of income going to the top decile. However, when we 'standardize' for household size the Netherlands receives the lowest value of all these countries on our indices on income inequality, clearly lower than what our indicators of the power distribution would lead us to expect. West Germany has an above-average inequality. However, the lowest deciles of the German income distribution appear to receive a relatively large proportion of income, something which is reflected in the lower value of the variance of logs as well as in the low proportion of the population living in relative poverty. The government budgets in these two countries seem to be relatively redistributive. This however is not the case in Switzerland, which probably also has a fairly high income inequality. The levels of unemployment have been low in this category of countries. For comparative purposes, the Swiss unemployment figures are misleading, since most of the so-called guest workers are probably excluded from the unemployment statistics.

The relationships between the indicators of inequality in the countries for which information is given in Table 9.2 and the distribution of power resources in these countries can be summarized by correlation coefficients. As our indicators of power resource distributions we will take union density and the 'weighted cabinet share for the left parties'. The latter measure is the product of the average left proportion of cabinet seats, the mean share of left seats in the parliament, and the time with left representation in government (cf. Chapter 3) but is unfortunately highly skewed. The two power resource indicators both have relatively large negative correlations with the indicators on inequality (Table 9.3). This consistent pattern is thus in agreement with my hypothesis that the relative position of the working class in terms of collective power resources affects the degree of inequality in capitalist democracies.

Table 9.3 Correlations between indicators of distribution of power resources and indicators of inequality in some OECD countries in the 1960s and 1970s

	Distribution of post-tax household income						
Distribution of power resources	Percentage to top decile	Gini	Variance	Tax redistribution	Percentage poor	Redistributive effects of gov't budget	Percentage unemployed 1959-78
	%				%		%
Union density	-0.78	-0.52	-0.39	-0.47	-0.71	-0.59	-0.37
Weighted cabinet share	-0.70	-0.62	-0.50	-0.78	-0.62	-0.64	-0.34

Levels of unemployment, however, appear to be only weakly related to the relative power position of wage-earners in the ten OECD countries for which we have comparable data. Apparently unemployment figures are affected by many factors of which political measures are only one part.

TOO MUCH WELFARE POLICY?

It is often assumed that welfare states have been developed in a spirit of political consensus. Thus, for instance, in the Swedish case it is argued that, because social policy measures were viewed as a solution to the problem of low birth rates in the 1930s, 'the Swedish welfare state was launched on the basis of political unity'.[31]

This interpretation of history must be questioned. The actual development of the Swedish welfare state has frequently involved political struggles over social policy issues. Political controversy concerning rules for public work projects for the unemployed forced two Social Democratic minority governments to resign in the 1920s. A proposed pension reform contributed to the fall of the Social Democratic government in 1936. Conflicts over policies for full employment and the supplementary pension scheme occurred in the 1950s. During the early postwar period, bourgeois spokesmen called for less ambitious employment measures than the full-employment policy advocated by the Social Democrats. The struggle over the supplementary pension scheme led to the resignation of the Social Democratic government in 1958 and to (so far) the only extra election to the Riksdag since the introduction of universal suffrage. Of six Social Democratic government resignations, four have thus been related to controversies involving the development of the welfare state.

Influenced by the Social Democrats' growing electoral support up through the early 1940s, the bourgeois parties however gravitated to the left. The Liberals, who adopted a new programme emphasizing 'social liberalism' in the mid-1940s, accepted the expansion of social insurance schemes.[32] Once social reforms have been implemented, they have also been generally accepted even by their earlier opponents. Social reform offensives and subsequent acceptance have moved the frontier of party conflicts in Swedish politics to the left. Higher taxes necessary to finance the reforms, however, have continuously generated controversy.

During the postwar period public expenditures in Sweden have risen sharply, from approximately one-third to slightly over one-half of GNP. A growing proportion of public expenditures has gone to business in the form of subventions and grants, but expenditures associated with the welfare state have also markedly increased. Simultaneously, the tax burden has grown, and since 1960 particularly for those taxes which are not progressive, primarily the value-added tax. Public expenditures and the level of taxation in Sweden are therefore among the highest in the Western countries.

The 1970 witnessed tax revolts and welfare backlashes in several Western countries. In Sweden, however, political controversies involving social insurance and employment policy were fairly low-keyed during most of the 1960s and 1970s. It must be noted for instance that, in contrast to British Conservatives and American Republicans, the Swedish bourgeois parties did not publicly attack the welfare state in the election campaigns of 1976 and 1979. On the contrary, the Liberals and the Centre Party in particular were anxious to portray themselves as supporters of welfare policies and as equally good guardians of the welfare state as the Social Democrats. To retain political credibility on this issue, throughout the 1970s the bourgeois governments largely continued previous Social Democratic social policies. However, at the same time they instituted changes, for example in taxation policies, which mostly benefited high-income households. In the context of increasing budget deficits, in the early 1980s bourgeois governments proposed and carried through significant cuts in various social policy programmes, including pensions, health insurance and unemployment insurance, something which again aroused strong political conflicts in the area of social policy.

The question of the extent of popular support for the Swedish welfare state, and thus the preconditions for more fundamental changes in its construction, is of both theoretical and political interest. To some extent, this question can be elucidated through an analysis of data on public opinion related to this complex of issues. Unfortunately, social scientists have made few attempts to describe public opinion concerning different aspects of the welfare state. Probably there are widely differing evaluations of its various components in the electorate. For example, the pension system is not a very controversial matter, whereas social assistance and certain types of allowances may be heavily criticized. Frequently attitude surveys have tried to cover the entire range of policies with a single question. The results are thus difficult to interpret. The distribution of responses is also affected by the phrasing of both the questions and the response alternatives, and therefore does not indicate very much about the absolute level of support for the welfare state. But since similar questions have been asked during different periods, this provides certain possibilities to illuminate changes in attitudes towards social policy.

The Swedish welfare state appears to have formed an important and positive element in Swedes' conceptions of their country. This comes out in the responses to a question posed to young people between the ages of eighteen and twenty-four in several Western countries in the winter of 1977-8: 'Do you think that (your country) has something to be proud of or not?' The proportion answering that their country could be proud of its social welfare was nearly two-thirds in Sweden, a little under one-half in the United Kingdom and much lower in the other Western countries (Table 9.4). Young people in West Germany and

Switzerland, in contrast, were most often proud of their standard of living, Americans of their science and technology, and French youth of their country's history and cultural heritage.[33]

Table 9.4 'Do you think that (your country) has something to be proud of or not?' Proportion mentioning social welfare among youth aged eighteen to twenty-four years in various countries

	%
Sweden	60
UK	45
West Germany	30
Switzerland	25
United States	24
France	11

Two questions in polls conducted by Sifo during the 1960s and 1970s suggest that popular support for social policy has not changed markedly during these two decades. One of these questions read: 'Sweden is known for its social policy. Is there some aspect of this social policy which you dislike or do you generally like it? Which of the following answers comes closest to your opinion?' The percentages choosing the alternative 'Social policy has gone too far; reliance on welfare and a poor sense of responsibility follow in its tracks' was 33 per cent in 1964 and 36 per cent in 1978 (Table 9.5). Another question dealt with the costs of social policy: 'Do you think that our current social programmes are too expensive and therefore ought to be reduced?' The proportion answering 'yes' was 34 per cent in 1967 and 39 per cent in 1978.

In the SCB election surveys the respondents since 1960 have been asked whether they agree or disagree with the statement; 'Social reforms have now gone so far in this country that in the future the government ought to reduce rather than increase allowances and assistance to the citizens.' The results show a fairly large stability in the distribution of responses (Table 9.6).[34] In the 1979 election there was some increase in the percentage agreeing with the statement. The 1968 election stands out as an exception when the proportion agreeing was low.

The proportion displaying a negative attitude to social policy as a response to the above question is substantially larger than in the two earlier questions, something which at least partly reflects the fact that it is easier for the respondents to agree than to disagree with statements of this sort. Unfortunately, we do not know which reforms the respondents have in mind when they agree with the statement. In view of the rapid expansion of the public sector since 1960, it is noteworthy that the opposition to additional social reforms does not seem to have increased up to 1976. This expansion however has been accompanied by several problems; for instance, there has been widespread discussion about 'fiddling' with earnings-related housing allowances. Attacks on social policy can therefore have gained a somewhat better basis at the end of the 1970s.

Table 9.5 Swedish attitudes towards social policy, 1964, 1967 and 1978

'Sweden is known for its social policy. Is there some aspect of this social policy which you dislike or do you generally like it? Which of the following answers comes closest to your opinion?'

	1964	1978
	%	%
Social policy is generally worth what it costs, but certain features ought to be expanded.	19	14
Social policy is generally satisfactory as it is, but means tests ought to apply to more benefits.	45	45
Social policy has gone too far; reliance on welfare and a poor sense of responsibility follow in its tracks.	33	36
Hesitant, don't know.	2	6
	100	100

'Do you think that our current social programmes are too expensive and therefore ought to be reduced?'

	1967	1978
	%	%
Yes	34	39
No	50	47
Don't know	16	14
	100	100

An analysis of the responses to the above statement on social reforms in the 1976 election survey indicates that the most negative views are found among farmers and small businessmen (Table 9.7). Middle-level salaried employees and social group I, which largely consists of high-level salaried employees, had a more negative attitude than workers, but the differences are not great. Thus among employees the attitude towards social reforms does not differ strongly between various socio-economic strata. Instead it is primarily the entrepreneurial groups which markedly deviate from the wage-earners. Attitudes towards social reforms are however clearly related to party preferences. The proportion who are negative to these reforms increases as we move from the Communists to the Conservatives.

Table 9.6 'Social reforms have gone so far in this country that in the future the government ought to reduce rather than increase allowances and assistance to citizens.'

	1960	1964	1968	1970	1973	1976	1979
	%	%	%	%	%	%	%
Agree	60	66	46	62	65	65	71
Disagree	40	34	54	39	35	35	29
	100	100	100	100	100	100	100

Table 9.7 Responses to the statement that social reforms have gone too far, by social group and party choice in 1976

	Workers	Social group II Salaried employees	Social group II Small businessmen	Farmers	Social group I
	%	%	%	%	%
Agree	56	62	72	85	65
Disagree	36	32	21	8	31
Don't know	8	6	7	7	4
	100	100	100	100	100
	Party choice				
	Comm.	SD	Lib.	Centre	Cons.
	%	%	%	%	%
Agree	27	44	73	78	84
Disagree	69	49	23	16	13
Don't know	4	8	4	7	3
	100	100	100	100	100

The data presented here suggest that, at least up to 1976, the opposition to welfare policy did not increase in Sweden. On the other hand, certain aspects of social policy, such as social assistance, have traditionally been viewed with considerable scepticism by the voters. However, since taxes have been a bone of contention during the entire postwar period, it seems reasonable to assume that Swedish voters have consciously opted for the welfare state. The electoral decline of the Social Democrats in the 1970s therefore can hardly be explained in terms of opposition to the welfare state.

. . . OR TOO LITTLE WELFARE?

If the voters did not turn their backs on the Social Democrats because of too much welfare policy, they may have instead done so because their welfare deteriorated or became more insecure. During the postwar period certain indicators, which reflect changes in the welfare of the working class, suggest that this interpretation is plausible.

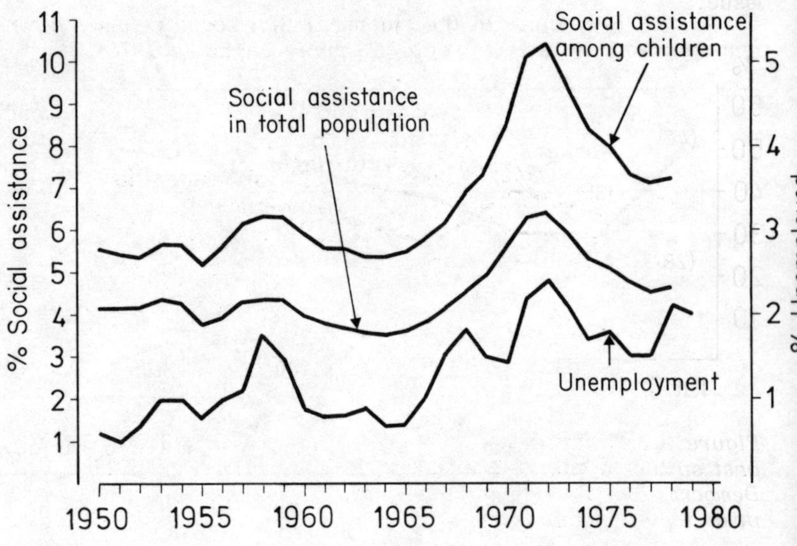

Figure 9.4 Percentage of unemployed persons and recipients of social assistance in population and among children up to sixteen years, 1950-79

Unemployment figures and data on means-tested social assistance are fairly good indicators of changes in the economic situation of the workers. The large majority of unemployed persons and recipients of social assistance are workers. After the economic recession in 1958 unemployment in Sweden was fairly low until the mid-1960s, when it began to climb sharply (Figure 9.4).[35] Following a brief economic upswing in 1969 unemployment rose again and remained at a high level during 1971-3.

The increase in unemployment in the early 1970s undercut one of the Social Democrats' most powerful political arguments, viz. that only they could guarantee full employment. In an interview survey a few months before the 1968 election Sifo inquired: 'What sort of government do you believe would be best suited to ensure employment in the country, a Social Democratic or a bourgeois government?' The responses reveal that the Social Democratic government enjoyed very strong confidence of the electorate on the employment issue prior to the 1968 election (Figure 9.5).[36] In the months before the elections in 1970 and in 1973, however, the alternative of a bourgeois government received a higher rating on this issue among the voters. Before the 1976 and 1979 election the Social Democrats had regained a lead on this issue. Half a year before the 1982 election the Social Democrats again had a record lead on the unemployment issue.

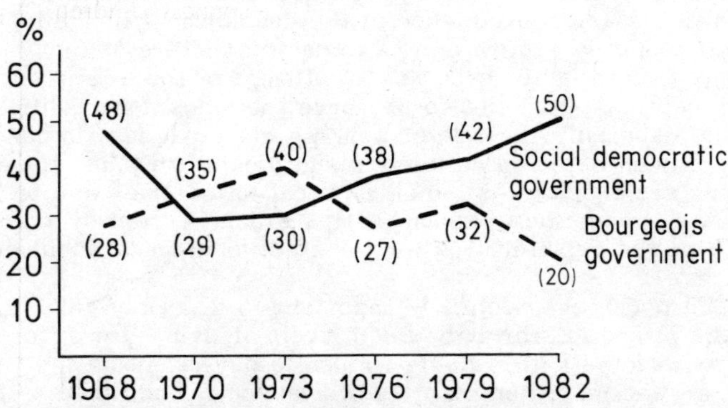

Figure 9.5 'What sort of government do you believe would be best suited to ensure employment in the country, a Social Democratic or bourgeois government?' Distribution of responses prior to the elections in 1968-82

Increases in means-tested social assistance are closely related to changes in unemployment and prices. In the mid-1960s the lowest figures during the postwar period for the proportion of recipients of social assistance were recorded. Subsequently, however, a rapid increase occurred, and in 1972 the social assistance rate was comparable to figures for the 1940s. The increase was especially pronounced among families with children, particularly those in the new suburbs with multi-family housing in the metropolitan areas. This increase in the social assistance rate was halted only by the introduction of a large programme of earnings-related housing allowances, at first allotted to families with children and later extended to all low-income groups.[37]

In the late 1960s and the early 1970s undoubtedly large sections of the working class were subject to growing economic pressures and increasing job insecurity. During these years the electorate and not least the core voters of the Social Democrats felt that the Social Democratic government had failed to increase and preserve the welfare of large groups of citizens. The election surveys show that the proportion of voters stating that the Social Democratic government's policy had benefited their own socio-economic group clearly decreased from the 1960s through the 1970s.[38] This decrease occurred also among those who had voted for the Social Democrats. Apparently it was not any too-ambitious efforts to expand welfare policy, but rather the failure of Social Democratic policy in preserving welfare which has been the central factor underlying the party's decline in the elections during the 1970s.

SOCIAL POLICY

Many social scientists have viewed the growth of the welfare state as a necessary consequence of the development of industrial society, of economic growth and of the age structure of the population. Others have seen it as an attempt of the dominating groups in capitalist societies to preserve their position. Political factors and especially the role of working-class parties, in contrast, have been depicted as fairly insignificant. In part, these conclusions are based on dubious empirical foundations and on too narrow a conception of social policy, which is often synonymous with public expenditures for the traditional social insurance programmes.

For social policy research it is important to describe and explain the processes through which levels of living are differentiated in society, and in doing so also to pay attention to public interventions other than traditional social insurance. Among the central tasks of social policy research is the analysis of how inequality among the citizens arises and how it can be counteracted. I have argued here for a research approach to the distribution of welfare in the capitalist democracies, which depart from the hypothesis that the distribution of power resources among the main collectivities in society is of essential importance for the distributive processes and for the forms and effects of public measures intervening in these processes. This hypothesis differs from both the pluralist theories and the Leninist interpretation of Marxian theory.

Surprisingly enough in social policy research, typologies, concepts or dimensions enabling us to describe the level of welfare-state development in different countries have not yet been formulated. The social policy literature however has hinted at two polar types of social policy systems. One is a limited 'marginal' type of social policy, which primarily seeks to assist the poorest citizens. The other is an 'institutional' social policy, which can be expected to play a major role in the distributive processes of society. Here I have attempted to specify the properties which can be assumed to characterize these two different ideal types of social policy.

Swedish social policy during the postwar period appears to have increasingly developed in the direction of an institutional social policy. Since such a social policy benefits the vast majority of households in one way or another, it can be expected to generate relatively strong political support among voters. Even if the political struggles over the introduction of social policy measures have often been intense, the measures have eventually been accepted by the parties and voters. This acceptance has been a part of the movement of political battle lines towards the left.

As distinct from several other Western countries, Sweden in the 1970s did not experience an intense 'welfare backlash'. The welfare state seems to be fairly firmly entrenched among the voters. The rapid expansion of certain allowance systems during the 1970s, however, has to some degree made them more vulnerable to political attacks. During the entire period, high taxes have been a major political issue. The Social Democratic setbacks in the elections since 1968 cannot be explained by increasing opposition to the welfare state among the voters, however. On the contrary, it seems to be the failure of welfare policy to ensure employment and the standard of living of workers and low-income groups which has been fundamental for the Social Democrats' losses.

The 1980s were ushered in by sharp attacks on major parts of Swedish welfare policy from conservative quarters and proposals by the bourgeois government for cutbacks in social policy measures. Thus social policy has re-emerged as a central issue of conflict in Swedish politics. In the following chapter we will return to the conflictual political scene in Sweden during the first half of the 1980s.

10 AFTER THE HISTORICAL COMPROMISE

The historical compromise of the 1930s lasted for roughly forty years. During the 1970s, however, the foundations of the compromise crumbled. As the 1980s began, the Swedes stood amidst the fragments of the old model, attempting to get their bearings as they searched for new solutions to serious economic problems. In this chapter we shall discuss the background to the disintegration of the historical compromise and the preconditions for alternative courses of political development in Sweden. Since labour's disadvantage in power resources in relation to business interests is probably smaller in Sweden than in other Western nations, an analysis of political possibilities in Sweden is of general interest. In the course of the discussion we shall summarize some of the arguments made in previous chapters.

THE END OF AN ERA

Briefly summarized, the orienting hypothesis of this study is that it is fruitful to view societal change as a result of citizen endeavours to solve important problems confronting them. A key part of these problems is generated by conflicts of interest in the sphere of production. These conflicts of interest tend to lead to cleavages and to the formation of collectivities or classes on the basis of the relationships to the means of production. The distribution of power resources between collectivities and classes affects the definition of social problems as well as the possible solutions to them. In the capitalist democracies, wage-earners generally have less power resources than those who control the means of production. The degree of the disadvantage in power resources of the wage-earners depends, however, on the extent and unity of their collective organizations, primarily unions and working-class-based political parties. Their disadvantage in power resources can thus vary significantly over time as well as between countries. The degree of disadvantage in power resources of wage-earners in relation to business interests is of key importance for the understanding of politics and distributive conflicts in the Western nations.

By underlining the basic importance of conflicts of interests generated in the sphere of production and the relative disadvantage in power resources of wage-earners, the approach developed here differs from the pluralist industrial model presently dominant in the social sciences. The assumption that the extent of subordination of wage-earners is not given by the mode of production but can vary significantly over time as well as between countries, is contrary to the Leninist interpretation of Marx. In contrast to neo-corporatist writers, who assume that the representation of wage-earners' interests through their organizations has become perverted and largely turned into a more or less successful social control of the members of these organizations, I have assumed that the interaction between labour, capital and the state that developed during the postwar period in countries like Sweden must be seen as a process of societal bargaining. In this bargaining process outcomes are not pre-determined but depend largely on the distribution of power resources between the parties. The relative strength and stability of left control over the government can significantly affect the actions of state representatives and thus the pattern of coalition formation in this tripartite bargaining.

The analyses in this book indicate that in Sweden, as well as in most other Western countries, classes and socio-economic cleavages continue to form a main basis for political life and distributive conflicts. We have repeatedly noted that the extent and unity of working-class-based organizations are of significance for the forms as well as for the outcomes of these conflicts. Upon closer inspection, Sweden - by many corporatist writers seen as the very apotheosis of the neo-corporatist model - fails to conform to the assumptions of this model.

Political developments in Sweden can however more easily be interpreted in terms of the power distribution model suggested here. As we have seen, at the turn of the century the growing labour movement could define the restriction of voting rights to the better-off strata as a central problem in Swedish society. In the Social Democratic Party during the interwar period, the reformist road to socialism was increasingly conceived of as three consecutive steps: political, social and economic democracy.

The first step, the introduction of universal suffrage in 1921, did not suffice. In a parliamentary speech in 1928, explicating the Social Democratic concept of Folkhemmet (the 'People's Home'), Per Albin Hansson, then leader of the opposition, stated: 'The Swedish society is not yet the good home for the people. To be sure, formal equality in political rights prevails here, but socially the class society remains and economically the dictatorship of the minority prevails.'[1] In the Social Democratic ideological tradition, the concept of Folkhemmet thus included not only political and social democracy, but also the abolition of the 'economic dictatorship of the minority'. Work on the second step in the development of the People's Home, a socially just distribution of welfare, could start when the labour movement gained a firm grip over governmental power. When this occurred in the 1930s, it generated a 'historical compromise' between the labour movement and business interests.

The separation of governmental and economic power was the most important prerequisite for the historical compromise concluded between labour and business interests in Sweden during the latter half of the 1930s. The formula for the compromise was that the labour movement 'admitted the necessity of maintaining favourable conditions for private enterprise' but could use governmental power to achieve full employment and a fairer distribution of economic growth. This formula led to a 'Swedish model' for the management of conflicts of interest between capital and labour which entailed benefits, but also disadvantages, for the wage-earners.

The erosion of the historical compromise of the 1930s began with the gradual emptying of its political formula. Since the 1960s the bourgeois parties were able to win votes by criticizing the shortcomings of the compromise's policy, problems such as centralization, regional imbalances and environmental degradation. Within the labour movement, criticism was also levelled against conditions at workplaces and the increasing concentration of ownership and power in the private sector of the economy. In addition, the prime advantages of the compromise, strong economic growth and full employment, became increasingly difficult to achieve.

But the compromise was also undermined by a slow change in the power relations which were once its prerequisite. The increase in power resources of course affected both business interests and labour, but on the whole it seems to have favoured the wage-earners. When the historical compromise emerged, the inferior position of the wage-earners vis-a-vis capital was still very sharp. During the postwar years their inferiority gradually decreased, primarily because of the spectacular increase in the wage-earners' propensity and capability to act collectively rather than individually, manifested in the rising level of unionization. As we have seen, the level of unionization in Sweden during the 1970s reached a unique world record.

During the postwar period the gradual increase in the power resources of the wage-earners provided the basis for efforts to advance their positions. The miners' strike in northern Sweden in 1969-70 and the subsequent wave of unofficial strikes contributed to the re-orientation of the labour movement. In the 1970s the inadequate influence of the wage-earners at the workplace became increasingly viewed as a serious problem in society. Not merely in theory and rhetoric but also through concrete proposals, the labour movement challenged managerial prerogatives based on control of company shares.

The labour movement's departure from the political formula of the historical compromise was marked by LO and the Social Democrats initiating a series of reforms aimed at limiting managerial prerogatives at the workplace. In connection with the enactment of the most comprehensive reform, the Joint Consultation Act (MBL) in 1976, LO terminated the Saltsjöbaden Agreement with SAF, the agreement which had been the symbolic cornerstone of the historical compromise. LO's proposal for wage-earners' funds in 1975 underscored that the labour movement intended to enter the struggle for power in the economy.

Simultaneously, the business community mobilized its forces. Within SAF, ever since the 1930s, there has been an internal conflict among proponents of a compromise strategy and the advocates of a confrontation strategy. Immediately after World War II, the advocates of a militant strategy had gained the upper hand and launched an intensive campaign - 'opposition to the planned economy' - against the postwar programme of the Social Democrats. When the controversy subsided after the 1948 election, a long period of co-operation with LO followed. During the 1970s the strategy of confrontation regained currency in SAF, something which was indicated in the election of its new chairman in 1976. In the autumn of the same year, the remnants of the preconditions for the compromise disappeared, when the Social Democrats lost governmental power. With a bourgeois government, SAF could mount a counter-offensive. The general lockout four years later underscored the fact that the historical compromise had definitely ceased to exist.

CONDITIONS FOR ELECTORAL SUPPORT

In what directions will Swedish politics develop after the demise of the historical compromise of the 1930's? Of central importance in this context are the long-term changes in the preconditions for bourgeois and socialist politics. What, then, are the basic differences between socialist and bourgeois politics? Central lines of cleavage between the blocs concern equality and the economic organization of production. Socialist politics can be assumed to aim at decreasing inequality among the citizens not only with respect to opportunities but also in terms of results and - in the long run - at replacing private ownership of the means of production by an order where the large private corporations ultimately are democratically governed. Bourgeois politics in the area of inequality range from those who want to create equal opportunities to those who desire greater inequalities. A fundamental feature of a bourgeois policy is the preservation of private ownership of the means of production.

Generally speaking, three circumstances affect the conditions for electoral support of the socialist bloc (and conversely the bourgeois bloc) and thus the future course of politics in Sweden. These circumstances concern the interest base of politics, how policy proposals are put across to the voters, and the content and consequences of the pursued policy.

In the first place, socialist politics must have a structural interest base in the population. This means that a sufficient proportion of the population must have such a position in society or such a social situation that - at least in principle - socialist policies can provide solutions to their problems. Second, these policies must be capable of being presented to the electorate so that the voters perceive of socialist policies as feasible solutions to their problems. Third the content and consequences of the policies of the socialist parties, especially when they are in government, must increase solidarity among the wage-earners and strengthen the voters' confidence that these parties have long-range solutions to their basic problems.

Changes in these three types of conditions need not all work in the same direction - combining either to improve or worsen the chances of success for socialist or bourgeois politics. Instead, we must expect that different changes may counteract one another. The effects of these changes can be deciphered in the electoral support for the two blocs, in shifts in the frontier of party conflict along the left-right axis, and in the capacity of the wage-earners for collective rather than individual action.

CHANGES IN CLASS STRUCTURE

A major change, which has gradually broadened the interest base of a socialist policy, is that growing proportions of the economically active population have become wage-earners. At the end of World War II, among economically active men nearly one out of four was still self-employed; the vast majority of them were farmers and a smaller portion were small businessmen. In the 1970s only about every tenth economically active male was self-employed. The remainder, over 90 per cent, were wage-earners. An overwhelming portion of the Swedish population therefore now finds itself in the same class situation. Clearly, socialist politics in principle are more in accord with the interests of wage-earners than with the interests of the self-employed.

Concurrently, however, among wage-earners there have occurred changes which affect the interest base of the politics as well as the possibilities of putting policies across to the voters. These changes are reflected in the distribution of wage-earners between different socio-economic strata and sectors of the economy. Since 1920 the percentage of workers in the electorate (social group III) has been largely constant, approximately 50 per cent. This also applies to the proportion of occupational categories classified as workers in census statistics up to 1965. Within these broad categories, however, important changes have taken place.

The decline in agricultural employment has been offset primarily by an increase of workers and salaried employees in the manufacturing and service sectors. The greatest relative increase among wage-earners since the 1930s has been among salaried employees. The proportions of persons employed in manufacturing rose until the mid-1960s but has subsequently fallen, a decline which has been accelerated by the crisis in Swedish industry.[2] These changes affect the wage-earners' situation on the labour market and at the workplace as well as their status.[3] Consequently, they influence the mobilizing possibilities of the parties.

Although salaried employees and workers are in the same class situation, their positions on the labour market and at the workplace are partly different. Traditionally, salaried employees have enjoyed much greater job security and possibilities of promotion than the workers. To some extent however these differences have decreased, partly because the tremendous growth of white-collar employees has altered the composition of the group as a whole. The major part of the new white-collar jobs are not positions where the employee exercises authority delegated from the employer. The expansion has probably occurred primarily in jobs involving staff functions, in the public sector and in less qualified jobs.[4] The new groups of salaried employees cannot be equated with the traditional white-collar employees, who were frequently the representatives and extended arms of management.

The differences between workers and salaried employees in their position on the labour market, as reflected in the risks of unemployment, have decreased. Up to the end of the 1960s unemployment almost always struck the workers. Since then younger salaried employees have frequently experienced unemployment.[5] Even if income differentials between salaried employees and workers have remained largely unchanged, differences have been reduced with regard to working hours, pensions, vacations and sickness benefits. Of course, white-collar occupations are still generally considered to offer more favourable conditions than worker occupations. Status differences in the original sense of respect for and deference to persons holding certain occupations, however, have declined markedly.[6] Major differences in the work environment and opportunities for personal development determined by the nature of the job persist.[7]

Changes in social stratification and occupational structure have thus affected the mobilizing possibilities of the party blocs in a variety of ways. Until the mid-1960s these changes clearly favoured the socialist bloc, in so far as the industrial sector grew whereas the agricultural sector shrank. Subsequently the picture becomes more complicated. During the 1970s there was some decline in the industrial sector while the service sector continued to grow. Foreign competition has contributed to the industrial decline, and the drop in industrial employment may become hastened by the increasing utilization of microcomputers in industrial production. These trends have been advantageous for the bourgeois bloc.

The significance of declining industrial employment however is often exaggerated. It is forgotten that the class base for socialist politics has been broadened and that the main features of social stratification have remained unaltered. Around half of the electorate still are workers, i.e., belong to social group III. The dissimilarities in the voting patterns of electors in different sectors of the economy have stemmed only partially from contextual factors related to the sectors of the economy. In the middle strata the new white-collar groups form a much less stable electoral base for the bourgeois bloc than the farmers once did. For the socialist bloc the decreasing proportion of industrial workers in social group III is probably more than outweighed by changes in the middle strata. Even if in the 1970s trends of development in the size of the various sectors of the economy, social stratification and class affiliation have become difficult to judge, the changes through the mid-1960s, on the whole, seem to have favoured the socialist bloc.

Public employees appear to vote for the socialist parties to a somewhat greater extent than persons employed in the private sector. Among higher-level salaried employees, this partially reflects the fact that political values influence the choice of employment in the public sector. The differences, however, can also be due to the vested interests of public employees in maintaining and expanding the public sector. The growth of public sector employment can therefore to some extent improve the mobilizing possibilities of the socialist parties.[8]

On the other hand, growing immigration during the postwar period has clearly worsened the mobilizing possibilities of the socialist parties. The proportion of foreign citizens in the population increased from roughly 1 per cent at the end of the war to 5 per cent in the 1970s. Most of the immigrants have been workers. The increasing immigration can lead to ethnic cleavages in the working class. The immigrants seldom vote in the country of their origin, where they formally have the right to vote. In Sweden as in several other countries, the factors causing immigration have in effect deprived considerable numbers of workers of the right to vote.

During the 1970s about 10 per cent of the members of LO have thus not been entitled to vote in parliamentary elections. In the county council and municipal elections, where immigrants received the right to vote in 1976, participation is much lower among immigrants than among Swedish-born voters.[9] The significance of the immigrants' right to vote is demonstrated by the fact that, while the socialist parties narrowly lost the parliamentary election in 1979, they received a slight majority of the votes simultaneously cast in the county council elections. The relative strength of the parties in the coming years is thus highly dependent upon whether the right to vote in parliamentary elections is extended to all permanent residents of Sweden or remains tied to citizenship.

The changing position of women on the labour market and in society can also be expected to affect the electoral support for the blocs. Housewives have traditionally been considered more conservative than their husbands.[10] The proportion of working women between the ages of twenty-five and forty-eight remained around 30 per cent until 1950 but increased to 37 per cent in 1960, further rose to 51 per cent in 1970, and totalled 80 per cent in 1979.[11] Even if roughly half of these women have part-time jobs, their entry into the labour market means that the majority of all women acquire experiences as wage-earners. These experiences are of a mixed nature but can generally be expected to improve the labour parties' mobilizing possibilities.[12] Certain changes in occupational roles, for instance the disappearance of large numbers of women in domestic service whose electoral participation was extremely low, can be assumed to have similar effects.

The interest base stemming from class affiliations of the voters can also be eroded if large groups of wage-earners acquire ownership interests. The probability of such a development is greatest in the area of housing. The housing policy pursued in Sweden until the beginning of the 1970s contributed to a decrease in the proportion living in single-family dwellings, from 54 per cent in 1945 to 42 per cent in 1975.[13] Since 1975 the proportion living in single-family dwellings has increased. The acceptance of market principles for the pricing of co-operative flats, along with experiments in other forms of occupier ownership of flats, have contributed to an increasing fragmentation of interests among wage-earners. Experiences from Denmark, for example, indicate that a housing policy which created a division of interests among those living in rented flats, owner-occupant flats and single-family dwellings can have serious repercussions on the electoral support of the Social Democratic party.[14]

PROSPERITY AND SOCIAL PROBLEMS

The notion that a rising standard of living and changing consumption patterns will cause budding socialism to wither on the vine has a long tradition. When workers at the beginning of the century could afford a ready-made suit, some observers believed that class unity and consciousness would dissolve. During the 1950s a leading thesis was that a rising standard of living, increased prosperity and new life-styles would lead the 'embourgeoisement' of the working class.[15] During the 1970s similar ideas cropped up in the notion of the 'commercialization' of the wage-earners in the 'gadget society'.

However, it has been shown that the theory of the embourgeoisement of the working class scarcely holds up when put to an empirical test.[16] The theory has glossed over the fact that it is not the size of income or consumption patterns but the conditions under which one earns an income which are ultimately decisive for the political allegiances of the voters.

It can be argued that, as such, a rising standard of living and secure employment ought to improve rather than detract from the possibilities of mobilizing support for socialist politics. Once minimum needs are satisfied, people's aspirations can grow to include influence at the workplace and personal development on the job. Efforts to satisfy these sorts of needs can lead people to question the present distribution of power in the economy. Obviously this does not happen automatically. Political alternatives must be formulated in a way which makes such a choice a realistic possibility.

Whereas the argument of the embourgeoisement of the working class assumes that material conditions of the workers will improve to the extent that workers will abandon the socialist parties, in the Swedish debate in recent years the same conclusion has been drawn on the basis of diametrically opposed assumptions. It is argued that economic growth has entailed serious problems and difficulties which will demobilize the working class. This line of argument is related to the realization in the 1960s in most Western countries that there was not a direct correlation between economic growth and the welfare of the people. The severed relationship between growth and welfare became apparent first with the increasing destruction of the environment.

In the 1960s, the years of record economic expansion and naive optimism in progress, critical voices had pointed out that welfare was an unfinished task. During the 1970s there was a swing of the pendulum among Swedish intellectuals. Welfare now suddenly seemed to be an impossibility. Social conditions and community life were seen as deteriorating. Critics pointed to growing numbers of people at the margins of society, the dissolution of the family, social isolation, the impoverishment of cultural life, and privatization instead of community involvement. Changing housing patterns were seen as undermining the possibilities of the labour parties winning voters by dispersing the core groups of the labour movement in the 'red company-towns' like chaff before the wind in a bourgeois Sweden. Economic growth, large-scale technology, urbanization and centralization were identified as the key forces behind this course of development.

To a significant extent, these warnings were justified. In other respects, however, the criticisms from many intellectuals were chiefly expressions of a newly awakened interest in social problems which had not yet been put in an adequate historical and comparative perspective.[17] We can here only discuss some of the problems which have a direct bearing on the capacity of the political blocs to gain electoral support.

One of the consequences of the increasing standard of living during the postwar period, in Sweden as in other industrial countries, has been an increase in the consumption of alcohol and in alcoholism. The liberalization of earlier restrictions on alcohol has contributed to this increase. In addition, the use of drugs has increased. If one were to judge from the amount of concern and debate surrounding alcohol and drugs in Sweden, one would think that the Swedes were being inundated with alcohol and drugs. Compared internationally, however, consumption of alcohol in Sweden is fairly low. Among twenty Western countries, Sweden ranked fifteenth in the consumption of alcohol in 1968-70.[18] In an international perspective drug abuse would also appear to be limited. It is instead the generally high level of social concern among the Swedes which generates the intensive debate on these issues.

The increases in alcoholism and drug abuse however have contributed to and exacerbated other problems, including criminality and phenomena which have been termed 'social elimination'. The concept of social elimination has been applied in a variety of ways. It is often used to describe persons who are not gainfully employed although for certain reasons they ought to be. The large increase in female employment has resulted in a rise in the proportion of economically active persons in the population during the 1970s. But among men there is an opposite trend. Since the early 1960s the proportion of men in the labour force has fallen somewhat in age groups over forty-five years. The decline in the labour force participation has been most pronounced among unmarried men. In ages over fifty-five years a definite decline has also occurred among married men. Among other things, this reflects the fact that increasing numbers in these age groups have received early retirement pensions. A serious symptom in this context is that during the 1960s the continuous increase in life expectancy in Sweden levelled off for men while it was maintained for women.

Early retirement pensions however need not be seen as an instrument for increased elimination from the labour market. It is possible that the need for early retirement pensions was very large even earlier, and that only when changes in legislation were introduced in 1970 was it possible to satisfy these needs. Early retirement pensions now function as a needs-tested lowering of the pension age, based on both medical criteria and labour market considerations.[19]

The concept of social elimination can also be used to describe the increase in the classic lumpenproletariat which has become noticeable in the metropolitan areas since the 1960s. The risks of entering the lumpenproletariat have increased somewhat through growing unemployment, greater frequency of divorces, increased alcoholism and drug abuse. Unmarried middle-aged and older men in the metropolitan areas are exposed to greater risks in this connection. This is perhaps the most important cause of the lower electoral participation in the metropolitan regions. The decline of the number of men in the labour force and the increase in the lumpenproletariat has hit primarily working-class groups, and thus to some extent has eroded the socialist parties' mobilizing possibilities.

During the postwar period the number of crimes committed has increased. Although violent crime has risen, property crime in particular has accelerated since the beginning of the 1960s.[20] The increasing crime rate reflects primarily increasing opportunities related to rising standards of living and urbanization, but is probably also partly related to growing alcoholism and drug abuse. Various forms of criminality, irrespective of whether they involve traditional types of stealing or sophisticated forms of theft through manipulations of taxes and allowances, weaken citizens' sense of solidarity with the community. In this way the prerequisites for electoral support of the labour parties are weakened.

On the whole, however, urbanization has probably had favourable effects on the mobilizing potential of the labour parties. As we have shown earlier, these parties encountered the greatest difficulties in winning voters in the rural areas. Traditionally, the towns and especially the big cities have furnished the labour movement with better preconditions for mobilizing the voters.

Urbanization is the result of migration. In contrast to what is commonly assumed, geographical mobility has not increased drastically during the postwar period. In Sweden figures on movements across parish boundaries have been consistently high from the 1910s until the 1960s. After the breakthrough of industrialism people have always had to move in order to get work. At least during the 1970s, those moving to new areas seem to have been active in unions and interested in politics almost to the same extent as others.[21]

During the postwar period the construction of new housing areas and the development of transport has significantly changed community life in the major cities. In a large measure social relations among neighbourhood residents have been replaced by contacts with friends and acquaintances in other parts of the metropolitan areas. This does not necessarily mean, however, that people's social relations have decreased or become less confined to their own socio-economic stratum. Also in the metropolitan areas workers seem to associate primarily with other workers.

A comparative study of the Nordic countries does not indicate that social relationships in Sweden are worse than in the other Nordic countries. In comparison with the average for the Nordic countries, the sense of community among neighbourhood residents, family ties and friendships seem to be slightly better in Sweden. Despite the increased frequency of divorces, children's relationships with their parents are probably not any worse in Sweden than in other industrial countries. A comparative study of youth between the ages of eighteen and twenty-four years asked, among other things: 'Whom do you talk to when you have worries?' The proportion stating that they usually talked with both their parents was higher in Sweden than in the United States, Britain, West Germany, France, Switzerland, Australia and Japan.[22]

EDUCATION AND CULTURE

Many changes have occurred in the area of education and culture affecting the potential support for the political blocs in diverse ways. One of the most far-reaching changes during the postwar period has been the extension of compulsory education. At the end of World War II compulsory schooling was limited to six years. Now the vast majority of young people continue their education for eleven or twelve years. The Swedish school system is now comprehensive and the teaching less authoritarian than before. The differences in the probabilities for working-class and middle-class youth to enter the universities, however, have not markedly decreased.[23] The values inculcated in the schools are heterogeneous. Yet one can probably expect that in the long-term perspective the higher level of education will have positive effects on the mobilizing possibilities of the socialist parties. Young people who are educated until the age of nineteen in the Swedish type of educational system are likely to have higher expectations regarding working life and equality than did working-class youths who until the 1950s entered the labour market around the age of fourteen.

The common assumption of a cultural decline in 'mass-media society' should not be uncritically accepted. A number of phenomena do not fit with this picture. Between 1950 and 1975, for instance, in Sweden the number of books borrowed per person from public and school libraries tripled. The number of participants in adult education study circles also tripled between 1960 and 1975.[24]

During the postwar period developments in mass media, including a growing bourgeois dominance of the daily press, has enhanced the bourgeois parties' possibilities of winning electoral backing. In the late 1970s the socialist newspapers had only 20 per cent of the total circulation. By delineating the limits of acceptability the daily press establishes norms and acts as a trend-setter also for radio and television, which are publicly owned. The mass media play an increasing role in shaping people's consciousness and in interpreting events in the surrounding world. In most other Western countries, however, the inferior position of the labour parties in terms of mass-media resources is much more pronounced than in Sweden. Yet the possibility to shape the social consciousness of voters via the mass media has become a powerful tool for business interests.

A frequently overlooked change, which has had negative effects for the mobilizing possibilities of the bourgeois parties, is the dwindling importance of church and religion. During its formative years the labour movement came to view the 'throne, altar and purse' as a trinity of its adversaries. In the Western European countries churchgoers voted in the 1970s for bourgeois parties to a considerably larger extent than those who seldom or never went to church. In Sweden the position of religion in the postwar period has been substantially eroded. Sweden is now perhaps the most secularized society among the Western countries.[25]

The trends of development discussed here are summarized in Table 10.1[26] The changes have occurred in very diverse areas and they have also operated in contradictory directions. Consequently an overall assessment of their effects is difficult. In my opinion, however, on the whole they have improved the preconditions for the labour parties to win the support of the electorate. In making this judgment, I attach major weight to the changes in class structure, the decline of the agricultural

Table 10.1 Summary of influences of postwar trends of development on preconditions for the electoral support of the socialist and bourgeois blocs

Area	Trend of development	Bloc favoured
Class structure	Proportion of wage-earners in population increases sharply; entrepreneurs decrease	Socialist
Social stratification	Fairly stable distribution of social strata; salaried employees increase	Contradictory
Branches of the economy	Manufacturing increases until about 1965, subsequently declines; agriculture decreases; service sector expands	Contradictory
Sector	Proportion of public employees increases	Socialist
Immigration	Proportion of immigrants without the right to vote in parliamentary elections increases; risk of ethnic cleavages	Bourgeois
Sex roles	Proportion of working women increases	Socialist
Housing	Single-family dwellings decrease up to the 1970s, then increase	Contradictory
Standard of living	Rising material standard; shorter working hours	Socialist
Labour force participation	Increasing number of men outside the labour force, especially unmarried men	Bourgeois
Social problems	Lumpenproletariat increases; increased drug abuse and alcoholism	Bourgeois
Crime	Increased crime rate, especially property crime	Bourgeois
Urbanization	Growing proportions of population in towns and cities	Socialist
Education	Longer compulsory education in comprehensive, non-authoritarian school system	Socialist

Table 10.1 (cont.)

Area	Trend of development	Bloc favoured
Mass media	Increasing bourgeois dominance of daily press	Bourgeois
Religion	Decline in religiosity and church attendance	Socialist

population and the rising standard of living. These changes have affected major sections of the population. The most important changes, with negative consequences for the mobilizing possibilities of the labour parties, and consequently improving the prospects of the bourgeois bloc, are probably trends of development in the areas of the media, housing and social deviation.

THE TIDES OF LEFT SUPPORT

Our discussion of the changes in the preconditions of the two blocs in winning electoral support leads to the question of how the electoral strength of the blocs has changed over the years. The differences between the socialist and bourgeois blocs in terms of the share of votes cast in the parliamentary elections since 1921 are characterized by long-term ebbs and flows (Figure 10.1). For the socialist bloc there are two high water marks in support, in the 1940 and 1968 elections. The two low points came in the 1956 and 1958 elections and in the 1976 election. The differences in the proportion of the electorate supporting the two blocs reveal the same pattern although somewhat subdued.

How does this long-term pattern of the ebb and flow of support square with the assumption that the mobilizing possibilities of the socialist bloc have improved during the postwar period? Should not these improvements have created a steadily increasing lead for the socialist bloc? It is however not reasonable to expect that a particular party or bloc can continue to increase its electoral lead over a very long period. If the losing side does not want to pursue purely demonstration politics, it is compelled to readjust its policy to that of the winning side. Instead, the improved mobilizing possibilities of the socialist bloc have been manifested in two other ways. The first is the marked increase in the wage-earners' capacity for collective rather than individual action, which is reflected in the increasing level of unionization and in co-operation between the unions. The second is that during the postwar years the Social Democrats could move the frontier of conflict in Swedish politics to the left.

The bloc or party in government has the political 'serve', and can introduce policies in order to move the battle line of politics in the direction it desires. During the 1930s the Social Democrats could overcome the opposition to state intervention in the economy. In the 1940s and 1950s the principal social insurance schemes and policies for full employment were accepted. The major conflicts in the 1960s focused on the expansion of the public sector and the resulting high level of taxation; by and large, the Social Democrats won these struggles, too. In contrast, they suffered losses in the controversies of the 1970s.

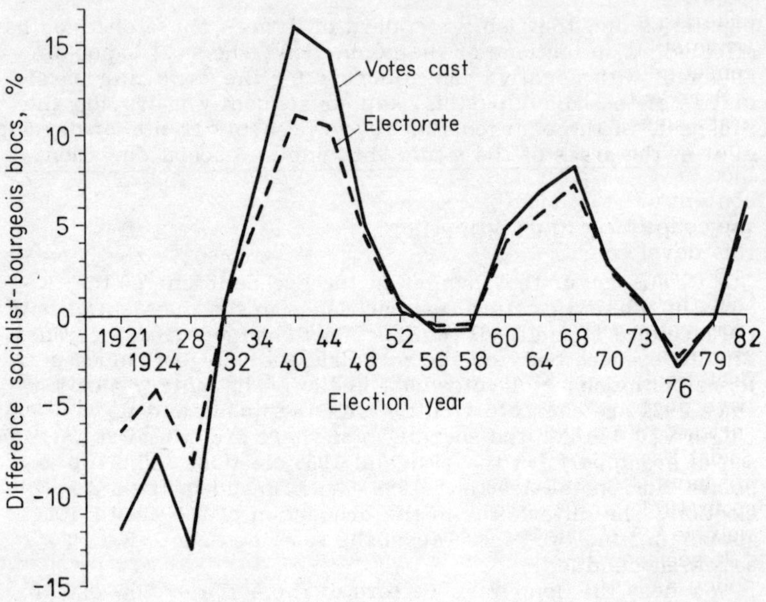

Figure 10.1 Difference between the socialist and bourgeois blocs in the proportion of votes cast and the proportion of the electorate supporting the blocs in parliamentary elections, 1921–82

Upon achieving government power in 1976 the bourgeois bloc could halt the leftward thrust in Swedish politics. During its second period in government the bourgeois parties clearly started to move the centre of gravity of political conflict towards the right, but they were defeated in the 1982 elections.

POLICY OUTPUTS AND CONSEQUENCES

Changes in the social structure shape the preconditions for the political struggle. Structural changes determine which actors emerge on the political scene, what interests they have, and what resources they can use to realize their interests. However structural changes occur slowly, and often maintain their direction for decades. Thus they cannot explain the rapid fluctuations in bloc strength during the 1960s and 1970s.

The structurally given preconditions for the political struggle do not always determine its outcome. The outcome also depends upon the skills and ability of the actors to utilize their possibilities. How actors use their possibilities is manifested in the content of the policies advocated by the parties and in the consequences of the policies they introduce when in government. In order to explain the shifts in party preferences of the electorate, we must thus therefore also analyse policy outputs and their consequences.

Here we shall focus on the question of why the Social Democrats since 1968 have experienced a series of election defeats in spite of the fact that the structural preconditions of the socialist bloc have probably not become worse. To what extent can the content of the policy of the Social Democratic government and the consequences of this policy for the electorate account for this development?

A common conception, especially among foreign observers, is that the decline of the Social Democrats during the 1970s stems from voter dissatisfaction with a swollen welfare state. However, as we have seen, the available data fail to confirm this interpretation. Even if the preconditions for attacking welfare policy have perhaps improved at the close of the 1970s, available time series data on the voters' views on social policy indicate that Social Democratic losses can hardly be explained by the electorate having become fed up with welfare policies. In 1979 as well as in 1976 the bourgeois parties campaigned for maintaining the welfare state, not for dismantling it.

It seems more plausible instead to view the failure of welfare policy as a central factor underlying the Social Democratic setbacks in the 1970s. In the preceding chapter we have examined various time series of statistics which reflect the changes in the economic situation of wage-earners. Most basic to the wage-earner's opportunities of making a living is the level of employment. The greatest strength of the Social Democrats during the postwar period has probably been that the voters regarded the party as the guarantee for full employment. As recently as the 1968 election a vast majority of the electorate saw the Social Democratic government as the best safeguard for full employment. But when unemployment problems mounted in the early 1970s, the voters' confidence in the Social Democrats on this score was undermined. As we have seen, the alternative of a bourgeois government ensuring employment at this time gained the confidence of the electorate.

The combination of deteriorating employment opportunities and rapid inflation (especially marked in rents and food prices) created economic strains on working-class families and forced a growing number to apply for means-tested social assistance. At the beginning of the 1970s the social assistance rate reached record levels for the postwar period. Young families with children were among the hardest hit. Swedish poverty moved from the northern forests to the new multi-family housing areas in suburbs of the cities.

The deteriorating opportunities of the voters to earn a living have probably been of importance for the growing dissatisfaction with policy outputs which can be discerned in the 1970s. As we have seen, there has been a drop by approximately 10 per cent during the 1970s, as compared with the previous decade, in the proportion of the electorate stating that government policies have benefited the socio-economic group to which they belong. Also, among Social Democratic voters we found a definite decline in the percentage who were satisfied with policy outputs. However, we do not have much evidence of growing opposition to the scope and costs of welfare policy in the 1970s. Thus it rather appears that voters deserted the Social Democrats mainly because the welfare policy failed to achieve important goals.

The long reign of the Social Democrats has also been a contributing factor to their electoral losses during the 1970s inasmuch as it caused many voters to associate the party with magisterial tendencies. A number of structural changes reinforced this perception. During the 1960s and 1970s democratic institutions were reformed with the aim of increasing efficiency through economies of scale. Thus the consolidation of local government units through the reforms of the 1960s, which was supported by all parties, resulted in the disappearance of three out of four independent communes. This entailed an enormous reduction in the number of political positions in local government. Up to 1962 the number of representative positions in local government has been estimated as between 150,000 and 200,000; by 1974 the number had dropped to around 42,000.[27] Through mergers of unions and amalgamation of branches, three out of four local branches in LO unions disappeared between 1960 and 1975. In union organizations a few instances of abuse of power by union officials have also occurred and have received wide publicity.

Even if there were good reasons for combining decision-making units, however, this process of consolidation has entailed considerable costs in the form of growing distance between decision-makers and the people. These organizational changes have meant a sharp reduction of people serving as intermediaries between citizens/members and the decision-makers, who now are most frequently full-time professionals. The changes have contributed to a common image of the LO as having too much power in society. The strong fundamental solidarity between union members and their organization as well as the members' confidence in the competence and effectiveness of union leadership are now mingled with a feeling that too many decisions in the trade union movement are made over the heads of its members.[28]

The political formula of the historical compromise was based on a deliberate effort to promote economic growth. Among other things, this entailed the collaboration of the labour movement in encouraging technological advances and labour mobility. With the emergence of environmentalist groups in the 1960s the Social Democrats thus found themselves in a defensive position. The young people involved in the environmentalist movement often viewed the Social Democratic Party as having merged with technocratic structures and big business. The Centre Party with its rural ties could win voters on environmental issues. During the 1970s the policy of encouraging labour mobility started to be questioned. Also on this issue the Centre Party could make electoral gains.

In the 1976 election the Social Democrats found themselves alone in defending a limited expansion of nuclear energy. In the final stages of the campaign this issue was probably decisive for the fall of the Social Democratic government. It took time for the Social Democratic Party to divorce itself from its earlier commitments and ties on the environmental issue. In the case of the workplace environment, however, the labour movement seized the initiative at an early point.

The reforms in the area of working life introduced in the 1970s aimed at expanding wage-earners' influence. The instruments to achieve this were partly the extension of wage-earners' rights through legislation, partly enlarging the sphere of union bargaining. The first approach was effective, for instance, when union safety stewards acquired the right to stop production in cases of health hazards for the workers. The second method, especially in the form of the Joint Consultation Act (MBL), threatens to become bogged down in extended negotiations. Broader bargaining rights, which are not combined with new power resources for the union organizations, only provide the unions with the right to delay decisions through negotiations. If a quick decision is necessary, management might make some concessions. Otherwise the number of negotiations multiplies but labour cannot appreciably influence decisions. Although it had several positive consequences for the unions, therefore, the Joint Consultation Act did not constitute a breakthrough for democracy in working life.

The proposals for wage-earners' funds, presented by LO in 1976 and later by TCO, signified a real possibility for fundamental changes in the distribution of power in the economy.[29] The concrete formulation of the ideas in the proposals however was incomplete and unclear on important points. The Social Democratic Party leadership chose to defend the goals of the funds but attempted to avoid a fight for their introduction. This stance probably caused disappointment among many party activists and confusions in the minds of the general electorate about party policy.

It is therefore probably the content and consequences of Social Democratic policy, not structural changes in society, which have been the major causes of the party's decline in the elections during the 1970s. The weaknesses of Social Democratic policy were not, as many believe, that it focused too much on welfare policy. On the contrary, voters became hesitant towards the Social Democrats primarily because welfare policy no longer fulfilled its major goals - among other things, full employment and a secure standard of living. Furthermore, the Social Democrats' commitments to the policy arising from the historical compromise made it difficult for the party to come to grips with the negative sides of the policy.

In spite of electoral defeats in the 1970s, in an international perspective the Swedish labour movement remains very strong. The 'secret' of the political and union strength of the Swedish labour movement is probably that the Social Democratic Party has largely remained a class party, which has pushed the basic interests of the working class, so that it has been able to maintain a good co-operation with a strong union movement.

Reformist parties in other countries have been less successful in their choice of strategy. Thus, for example, the British Labour Party appears to have been wooing marginal voters to the extent that it has never been able fully to mobilize the working-class vote but has instead come into serious conflicts with the unions and eventually to a severe internal split. The Danish Social Democrats have compromised working-class interests in weak governments, something which has generated splits between the party and the unions. The Norwegian social democrats decided to fight a major battle on an issue cutting across class lines, the entry into the European Economic Community, a decision which divided the party and alienated especially younger voters. By and large, the Swedish Social Democrats have managed to avoid such a fate. In Sweden the left-right dimension remains the major line of conflict along which the most important struggles will be fought in the coming years. The international economic crises form the backdrop of these struggles.

THE WAVE OF CONSERVATISM

In Swedish politics the historical compromise of the 1930s came to an end in a period when the Western countries entered the deepest economic crisis since the Great Depression. The crisis which began in the 1970s was marked by tens of millions of unemployed, double-digit inflation and zero economic growth. In order to gain perspective on the future alternatives in Swedish politics, it is worthwhile to examine Swedish problems and prospects in an international context.

The economic crisis in the Western countries has once again made controversial issues out of questions which many thought had been solved since Keynesian economic principles had begun to be applied during the postwar period. As is well-known, the Keynesian economic policy was based on the government's assuming the responsibility for maintaining relatively high levels of economic activity and employment, primarily through measures to stimulate demand. In Sweden Ernst Wigforss and the Social Democratic government in 1932 had already begun to apply this sort of policy a few years before Keynes himself formulated its principles in his major theoretical work. With some exceptions, such as the United States, Keynesian ideas on economic policy came to influence government policy in the Western countries during the postwar period. They contributed to lower levels of unemployment than had been normal in the interwar period.

The intellectual and political reactions to the economic crisis of the Western countries reflect divergent lines of thought concerning the functioning of markets and the relationship between politics and markets. Markets can be viewed as arenas where people compete for worldly goods and where their initial positions and opportunities are determined by a highly unequal distribution of economic and other resources at their control. The distribution created through the markets is therefore unequal and reflects the initial resources of people. The labour movement can be seen as an organized attempt by those who are weakest on the different markets in society collectively to counteract the distribution resulting from market forces. By joining together, individuals who are weak on the markets can improve their position in the distributive struggle.

From this perspective the fact that the government, by accepting Keynesian principles for economic policy, takes responsibility for maintaining the level of economic activity and employment, signifies a major advance for a labour movement. Besides being an important goal in itself, a low level of unemployment also increases the economic and political strength of the wage-earners. Sweden was the country where this type of policy was used most extensively and successfully.

In the 1970s the Keynesian economic policy failed to cope with unemployment and rising prices. Economic stagnation thus combined with inflation, producing stagflation. The previously effective instruments of economic policy were difficult to apply, since efforts to reduce unemployment through measures stimulating demand could fan inflation. In this predicament the governments of many Western countries tried to reduce the rate of inflation by accepting a considerably higher level of unemployment than they had previously done.

Political reactions of this sort to the economic crisis were guided by economic theories, which view the market as principally a natural, self-regulating system. In order not to disturb the self-regulating mechanisms of the market, the government should intervene as little as possible. Instead, it should concentrate on creating an institutional environment where the self-regulating forces of the market can operate. According to this view, in the long run all groups of citizens derive the greatest advantages by allowing the market to function freely and by accepting its distribution of the rewards of society.

These ideas are fundamental for the 'monetarist' school, which argues that inflation is due primarily to the government permitting the amount of money in circulation to increase faster than productivity. To attain economic balance and a healthy economy, the state should therefore strictly control the money supply. When the government contracts the money supply, economic activity declines and unemployment increases. This drastic cure is necessary, however, in order to break the inflationary spiral based on expectations of continued price increases. According to the monetarist teaching, in order to restore economic equilibrium the government must explicitly - and also for the future - relinquish all responsibility for the overall level of economic activity and employment.

In relation to Keynesian principles, this economic theory thus entails a reformulation of the goals of economic policy with respect to both employment and distribution. It formed an important intellectual underpinning of the wave of conservatism which influenced the economic policies in many Western countries since the latter half of the 1970s, perhaps most strikingly in Britain under the Thatcher government.

In recent years competing views of the causes of inflation have begun to gain ground among social scientists. Roughly summarized, these views hold that inflation is a reflection of the distributive conflicts waged in society.[30] When different interest groups threaten to utilize their power resources in backing up their claims for a larger share of the pie, the government 'settles' the conflicts by artificially making the pie larger, i.e., by increasing the money supply. As an emergency solution, inflation has some advantages. Even if its redistributive effects are sizeable, they are difficult to interpret and not immediately apparent. As a result, it is easier to avoid open and intense distributive conflicts.

The view of inflation as the outcome of distributive conflicts in society points to clear difficulties in the formula of the monetarist school for reinstating economic balance. The wage-earners can hardly be persuaded to accept voluntarily the market's outcome of the distributive conflicts, since they have formed the trade union movement precisely in order to counteract these effects. If the government cannot settle the distributive conflicts, at least temporarily, say, by increasing the money supply, they will appear in other forms, such as severe industrial disputes. Open conflicts of this type can be avoided only if unemployment increases drastically or if the government introduces measures to weaken the trade union movement, a solution which some proponents of the monetarist theory do not shun. The party in government which implements such policies however risks major losses at the polls. Such a policy therefore can produce deadlocks instead of effective solutions to economic problems, something which is illustrated by developments in Britain around the turn of the decade.

Up to the end of the 1970s the monetarist theories had limited influence on Swedish economic policy. The remedies set forth by these theories, however, cast light on a fundamental problem which is especially important in Sweden. As long as the political and union organizations of the wage-earners are weak, the wage-earners generally must accept the distribution resulting from market forces. But when their organizations grow in strength, they can offer resistance and consequently 'disturb' the free play of market forces. The question, then, is whether, and by what means, the strongly organized wage-earners can be induced to forgo using their full strength so that an economic system based on private ownership of the means of production may function effectively. Why should wage-earners make sacrifices and refrain from utilizing their collective power resources only to maintain a system where the power resources of other interest groups may freely assert themselves?

In Sweden the discussion of this problem since the late 1970s has revolved around the question of how to finance the investments which are necessary for the renewal and expansion of export industries. The traditional solution to providing industry with capital for investments in an economy based on private ownership is to increase company profits and investment incentives. For this to occur, wage-earners must restrict their wage demands and accept reductions in real wages. Taxes on investment profits must be reduced and tax revenue used to support private firms. Solutions of this type have been advocated by the bourgeois parties and the employers. What, then, are the alternative solutions to the economic crisis and political development in Sweden during the coming years?

THE ALTERNATIVES

The strength of the labour movement in a country can be expected to influence the nature of the attempts to surmount the economic crisis. The unique feature of the Swedish situation is the high level of unionization of wage-earners and a well-developed co-operation between union organizations. In addition to a host of other factors which shape the conditions for development in Sweden - external relations are important here - the degree of unity among wage-earners will be of major, perhaps decisive, importance.

One possible course of development is that trade union strength and the co-operation between various groups of wage-earners will be undermined. The control of the government offers opportunities to weaken or strengthen the position of the trade union movement and co-operation between union organizations. In this context, relations between LO and TCO are of special interest. During the 1970s the Social Democrats in government could facilitate co-operation between the two organizations by, among other means, proposals for strengthening the position of wage-earners at the place of work, which received the backing of both LO and TCO. The Social Democratic government's tax proposals paved the way for efforts to co-ordinate the collective bargaining of LO and the cartel of salaried employees in the private sector.

By contrast, the bourgeois government's proposals in the area of taxation, for example the indexation of taxes, were supported by TCO but heavily criticized by LO. These tax proposals contributed to breaking up the co-operation between LO and the salaried employees in the private sector during the wage negotiations in 1979-80. In the 1980s the Swedish Employers' Confederation (SAF) withdrew its support of economy-wide bargaining, which had helped to unify the unions under the leadership of the LO. Instead, SAF wanted to return to wage negotiations on the level of industries and firms. The SAF also wanted the LO to give up the solidaristic wage policy and to accept larger wage differences between workers. At the same time the Conservative Party in particular began to heavily criticize the union movement and proposed legislation limiting union rights.

However, even if co-operation between LO and TCO can be impaired, the organizational strength of the unions in terms of their membership will scarcely be eroded in the foreseeable future. Thus in the coming years also we must reckon with very strong but perhaps somewhat less united union organizations.

The continued existence of strong and relatively united union organizations ensures that the material interests of wage-earners will be effectively represented in societal bargaining, including the formation of economic policy. In this context it is important to remember that the question of co-operation or conflict between unions and the government is basically determined by the distributive policy, in a broad sense, pursued by the government, not by its party composition. On the other hand, there is of course a relationship between the political composition of a government and its distributive policy. Since open conflicts are costly, unions will try as far as possible to reach acceptable solutions through negotiations. The strike is the last resort.

If the Swedish bourgeois parties are to stay in office for a prolonged period, a bourgeois government must succeed in establishing a stable co-operation with the wage-earners, whose interests are represented by the unions. It must also pursue a policy which produces an enduring confidence among the voters. In comparison with the Social Democratic government which came to power in 1932, the bourgeois governments during the years 1976-82 failed on these counts. Opinion polls have disclosed a varying but generally fairly weak support for the bourgeois parties. Co-operation with the wage-earners' organizations has encountered serious difficulties.

The economic crisis did of course complicate the situation for the bourgeois governments. The Social Democratic experiences from the 1930s, however, indicate that an economic crisis need not prevent a government from strengthening its position among the voters. What is essential here is the strategy selected by the government in attempting to overcome the crisis. The strategy of the bourgeois government consisted of, among other things, demanding sacrifices by the wage-earners and of favouring business interests and shareholders. Even if there has been a considerable willingness among wage-earners to make sacrifices, they were not able to accept the terms of the government's crisis policy.

In addition, the bourgeois coalition governments, composed of three parties, found it difficult to agree on measures to combat the crisis. The separation into three parties is an asset in winning votes when the bourgeois bloc is in opposition, because the three parties can project distinctive profiles and attract a broad spectrum of voters. In government, however, the division is a disadvantage. Since cabinet decisions often have different political consequences for the three parties, conflicts of interests are built into the government - which impedes effective action. Although each party is in the minority in the government, in practice it has the right to veto cabinet decisions.

The difficulties of bourgeois governments in taking united action came to the fore on the issue of nuclear energy, which led to the fall of the first bourgeois coalition cabinet in the autumn of 1978. Party dissensions also came to the surface on taxation and other economic matters and led to a break in the three-party coalition government in May 1981.

The election in 1982 brought a Social Democratic government to power. What does this victory signify for the future? There is a clear possibility of a period of frequent alternations between Social Democratic and bourgeois governments. The decisive factor in this connection is if the Social Democratic Party can formulate a successful programme for overcoming the crisis, which can gain the confidence of the voters. The difficulties in formulating a solution to the crisis are immense. Moreover, attempts to rectify the situation can necessitate measures which are not popular in the short run. If such a policy is not effective in the long run, it can deplete the party's fund of goodwill among the voters.

The most serious risk which a Social Democratic government runs here is to find itself forced to introduce measures which one-sidedly hit the workers. In this instance the Social Democratic government could be headed for a collision with LO. Such a development was close to happening during the attempts at a wage freeze in 1949-50. In the 1950s, however, the active labour market policy formulated by the LO economists, Gösta Rehn and Rudolf Meidner, salvaged the unity of the labour movement. A dissolution of the collaboration between LO and the Social Democratic Party would create a situation in Sweden similar to that in Denmark and Britain, where a weak Social Democratic government attempts to extricate the country from its economic difficulties with a policy which does not have the backing of the trade union organizations.

What are the possibilities of the Social Democrats' once again gaining a firm grip on governmental power? In my opinion, the structural conditions for this are fairly favourable. The problem is instead whether the Social Democratic Party will be able to utilize these possibilities. A social movement which from an inferior power position wants to change society must indicate the means of achieving this and imbue people with the hope that social change is feasible. To unify and strengthen the movement, the Social Democratic Party must be able to formulate a 'provisional Utopia' and through political action demonstrate that it is possible to move in the direction of this Utopia.[31]

A NEW HISTORICAL COMPROMISE?

The provisional Utopias espoused by the Social Democrats have shifted through the years but they have had a common foundation: equality. During the breakthrough of industrialism towards the end of the nineteenth century, for many workers universal suffrage - the first step - must have seemed too bold an aspiration. How would the common people be able to occupy the place of the powers that be? Within a few decades, however, the workers had been mobilized behind the demand of political democracy. For those who faced recurrent unemployment, insecurity and a society ridden with class distinctions, the second step towards full employment and social justice must have also appeared very remote.

Per Albin Hansson, leader of the Social Democratic Party, concluded his May Day speech in 1930 by expressing his conviction that 'in a not too distant future' the people would rally to the cause of fundamental reform of society, creating democracy in all areas - that is, also social and economic democracy. 'I believe in the people, their sound instincts and ability to ultimately take their destiny into their own hands.'[32] Fifty years later the Swedish labour movement probably has better possibilities to move towards economic democracy than is the case in any other Western country, yet it has been hesitant to turn its full energies to the task.

In the 1970s the provisional Utopia of economic democracy was formulated in the proposal for 'löntagarfonder', wage-earners' funds. This proposal was prompted by the question of how the unions would be able to continue with the solidaristic wage policy, the basic principles of which are wages according to the nature of the job, not according to the profitability of the firm, and decreasing wage differentials. By critics on the left the solidaristic wage policy has often been disparaged as 'socialism in one class'.[33] It implied, however, that workers had come to accept that their interests encompassed the whole working class and not primarily occupational or sectional groups. Further, the solidaristic wage policy generated a union organization capable of action on the basis of class, i.e., a strong union confederation. To a large extent also the unions of the salaried employees came to accept the basic principles of the solidaristic wage policy.

In the late 1960s the solidaristic wage policy was seen as threatened by the high profits which it left largely untouched in some industrial firms and by the increasingly skewed distribution of capital which it helped to generate. In this situation the Swedish unions did not return to a 'trade unionistic' strategy with a focus on safeguarding the short-term economic interests of their members. Instead, the unions moved forward to question the basis for the capitalist system, the private ownership of shares which determine the voting rights in economic decision-making.

The first proposal on the funds came in 1975 from a committee within the LO, led by Rudolf Meidner.[34] The funds were given three basic goals: to support the solidaristic wage policy of the unions, to counteract the concentration of ownership and power in industry, and to strengthen the influence of wage-earners in industry through the ownership of shares. The movement forward, however, came to be a rather complicated journey.

The original fund proposal contained some principles which the Social Democratic Party found difficult to accept. The most important of these was the idea that the private companies would have to issue shares to the funds in proportion to their profits and that the unions would appoint the majority on the boards of the funds. The party therefore chose to support the goals of the funds but attempted to bury temporarily the proposal in union-party committees and a parliamentary commission. In 1978 a revised proposal was put forward by the LO and the Social Democratic Party. In the deepening economic crisis, a fourth goal had now been added for the funds: to provide Swedish industry with investment capital. Again, however, the party had to withdraw the proposal for the construction of the funds. Only in 1981 could the congresses of the LO and the Social Democratic Party agree on the basic principles of the funds. In the 1982 election campaign the Social Democratic Party for the first time committed itself to establishing a system of wage-earners' funds. The technical details of the system were however left open.

According to the principles accepted by the congresses, the funds are to be financed partly through the sharing of excess profits of companies and partly through an increase in the social security contributions of all employers. The latter increase will be taken into account by the unions in future wage negotiations. The money will be paid into the pensions system, and from there transferred to twenty-four regional funds. The purpose of the funds is to buy shares in private firms, primarily in the larger ones. Since the amount of capital controlled by the funds within a decade or two can rival the size of the total stock now in private hands, the presence of the funds on the capital market is of great significance. According to the proposal, the funds will be governed by boards elected directly by the wage-earners. In the first stage of their development, however, the unions will appoint the majority on the boards of the funds.

When the funds begin to buy shares in the companies, their representation on the shareholders' meeting will be evenly divided between the employees in the firm and the fund. When the employees have received 20 per cent of the representation at the shareholders' meeting, the remaining shares will be controlled by the funds. The funds will be allowed to buy shares in all firms which are willing to sell shares to them, including firms outside their own region. In relation to the firms which the funds will eventually control, they will act in principle as holding companies, leaving the firms the initiative and freedom to plan and direct their production within very wide limits. Thus the employees in the firms will have relatively good opportunities to influence conditions at their place of work. To create pressures for economic efficiency on the funds, they will be required to pay an interest to the pensions system for the money which they receive from the funds. If the funds are not able to pay this interest, they will be cut off from further funding.

The above basic principles would thus appear to give the funds several advantages as tools for moving Sweden in the direction of economic democracy. The structure of the funds is relatively decentralized. They will provide opportunities for influences from national and regional levels as well as for the employees at the level of the firm. Unions will retain their traditional role of handling wage policy and of safeguarding the interests of the employees at the workplace. The system also provides opportunities to achieve the desired amount of pressures for economic efficiency. Since the funds are to buy shares on the capital market, basically on the same terms as other buyers of shares, this can be expected to decrease the risks of severe backlashes from business interests in the transition period.

The attacks against the fund proposals have focused on two key issues: economic inefficiency and a concentration of economic power in the hands of union and party 'bosses'. Thus it has been argued that only private enterprise has proved itself to be economically effective, and that any form of collective ownership of industry is bound to fall prey to short-term considerations, for example, the protection of employment in firms and branches with economic difficulties at the expense of long-term investments for future jobs. The questions of how to achieve economic efficiency and how to balance the necessity of economic returns with other needs of the employees obviously demand serious consideration of the architects of an economic democracy. The very effective attacks from business interests and others, for example neoclassical economists, that the funds will not democratize the the economic power but will lead instead to the concentration of economic power in new hands, has been possible primarily because of ambiguities and ineptness in the handling of this issue by the proponents of the funds.

The original proposals from 1975-6 came close to the traditional syndicalist idea that the unions are to take over industry. Such a proposal would imply a very difficult 'double role' for the unions as both representatives of the employees and as the owners of the firms. It also gave the opportunity to the opponents of economic democracy to point to inadequacies in union democracy and to fan a growing unpopularity of the unions.

The group which drafted the revised proposals for the funds saw the interests of workers, especially those in manufacturing, for a humanization of working life as threatened by consumer interests in the efficiency of production. Therefore they sought to safeguard producer interests by limiting the right to vote in the elections to the regional boards of the funds to the wage-earners and did not want to extend suffrage to all citizens. Such a proposal, however, is not effective since it would exclude primarily pensioners, housewives, students and the handicapped but would include managers and salaried employees as well as capital owners and persons working on their own account, most of whom formally are wage-earners. It is also impossible to find a democratically acceptable way of delineating the right to vote to individuals who can be described as wage-earners. The humanization of working life has to take place with the consent of the citizens and cannot be ensured through restrictions of suffrage.

This part of the proposal, however, put the labour movement on the defensive in an area which could have provided the most effective line of attack. A proposal for universal and equal suffrage to the boards of the funds would clarify the concept of economic democracy and would sharply contrast with the presently so obviously undemocratic decision-making procedures in industry. Because of its obvious democratic legitimity, a universal suffrage to the boards of the funds is also one of the best ways of safeguarding the future of economic democracy in the face of shifting electoral winds.

What is new in the situation at the beginning of the 1980s is that economic democracy can provide a possible solution to a major problem in society, the economic crisis. Through gradually abolishing competition among themselves, the wage-earners have decreased their disadvantage in power resources in relation to business interests. This eliminates one of the basic preconditions for an economy based on private control of the major corporations: the ability of capital to control the level of wages and ensure sufficient corporate profits. The efforts to solve the current economic crisis must take into account the changes in the power relations in Swedish society which have occurred since the 1930s. In this situation arguments on moral grounds that wage-earners must observe restraint and make sacrifices are inadequate in avoiding severe conflicts between labour and capital. Economic democracy can constitute a viable alternative inasmuch as it gives wage-earners something essential in return for their restraint and sacrifices - influence over the large private companies.

For the Swedish labour movement the wage-earners' funds can be a crucial component in a strategy to overcome the economic crisis. Instead of appealing to the unions for restraint and sacrifices, through the funds the party can devise a policy affording citizens and wage-earners possibilities of economic democracy in exchange for their sacrifices.

The contours of a new historical compromise, based on a narrowing of the difference in power resources between labour and capital, again develop around two legs. The first consists of the citizens and wage-earners making the sacrifices which are necessary for the Swedish economy to pull through the crisis. The second is that private capital interests accept that the citizens and wage-earners unite in democratic forms and through ownership of shares acquire influence in and over the major corporations.

It remains to be seen whether or not the debate on wage-earners' funds in Sweden will lead to legislation constituting a significant step in the direction of economic democracy. Yet the Swedish case has clear implications for the relative fruitfulness of competing theoretical approaches to the understanding of the development of free-enterprise or capitalist democracies. It points to the inadequacy of approaches originating in pluralist assumptions about industrial society. Further, it draws attention to the serious limitations of models based on neo-corporatism and on functionalist or Leninist interpretations of Marxism. In this context a theoretical approach with distinct advantages is one which starts from the hypotheses that in Western nations conflicts of interest are generated by the subordinate position of the wage-earners in the mode of production and that this degree of subordination can vary as a result of the capacity of wage-earners to act collectively.

APPENDIX

Table A1 The popular vote in Sweden 1910–82

Year	Type of election[1]	Electoral participation, of eligible voters	Conservatives[2]	Centre Party[3]	Liberals[4]	CDU	Social Democrats	Left Socialists	Socialists[5]	Communists	Others[6]	Total
		The relative distribution of valid ballots cast										
	%	%	%	%	%	%	%	%	%	%	%	%
1910	L	50.8	40.1	–	42.5	–	16.8	–	–	–	0.8	100
1911	P	57.0	31.2	–	40.2	–	28.5	–	–	–	0.1	100
1912–1914[7]	L	54.8	40.8	–	32.5	–	26.6	–	–	–	0.1	100
1914s[8]	P	69.9	37.7	0.0	32.2	–	30.1	–	–	–	0.0	100
1914a[8]	P	66.2	36.5	0.2	26.9	–	36.4	–	–	–	0.0	100
1916, 1918[7]	L	53.5	35.9	4.5	26.5	–	29.9	3.2	–	–	0.0	100
1917	P	65.8	24.7	8.5	27.6	–	31.1	8.1	–	–	0.0	100
1919	L	63.3	24.9	13.2	25.4	–	30.5	5.8	–	–	0.2	100
1920	P	55.3	27.9	14.2	21.8	–	29.7	6.4	–	–	0.0	100
1921	P	54.2	25.8	11.1	19.1	–	36.2	3.2	–	4.6	0.0	100
1922[9]	L	38.2	31.8	11.9	17.1	–	32.9	1.8	–	4.5	0.0	100
1924	P	53.0	26.1	10.8	16.9	–	41.1	–	–	5.1	0.0	100
1926[9]	L	49.8	28.9	11.7	16.1	–	39.0	–	–	4.1	0.2	100
1928	P	67.4	29.4	11.2	15.9	–	37.0	–	–	6.4	0.1	100
1930[9]	L	58.2	28.4	12.5	13.5	–	41.4	–	2.8	1.2	0.2	100
1932	P	68.6	23.5	14.1	11.7	–	41.7	–	5.3	3.0	0.7	100
1934[9]	L	63.6	24.2	13.3	12.5	–	42.1	–	4.0	2.8	1.1	100
1936	P	74.5	17.6	14.3	12.9	–	45.9	–	4.4	3.3	1.6	100
1938	L	66.0	17.8	12.6	12.2	–	50.4	–	1.9	3.8	1.3	100
1940	P	70.3	18.0	12.0	12.0	–	53.8	–	0.7	3.5	0.0	100
1942	L	66.9	17.6	13.2	12.4	–	50.3	–	0.1	5.9	0.5	100
1944	P	71.9	15.9	13.6	12.9	–	46.7	–	0.2	10.3	0.4	100
1946	L	72.0	14.9	13.6	15.6	–	44.4	–	–	11.2	0.3	100
1948	P	82.7	12.3	12.4	22.8	–	46.1	–	–	6.3	0.1	100
1950	L	80.5	12.3	12.3	21.7	–	48.6	–	–	4.9	0.2	100
1952	P	79.1	14.4	10.7	24.4	–	46.1	–	–	4.3	0.1	100
1954	L	79.1	15.7	10.3	21.7	–	47.4	–	–	4.8	0.1	100
1956	P	79.8	17.1	9.4	23.8	–	44.6	–	–	5.0	0.1	100
1958 1/6	P	77.4	19.5	12.7	18.2	–	46.2	–	–	3.4	0.0	100
1958 21/9	L	79.2	20.4	13.1	15.6	–	46.8	–	–	4.0	0.1	100
1960	P	85.9	16.5	13.6	17.5	–	47.8	–	–	4.5	0.1	100
1962	L	81.0	15.5	13.1	17.1	–	50.5	–	–	3.8	0.0	100
1964	P	83.9	13.7	13.2	17.0	1.8	47.3	–	–	5.2	1.8[10]	100
1966	L	82.8	14.7	13.7	16.7	1.8	42.2	–	–	6.4	4.4[11]	100
1968	P	89.3	12.9	15.7	14.3	1.5	50.1	–	–	3.0	2.6[12]	100
1970	P	88.3	11.5	19.9	16.2	1.8	45.3	–	0.4	4.8	0.0	100
1973	P	90.8	14.3	25.1	9.4	1.8	43.6	–	0.4	5.3	0.2	100
1976	P	91.8	15.6	24.1	11.1	1.4	42.7	–	0.3	4.8	0.1	100
1979	P	90.7	20.3	18.1	10.6	1.4	43.2	–	0.2	5.6	0.6[13]	100
1982	P	91.4	23.6	15.5	5.9	1.9	45.6	–	–	5.6	1.9[14]	100

Notes

1 L = local election, P = parliamentary election (Lower Chamber election up to 1970).
2 Before 1969, Högern (including Liberala Försvarsvänner); since 1969, Moderata Samlingspartiet.
3 Before 1957, the Agrarians (Bondeförbundet, including Jordbrukarnas Riksförbund).
4 Before 1934, Liberala (samlings-) partiet and Frisinnade Folkpartiet; since 1934, Folkpartiet.
5 1929-34, Kilbom Communists; 1970-9, SKP.
6 During the 1930s and 1940s includes Nazi parties.
7 Elections in half of the constituencies for the respective year.
8 s = elections in March and April 1914, a = election in September 1914.
9 Election in Stockholm the following year.
10 Medborgerlig Samling (Citizens Rally for Co-operation between Bourgeois Parties), 1.8%.
11 Borgerlig Trepartisamverkan, 2.6%; Mittensamverkan, 1.7%.
12 Borgerlig Trepartisamverkan, 1.7%; Mittensamverkan, 0.9%.
13 Apk 0.2%.
14 Environmentalist Party, 1.7%. Apk, 0.1%.

Sources: SOS, 'Allmänna Valen' 1979, vol. 1, pp. 12-13; and Hadenius et al., 'Sverige efter 1900', pp. 286-7.

Table A2 Distribution of seats in Riksdag, 1929–82

	1929		1933		1937		1941		1945		1949		1953		1957		1959		1961		1965		1969		1971	1974	1976	1979	1982
	LC	UC	LC	UC	LC	UC	LC	UC	LC	UC	LC	UC	LC	UC	LC	UC	LC	UC	LC	UC	LC	UC	LC	UC					
Cons.	73	49	58	50	44	45	42	35	39	30	23	24	31	20	42	13	45	16	39	19	33	26	32	25	41	51	55	73	86
Lib.	32	31	24	23	27	16	23	15	26	14	57	18	58	22	58	30	38	32	40	33	43	26	34	26	58	34	39	38	21
Centre	27	17	36	18	36	22	28	24	35	21	30	21	26	25	19	25	32	22	34	20	36	19	39	20	71	90	86	64	56
SD	90	52	104	58	112	66	134	75	115	83	112	84	110	79	106	79	111	79	114	77	113	78	125	79	163	156	152	154	166
Soc.			6	1	6	1	–	–	–	–	–	–	–	–	–	–	–	–	–	–	–	–	–	–	–	–	–	–	–
Comm.	8	1	2	–	5	–	3	1	15	2	8	3	5	4	6	3	5	2	5	2	8	2	3	1	17	19	17	20	20
	230	150	230	150	230	150	230	150	230	150	230	150	230	150	231	150	231	151	232	151	233	151	233	151	350	350	349	349	349

Notes
LC = Lower Chamber, UC = Upper Chamber. The Conservatives' figure for 1937 includes two Conservative-minded 'Independents' and the figures for 1941–53 include one. The Liberals' figure for 1937 includes one 'Liberal Independent'. The three representatives for the Citizen Rally in the Lower Chamber in 1965 have been assigned to the Conservatives, Liberals and Centre Party respectively. The latter representative however was not accepted by the Centre Party parliamentary group. The Citizens Rally representative in the Upper Chamber in 1965 has been assigned to the Conservatives since he was elected on a Conservative slate.

Source: SOS, 'Riksdagsmannavalen'.

Table A3 Swedish cabinets, 1911-82

Period in office	Prime minister	Party composition
7 October 1911- 17 February 1914	K. Staff	Liberal
17 February 1914- 30 March 1917	Hj. Hammarskjöld	Conservative
30 March 1917- 19 October 1917	C. Swartz	Conservative-caretaker
19 October 1917- 10 March 1920	N. Edén	Liberal-Social Democratic coalition
10 March 1920- 27 October 1920	Hj. Branting	Social Democrat
27 October 1920- 13 October 1921	G. de Geer/ O. von Sydow	Caretaker
13 October 1921- 19 April 1923	Hj. Branting	Social Democrat
19 April 1923- 18 October 1924	E. Trygger	Conservative
18 October 1924- 7 June 1926	Hj. Branting/ R. Sandler	Social Democrat
7 June 1926- 2 October 1928	C.G. Ekman	Prohibitionist/Liberal coalition
2 October 1928- 7 June 1930	A. Lindman	Conservative
7 June 1930- 24 September 1932	C.G. Ekman/ F. Hamrin	Liberal (Prohibitionist)
24 September 1932- 19 June 1936	P.A. Hansson	Social Democrat
19 June 1936- 28 September 1936	A. Pehrsson	Agrarian
28 September 1936- 13 December 1939	P.A. Hansson	Social Democratic-Agrarian coalition
13 December 1939- 31 July 1945	P.A. Hansson	National coalition
31 July 1945- 1 October 1951	P.A. Hansson/ T. Erlander (11 Oct. 1946)	Social Democrat
1 October 1951- 31 October 1957	T. Erlander	Social Democratic-Agrarian coalition
31 October 1957- 20 September 1976	T. Erlander/ O. Palme (14 Oct. 1969)	Social Democrat
7 October 1976- 5 October 1978	T. Fälldin	Conservatives/Liberals/Centre Party
18 October 1978- 17 September 1979	O. Ullsten	Liberal
12 October 1979- 8 May 1981	T. Fälldin	Conservatives/Centre Party/Liberals
22 May 1981- 20 September 1982	T. Fälldin	Centre Party/Liberals
8 October 1982-	O. Palme	Social Democrat

Table A4 Party choice by social group in the elections 1956-79

Party choice	Social group I							
	1956	1960	1964	1968	1970	1973	1976	1979
	%	%	%	%	%	%	%	%
Communists	0	0	0	1	1	2	6	7
Soc. Democrats	4	10	8	14	15	16	17	20
Centre	0	4	4	17	12	21	19	14
Liberals	40	23	31	27	36	16	17	15
Conservatives	56	63	48	39	33	41	40	43
CDU*			3	1	1	2	1	1
Other			6	1	2	2		
Total	100	100	100	100	100	100	100	100
N	(73)	(73)	(140)	(180)	(228)	(183)	(199)	(584)

Party choice	Social group II: farmers							
	1956	1960	1964	1968	1970	1973	1976	1979
	%	%	%	%	%	%	%	%
Communists	0	1	0	0	0	0	1	0
Soc. Democrats	14	7	7	6	5	9	9	6
Centre	49	70	65	62	70	68	68	73
Liberals	15	5	13	9	7	5	5	5
Conservatives	22	17	13	19	15	17	16	14
CDU*			2	3	3	1	1	2
Other			0	1	0	0		
Total	100	100	100	100	100	100	100	100
N	(129)	(158)	(266)	(218)	(275)	(179)	(148)	(314)

Party choice	Social group II: small businessmen							
	1956	1960	1964	1968	1970	1973	1976	1979
	%	%	%	%	%	%	%	%
Communists	0	1	1	1	1	2	1	2
Soc. Democrats	21	19	26	32	28	21	21	20
Centre	5	17	18	25	33	38	27	25
Liberals	48	34	36	23	22	16	22	12
Conservatives	26	29	16	17	13	21	27	39
CDU*			2	2	1	2	2	2
Other			1	0	2	0		
Total	100	100	100	100	100	100	100	100
N	(75)	(122)	(198)	(205)	(251)	(137)	(150)	(465)

Table A4 (cont.)

Party choice	Social group II: middle-level salaried employees							
	1956	1960	1964	1968	1970	1973	1976	1979
	%	%	%	%	%	%	%	%
Communists	1	1	1	2	4	3	4	4
Soc. Democrats	37	42	46	47	41	37	38	37
Centre	2	6	6	14	20	28	20	14
Liberals	42	31	27	22	22	12	19	18
Conservatives	18	20	16	13	12	17	17	25
CDU*			1	1	1	3 }	2	2
Other			3	1	0	0 }		
Total	100	100	100	100	100	100	100	100
N	(171)	(245)	(545)	(631)	(912)	(561)	(816)	(1943)

Party Choice	Social group III							
	1956	1960	1964	1968	1970	1973	1976	1979
	%	%	%	%	%	%	%	%
Communists	3	3	5	2	4	5	5	5
Soc. Democrats	73	77	72	74	67	67	62	66
Centre	3	6	9	12	16	18	20	14
Liberals	17	10	9	7	8	4	7	7
Conservatives	4	3	4	4	2	4	4	7
CDU*			1	2	2	2	2	1
Other								
	100	99	100	100	99	100	100	100
	(480)	(912)	(1265)	(1403)	(1903)	(1129)	(1203)	(3182)

* = Christian Democratic Union

Table A5 Composition of votes from the various social groups for the parties in the elections 1956–79

Party	Social group	Election year 1956	1960	1964	1968	1970	1973	1976	1979
		%	%	%	%	%	%	%	%
Conservative	I	30	25	25	25	24	27	24	20
	III	14	13	17	17	13	12	17	19
	N	(138)	(181)	(265)	(286)	(319)	(282)	(329)	(1278)
Liberal	I	12	8	10	13	16	16	12	11
	III	35	33	29	28	29	27	28	29
	N	(239)	(212)	(408)	(370)	(519)	(183)	(288)	(759)
Centre	I	0	2	1	6	3	6	8	7
	III	14	22	22	35	39	34	42	37
	Farmers	77	57	48	29	23	21	19	20
	N	(83)	(194)	(359)	(469)	(822)	(582)	(565)	(1171)
Social Democratic	I	1	1	1	2	2	3	5	4
	III	78	78	74	72	71	72	68	67
	N	(454)	(663)	(1248)	(1458)	(1801)	(1047)	(1111)	(3140)
Communist	I	0		0	5	2	3	7	13
	III	88		84	54	63	65	56	45
	N	(40)		(67)	(39)	(142)	(98)	(103)	(311)

NOTES

CHAPTER 2 THE DEMOCRATIC CLASS STRUGGLE

1 The extent of agreement of course depends upon what writers we include in the pluralist industrial model. This tradition appears to have at least three important parts: structural functionalism; the assumption that industrial technology is the prime mover of societal change; and the extension of a market bargaining model into interest representation. The by now 'classical' presentation of basic ideas in this tradition was given in C. Kerr et al., 'Industrialism and Industrial Man'. Other sources include R.A. Dahl, 'Who Governs?'; R. Dahrendorf, 'Class and Class Conflict in Industrial Society'; C. Kerr, 'Marshall, Marx and Modern Times'; Wilbert E. Moore, 'Industrialization and Labour'; T. Parsons, 'Societies: Evolutionary and Comparative Perspectives'; W.W. Rostow, 'The Stages of Economic Growth'; and Herbert Tingsten, 'Demokratins Problem'.

Criticism of the pluralist industrial model can be found, e.g., in J.H. Goldthorpe, Theories of Industrial Society, J.H. Goldthorpe et al., 'The Affluent Worker'; R.R. Alford and R. Friedland, Political Participation and Public Policy; L.J. Sharpe, American Democracy Reconsidered, and P. Bachrach and M.S. Baratz, 'Power and Poverty'. Also among writers close to the pluralist industrial tradition, different aspects of the model have been criticized; cf., e.g., R. Bendix, 'Nation-building and Citizenship'.

2 V.I. Lenin, 'State and Revolution'. For an entertaining criticism of the Leninist interpretation of Marxism see F. Parkin, 'Marxism and Class Theory: A Bourgeois Critique'.

3 Significant writings on the neo-corporatist theme can be found in Philippe C. Schmitter and Gerhard Lembruch, 'Trends Towards Corporatist Intermediation' and Gerhard Lembruch and Philippe C. Schmitter, 'Patterns of Corporatist Policy Making'. See also Philippe C. Schmitter, Interest Intermediation and Regime Governability; Claus Offe, The Attribution of Public Status to Interest Groups; and C. Crouch, 'Class Conflict and the Industrial Relations Crisis'.

4 Leo Panitch, Recent Theorizations of Corporatism, p. 159.

5 Philippe C. Schmitter, Still the Century of Corporatism?

6 In outlining the two subtypes of corporatism, state and societal, Schmitter often stretches the meaning of words in order to fit the societal variety under the heading of corporatism. Thus he exemplifies that de facto 'compulsory' membership can be based on social pressure and provision of essential services. In the normal meaning of words, these examples would appear to form the basis for voluntary rather than for compulsory membership. These definitional niceties, however, appear to have been largely overlooked by corporatist writers. The crucial issue here is what affects the decision of the individual wage-earner to join the union. If unions are represented in statutory bodies such as the Chambers of Labour in Austria and the Swedish Labour Market Board, or if union activists at the workplace level are elected to the leading positions of statutory organs like the German Betriebsräte (works' councils), this does not in itself affect the principle of voluntary membership.

7 Schmitter, Still the Century of Corporatism?, pp. 24-5.

8 Thus, Schmitter, Still the Century of Corporatism?, in his characteristic style, writes that

> once the new collective actors begin to acquire resources and organizational properties of their own and once the state has expanded the scope and volume of its policy interventions, the mode of interest mediation may become molded from 'within' and 'from above', so to speak, in relative independence from the conditions of civil society and even in disregard for the preferences and interests of the individuals, firms, sectors, classes, and so on whose interests are supposedly being represented. Michels was perhaps the first to stress these emergent properties of modern bureaucratic organizations, but his comments on the Iron Law of Oligarchy have now been extensively supplemented by the vast literature on the importance of organizational routines, standard operating procedures, goal displacement, incrementalist strategies, cooptation, professional norms, administrative leadership, diffusion of innovations, incentive structures, manipulation of client preferences, selective benefits and so forth. Interest associations, even in the rare instances in which they are non-monopolistic in their coverage and voluntaristic in their member support, are no less (and possibly more) susceptible to acquiring these properties than business and governmental organizations.

9 Philippe C. Schmitter, Reflections on Where the Theory of Neo-corporatism Has Gone and Where the Praxis of Neo-corporatism May be Going, pp. 266-73.
10 Panitch, op.cit., p. 173. See also Leo Panitch, The Limits of Corporatism.
11 B. Jessop, Corporatism, Parliamentarism and Social Democracy.
12 Ibid., p. 207.
13 Ibid., p. 211.
14 One example of use by 'pluralist industrial' scholars is H. Wilensky, 'The "New" Corporatism: Centralization and the Welfare State'.
15 Quoted in R. McKenzie and A. Silver, 'Angels in Marble', p. 4.
16 This and the following section draw on Walter Korpi, 'The Working Class in Welfare Capitalism', Chapter 2; and Power, Exchange and Inequality.
17 In this context, cf., e.g., C.J. Friedrich, 'Man and his Government', p. 203, on the 'rule of anticipated reactions'.
18 The pluralist approach to the study of power focuses on participation in the making of key decisions (e.g., R.A. Dahl, 'Who Governs?'). It therefore has come to neglect C.J. Friedrich's (op. cit., Chapter 11) observation that 'power hides' and tends to overlook a large part of apparently routine decisions which yet are based on power and have important consequences.
19 A basic principle of Swedish labour law has been that 'the employed person is obligated to submit to management' (F. Schmidt, 'Tjänsteavtalet', p. 105).
20 Similar assumptions are made in G. Esping-Andersen et al., Modes of Class Struggle and the Capitalist State.
21 A. Pizzorno, in Political Exchange and Collective Identity in Industrial Conflict, has referred to similar practices as 'political exchange'. C. Crouch, op. cit., has coined the term 'bargained corporatism'.
22 The following discussion draws on Korpi, 'The Working Class in Welfare Capitalism', Chapter 1.
23 For a discussion of these tendencies, see J.H. Goldthorpe and P. Bevan, The Study of Social Stratification in Britain: 1946-1976.
24 Parkin, op. cit., p. 9.
25 For discussions and reviews, see A. Lijphart, Political Parties: Ideologies and Programs; and G. Bingham Powell, Voting Turnout in Thirty Democracies; and R. Rose and D.W. Urwin, Social Cohesion, Political Parties and Strains in Regimes.
26 Lijphart, Language, Religion, Class and Party Choice, p. 320. Lijphart claims that his is a 'crucial test' of the relative importance of these three variables. The logic of his test must, however, be questioned, since Lijphart excludes from the test those nations where religious and ethnic cleavages are

unimportant. In most of these countries at least the cleavage between frequent and infrequent churchgoers is a potential one.

CHAPTER 3 WORKING-CLASS MOBILIZATION

1 This limitation is made necessary because of the difficulties involved in the comparative study of the power resources of business interests, e.g., the distribution of property. A promising study of the organizational efforts of business interests directed by Philippe C. Schmitter and Wolfgang Streeck is under way. In 'The Social Democratic Image of Society', Francis G. Castles draws attention to the significance of the party structure among bourgeois parties for the distribution of political power.

2 The following discussion draws on S. Rokkan, Nation-Building, Cleavage Formation and the Structuring of Mass Politics. Some of these factors are discussed in Michael Shalev and Walter Korpi, Working Class Mobilization and American Exceptionalism.

3 The discussion in the following paragraphs draws upon Shalev and Korpi, op. cit.

4 The classical study on this problem is of course W. v. Sombart's 'Why Is There No Socialism in the United States?', originally published in 1906. Further references are found in Shalev and Korpi, op. cit.

5 J. Karbel, The Reason Why, p. 23.

6 The exact years in the first two periods differ somewhat between some of the countries.

7 G.S. Bain and F. Elsheikh, 'Union Growth and the Business Cycle', p. 94.

8 In a survey among Swedish metal workers in 1966-7 a question about the reasons for membership in the union drew the following response distribution: 'I felt obliged to join', 8 per cent; 'I was not interested but joined none the less', 9 per cent; 'I personally benefit from being a member of the union', 37 per cent; and 'I think that one should be solidaristic with the labour movement', 41 per cent (Korpi, 'The Working Class in Welfare Capitalism', p. 171). A parallel question to a sample of members in the whole of the LO in 1974 gave the following distribution of responses: 'I joined because most others are members', 7 per cent; 'I felt obliged to join the union', 18 per cent; 'I myself benefit from being a member', 45 per cent; 'I think that one should be solidaristic with the labour movement', 27 per cent (L. Lewin, 'Hur Styrs Facket?', p. 142).

9 See, e.g., G. Bingham Powell, Voting Turnout in Thirty Democracies; A. Lijphart, Language, Religion, Class and Party Choice; R. Rose and D. Urwin, Social Cohesion, Political Parties and Strains in Regimes; and Richard Rose, Comparability in Electoral Studies.

10 Cf. R.R. Alford, Class Voting in the Anglo-American Political Systems. For a discussion of this type of measures, see Walter Korpi, Some Problems in the Measurement of Class Voting. The relative importances of different bases of cleavage are difficult to quantify in a satisfactory manner. Values on the Alford index depend, inter alia, on the dichotomization of the independent and the dependent variables as well as on the particular data set used. Other techniques of quantification can yield quite different results; cf., e.g., Rose, op. cit.

11 Data on 'class voting' are taken from the first version of G.B, Powell's paper, op. cit; in the published version some of the data were slightly revised.

12 Data based on T.T. Mackie and R. Rose, 'The International Almanac of Electoral History' and their successive updates in the 'European journal of Political Research', 1973-81.

13 In this table, 'Working-class mobilization' is based on the combined rank order of the percentage of unionization and left proportion of the electorate 'Weighted cabinet share': low = 0.00-10; medium = 0.11-0.30; High = 0.31-0.50. 'Time with left representation in cabinet': low = 0-24%; medium = 25-74%; high = 75-100%. Splits within the labour movement are those described

in standard sources on comparative labour movements. Party splits are defined in terms of the average share of the total left vote held by the largest party in the period 1946-76. A major split implies a share of about 50%. The data are taken from Walter Korpi and Michael Shalev, Strikes, Power and Politics in the Western Nations, 1900-1976.

14 Cf M.G. Schmidt, Does Corporatism Matter?; G. Lehmbruch, Introduction: Neo-corporatism in Comparative Perspective; and Philippe C. Schmitter, Interest Intermediation and Regime Governability in Contemporary Western Europe and North America.

15 A. Downs, 'An Economic Theory of Democracy'.

16 The discussion in this and the following two sections draws upon Korpi, 'The Working Class in Welfare Capitalism'.

17 E. Wigforss, 'Minnen', p. 111.

18 This 'political' explanation of the 'withering away of the strike' was first presented in 1975 in Walter Korpi, Sweden: Conflict, Power and Politics in Industrial Relations. Cf. also Chapter 8 below.

19 E. Wigforss, Den Ekonomiska Makten ska Flyttas från Kapitalet till Arbetet, pp. 391-2.

20 Philippe C. Schmitter, Still the Century of Corporatism?, p. 13.

21 Korpi, 'The Working Class in Welfare Capitalism', pp. 301-5.

22 For a discussion of union party relations in Sweden, cf. N. Elvander, In Search of New Relationships.

23 For an analysis of unofficial strikes in Sweden during the postwar period, see Walter Korpi, Unofficial Strikes in Sweden.

CHAPTER 4 ELECTORAL PARTICIPATION

1 An excellent discussion of political participation is found in R.R. Alford and R. Friedland, Political Participation and Public Policy. See also, e.g., S.M. Lipset, 'Political Man', Chapter 6; Lester Milbraith and M.L. Goel, 'Political Participation'; Sidney Verba et al., 'Participation and Political Equality'; Sten Johansson, 'Politiska Resurser'.

2 E.g., Philip E. Converse, Some Priority Variables in Comparative Electoral Research, pp. 730-3.

3 E.g., Herbert Tingsten, 'Political Behaviour', pp. 147-8, 177-81, 230-1.

4 For good comparative surveys and discussions of electoral participation see G. Bingham Powell, Voting Turnout in Thirty Democracies, and Ivor Crewe, Electoral Participation.

5 The data on electoral participation are taken from T.T. Mackie and R. Rose, 'The International Almanac of Electoral History'.

6 See, e.g., Tingsten, op. cit., pp. 29 and 220 on Austria, p. 219 on Switzerland and p. 221 on the United States.

7 Walter Dean Burnham, The Appearance and Disappearance of the American Voter.

8 Verba et al., op. cit., Chapter 7.

9 According to Verba et al., op. cit., Chapter 7, voting participation in Japan is fairly similar in various socio-economic strata despite a relatively low turnout. However, their results can be largely due to the fact that they measured electoral participation in Japan with a very imprecise question: 'How often have you voted in national elections: have you voted every time, most of the time, or rarely?' (p. 341). In Austria and the United States the question pertained to a specific election. The more imprecise the measurement, the weaker the correlation it will show. In Britain, in spite of relatively low turnouts in recent elections, participation rates between different socio-economic categories appear to be relatively small. In the elections in October 1974 the proportion of non-voters can be estimated at 14 per cent in the manual occupational grades and at 11 per cent in the non-manual occupational grades (calculations based on data given in Ivor Crewe, et al., Non-voting in British General Elections 1966-October 1977).

10 The label 'Cossack election' is based on a series of election posters issued

by Conservative circles which portrayed the Social Democrats as bands of Russian Cossacks.

11 The classification into 'social groups' used in this book has a long tradition in Swedish statistics. It was created by officials at the Central Bureau of Statistics for use in an analysis of the general election in 1911. The classification divides the electorate into an 'upper middle class', termed social group I; the 'middle class', termed social group II; and the working class, termed social group III. Social group I consists of professional people, owners of large business firms, landed proprietors, senior managerial and executive employees in private business and senior civil servants. Social group II consists of middle-level salaried employees, independent artisans, owners of small business firms, shopkeepers and independent farmers. Social group III consists of manual workers, farm and forestry workers, small and tenant farmers, and lower-grade salaried employees.

Social group I also includes university students, housewives married to men with occupations in that social group, and pensioners who have retired from such jobs. Housewives and pensioners in the other social groups are classified accordingly.

The index of class participation constitutes a parallel to R.R. Alford's well-known index of class voting ('Party and Society', pp. 79-80). Through 1958 the figures are based on the official statistics on general elections which contained the turnout rates of various occupational categories based on total counts or very large samples of election registers. This information is not available for the 1932 election. Occupational categories with the following codes are assigned to social groups I-II and social group III respectively: the 1921 election, 1-19 and 20-6 respectively; the 1924 and 1928 elections, 1-21 and 22-6 respectively, the 1936 and 1940 elections, 1-21 and 22-30 respectively; and the 1944 and 1948 elections, 1-12 and 13-18 respectively. In the elections from 1952 to 1958 the 'no occupation indicated' category has been excluded.

For the elections from 1960 to 1976 the interview surveys of SCB have provided the data. These surveys are based on samples of 1,500-3,700 persons, the voting participations of whom were taken from the election registers. In the 1956 election, when the first interview survey was conducted, it indicated a class differential of 4.5 per cent, while the official statistics showed 5.7 per cent.

12 See, e.g., 'Riksdagsmannavalen', 1925-8, pp. 57-8.

13 Statements about the character of densely populated communities are from the 1930 'Census of the Population', vol. 1, pp. 122-37. In this context a difficult problem is to be able sufficiently to isolate company towns and industrial communities in the election statistics. According to our classification, the voting turnout among working-class men in these industrial communities was 70 per cent in the 1928 election.

14 G. Ahlberg, 'Befolkningsutveckling och Urbanisering i Sverige 1911-50', Table XII. The voting turnout among working-class men in these communities was 69 per cent in the 1928 election.

15 Cf. Verba et al., op. cit.,Chapter 12; Elina Haavio-Mannila, Sex Roles in Politics; Riitta Jallinoja, Miehet ja Naiset; and Gerald Pomper, 'Voters' Choice', Chapter 4. For voting in the United States, cf. Raymond E. Wolfinger and Steven J. Rosenstone, 'Who Votes?', Chapter 3.

16 Tingsten, op. cit., Chapter 1.

17 The official statistics on voting turnout (e.g. SOS, 'Allmänna Valen 1976', vol. 3, Special Studies) are currently based on interviews in connection with the Labour Force Surveys (AKU), which are subsequently complemented by data on electoral participation from the national register of voters. As studies of electoral participation, these data are deficient for the following reasons: (a) Persons not responding in the Labour Force Surveys are not included despite the fact that non-voting can be expected to be especially large in this group. (b) The classification of occupations used here (based on the International Standard Classification of Occupations) is irrelevant for this purpose as well as for most others. Instead, available

socio-economic classifications of occupations ought to be used. (c) Divorced persons, widows, widowers and single persons are combined into one category of unmarried persons despite major differences among them.

18 E.g. Walter Korpi, 'Fattigdom i Välfärden', and Social Policy and Poverty in Postwar Sweden.

19 These figures on the differences with respect to employed women and the figures on unemployed persons are based on a re-analysis of data from the SCB electoral participation studies (SOS, 'Allmänna Valen', 1973 and 1976 respectively, Special Studies).

20 See, e.g., Harald Swedner, Sextiotalets politik lade Grunden till Valförlusten.

21 An example is Jan Lindhagen, Åren vi Förlorade, and Men å Andra Sidan.

22 In computing the predicted electoral participation, I have assumed the following probabilities of voting in various sub-categories: men and women between the ages of 18 and 34 years, 0.925; married men and women between the ages of 35 and 64 years, 0.960; married men and women over 64 years, 0.940; unmarried men between the ages of 35 and 64 years, 0.870; unmarried men over 64 years, 0.800; unmarried women between the ages of 35 and 64 years, 0.880; unmarried women over 64 years, 0.820; divorced men, 0.750; widowers 0.850; divorced women, 0.790; widows, 0.850. The defects in the election statistics compiled by SCB make it necessary to rely on plausible estimates. The probabilities given above have been selected so that they generate the actual voting turnout in the 1976 election, given the relative distributions of these sub-categories in the population according to the 1975 census.

23 See, e.g., Nader Fatahi and Harald Swedner, 'Olika Samhällsklassers Deltagande i de Politiska Valen i Göteborg Åren 1921-1976'.

24 SOS, 'Allmänna Valen', 1979, vol. 1, p. 22. The proportion of invalid votes, most of them blank ballots, was 0.6 per cent in the whole country, 0.9 per cent in Stockholm and 1.0 per cent in Gothenburg. O. Petersson, 'Väljarna och Valet 1976', p 254, however does not find any strong evidence that non-voting is a deliberate act of protest.

25 The number of respondents in the different groups is as follows:

Social group	Men by age 18-34	Men by age 35-64	Men by age 65-80	Women by age 18-34	Women by age 35-64	Women by age 65-80
I	65	112	22	23	42	15
II (excluding farmers)	106	208	69	184	208	52
Farmers	9	45	37	8	30	32
III	258	331	136	184	297	97

26 J.S. Mill, 'On Representative Government'.

27 Tingsten, op. cit., p. 225; Joseph A. Schumpeter, 'Capitalism, Socialism and Democracy'. Cf also, e.g., Bernard Berelson et al., 'Voting' and William Kornhauser, 'The Politics of Mass Society'.

28 Thus, e.g., Richard Rose, 'Electoral Behaviour: A Comparative Handbook', almost entirely neglects electoral participation. In the 1980s, however, at least two comparative studies on participations have been published: Crewe, op. cit., and Powell, op. cit. Walter Dean Burnham has provided a highly perceptive and interesting analysis of The Appearance and Disappearance of the American Voter.

29 Verba et al., op. cit., Chapters 9 and 10.

30 Comparative data on women's political participation can be found in Verba et al., op. cit., Chapter 12. For Scandinavian attempts to explain these differences, see, e.g., Maud Eduards, 'Kvinnor och Politik'; Beatrice Halsaa Albrektsen, 'Kvinner og Politisk Deltagelse'.

CHAPTER 5 SOCIAL ROOTS OF PARTY PREFERENCES

1 See e.g., B. Särlvik, Sweden: The Social Bases of the Parties in a Developmental Perspective; Richard Rose, Comparability in Electoral Studies, p. 17; Sten Berglund and Ulf Lindström, 'The Scandinavian Party System(s)'. Religious and linguistic cleavages have been of some importance in Norway, however. John D. Stephens, in The Consequences of Social and Structural Change for the Development of Socialism in Sweden, offers a broad and interesting study of social background and changes in party preferences in Sweden during the postwar period.

2 Särlvik, op. cit., pp. 415-19; Walter Korpi, 'The Working Class in Welfare Capitalism', pp. 312-17.

3 Olof Frändén, 'Who Were the Young Leftists', has examined the political socialization process in Sweden.

4 The path coefficients here are relatively low. The three social groups and a five-category party scale (Communists, Social Democrats, No answer, Liberals + Centre, Conservatives) have been used.

5 The strong correlation between the husband's and the wife's own social group makes it difficult to distinguish their effects on party preferences. Robert Erikson, Om Socio-ekonomisk Indelning av Hushåll, discusses characteristics of husbands and wives as indicators of a household's socio-economic position.

6 Korpi, op. cit., p. 304.

7 R.R. Alford, 'Party and Society', pp. 79-80. For a discussion, see, e.g., Walter Korpi, Some Problems in the Measurement of Class Voting.

8 Occupational categories are based on the classification into social group used in the Election Surveys through 1976 and the new socio-economic classification of occupations used in the Party Sympathy Surveys. In principle they should, however, be comparable (G. Carlsson et al., Socio-ekonomisk Gruppering). The terms 'middle strata' and 'middle class' are of course misleading for big businessmen and the uppermost echelons of salaried employees, but their proportion of social group I is fairly small. L. Lewin, et al., 'The Swedish Electorate 1887-1968', have made a valiant attempt to analyse changes in the relationship between social position and voting over time using ecological data.

9 The figures for the 1979 election are taken from the Party Sympathy Survey carried out two months after the election. Data for the previous elections come from the series of Election Surveys, which have been done in connection with the elections since 1956. In the latter series the classification of occupations has changed somewhat over the years. The occupational classification used in the Party Sympathy Survey should give a categorization into manual and non-manual occupations similar to that used in the Election Surveys. In the 1979 Election Survey the proportion voting socialist was estimated to be 69 per cent for workers and 32 per cent for the non-manuals. This survey had a sample of 2,816 respondents, compared with 9,000 respondents in the Party Sympathy Survey from the 1979 election.

10 These series of figures possibly contain a statistical error. Since 1956 the number of employed married women has increased very sharply. Thus a growing number of women have been classified according to their own occupation rather than their husbands'. However, as seen by earlier reported data, the husband's social position is at least as important in determining the party preference of a married woman as her own occupation. When S. Holmberg, 'Svenska Väljare', pp. 316-21, computes 'class voting' indices separately for each sex, he finds that, although index values generally are lower for women, the pattern reported here appears among men as well as among women.

11 Markku Haranne, Dialectics between Occupational and Party Structures: Finland since World War II.

12 Henry Valen, 'Valg og Politikk', pp. 130-2.

13 The more dramatic changes among young voters than among the entire electorate is due partly to the greater volatility among younger voters in

party choice, but also to the larger amount of random variation in the measurement of their party preferences resulting from a smaller number of respondents.

14 Robert Erikson, 'Uppväxtförhållanden och Social Rörlighet', pp. 83-7.

15 Ibid., p. 76.

16 D. Butler and D. Stokes, 'Political Change in Britain', pp. 98-101. This study, however, adopts more stringent criteria in defining the socially mobile, i.e., not only occupational data for the voter and father but also the voter's perceptions of his and his father's class. Rune Åberg, Social Mobility and Class Structuration, discusses social mobility and party preferences.

17 Korpi, 'The Working Class in Welfare Capitalism', p. 321.

18 S.M. Lipset, 'Political Man', Chapter 4 argues that communist voting among the workers stems from authoritarian personality traits, and Erik Allardt, that some types of communist voting originate in anomie (cf. E. Allardt, Types of Protest and Alienation; A Theory of Solidarity and Legitimacy Conflicts; and Patterns of Class Conflict and Working Class Consciousness in Finnish Politics).

19 Lipset, op. cit., Chapter 4.

20 Allardt, op. cit.

21 The discussion in this section is documented in Walter Korpi, Working Class Communism in Western Europe.

22 The metal-workers' survey was carried out during the winter of 1966-7 and is documented in Korpi, 'The Working Class in Welfare Capitalism' pp. 369-72. The analysis here is confined to Swedish-born men. The miners' survey was commissioned by the Swedish Broadcasting Corporation and was conducted during the autumn of 1970, one year after the LKAB miners' strike, by the author in co-operation with the Audience and Programme Research Department. The sample consisted of 750 workers. The rate of non-response to the mailed anonymous questionnaire was 6 per cent. Of the respondents, 26 per cent failed to report their party preference.

23 Cf. also Korpi, 'The Working Class in Welfare Capitalism', pp. 311-17. Among the metal-workers, the bourgeois sympathizers also own a house and car more often than others.

24 Farmers have been excluded from the analysis.

25 E.g., Lipset, op. cit., Chapter 7.

26 Valen, op. cit., pp. 107-11.

27 Robert Erikson, 'Yrkesval och Officersrekrytering', p. 75 and Appendix G, Table 87, found a definite correlation between the desire for government employment (rather than a job in a private company) and leftist political attitudes among conscripts in military officer training.

28 O. Petersson, 'Väljarna och Valet 1976', pp. 37-9.

29 Linnea Gillwik, 'Småhuslyckan - Finns Den?', analyses activities and social relations in residential areas with single-family dwellings.

30 Butler and Stokes, op. cit., pp. 102-4, found a slight increase in identification with the middle class but no changes in party allegiances among those whose level of housing improved.

31 E.g., Seymour Martin Lipset, Industrial Proletariat in Comparative Perspectives.

32 Gösta Esping-Andersen, 'Social Class, Social Democracy and State Policy'.

CHAPTER 6 ELECTORAL GEOGRAPHY

1 C.G. Janson, 'Mandattilldelning och Regional Röstfördelning'; Gösta Carlsson, Partiförskjutningar som Tillväxtprocesser; Göran Gustafsson, 'Partistyrka och Partistyrkeförskjutningar'; Lars Ricknell, Politiska Regioner. For a general survey of the geography of elections, see, e.g., P.J. Taylor and R.J., Johnston, 'Geography of Elections'.

2 The geographical distribution of church attendance in Sweden is discussed in B. Gustafsson, The Established Church and the Decline of Church

Attendance in Sweden, p. 314.
3 Carlsson, op. cit.; Janson, op. cit., Chapter 6.
4 Carlsson, op. cit.
5 G. Carlsson, et al., Socio-ekonomiska Grupperingar.
6 In computing the expected socialist voting percentage in the 1979 election, I have attempted to replicate Carlsson's methods for the three earlier elections. The distribution of occupations in the constituencies has been estimated on the basis of the 'Surveys of Living Conditions' in Sweden (ULF) carried out by SCB. Only Swedish citizens between the ages of 18 and 74 in the 1977-8 surveys are included here. In addition, I have utilized the Party Sympathy Survey from November 1979 and the methods study of party preferences in connection with the 1979 election. The total number of interviews is 31,700. Ten occupational categories (formed by collapsing the categories in the socio-economic classification code, the SEI code) have been used in computing the expected socialist percentages. The occupational categories and the expected probabilities of electoral participation and socialist voting in the 1979 election, based on Party Sympathy Surveys, are reproduced in the table.

Occupational category	SEI code	Probability of electoral participation	Probability of voting socialist
Assistants, etc.	1	0.92	0.7007
Unskilled labourers	2	0.92	0.6608
Skilled labourers	3-4	0.92	0.7089
Low- and middle-level salaried employees	5-7	0.94	0.4293
Technicians, Engineers, etc.	8	0.94	0.3663
Higher-level salaried employees	9-10	0.98	0.2795
Farmers	11-12	0.94	0.0413
Small businessmen	13-14	0.94	0.2066
Big businessmen	15	0.98	0.0535
Students	19(20)	0.94	0.4423

The variances in the socialist voting percentages between the constituencies for the four elections were:

	1911	1924	1940	1979
	%	%	%	%
Actual	178.6	150.3	77.2	45.7
Expected	31.8	49.0	36.7	4.0
Difference (actual-expected)	92.0	51.9	30.4	33.6

Some of the changes in predicted variance between the elections are, of course, due to differences in computing methods.

Janson, op. cit., p. 185, has computed similar expected values for the 1948 election. However, his results for certain constituencies differ from the trends which emerge here, something which can be due to his use of partly different bases for computations.

7 E.g., Jan Lindhagen and Macke Nilsson, 'Hotet mot Arbetarrörelsen'; Jan Lindhagen, Åren vi Förlorade, and Men å Andra Sidan.
8 Robert Erikson, On Measuring Errors in Comparative Surveys; Robert M. Hauser, Context and Consex.
9 Herbert Tingsten, 'Political Behaviour', pp. 177-80.
10 Ibid., p. 231.
11 A British analysis based on a very large number of interviews shows that the proportion voting Labour among working-class voters tends to increase with the increase of the proportion of working-class voters in the constituency (D. Butler and D. Stokes, 'Political Change in Britain', pp. 182-9). For descriptions of similar studies, see Taylor and Johnston, op. cit., Chapter 5. C.N. Tate, Individual and Contextual Variables in British Voting Behaviour, has criticized Butler and Stoke's interpretation of their results.
12 Quoted from G. Fredriksson et al., 'Per-Albin-linjen', pp. 7-8.
13 The categorization of the communes is based on employment by sector of the economy of the resident population according to the 1975 census, where we have divided the economically active persons into three categories: industrial employment (manufacturing, mining, construction and utilities), service employment (distribution, transport, banking, government and public services), and other type of economic activity. In the metropolitan communes suburban communes are also included (e.g., for Stockholm the entire county of Stockholm is included with the exceptions of Norrtälje, Södertälje and Nynäshamn) all of which have very high proportions employed in the service sector. Industrial communes and partly industrialized communes have been defined solely on the basis of the proportion in industrial jobs. The mixed communes also comprise, among others, agricultural and sparsely populated communes.
14 Walter Korpi, 'The Working Class in Welfare Capitalism', pp. 182-3.
15 The figures to 1975 are based on census statistics; those for 1979, on the Labour Force Surveys.
16 The proportions of voters by social groups have been computed on the basis of official election statistics from 1924 to 1948. The data for 1952 are taken from C.G. Janson, Stadens Struktur, p. 306. The figures for 1979 come from surveys of living conditions carried out by SCB (see note 6 above).
17 Janson, Stadens Struktur, pp. 306-7. Some commentators, who claim that the homogeneous working-class districts in the metropolitan centres previously were a major prerequisite for the mobilizing capability of the labour movement, explain in the next breath that the Social Democratic setbacks in the metropolitan regions during the 1970s were a result of growing social segregation.

CHAPTER 7 VOTERS ON THE MOVE

1 For a survey of the development of the Swedish party system, see B. Särlvik, Sweden: The Social Bases of Parties in a Developmental Perspective; and Per Erik Back and Sten Berglund, 'Det Svenska Partiväsendet', Chapter 2. The Citizens Rally ('Medborgerlig Samling'), which campaigned to increased co-operation between the bourgeois parties and hardly can be designated as a party, was also represented in the Riksdag for a number of years in the 1960s.
2 The changes in partisan choice can be expressed, e.g., as average percentage of change in the party's share of the vote between two consecutive elections during a period of years. In the elections between 1938 and 1950 the Social Democrats' electoral support changed on an average of 2.8 per cent. This average was 2.0 per cent during 1950-60, it was 4.7 per cent during 1960-70 and 1.0 per cent during 1970-9. M. Pedersen, Changing Patterns of Electoral Volatility, shows that the swings in electoral support since the 1950s have been less dramatic in Sweden than in many other European countries, especially Norway and Denmark.

3 Sören Holmberg and Olof Petersson, 'Inom Felmarginalen', Chapters 3-5, have an insightful discussion of the problems of reliability in political opinion polls in Sweden. Experience shows that certain biases exist in the responses to interview questions concerning party preferences. For example, the results often overestimate the support of the Social Democrats and underestimate Communist Support. The estimates based on these surveys are usually corrected for such biases.

4 The voter polls conducted by Sifo are based on the question: 'What party do you think is best today?' This type of question with affective overtones can be expected to produce sharper swings in opinion than SCB's Party Sympathy Surveys, which inquire: 'What party would you vote for if there were an election in the next few days?' Sifo's polls are based on a sample of 1,000-1,500 persons, whereas SCB's sample consists of 9,000 persons. Sifo excludes a substantial portion of the electorate, including all persons over seventy years of age, from its sampling frame. By using personal interview and simulated election ballots, however, Sifo has a lower proportion who refuse to disclose their party preference than SCB, which uses telephone interviews. Sifo's election forecasts are based on better methods than are its voter polls. SCB's survey techniques may possibly result in the underestimation of changes in party choice. See Holmberg and Petersson, op. cit., Chapter 4. The methods and results of SCB's Party Sympathy Surveys have been reported in 'Statistiska Meddelanden', serie Be.

5 The results of these election surveys, carried out by SCB with the collaboration of Bo Särlvik, Olof Petersson and Sören Holmberg, are presented in the series 'Sveriges Officiella Statistik: Allmänna Val' for the particular election and in O. Petersson, 'Väljarna och Valet 1976'.

6 Sources SOS, 'Allmänna Valen 1976', vol. 3, pp. 139-40 and SCB's Party Sympathy Survey, November 1979.

7 S. Holmberg, 'Svenska Väljare', p. 45. Elections to the Riksdag are traditionally held on the third Sunday in September.

8 Petersson, op. cit., p. 169. Data for the 1979 election from SCB's Party Sympathy Survey.

9 In the parliamentary elections between 1964 and 1979 the average percentages of non-voting by party choice in the preceding election were 2.6 per cent for the Conservatives, 3.2 per cent for the Centre Party, 3.8 for the Liberals, 2.9 for the Social Democrats and 3.5 for the Communists.

10 Petersson, op. cit., pp. 174 and 271.

11 The average percentages of low confidence in the parties and politicians in the elections between 1968 and 1976 were 14 per cent among those voting for the Social Democrats, 27 per cent among Communist voters, 24 per cent among voters for the Centre Party, 23 per cent among Liberal voters, and 21 per cent among Conservative voters (Petersson, op. cit., p. 261). The low average for Social Democratic voters is probably due to their party being in power until the autumn of 1976. Between 1976 and 1979 confidence decreased among voters for all parties except Communist voters. The decrease was strongest among Social Democrats.

12 In these calculations, switches to and from the minor parties have not been included. Furthermore, the figures refer only to voters who were eligible in both elections. Only changes of at least 0.2 per cent have been reported here.

13 According to the Party Sympathy Survey in November 1979, non-voting amounted to 3.2 per cent among the bourgeois voters in the 1976 election and 2.1 per cent among Social Democratic and Communist voters. On the basis of a smaller sample, Holmberg, op. cit., p. 57, finds however that the Social Democrats were the primary losers on the decrease in participation.

14 Petersson, op. cit., pp. 191-5.

15 The so-called 'affairs', which attracted much attention in the media during the spring of 1976, included the chairman of the Transport Workers' Union vacationing in the Canary Islands (at a holiday facility owned and used by the Swedish Employers' Confederation) at the same time as LO called for a

tourist boycott of Franco's Spain, the attempts of labour movement officials clandestinely to transfer funds to the Finnish Social Democratic Party, and the taxation case of Ingmar Bergman.

16 SCB's data on changes in voting intentions during the weeks before the 1976 election come from a methods study complementing the regular Party Sympathy Surveys. These day-by-day data on changes in estimates of voting intentions for each party have been obtained by basing the estimate of voting intentions on the interviews conducted up to a specific day and subtracting from this figure the estimate based on the completed set of interviews. Since the interviews are not randomly distributed over days, trends may possibly emerge through methodological artefacts. To control for this, at my request SCB has produced comparable data from the Party Sympathy Surveys in February, May and November 1976, where however similar trends do not occur.

17 Petersson, op. cit., pp. 188, 190, 201 and 220.

18 Forskningsgruppen för samhälls- och informationsstudier, Undersökningsmaterial Över en Serie Opinionsmätningar, see also S. Holmberg et al., 'Väljarna och Kärnkraften'.

19 Holmberg, op. cit., pp. 61-8.

20 A. Downs, 'An Economic Theory of Democracy'.

21 Korpi, 'The Working Class in Welfare Capitalism', pp. 310-7, and B. Särlvik, 'Electoral Behaviour in the Swedish Multiparty System'.

22 Cf. R. Inglehardt, 'The Silent Revolution', and Seymour Martin Lipset, Industrial Proletariat in Comparative Perspectives.

23 Holmberg et al., op. cit., pp. 146, 149; and Evert Vedung, 'Kärnkraften och Regeringen Fälldins Fall', pp. 169-72.

24 See, inter alia, B. Särlvik, Partibyten som Mått på Avstånd och Dimensioner i Partisystemet, and Mapping the Party Space; Petersson, op. cit., Chapter 3; M. Lindén, Political Dimensions and Relative Party Positions; D. Stokes, Spatial Models of Party Competition; and I Budge et al., 'Party Identification and Beyond'.

25 The analysis of dimensions has entailed the following technical procedures. For each of the two tables on changes in partisan choice (the first covering the period 1958-68 and the second for 1976-9), we have first constructed an index of similarity-dissimilarity between the parties by comparing the actual switches between the parties and the predicted switches, assuming that those who change parties choose the new party irrespective of their original party. Subsequently a log-linear analysis of a matrix without diagonal values has been employed (Yvonne Bishop et al., 'Discrete Multivariate Analysis', pp. 177-210). In this way two values have been computed for each party, one for outflows and one for inflows. The average of these two values has been used as input for a dimensions analysis according to the 'smallest space' model, utilizing the MINISSA program.

The dimension analyses show that two dimensions can completely account for the input data (coefficient of stress = 0) for both the years 1958-68 and 1976-9. The first is the left-right dimension. The second dimension, and in both cases the less significant one, places the Centre Party and the Liberals on opposite sides of the other three parties, which receive almost identical values. This second dimension is difficult to interpret. The peculiar results for the Centre Party and the Liberals can arise from the nearness of these two parties, which means that one of them is bypassed, especially in partisan changes by bourgeois voters. Figure 7.12 depicts only the positions of the parties along the first dimension.

26 Holmberg, op. cit., pp. 198-9.

27 In the period 1958-68 we find hardly any switches between the Centre Party and the Communists, but during the years 1976-9 4 per cent of the Centre Party defectors have gone over to the Communists, while 9 per cent of the Communist defectors have changed to the Centre Party and 4 per cent to the Liberals. This change can also be partly due, however, to the fact that in the 1970s the electoral support of the Communist Party has increasingly come from middle-class voters.

28 Holmberg, op. cit., pp. 103ff. Holmberg's dimensional analysis based on preference orderings of parties also indicates that the left-right dimension was much more important than the issue of nuclear energy in voters' preferences for the parties.

29 The percentages in parentheses in this and the following tables indicate that the number of respondents was 16-29 individuals.

30 For Gothenburg and Malmö, which do not have a county council the comparison is with the 1979 parliamentary election.

31 In Tables 7.5 and 7.6 the calculations are based on data from the Party Sympathy Survey in May 1980.

32 Before World War II, employment among women with young children seems to have been more common in working-class families than in the higher socio-economic strata. During the postwar years, however, these differences appear to have decreased (Robert Erikson, 'Uppväxtförhållanden och Social Rörlighet', pp. 58 and 160). The data on young people's perceptions of sex roles are from Youth Bureau, 'The Youth of the World and Japan', pp. 9 and 44-5.

33 E.g. Rita Liljeström, Jämställdhet, Arbetarklass och Välfärdskapitalism.

34 The idea of the authoritarian or irrational working class has been influential in social research (e.g. S.M. Lipset, 'Political Man', Chapter 4; E. Allardt, Types of Protest and Alienation). An analysis of available data on differences between socio-economic strata concerning cultural values indicates that these assumptions do not have any firm empirical foundation (Walter Korpi, Working Class Communism in Western Europe: Rational or Non-rational?). Connie Svenning and Marianne Svenning, 'Daghemmen, Jämlikheten och Klassamhället', p. 181, however, present data revealing that Swedish workers more frequently agree with statements on sex roles of a traditional nature.

35 Petersson, op. cit., pp. 256-65; Kurt Törnqvist, 'Opinion 80', pp. 10-14; and Holmberg, op. cit., Chapter 9, find that after 1976 the previously very high confidence of Social Democrats has dropped markedly, but also that the confidence of bourgeois voters has further declined.

36 This need not be the case in countries with weak class voting: see James DeNardo, Turnout and the Vote.

37 For an excellent analysis of electoral change in Norway in the post-war period see Henry Valen, 'Valg og Politikk'.

38 See e.g. Inglehardt, op. cit., and Lipset, Industrial Proletariat in Comparative Perspectives.

CHAPTER 8 THE POLITICS OF INDUSTRIAL CONFLICT

1 This chapter is based largely on Walter Korpi and Michael Shalev, Strikes, Industrial Relations and Class Conflict in Capitalist Societies; Walter Korpi and Michael Shalev, Strikes, Power and Politics in the Western Nations, 1900-1976; Walter Korpi, 'The Working Class in Welfare Capitalism', Chapter 4; and Walter Korpi, Sweden: Conflict, Power and Politics in Industrial Relations. I am however alone responsible for the interpretations made here.

2 Clark Kerr et al., 'Industrialism and Industrial Man', p. 209.

3 C. Kerr, 'Labour and Management in Industrial Society', p. xx. Kerr had however earlier expressed more structural views on industrial conflict, to the effect that it cannot be eliminated.

4 Ralph Dahrendorf, 'Class and Class Conflict in Industrial Societies', pp. 267-76.

5 J.T. Dunlop, 'The Industrial Relations System'; Arthur M. Ross and Paul I Hartman, 'Changing Patterns of Industrial Conflict'. Among the several factors Ross and Hartman mention as contributing to the decline of strikes is labour's political activity, which may provide an effective alternative to collective bargaining for increasing the standard of living of the workers, but which also may discourage strikes through fear of their electoral reper-

cussions on the labour parties.

In another theoretical approach, common especially among American economists, industrial conflict has been analysed as a bargaining process between labour and management, usually at company level. In that perspective labour disputes have been regarded as a result of 'faulty negotiations' (J.R. Hicks, 'The Theory of Wages'). The manner in which the business cycles influence the bargaining process and the frequency of industrial conflict has also been studied (cf., e.g., Orley Ashenfelter and George E. Johnson, Bargaining Theory, Trade Unions and Industrial Strike Activity).

6 H.A. Clegg, 'Trade Unionism under Collective Bargaining', and A. Flanders, 'Management and Unions'.

7 Clegg, op. cit., p. 82.

8 This view permeated the work of the Donovan Commission on industrial relations.

9 Edward Shorter and Charles Tilly, 'Strikes in France, 1830-1968'.

10 E.g. Richard Hyman, 'Strikes', and 'Industrial Relations'.

11 M.G. Schmidt, Does Corporatism Matter?, p. 257; G. Lehmbruch, Introduction: Neo-corporatism in Comparative Perspective, p. 6; and Leo Panitch, Recent Theorizations on Corporatism.

12 The main body of data is taken from original publications. A more detailed description of the data collection shall be given by Michael Shalev in forthcoming publications. The data for relative involvement in Figure 8.1 are partially smoothed by the use of weighted five-year moving averages, with weights 0.1, 0.2, 0.4, 0.2, 0.1.

13 Depending on the data supply and political conditions in the different countries, our data up to 1938 may refer to somewhat different periods in different countries.

14 Comparison between countries with regard to number of conflicts is unreliable, as custom regarding the registration of small conflicts varies from one country to another. These data are not presented here.

15 Economic growth here refers to annual changes in gross domestic product per capita. The correlation between economic growth and volume of conflict is 0.03, and with involvement in conflict, 0.13.

16 The correlation between GDP per capita and volume of conflict is 0.06, and with involvement in conflict, 0.24.

17 For an analysis of industrial relations on the level of the workplace in the Swedish metal-working industry and some comparisons with the United Kingdom, see Walter Korpi, Unofficial Strikes in Sweden, and Workplace Bargaining, the Law and Unofficial Strikes.

18 This 'political' explanation of long-term changes in the level of industrial conflict was presented in a paper (Walter Korpi, Sweden: Conflict, Power and Politics in Industrial Relations) at an international industrial relations conference held at Harvard University in 1975.

19 P.K. Edwards, 'Strikes in the United States 1881-1974', pp. 220 and 223, misinterprets this classification to be based on the patterns of strikes. Industrial conflict in this context however is a dependent variable, and the classification of countries is based on independent variables.

20 Korpi, 'The Working Class in Welfare Capitalism', Chapters 4 and 9.

21 Data on union membership are from the 'Yearbook of Swedish Statistics' and include also members of white-collar unions. Unemployment figures are from the following sources: 1962-80, from labour force surveys; 1956-61, from statistics on unemployment among members of unemployment insurance bodies; and 1911-55, from registered unemployment among union members. Unemployment figures for 1894-1911 are estimated from data on employment variations in mining and the engineering industry, based on the regression of deviations from the trend in these employment figures for 1911-39. The Durbin-Watson statistic indicates the presence of trends in the residuals. The equation tends to give too low estimates before 1900 and in 1955-70, too high estimates in 1930-7.

22 For a study of the development of industrial conflict in the United Kingdom,

see J.E. Cronin, 'Industrial Conflict in Modern Britain'.

23 During the postwar period the Icelandic union movement has been relatively strong but the political splits within the left have persisted. The socialist parties have from time to time participated in the government on a politically relatively weak basis. The level of industrial conflict has been very high. Cf. Walter Korpi, Labour Movements and Industrial Relations.

24 Edwards, op. cit., pp. 234-5.

25 Geoffrey K. Ingham, 'Strikes and Industrial Conflict', has attempted to explain differences in levels of employer organizations between the United Kingdom and Scandinavia in terms of structural characteristics facilitating employer organization. While such factors probably are of relevance, my hypothesis is thus that it is the threat from a strong and unified union movement which is most effective in inducing employers to organize.

26 For a discussion of such factors cf. Michael Shalev and Walter Korpi, Working Class Mobilization and American Exceptionalism.

27 Jürg K. Siegenthaler, Current Problems of Trade Union and Party Relations in Switzerland.

28 Andrew Martin, 'The Politics of Economic Policy in the United States', contains a fruitful discussion of these questions.

29 E.g., Ashenfelter and Johnson, op. cit.; Douglas A. Hibbs, Industrial Conflict in Advanced Industrial Societies. Cf. also, however, Martin Paldam and Peder J. Pedersen, The Macro-model Explaining Industrial Conflict, where this association is not found.

30 Cf. Christopher Hewitt, 'The Effect of Political Democracy and Social Democracy on Equality in Industrial Societies. The sources of the figures on unemployment and redistribution used here are further discussed in Chapter 9.

31 We have here taken as the dependent variable the log of relative volume of conflict, which gives a somewhat better fit with the theoretical model than the actual figures for volume of conflict.

32 The former view prevails, e.g., in the so-called McCracken Report (Paul McCracken, 'Towards Full Employment and Price Stability'). The latter view has been developed in Fred Hirsch and John H. Goldthorpe, 'The Political Economy of Inflation'.

CHAPTER 9 SOCIAL POLICY

1 Richard Jackman, 'Politics and Social Equality'; Harold Wilensky, 'The Welfare State and Equality'; Hugh Heclo, 'Modern Social Politics in Britain and Sweden'; and F. Parkin, 'Class, Inequality and the Political Order'.

2 Göran Therborn et al., Sweden Before and After Social Democracy; Richard Scase, 'Social Democracy in Capitalist Society'; Ralph Miliband, 'The State in Capitalist Society'; Claus Offe, Advanced Capitalism and the Welfare State; Ian Gough, 'The Political Economy of the Welfare State'; Norman Ginsburg, 'Class, Capital and Social Policy'.

3 Christopher Hewitt, The Effect of Political Democracy and Social Democracy on Equality in Industrial Societies; Francis G. Castles, 'The Social Democratic Image of Society'; John D. Stephens, 'The Transition from Capitalism to Socialism'.

4 At the Swedish Institute for Social Research, Gösta Esping-Andersen and I are presently involved in a comparative research project on social policy in eighteen OECD countries. This chapter incorporates sections of Walter Korpi, Social Policy and Distributional Conflict in Capitalist Democracies.

5 Asa Briggs, The Welfare State in Historical Perspective; Peter Flora, On the Development of Western European Welfare States.

6 Seebohm Rowntree and G.R. Lavers, 'Poverty: A Study of Town Life'.

7 The absolute definition of poverty in the United States is based on the work of Mollie Orshansky, Counting the Poor, and is discussed in A.B. Atkinson, 'The Economics of Inequality', Chapter 10; and Walter Korpi, Approaches to the Study of Poverty in the United States. Social assistance as a defini-

tion of poverty is discussed in Walter Korpi, 'Fattigdom i Välfärden', and Social Policy and Poverty in Postwar Sweden.

8 The concept of power resources is discussed in Chapter 2.

9 The theory of human capital is developed, inter alia, in Gary S. Becker, 'Human Capital'. Alternative approaches are outlined, e.g., in Lester Thurow, 'Generating Inequality', and in Peter B. Doeringer and Michael J. Piore, 'Internal Labor Markets and Manpower Analysis'.

10 The now classic presentation of this theory was made in Kingsley Davis and Wilbert E. Moore, Some Principles of Stratification.

11 E.g., Gerhard E. Lenski, 'Power and Privilege'.

12 Sten Johansson, 'Om Levnadsnivåundersökningen'.

13 Cf., e.g., Flora, op. cit., and Peter Flora and Arnold J. Heidenheimer, 'The Development of Welfare States in Europe and America'.

14 E.g., Wilensky, op. cit. Some studies (e.g., Jackman, op. cit.) also use as a dependent variable an index of income inequality among branches of the economy or sectors, something which is irrelevant when one wants to describe inequality among individuals and households.

15 The ILO measure of 'social security spending' includes medical care expenditures covered by social insurance, cash sickness benefits, unemployment insurance, statutory old-age pensions, occupational injury benefits under social insurance, and family allowances (ILO, 'The Cost of Social Security').

16 Jens Alber, The Growth of Social Insurance Schemes in Western Europe.

17 Richard Titmuss, 'Essays on "the Welfare State"', pp. 34-55.

18 Richard Titmuss, 'Commitment to Welfare', p. 116.

19 The figure is a modified version of Sten Johansson, Välfärdsbegrepp och Välfärdsmätning.

20 Harold Wilensky and C. Lebeaux, 'Industrial Society and Social Welfare' and Richard Titmuss, 'Social Policy', pp. 30-1.

21 E.g., Roland Spånt, 'Den Svenska Inkomstfördelningens Utveckling'.

22 Wilensky, op. cit.

23 Wilensky's dependent variable of 'the welfare backlash' therefore has low reliability and validity.

24 Malcolm Sawyer, 'Income Distribution in the OECD Countries'. Cf. also T. Stark, 'The Distribution of Income in Eight Countries'.

25 OECD, 'Public Expenditure on Income Maintenance Programs', pp. 64-8. For one-person households the poverty line is set at two-thirds of the average per capita income and for three-person households, at 125 per cent of the per capita income.

26 Toshiaki Tachibanaki, A Note on the Impact of Income Tax Redistribution.

27 Hewitt, op. cit.

28 For a perceptive discussion of the political context of unemployment, see Andrew Martin, 'The Politics of Economic Policy in the United States'.

29 In Table 9.2 unemployment measures are adjusted to US standards except for figures given within parentheses, which are national definitions and thus are not directly comparable with the remaining data.

30 There are some indications that the Japanese data used by Sawyer may underestimate the level of inequality. Stark, op. cit., Chapter 7, finds that in 1956-73 income inequality has been clearly higher in Japan than in the United Kingdom. Generally we can expect that variations in female labour force participation will affect differences in income equality between countries, something which is of relevance, e.g., in the case of the Netherlands.

31 Hans L. Zetterberg, 'En Socialpolitik för Åttiotalet', p. 115.

32 Diane Sainsbury, 'Swedish Social Democratic Ideology and Electoral Politics 1944-1948', discusses the political parties' positions on the expansion of social insurance schemes in the election campaigns during 1944-8.

33 The data in Tables 9.4 and 9.5 are taken from Zetterberg, op. cit.

34 I wish to thank Bo Särlvik, Sören Holmberg and Olof Petersson for providing me with these computations. The choice of alternative answers to the questions has been slightly modified during the different elections. Since

the alternative 'Don't know' has not been included for all elections the percentages are based only on those who agree or disagree with the statement.

35 The unemployment figures refer to unemployed persons in manufacturing according to unemployment insurance statistics.

36 Hans L. Zetterberg, Det Svenska Valet 1976, and later figures.

37 Changes in social assistance are analysed in Korpi, Social Policy and Poverty in Postwar Sweden, and Karin Tengvald, 'Samhällets Krav och de Fattigas Resurser'. Lars Jonung and Eskil Wadensjö, The Effects of Unemployment, Inflation and Real Income Growth on Government Popularity in Sweden, show that support for the Social Democrats during the period 1967-76 was affected by changes in unemployment and prices.

38 O. Petersson, 'Väljarna och Valet 1976', p. 264.

CHAPTER 10 AFTER THE HISTORICAL COMPROMISE

1 G. Fredriksson et al., 'Per-Albin-linjen', p. 26.

2 Election statistics make it possible to describe the distribution of 'social groups' among the population included in the electoral registers. During the period 1924-48 the distribution was fairly stable, approximately 5 per cent for social group I, 40 per cent for social group II, and 55 per cent for social group III. I have used the SCB Level of Living Surveys for 1977 and 1978 to estimate the distribution of socio-economic strata according to the SEI Classification (G. Carlsson et al., Socio-ekonomiska Grupperingar, p. 385) among Swedish citizens between the ages of eighteen and seventy-four years. The resulting distribution is roughly 10 per cent in social group I (SEI categories 9, 10 and 15), 36 per cent in social group II (SEI categories 6-8, 11-14), 50 per cent in social group III (SEI categories 1-5) and 4 per cent students. Social group III is over-represented among the immigrants, who have not been included here but have increased markedly since 1948. Göran Therborn, 'Klasstrukturen i Sverige 1930-80', has charted the changes in occupational groups, based on census statistics, since the 1930s.

3 The distinction made here between the situations of individuals in terms of class, market, work and status is reminiscent of D. Lockwood, 'The Black-coated Worker', pp. 201-13. While Lockwood defines class situation in terms of market and work situations, I distinguish between these three situations and view class in terms of relationships to the means of production. These analytical concepts can in part be traced back to Max Weber's original division of class, status and party which he saw as different aspects of power.

4 For a discussion, see Walter Korpi, 'The Working Class in Welfare Capitalism', p. 84. Changes in the position of the salaried employee are probably related more to the composition of new white-collar jobs than to a 'proletarization' of earlier white-collar positions.

5 Rune Åberg, Social Mobility and Class Structuration.

6 See John H. Goldthorpe and P. Bevan, The Study of Social Stratification in Great Britain: 1946-1976, for distinctions in the interpretation of the concept of status.

7 Korpi, op. cit., pp. 139-42.

8 Public employees are very strongly represented among politically elected office holders.

9 Tomas Hammar, 'Sveriges Första Invandrarval', has studied the electoral participation of immigrants.

10 See e.g. S.M. Lipset, 'Political Man', p. 231.

11 See SCB, 'Levnadsförhållanden', p. 107 and SCB, 'Arbetskraftsundersökningen'. Approximately 40 per cent of the women in the labour force had part-time jobs in 1979. The largest increase in labour force participation among women has occurred among those with children under seven years of age; their participation rose from 39 per cent in 1963 to 72 per cent in 1979.

12 See Rita Liljeström et al., 'Roller i Omvandling', for examples of the job experiences of working women.

13 A considerable proportion of the decline, of course, reflects the shrinking of the agricultural sector.

14 The Danish and Swedish experiences in housing policy are analysed in Gösta Esping-Andersen, 'Social Class, Social Democracy and State Policy'.

15 It was suggested, for example, that when workers switched from beer to wine this was an indication of changing life styles and a sign of the disappearing class-consciousness (Tage Erlander, 'Tage Erlander 1955-1960', pp. 146-8).

16 J.H. Goldthorpe et al., 'The Affluent Worker'; R.F. Hamilton, 'Class and Politics in the United States'.

17 An early critique of the naive optimism in economic progress is found in Gunnar Inghe and Maj-Britt Inghe, 'Den Ofärdiga Välfärden'.

18 Per capita consumption of alcohol converted into litres of pure alcohol in 1968-70 was estimated as the following amounts: France, 16.1; Portugal, 15.2; Italy, 13.7; Spain; 11.9; Austria, 10.8; Switzerland, 10.3; West Germany, 10.1; Belgium, 8.4; Australia, 8.2; New Zealand, 7.3; Denmark, 7.0; Canada, 6.4; Britain, 6.2; United States, 6.0; Sweden, 5.8; Netherlands, 5.3; Finland, 4.4; Ireland, 4.4; Norway, 3.5; Iceland, 2.8; and Israel, 2.1 litres (K. Bruun et al., 'Alcohol Control Policies in Public Health Perspective', p. 76).

19 The concept of social elimination is discussed in Hans Berglind and Anna-Lena Lindquist, 'Utslagningen på Arbetsmarknaden'. The trends in life expectancy of men and women are discussed in G. Carlsson et al., 'Liv och Hälsa', pp. 94ff. An analysis of early retirement pensions is found in Peter Hedström, 'Förtidspension - Välfärd eller Ofärd?'

20 SCB, 'Levnadsförhållanden', pp. 214-15, 254.

21 Data on urbanization and labour mobility are presented in Rune Åberg, 'Flyttarna och Arbetsmarknaden', pp. 9-12 and in A. Jacobsson, 'Om Flyttningar i Sverige', p. 97. Åberg's interesting study of the causes and consequences of labour mobility indicates that moving does not have pronounced negative effects on union and political activity (Åberg, op. cit., pp. 116-21). Long-distance mobility, indicated by the proportion who have lived in more than one locality during their childhood, has however increased among generations born after 1930 (Robert Erikson, 'Uppväxtförhållanden och Social Rörlighet').

22 Analyses of social relations in different types of residential areas in Sweden are contained in Åke Daun, 'Förortsliv'; Börje Hanssen, 'Familj, Hushåll, Släkt'; David Popenoe, 'The Suburban Environment; Sweden and the United States'; and Korpi, op. cit., pp. 181-4. In his comparative study of welfare in the Nordic countries, E. Allardt, 'Att Ha, att Älska, att Vara', pp. 97-108, also deals with social relations. The distribution of the response to the question about discussions with parents is found in Youth Bureau, 'The Youth of the World and Japan', pp. 36-7, 70-1.

23 Kjell Härnqvist and Allan Svensson, 'Den Sociala Selektionen till Gymnasiet'.

24 SCB, 'Levnadsförhållanden', pp. 158, 264. The number of books per person borrowed from public libraries increased from 3.9 in 1950 to 6.5 in 1965 and to 11.2 in 1975. The proportion of adults participating in voluntary study circles in their leisure time increased from 22 per cent in 1968 to 33 per cent in 1981.

25 R. Inglehart, 'The Silent Revolution', pp. 216-29, provides data on the relationship between religious activity and voting in several Western countries. In Sweden the proportion of baptized children during the years 1970-5 was slightly over 80 per cent whereas the proportion of civil marriages increased from 16 to 31 per cent and proportions of confirmations declined from 81 to 74 per cent (SCB, op. cit., p. 58). In a comparative study in 1977-8 young people between the ages of eighteen and twenty-four years were asked about their religious convictions. The proportions stating they were not religious were 71 per cent in Japan, 68 per cent in Sweden, 41 per cent in France, 35 per cent in Australia, 14 per cent in Britain,

10 per cent in United States, 7 per cent in Switzerland and 5 per cent in West Germany. See Youth Bureau, op. cit., pp. 36-7.

26 To avoid misinterpretations it should be pointed out that such trends as increasing drug abuse and crime do not of course lead to bourgeois voting. They do however, reduce the socialist bloc's mobilizing possibilities and thus indirectly benefit the bourgeois bloc.

27 SOU 1975: 41, pp. 23, 28; Göran Gustafsson, 'Partistyrka och Partistyrke-förskjutningar'.

28 Problems of union democracy are discussed in more detail in Korpi, op. cit., Chapter 8. The electorate's perceptions of the power of groups and organizations are described in O. Petersson, 'Väljarna och Valet 1976', pp. 110-14.

29 Rudolf Meidner et al., 'Employee Investment Funds'; LO, 'Kollektiv Kapitalbildning genom Löntagarfonder'; TCO, 'Löntagarkapital genom Fonder'.

30 These ideas are developed in F. Hirsch and J.H. Goldthorpe, 'The Political Economy of Inflation'. The following discussion of the monetarist views has benefited from a critical review of these ideas in J.H. Goldthorpe, Problems of Political Economy after the End of the Post-War Period.

31 For a discussion of the concept of 'provisional Utopias' as formulated by the late Ernst Wigforss, see Timothy Tilton, A Swedish Road to Socialism. Ulf Himmelstrand et al., 'Beyond Welfare Capitalism', offer an interesting analysis of preconditions for political developments in Sweden.

32 Fredriksson et al., op. cit., p. 9.

33 E.g., Leo Panitch, The Limits of Corporatism.

34 Meidner, op. cit.

BIBLIOGRAPHY

Åberg, Rune, Social Mobility and Class Structuration; 'Acta Sociologica', 22 (3), pp. 247-71, 1979.

Åberg, Rune, 'Flyttarna och Arbetsmarknaden. En Studie av Flyttningars Orsaker och Konsekvenser', Stockholm, Prisma och Institutet för Social Forskning, 1980.

Ahlberg, G., 'Befolkningsutveckling och Urbanisering i Sverige 1911-50', Stockholm, Stockholms kommunalförvaltning, 1953.

Alber, Jens, The Growth of Social Insurance Schemes in Western Europe: Has Social Democracy Made a Difference? Paper presented at the XIth World Congress of the International Political Science Association in Moscow, 1979.

Albrektsen, Beatrice Halsaa, 'Kvinner og Politisk Deltagelse', Oslo, Pax, 1977.

Alford, R.R., 'Party and Society', Chicago, Rand McNally, 1963.

Alford, R.R., Class Voting in the Anglo-American Political Systems, pp. 67-94 in S.M. Lipset and S. Rokkan (eds), 'Party Systems and Voter Alignments', New York, Free Press, 1967.

Alford, R.R., and Friedland, R., Political Participation and Public Policy, pp. 429-79 in A. Inkeles et al. (eds), 'Annual Review of Sociology', Palo Alto, Annual Review, 1975.

Allardt, E., A Theory on Solidarity and Legitimacy Conflicts, pp. 78-960, in E. Allardt and Y. Littunen (eds), 'Cleavages, Ideologies and Party Systems', Helsinki, Transactions of the Westermarck Society, 1964.

Allardt, E., Patterns of Class Conflict and Working Class Consciousness in Finnish Politics, pp. 97-131, in E. Allardt and Y. Littunen (eds), 'Cleavages, Ideologies and Party Systems', Helsinki, Transactions of the Westermarck Society, 1964.

Allardt, Erik, Types of Protest and Alienation, pp. 45-63 in Erik Allardt and Stein Rokkan (eds), 'Mass Politics: Studies in Political Sociology', New York, Free Press, 1970.

Allardt, E., 'Att Ha, att Älska, att Vara. Om Välfärd i Norden', Lund, Argos, 1975.

Ashenfelter, Orley, and Johnson, George E., Bargaining Theory, Trade Unions and Industrial Strike Activity, 'American Economic Review', 59, pp. 35-49, 1969.

Atkinson, A.B., 'The Economics of Inequality', Oxford, Clarendon Press, 1975.

Bachrach, P., and Baratz, M.S., 'Power and Poverty', London, Oxford University Press, 1970.

Back, Per Erik, and Berglund, Sten, 'Det Svenska Partiväsendet', Stockholm, AWE/Gebers, 1978.

Bain, G.S. and Elsheikh, F., 'Union Growth and the Business Cycle', Oxford, Basil Blackwell, 1976.

Barry, Brian (ed.), 'Power and Political Theory', New York, John Wiley, 1975.

Becker, Gary S., 'Human Capital', New York, John Wiley, 1964.

Bendix, R., 'Nation-building and Citizenship', New York, John Wiley, 1964.

Bendix, R., and Lipset, S.M., 'Class, Status and Power: Social Stratification in Comparative Perspective', New York, Free Press, 1966.

Berelson, Bernhard, Lazarsfeld, Paul F. and Mcphee, William N., 'Voting', Chicago, University of Chicago Press, 1954.

Berglind, Hans, and Lindquist, Anna-Lena, 'Utslagningen på Arbetsmarknaden', Lund, Studentlitteratur, 1975.

Berglund, Sten, and Lindström, Ulf, 'The Scandinavian Party System(s)', Lund Studentlitteratur, 1978.
Bishop, Yvonne, Fienberg, Stephen E. and Holland, Paul W., 'Discrete Multivariate Analysis: Theory and Practice', Cambridge, Mass., MIT Press, 1975.
Briggs, Asa, The Welfare State in Historical Perspective, 'European Journal of Sociology', 2 (2), pp. 221-58, 1961.
Bruun, K., et al., 'Alcohol Control Policies in Public Health Perspective', Helsinki, Finnish Foundation for Alcohol Studies, vol. 25, 1975.
Budge, I., Crewe, I. and Farlie, D. (eds), 'Party Identification and Beyond: Representations of Voting and Competition', London, John Wiley, 1976.
Burnham, Walter Dean, The Appearance and Disappearance of the American Voter: A Historical Overview, in Richard Rose (ed.), 'Electoral Participation: A Comparative Analysis', London, Sage, 1980.
Butler, D., and Stokes, D., 'Political Change in Britain', Harmondsworth, Penguin, 1969.
Carlsson, Gösta, Partiförskjutningar som Tillväxtprocesser, 'Statsvetenskaplig Tidskrift', 45, pp. 172-213, 1963.
Carlsson, G., et al., Socio-ekonomiska Gruppering, 'Statistisk Tidskrift', 12 (5), pp. 381-401, 1974.
Carlsson, G., et al., 'Liv och Hälsa. En Kartläggning av Hälsoutvecklingen i Sverige', Stockholm, Liber, 1979.
Castles, Francis G., 'The Social Democratic Image of Society. A Study of the Achievements and Origins of Scandinavian Social Democracy in Comparative Perspective', London, Routledge & Kegan Paul, 1978.
Clegg, H.A., 'Trade Unionism under Collective Bargaining', Oxford, Basil Blackwell, 1976.
Converse, Philip E., Some Priority Variables in Comparative Electoral Research, pp. 727-45 in R. Rose (ed.), 'Electoral Behavior: A Comparative Handbook', New York, Free Press, 1974.
Converse, Philip E., 'The Dynamics of Party Support', Beverly Hills, Cal., Sage, 1976.
Crewe, Ivor, Electoral Participation, pp. 216-63 in D. Butler, H.R. Penniman and A. Ranney (eds), 'Democracy at the Polls: A Comparative Study of Competitive National Elections', Washington, DC, American Enterprise Institute, 1981.
Crewe, Ivor, Fox, Tony and Alt, Jim, Non-voting in British General Elections 1966-October 1977, in Colin Crouch (ed.), 'Participation in Politics', London, Croom Helm, 1977.
Cronin, J.E., 'Industrial Conflict in Modern Britain', London, Croom Helm, 1979.
Crouch, C., 'Class Conflict and the Industrial Relations Crises', London, Heinemann, 1977.
Crouch, C., and Pizzorno, A., 'The Resurgence of Class Conflict in Western Europe since 1968', London, Macmillan, 1978.
Dahl, R.A., 'Who Governs? Democracy and Power in an American City', New Haven, Conn., Yale University Press, 1961.
Dahrendorf, R., 'Class and Class Conflict in Industrial Society', Stanford, Cal., Stanford University Press, 1959.
Dahrendorf, Ralph, 'Life Chances: Approaches to Social and Political Theory', London, Weidenfeld & Nicolson, 1979.
Daun, Åke, 'Förortsliv. En Etnologisk Studie av Kulturell Förändring', Stockholm, Prisma, 1974.
Davis, Kingsley, and Moore, Wilbert E., Some Principles of Stratification, in R. Bendix and S.M. Lipset (eds), 'Class, Status and Power', New York, Free Press, 1945, 1966.
DeNardo, James, Turnout and the Vote, 'American Political Science Review', 74 (June), pp. 406-20, 1980.
Doeringer, Peter B., and Piore, Michael J., 'Internal Labor Markets and Manpower Analysis', Lexington, Mass., D.C. Heath, 1971.
Downs, A., 'An Economic Theory of Democracy', New York, Harper & Row, 1957.
Dunlop, J.T., 'The Industrial Relations System', New York, Holt, 1958.
Eduards, Maud, 'Kvinnor och Politik', Stockholm, Liber. 1977.

Edwards, P.K., 'Strikes in the United States 1881-1974', Oxford, Basil Blackwell, 1981.

Elvander, N., In Search of New Relationships: Parties, Unions and Salaried Employees' Associations in Sweden, 'Industrial and Labour Relations Review', vol. 28 (October), pp. 60-74,

Erikson, Robert, Yrkesval och Officersrekrytering, Stockholm, MPI Report, no. 31 (stencil), 1964.

Erikson, Robert, 'Uppväxtförhållanden och Social Rörlighet', Stockholm, Allmänna Förlaget, 1971.

Erikson, Robert, On Measuring Errors in Comparative Surveys, 'Statistisk Tidskrift', no. 2, pp. 101-10, 1979.

Erikson, Robert, Om Socio-ekonomisk Indelning av Hushåll, 'Statistisk Tidskrift', no. 1 (forthcoming).

Erlander, Tage, 'Tage Erlander 1955-1960', Stockholm, Tiden, 1976.

Esping-Andersen, Gösta, 'Social Class, Social Democracy and State Policy', Copenhagen, New Social Science Monographs E8, 1980.

Esping-Andersen, Göstä, Friedland, Roger, and Wright, Erik Olin, Modes of Class Struggle and the Capitalist State, 'Kapitalistate', no. 3, pp. 186-219, 1976.

Fatahi, Nader, and Swedner Harald, 'Olika Samhällsklassers Deltagande i de Politiska Valen i Göteborg åren 1921-1976', Stockholm; Gruppen för Samhällsstudier, Socialdemokraterna, 1979.

Flanders, A., 'Management and Unions', London, Faber & Faber, 1970.

Flora, Peter, On the Development of the Western European Welfare States, paper presented at the World Congress of the International Political Science Association in Edinburgh, 1976.

Flora, Peter, and Heidenheimer, Arnold J., 'The Development of Welfare States in Europe and America', New Brunswick, N.J., Transaction Press, 1980.

Forskningsgruppen för Samhälls-och Informationsstudier, Undersökningsmaterial Över en Serie Opinionsmätningar, Stockholm (stencil), 1976.

Fredriksson, G., Strand, D., and Södersten, B., 'Per-Albin-linjen', Stockholm, Pan, Norstedts, 1970.

Friedrich, C.J. 'Man and His Government', New York, McGraw-Hill, 1963.

Frändén, Olof, 'Who Were the Young Leftists? Psychological Antecedents of Party Preference', Stockholm, Stockholms universitet, Sociologiska institutionen (Research Report no. 8, Project Metropolitan), 1977.

Galbraith, J.K., 'The New Industrial State', New York, Signet Books, 1967.

Gillwik, Linnéa, 'Småhuslyckan - Finns Den?' Stockholm, Byggforskningsrådet, 1979.

Ginsberg, Norman, 'Class, Capital and Social Policy', London, Macmillan, 1979.

Goldthorpe, J.H., Social Stratification in Industrial Society, in R. Bendix and S.M. Lipset (eds), 'Class, Status and Power', New York, Free Press, 1966.

Goldthorpe, J.H. Problems of Political Economy after the End of the Post-War Period. Unpublished manuscript.

Goldthorpe, J.H., Theories of Industrial Society: Reflections on the Recrudescence of Historicism and the Future of Futurology, 'European Journal of Sociology', 12, pp. 263-88, 1971.

Goldthorpe, J.H., Political Problems of the New Laissez-Faire (manuscript), 1981.

Goldthorpe, John H., and Bevan, P., The Study of Social Stratification in Great Britain: 1946-1976, 'Social Science Information', 16 (3/4), pp. 279-334, 1977.

Goldthorpe, J.H., et al., 'The Affluent Worker: Industrial Attitudes and Behaviour', London/Cambridge, Cambridge University Press, 1968.

Goldthorpe, J.H. et al., 'The Affluent Worker in the Class Structure', London/Cambridge, Cambridge University Press, 1969.

Gough, Ian, 'The Political Economy of the Welfare State', London, Macmillan, 1979.

Gustafsson, Berndt, Det Religiösa Livet, in Edmund Dahlström (ed.), 'Svensk Samhällsstruktur i Sociologisk Belysning', Stockholm, Svenska Bokförlaget/Norstedts, pp. 313-47, 1965.

Gustafsson, B., The Established Church and the Decline of Church Attendance in Sweden, in N. Birnbaum and G. Lenzer (eds), 'Sociology and Religion', Englewood Cliffs, N.J., Prentice-Hall, pp. 360-6, 1969.

Gustafsson, Gunnel, Models and Effects of Local Government Mergers in Scandinavia, 'West European Politics', 3 (October), pp. 339-57, 1980.

Haavio-Mannila, Elina, Sex Roles in Politics, 'Scandinavian Political Studies', 5, pp. 209-40, Oslo, Universitetsforlaget, 1970.

Hadenius, Stig, Wieslander, Hans, and Molin, Björn, 'Sverige efter 1900', Stockholm, Aldus, 1971.

Hamilton, R.F., 'Class and Politics in the United States', New York, John Wiley, 1972.

Hammar, Tomas, 'Sveriges Första Invandrarval', Stockholm, Publica, 1979.

Hanssen, Börje, 'Familj, Hushåll, Släkt', Stockholm, Giglund, 1978.

Haranne, Markku, Dialectics between Occupational and Party Structures: Finland since World War II, 'Acta Sociologica', 23 (2-3), pp. 83-96, 1980.

Hauser, Robert M., Context and Consex: A Cautionary Tale, 'American Journal of Sociology', 75 (4), pp. 647-64, 1970.

Heclo, Hugh, 'Modern Social Politics in Britain and Sweden', New Haven, Conn., Yale University Press, 1974.

Hedström, Peter, 'Förtidspension - Välfärd eller Ofärd?' Stockholm, Institutet för Social Forskning, 1980.

Hewitt, Christopher, The Effect of Political Democracy and Social Democracy on Equality in Industrial Societies: A Cross-National Comparison, 'American Sociological Review', 42 (June), pp. 450-64, 1977.

Hibbs, Douglas A., Industrial Conflict in Advanced Industrial Societies, 'American Political Science Review', 70 (September), pp. 1033-58, 1976.

Hibbs, Douglas A., On the Political Economy of Long-run Trends in Strike Activity, 'British Journal of Political Science', 7, pp. 153-77, 1978.

Hicks, J.R., 'The Theory of Wages', New York, Peter Smith, 1975.

Himmelstrand, Ulf, et al., 'Beyond Welfare Capitalism', London, Heinemann, 1981.

Hirsch, Fred, and Goldthorpe, John H. (eds), 'The Political Economy of Inflation', Oxford, Martin Robertson, 1978.

Holmberg, S., 'Svenska Väljare', Stockholm, Publica, 1982.

Holmberg, Sören, and Petersson, Olof, 'Inom Felmarginalen. En bok om Politiska Opinionsundersökningar', Stockholm, Publica, 1980.

Holmberg, S., Westerståhl, J., and Branzén, K., 'Väljarna och Kärnkraften', Stockholm, Liber, 1977.

Hyman, Richard, 'Strikes', London, Fontana, 1972.

Hyman, Richard, 'Industrial Relations: A Marxist Introduction', London, Macmillan, 1975.

Härnqvist, Kjell, and Svensson, Allan, 'Den Sociala Selektionen till Gymnasiet', Stockholm, Allmänna förlaget (SOU 1980: 30), 1980.

ILO, 'The Cost of Social Security', Geneva, ILO, 1972.

Ingham, Geoffrey, K., 'Strikes and Industrial Conflict: Britain and Scandinavia' London, Macmillan, 1974.

Inghe, Gunnar, and Inghe, Maj-Britt, 'Den Ofärdiga Välfärden', Stockholm, Tiden/Folksam, 1968.

Inglehardt, R., 'The Silent Revolution: Changing Values and Political Styles Among Western Publics', Princeton, NJ., Princeton University Press, 1977.

Isberg, Magnus, et al., 'Partierna inför Väljarna', Stockholm, Allmänna förlaget, 1974.

Jackman, Richard, 'Politics and Social Equality: A Comparative Analysis', New York, John Wiley, 1975.

Jacobsson, A., 'Om Flyttningar i Sverige', Stockholm, SCB, 1970.

Jallinoja Riitta, Miehet ja Naiset, in Tapani Valkonen et al., 'Suomalaiset. Yhtesiskunnan Rakenne Teollistumisen Aikana', Helsinki, Werner Söderström OY, 1980.

Janson, C.G., 'Mandattilldelning och Regional Röstfördelning', Stockholm, Esselte, 1961.

Janson, Carl Gunnar, Stadens Struktur, in Edmund Dahlströms (ed.),

'Svensk Samhällsstruktur i Sociologisk Belysning', Stockholm, Svenska Bokförlaget/Norstedts, 1965.
Jessop, B., Corporatism, Parliamentarism and Social Democracy, pp. 185-212 in Ph. C. Schmitter and G. Lehmbruch (eds), 'Trend Towards Corporatist Intermediation', Beverly Hills, Cal., Sage, 1979.
Johansson, Sten, 'Om Levnadsnivåundersökningen', Stockholm, Allmänna Förlaget, 1970.
Johansson, Sten, 'Politiska Resurser', Stockholm, Allmänna Förlaget, 1971.
Johansson, Sten, Välfärdsbegrepp och Välfärdsmätning, 'Statistisk Tidskrift', no. 2, 1972.
Jonung, Lars, and Wadensjö, Eskil, The Effects of Unemployment, Inflation and Real Income Growth on Government Popularity in Sweden, 'Scandinavian Journal of Economics', 81 (2), pp. 343-53, 1979.
Karabel, J. The Reason Why, 'New York Review of Books', vol. 26 (February), pp. 22-7, 1979.
Kerr, C., 'Labour and Management in Industrial Society', New York, Anchor Books, 1964.
Kerr, C., 'Marshall, Marx and Modern Times: The Multidimensional Society', Cambridge, Cambridge University Press, 1968.
Kerr, Clark, et al., 'Industrialism and Industrial Man', Cambridge, Mass., Harvard University Press, 1960.
Kornhauser, William, 'The Politics of Mass Society', London, Routledge & Kegan Paul, 1960.
Korpi, Walter, Working Class Communism in Western Europe: Rational or Non-rational? 'American Sociological Review', 36 (December), pp. 971-84, 1971.
Korpi, Walter, 'Fattigdom i Välfärden. Om Människor med Socialhjälp', Stockholm, Tiden, 1972.
Korpi, Walter, Some Problems in the Measurement of Class Voting, 'American Journal of Sociology', 78 (November), pp. 627-42, 1972.
Korpi, Walter, Social Policy and Poverty in Postwar Sweden, 'Acta Sociologica', 18 (2-3), pp. 120-41, 1975.
Korpi, Walter, 'The Working Class in Welfare Capitalism: Work, Unions and Politics in Sweden', London, Routledge & Kegan Paul, 1978.
Korpi, W., Workplace Bargaining, the Law and Unofficial Strikes: The case of Sweden, 'British Journal of Industrial Relations', vol. 16 (November), pp. 355-68, 1978.
Korpi, Walter, Power, Exchange and Inequality, paper presented at the XIth World Congress of the International Political Science Association in Moscow (mimeo), 1979.
Korpi, Walter, 'Fonder för Ekonomisk Demokrati', Stockholm, Sveriges Kommunaltjänstemannaförbund, 1980.
Korpi, Walter, Approaches to the Study of Poverty in the United States: Critical Notes from a European Perspective, in Vincent T. Covello (ed.), 'Poverty and Public Policy: An Evaluation of Social Science Research', Boston, G.K. Hall & Co. 1980.
Korpi, Walter, Social Policy and Distributional Conflict in Capitalist Democracies. A Preliminary Comparative Framework, 'West European Politics', 3 (October), pp. 296-316, 1980.
Korpi, Walter, Unofficial Strikes in Sweden, 'British Journal of Industrial Relations', 19 (March), pp. 66-86, 1981.
Korpi, W., Labour Movements and Industrial Relations, pp. 308-23 in F. Wisti (ed.), 'Nordic Democracy', Copenhagen, Det Danske Selskap, 1981.
Korpi, W., Sweden: Conflict, Power and Politics in Industrial Relations. Paper presented at an international industrial relations conference at Harvard, 1975. Revised version pp. 185-217 in P.B. Doeringer, P. Gourevitch, P. Lange and A. Martin (eds), 'Industrial Relations in International Perspective', London, Macmillan, 1981.
Korpi, Walter, and Shalev, Michael, Strikes, Industrial Relations and Class Conflict in Capitalist Societies, 'British Journal of Sociology', 30 (June), pp. 164-87, 1979.
Korpi, Walter, and Shalev, Michael, Strikes, Power and Politics in the Western

Nations, 1900-1976, in Maurice Zeitlin (ed.), 'Political Power and Social Theory', vol. 1, 1980.
Lehmbruch, G., Introduction: Neo-corporatism in Comparative Perspective, pp. 1-28 in Lehmbruch, G. and Schmitter, Ph. C. (eds), 'Patterns of Corporatist Policy Making', Beverly Hills, Cal., Sage, 1982.
Lenin, V.I., 'State and Revolution', in 'Selected Works' (one-volume edition), London, Lawrence and Wishart, 1969.
Lenski, Gerhard E., 'Power and Privilege', New York, McGraw-Hill, 1966.
Lerner, D., 'The Passing of Traditional Society: Modernization in the Middle East', New York, Free Press, 1958.
Lewin, L., 'Hur Styrs Facket?', Stockholm, Rabén & Sjögren, 1977.
Lewin L., Jansson, B., and Sörbom, D., 'The Swedish Electorate 1887-1968', Stockholm, Almqvist & Wiksell, 1972.
Lijphart, A., Language, Religion, Class and Party Choice: Belgium, Canada, Switzerland and South Africa Compared, pp. 283-328 in R. Rose, 'Electoral Participation: A Comparative Analysis', Beverly Hills, Cal., Sage, 1980.
Lijphart, A., Political Parties, Ideologies and Programs, pp. 26-51 in D. Butler, H.R. Penniman and A. Ranney (eds), 'Democracy at the Polls: A Comparative Study of Competitive National Elections', Washington, DC, American Enterprise Institute, 1981.
Liljeström, Rita, Jämställdhet, Arbetarklass och Välfärdskapitalism, in Ann-Sofie Kälvemark (ed.), 'Jämställdhetsperspektiv i Forskningen', Stockholm, Riksbankens Jubileumsfond, 1980.
Liljeström, Rita, et al., 'Roller i Omvandling', (SOU 1977:71), 1977.
Lindén, M., Political Dimensions and Relative Party Positions: A Factor Analytical Study of Swedish Attitude Data, 'Scandinavian Journal of Psychology', vol. 16, 1975.
Lindhagen, Jan, Åren vi Förlorade, 'Tiden', 68, pp. 558-77, 1976.
Lindhagen, Jan, Men å Andra Sidan, 'Tiden', 69, pp. 470-93, 1977.
Lindhagen, Jan, and Nilsson, Macke, 'Hotet mot Arbetarrörelsen', Stockholm, Tiden, 1970.
Lipset, S.M., 'Political Man', London, Mercury Books, 1960.
Lipset, Seymour Martin, Industrial Proletariat in Comparative Perspectives, in J. Triska and C. Gati (eds), 'Labour in Socialist Societies. Blue Collar Workers in Eastern Europe', London, Allen & Unwin, 1980.
LO, 'Kollektiv Kapitalbildning genom Löntagarfonder. Rapport till LO-kongressen', Stockholm, Landsorganisationen, 1976.
Lockwood, D., 'The Blackcoated Worker', London, Allen & Unwin, 1958.
Marklund, Staffan, and Åberg, Rune (eds), 'Framtidens oönskade sociala förhållanden', Umeå, Umeå University, Institute of Sociology, 1980.
Martin, Andrew, 'The Politics of Economic Policy in the United States: A Tentative View from a Comparative Perspective', Beverly Hills, California, Sage, 1973.
McCracken, Paul, 'Towards Full Employment and Price Stability', Paris, OECD, 1977.
McKenzie, R., and Silver, A., 'Angels in Marble; Working class Conservatives in Urban England', London, Heinemann, 1968.
Mackie, T.T., and Rose, R., 'The International Almanac of Electoral History', London, Macmillan, 1974.
Meidner, Rudolf, et al., 'Employee Investment Funds', London, Allen & Unwin, 1978.
Milbraith, Lester, and Goel, M.L., 'Political Participation', Chicago, Rand, McNally, 1977.
Miliband, Ralph, 'The State in Capitalist Society', London, Weidenfeld and Nicolson, 1969.
Mill, J.S., 'On Representative Government', London, Encyclopedia Britannica, 1952.
Moore, Wilbert E., 'Industrialization and Labour', Ithaca, NY., Cornell University Press, 1951.
OECD, 'Public Expenditure on Income Maintenance Programs', Paris, OECD, 1976.

Offe, Claus, Advanced Capitalism and the Welfare State (mimeo), 1972.
Offe, Claus, The Attribution of Public Status to Interest Groups: Observations on the West German Case, pp. 123-58 in Suzanne D. Berger (ed.), 'Organizing Interests in Western Europe', Cambridge, Cambridge University Press, 1981.
Orshansky, Mollie, Counting the Poor: Another Look at the Poverty Profile, 'Social Security Bulletin', vol. 28, 1965.
Paldam, Martin and Pedersen, Peder J., The Macro-model Explaining Industrial Conflict - a Comparative Study of 17 Countries 1948-1975, Århus, Århus universitet, Ekonomiska institutet (Memo 1980-6), 1980.
Panitch, Leo, Recent Theorizations of Corporatism: Reflections on a Growth Industry, 'British Journal of Sociology', 31 (June), pp. 159-87, 1980.
Panitch, Leo, The Limits of Corporatism, 'New Left Review', no. 125 (January-February); pp. 21-44, 1981.
Parkin, Frank, 'Class, Inequality and the Political Order', London, MacGibbon & Kee, 1971.
Parkin, F., 'Marxism and Class Theory: A Bourgeois Critique', New York, Columbia University Press, 1979.
Parsons, T., 'Societies: Evolutionary and Comparative Perspectives', Englewood Cliffs, NJ, Prentice-Hall, 1966.
Pedersen, M., Changing Patterns of Electoral Volatility in European Party Systems, 1948-1977, 'European Journal of Politics', vol. 5, pp. 100-20, 1979.
Petersson, O., 'Väljarna och Valet 1976' (Valundersökningar, Report No. 2), Stockholm, Statistiska Centralbyrån, 1977.
Pizzorno, A., Political Exchange and Collective Identity in Industrial Conflict, pp. 277-98 in C. Crouch and A. Pizzorno (eds), 'The Resurgence of Class Conflict in Western Europe since 1968', vol. 2, London, Macmillan, 1978.
Pomper, Gerald, 'Voters' Choice. Varieties of American Political Behavior', New York, Harper & Row, 1975.
Popenoe, David, 'The Suburban Environment; Sweden and the United States', Chicago, University Press, 1977.
Powell, G. Bingham, Jr, Voting Turnout in Thirty Democracies: Effects of the Socio-economic, Legal and Partisan Environments, in Richard Rose (ed.), 'Electoral Participation: A Comparative Analysis', London, Sage, 1980.
Ricknell, Lars, Politiska Regioner, Umeå, Umeå University, Department of Statistics, (stencil), 1976.
Rokkan, Stein, Numerical Democracy and Corporate Pluralism, pp. 70-115 in R.A. Dahl (ed.), 'Political Opposition in Western Democracies', New Haven, Conn., Yale University Press, 1966.
Rokkan, Stein, Nation-Building, Cleavage Formation and the Structuring of Mass Politics, pp. 72-144 in S. Rokkan, 'Citizens, Elections, Parties', Oslo, Universitetsforlaget, 1970.
Rose, Richard (ed.), 'Electoral Behavior: A Comparative Handbook', New York, Free Press, 1974.
Rose, Richard, Comparability in Electoral Studies, pp. 3-28 in Richard Rose (ed.), 'Electoral Behavior: A Comparative Handbook', New York, Free Press, 1974.
Rose, R., and Urwin, D.W., Social Cohesion, Political Parties and Strains in Regimes, 'Comparative Political Studies', vol. 2 (April), pp. 7-67, 1969.
Ross, Arthur M., and Hartman, Paul I., 'Changing Patterns of Industrial Conflict', New York, John Wiley, 1960.
Rostow, W.W., 'The Stages of Economic Growth', Cambridge, University Press, 1960.
Rowntree, Seebohm, and Lavers, G.R., 'Poverty: A Study of Town Life', London; Macmillan, 1901.
Rudebeck, Lars, Det Politiska Systemet i Sverige, in Edmund Dahlström (ed.), 'Svensk Samhällsstruktur i Sociologisk Selysning', Stockholm, Svenska Bokförlaget/Norstedts, 1965.
Rydenfeldt, Sven, 'Kommunismen i Sverige', Lund, Gleerup, 1954.
Sainsbury, Diane, 'Swedish Social Democratic Ideology and Electoral Politics 1944-1948', Stockholm, Almqvist & Wiksell International, 1980.

Särlvik, Bo, Partibyten som Mått på Avstånd och Dimensioner i Partisystemet, 'Sociologisk Forskning', 5(1), pp. 35-82, 1968.
Särlvik, Bo, Electoral Behaviour in the Swedish Multiparty System, Gothenburg University, Statsvetenskapliga Institutionen (stencil), 1970.
Särlvik, Bo, Sweden: The Social Bases of the Parties in a Developmental Perspective, pp. 371-436 in Richard Rose (ed.), 'Electoral Behavior: A Comparative Handbook', New York, Free Press, 1974.
Särlvik, Bo, Mapping the Party Space. Distance, Evaluations and Ideological Perspectives, paper presented at the Xth World Congress of the International Political Science Association in Edinburgh, 1976.
Särlvik, Bo, Recent Electoral Trends in Sweden, in Karl H. Cerny (ed.), 'Scandinavia at the Polls. Recent Political Trends in Denmark, Norway, and Sweden', Washington, DC, American Enterprise Institute for Public Policy Research, 1977.
Sawyer, Malcolm, 'Income Distribution in the OECD Countries', Paris, OECD, 1976.
Scase, Richard, 'Social Democracy in Capitalist Society', London, Croom Helm, 1977.
SCB, 'Levnadsförhållanden. Utveckling och Nuläge 1976', Stockholm, Statistiska Centralbyrån, 1977.
SCB, Partisympatiundersökningen, 'Statistiska Meddleanden', Serie Be, Stockholm, Statistiska Centralbyrån, 1972-81.
SCB, 'Arbetskraftsundersökningen. Årsmedeltal, 1979', Stockholm, Statistiska, Centralbyrån, 1980.
Schmidt, F., 'Tjänsteavtalet', Stockholm, Norstedts, 1968.
Schmidt, M.G., Does Corporatism Matter? Economic Crises, Politics and Rates of Unemployment in Capitalist Democracies in the 1970s, pp. 237-58 in G. Lehmbruch and Ph. C. Schmitter (eds), 'Patterns of Corporatist Policy-Making', Beverly Hills, Cal., Sage, 1982.
Schmitter, Philippe C., Still the Century of Corporatism? pp. 7-53 in Philippe C. Schmitter and Gerhard Lembruch (eds), 'Trends Towards Corporatist Intermediation', Beverly Hills, Cal., and London, Sage, 1979 (originally published in 'Review of Politics', January 1974).
Schmitter, Philippe C., Interest Intermediation and Regime Governability in Contemporary Western Europe and North America, pp. 285-330 in Suzanne D. Berger (ed.), 'Organizing Interests in Western Europe', Cambridge, University Press, 1981.
Schmitter, Ph. C., Reflections on Where the Theory of Neo-corporatism has Gone and Where the Praxis of Neo-Corporatism May be Going, pp. 259-79 in G. Lehmbruch and Ph. C. Schmitter (eds), 'Patterns of Corporatist Policy-Making', Beverly Hills, Cal., Sage, 1982.
Schmitter, Philippe C., and Lehmbruch, Gerhard (eds), 'Trends Towards Corporatist Intermediation', Beverly Hills, Cal., and London, Sage, 1979.
Schumpeter, Joseph A., 'Capitalism, Socialism and Democracy', New York, Harper & Row, 1947.
Shalev, Michael, and Korpi, Walter, Working Class Mobilization and American Exceptionalism, 'Economic and Industrial Democracy', 1 (1), pp. 31-61, 1980.
Sharpe, L.J., American Democracy Reconsidered, 'British Journal of Political Science', vol. 3, pp. 129-67.
Shorter, Edward, and Charles Tilly, 'Strikes in France, 1830-1968', London, Cambridge University Press, 1974.
Siegenthaler, Jürg K., Current Problems of Trade Union and Party Relations in Switzerland. Reorientation versus Inertia, 'Industrial and Labour Relations Review', 28, pp. 264-81, 1975.
Sjöström, Kurt, 'Socialpolitiken i det Kapitalistiska Samhället. Inledning till en Marxistisk Analys', Stockholm, Arbetarkultur, 1974.
Sombart, W. V., 'Why Is There No Socialism in the United States?', White Plains, NY, M.E. Sharpe, 1976.
SOS, 'Riksdagsmannavalen', Stockholm, Statistiska Centralbyrån, 1921-68.
SOS, 'Allmänna Valen', Stockholm, Statistiska Centralbyrån, 1970-9.
SOS, 'Folkräkningen 1930', vol. 1, Stockholm, Statistiska Centralbyrån, 1933.

Spånt, Roland, 'Den Svenska Inkomstfördelningens Utveckling', Uppsala, Studia Oeconomica Uppsaliensia, no. 4, 1976.
Stark, T., 'The Distribution of Income in Eight Countries', London, HMSO, 1977.
Stephens, John D., The Consequences of Social Structural Change for the Development of Socialism in Sweden, PhD, dissertation, Yale University, 1976.
Stephens, John D., 'The Transition from Capitalism to Socialism', London, Macmillan, 1979.
Stokes, B., Spatial Models of Party Competition, 'American Political Science Review', 57, pp. 365-77, 1963.
Svenning, Conny, and Svenning, Marianne, 'Daghemmen, Jämlikheten och Klassamhället', Lund, Liber, 1980.
Svenska Industritjänstemannaförbundet, 'SIFs Lönepolitik. Lön 80. Slutrapport från Lönepolitiska Utredningen', Stockholm, Svenska Industritjänstemannaförbundet, 1977.
Swedner, Harald, Sextiotalets Politik lade Grunden till Valförlusten, 'LO-tidningen', no. 50 p. 6, 1979.
Tachibanaki, Toshiaki, A Note on the Impact of Income Tax Redistribution, 'Review of Income and Wealth', Series 27 (September), 1981.
Tate, C.N., Individual and Contextual Variables in British Voting Behaviour: An Exploratory Note, 'American Political Science Review', 68 (December), pp. 1656-62, 1974.
Taylor, C. L., and Hudson, M.C., 'World Handbook of Political and Social Indicators', New Haven, Conn., Yale University Press, 1972.
Taylor, P.J., and Johnston, R.J., 'Geography of Elections', London, Croom Helm, 1979.
TCO, 'Löntagarkapital Genom Fonder - ett Principförslag. Rapport till TCO-kongressen', Stockholm, Tjänstemännens Centralorganisation, 1979.
Tengvald, Karin, 'Samhällets Krav och de Fattigas Resurser', Uppsala, Sociologiska institutionen, Uppsala universitet, 1976.
Therborn, Göran, The Rule of Capital and the Rise of Democracy, 'New Left Review', no. 103 (May-June), pp. 3-41, 1977.
Therborn, Göran, 'Klasstrukturen i Sverige 1930-80'. Stockholm, Zenit, 1981.
Therborn, Göran, et al., Sweden Before and After Social Democracy: A First Overview, 'Acta Sociologica', vol. 21 (supplement), pp. 37-58, 1978.
Thurow, Lester, 'Generating Inequality: Mechanisms of Distribution in the US Economy', New York, Basic Books, 1975.
Tilton, Timothy, A Swedish Road to Socialism: Ernst Wigforss and the Ideological Foundations of Swedish Social Democracy, 'American Political Science Review', 73, pp. 505-20, 1979.
Tingsten, Herbert, 'Political Behaviour: Studies in Election Statistics', London, King & Son, 1937.
Tingsten, Herbert, 'Demokratins Problem', Stockholm, Norstedts/Aldus, 1945, 1960.
Titmuss, Richard, 'Essays on "the Welfare State"', London, Unwin Brothers, 1958.
Titmuss, Richard, 'Commitment to Welfare', London, Unwin Brothers, 1968.
Titmuss, Richard, 'Social Policy', London, Allen & Unwin, 1974.
Törnqvist, Kurt, 'Opinion 80', Stockholm, Beredskapsnämnden för Psykologiskt Försvar, 1980.
United Nations, 'Yearbook of National Account Statistics 1966', New York, United Nations, 1967.
United Nations, 'Yearbook of National Account Statistics 1978', New York, United Nations, 1979.
Valen, Henry, 'Valg og Politikk', Oslo, NKS-forlaget, 1981.
Vedung, Evert, 'Kärnkraften och Regeringen Fälldins Fall', Stockholm, Rabén & Sjögren, 1979.
Verba, Sidney, Nie, Norman H., and Kim Jae-on, 'Participation and Political Equality: A Seven-nation Comparison', Cambridge, Cambridge University Press, 1978.

Wigforss, E., Den Ekonomiska Makten ska Flyttas från Kapitalet till Arbetet, 'Tiden', vol. 66 (7), pp. 390-5, 1975.
Wilensky, Harold, 'The Welfare State and Equality: The Roots of Public Expenditures', Berkeley, Cal., University of California Press, 1975.
Wilensky, Harold, 'The "New" Corporatism: Centralization and the Welfare State', Beverly Hills, Cal., Sage, 1976.
Wilensky, Harold and Lebeaux, C., 'Industrial Society and Social Welfare', New York, Russell Sage Foundation, 1958.
Winkler, J.T., Corporatism, 'European Journal of Sociology', 17 (1), 1976.
Wolfinger, Raymond E., and Rosenstone, Steven J., 'Who Votes?' New Haven, Conn., Yale University Press, 1980.
Wrong, Dennis, 'Power. Its Forms, Bases and Uses', New York, Harper, 1979.
Youth Bureau, 'The Youth of the World and Japan. The Findings of the Second World Youth Survey', Tokyo, Prime Minister's Office of Japan, 1978.
Zetterberg, Hans L., Det Svenska Valet 1976, 'Indikator', Stockholm, Sifo, 1976.
Zetterberg, Hans L., En Socialpolitik för Åttiotalet, in 'Inför SAF-kongressen 1980. Expertrapporter', vol. 2, pp. 106-31, Stockholm, Svenska arbetsgivareföreningen, 1980.

SUBJECT INDEX

NAME INDEX